CHILTON'S REPAIR & TUNE-UP GUIDE

VOLKSWAGEN 1949 to 1971

Beetle • Karmann Ghia • Bus • Fastback • Squareback

Vice President and General Manager JOHN P. KUSHNERICK
Managing Editor KERRY A. FREEMAN, S.A.E.
Senior Editor RICHARD J. RIVELE, S.A.E.

CHILTON BOOK COMPANY
Radnor, Pennsylvania
19089

SAFETY NOTICE

Proper service and repair procedures are vital to the safe, reliable operation of all motor vehicles, as well as the personal safety of those performing repairs. This book outlines procedures for servicing and repairing vehicles using safe, effective methods. The procedures contain many NOTES, CAUTIONS and WARNINGS which should be followed along with standard safety procedures to eliminate the possibility of personal injury or improper service which could damage the vehicle or compromise its safety.

It is important to note that repair procedures and techniques, tools and parts for servicing motor vehicles, as well as the skill and experience of the individual performing the work vary widely. It is not possible to anticipate all of the conceivable ways or conditions under which vehicles may be serviced, or to provide cautions as to all of the possible hazards that may result. Standard and accepted safety precautions and equipment should be used when handling toxic or flammable fluids, and safety goggles or other protection should be used during cutting, grinding, chiseling, prying, or any other process that can cause material removal or projectiles.

Some procedures require the use of tools specially designed for a specific purpose. Before substituting another tool or procedure, you must be completely satisfied that neither your personal safety, nor the performance of the vehicle will be endangered.

Although the information in this guide is based on industry sources and is as complete as possible at the time of publication, the possibility exists that the manufacturer made later changes which could not be included here. While striving for total accuracy, Chilton Book Company cannot assume responsibility for any errors, changes, or omissions that may occur in the compilation of this data.

PART NUMBERS

Part numbers listed in this reference are not recommendations by Chilton for any product by brand name. They are references that can be used with interchange manuals and aftermarket supplier catalogs to locate each brand supplier's discrete part number.

ACKNOWLEDGMENTS

The Chilton Book Company expresses its appreciation to Volkswagen of America, Englewood Cliffs, New Jersey for their valued assistance and cooperation.

Published in Radnor, Pennsylvania 19089, by Chilton Book Company

Manufactured in the United States of America
Revised May 1974
Twentieth Printing, August 1983

Chilton's Repair & Tune-Up Guide: Volkswagen 1949–71
ISBN 0-8019-5624-2
ISBN 0-8019-5796-6 pbk.
Library of Congress Catalog Card No. 74-154691

CONTENTS

Quick Reference Specifications For Your Vehicle

Fill in this chart with the most commonly used specifications for your vehicle. Specifications can be found in Chapters 1 through 3 or on the tune-up decal under the hood of the vehicle.

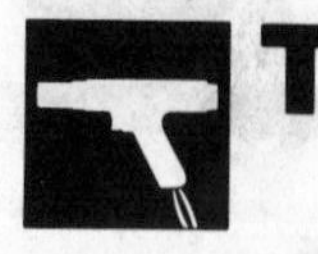

Tune-Up

Firing Order ______

Spark Plugs:

Type ______

Gap (in.) ______

Point Gap (in.) ______

Dwell Angle (°) ______

Ignition Timing (°) ______

Vacuum (Connected/Disconnected) ______

Valve Clearance (in.)

Intake ______ **Exhaust** ______

Capacities

Engine Oil (qts)

With Filter Change ______

Without Filter Change ______

Cooling System (qts) ______

Manual Transmission (pts) ______

Type ______

Automatic Transmission (pts) ______

Type ______

Front Differential (pts) ______

Type ______

Rear Differential (pts) ______

Type ______

Transfer Case (pts) ______

Type ______

FREQUENTLY REPLACED PARTS

Use these spaces to record the part numbers of frequently replaced parts.

PCV VALVE	OIL FILTER	AIR FILTER
Manufacturer ______	Manufacturer ______	Manufacturer ______
Part No. ______	Part No. ______	Part No. ______

General Information and Maintenance

MODEL IDENTIFICATION

To the casual observer, it would appear that the appearance of the Volkswagen "beetle" has not changed since the car was first sold in this country in 1949. However, there have been hundreds, if not thousands, of changes made on the inside and outside of this seemingly perpetual automotive design. Because so many changes were made during an actual model run, the only sure way of telling the year of a Volkswagen is by looking at the chassis number of the vehicle.

The accompanying chart gives the yearly chassis numbers, exterior and interior body changes, and the mechanical changes that apply to all Volkswagen beetle models since the first two were sold here in 1949.

Volkswagen models are further differentiated by type. Type 1 is the beetle and Karmann Ghia. Type 2 is the transporter, or bus and truck, series. Type 3 is the Fastback and Squareback. Type 4 is the 411 sedan and wagon. The current model numbers are as follow:

Model Number (LHD)	*Description*
• 111	VW 1300A sedan, 1971 1600 sedan
• 115	VW 1300A sedan with folding sunroof
• 113	VW 1500 sedan, 1971 1600 Super Beetle
• 117	VW 1500 sedan with steel sunroof
• 141	VW 1500 Karmann Ghia Convertible
• 143	VW 1500 Karmann Ghia Coupe
• 151	VW 1500 Convertible (4-seater)
• 211–215	Delivery Van
• 221–225	Micro Bus
• 231–237	Kombi
• 241	Deluxe Micro Bus (9-seater)
• 251	Deluxe Micro Bus (7-seater)
• 261–267	Pick-up
• 271–273	Ambulance
• 281–285	Micro Bus (7-seater)
• 311	Fastback sedan (1600TL)
• 313	Fastback sedan with steel sunroof
• 315	1600A sedan
• 317	1600A sedan with steel sunroof
• 343	1600L Karmann Ghia Coupe
• 345	1600L Karmann Ghia Coupe with steel sunroof
• 361	1600L Squareback sedan
• 363	1600L Squareback sedan with steel sunroof
• 365	1600A Squareback sedan
• 367	1600A Squareback sedan with steel sunroof
• 411	411 Four door sedan
• 411	411 Three door sedan (wagon)

Chassis Number

The chassis number is on the frame tunnel under the back seat in the type 1 and 3. In

Type 1 chassis number location

the type 2, the chassis number is on the right engine cover plate in the engine compartment.

Beginning with the 1965 model year, a nine-digit serial number system was instituted. In this system, the first two numbers are the first two digits of the car's model number and the third digit stands for the car's model year—"5" stands for 1965, "8" stands for 1968, etc. A tenth digit was added when production passed one million.

Identification Plate

The identification plate carries the vehicle serial number and paint, body, and assembly codes. It is behind the spare tire in the luggage compartment on type 1 models, and on the right side of the overhead air duct in early type 2 vehicles. The type 3 identification plate is next to the hood latch, in front of the spare tire in the luggage compartment. Starting 1970, all models have an identification plate on top of the driver's side of the instrument panel. This plate may be seen through the windshield.

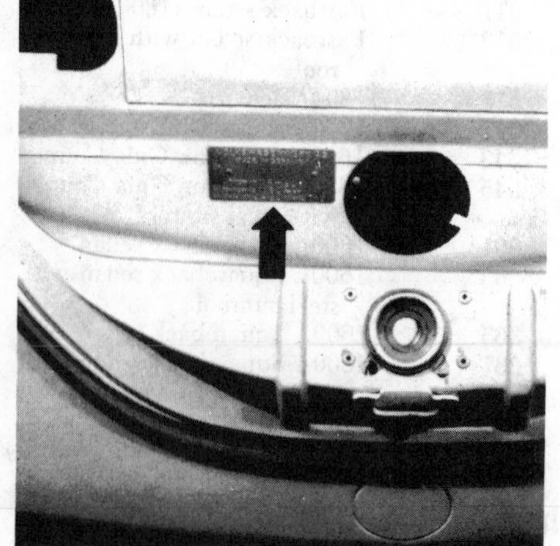

Type 1 identification plate location

Engine Number

On type 1 and 2 vehicles, which have the upright engine fan housing, the engine number is on the crankcase flange for the generator support. The number can readily be seen by looking through the center of the fan belt. On type 3 engines, which have the fan on the end of the crankshaft, the number is along the crankcase joint between the oil cooler and the air cleaner. The engine can be identified by the letter preceding the serial number. Refer to the Engine Identification Chart.

Type 1 engine number location

HISTORICAL HIGHLIGHTS

In 1932, Ferdinand Porsche produced prototypes for the NSU company of Germany. These led to the design of the Volkswagen. The prototypes had a rear, air-cooled engine, torsion-bar suspension, and the spare tire mounted at an angle in the front luggage compartment. In 1936, Porsche produced three Volkswagen prototypes, one of which was a 995 cc., horizontally-opposed, four-cylinder automobile. In 1945 Volkswagen production began and 1,785 beetles were built. The Volkswagen convertible was introduced in 1949, the year when only two Volkswagens were sold in the entire U.S.A. The year 1950 marked the beginning of the sunroof models and the transporter series. The Volkswagen Karmann Ghia was introduced in 1956, and is still of the same basic styling format. The "big" Volkswagen, the 1500 Squareback, was introduced in Europe in 1961, and sold in the U.S.A. in 1966 as a member of the new type 3 series (Fastback and Squareback). The type 4 was introduced to the U.S.A. with the 1971 model line.

Engine Identification

Common Designation	Number Of Cylinders	C.C. Displacement (cu.in.)	Type Engine	Type Vehicle	Engine Code Letter	Year
–	4	1,131 (69.02)	Upright fan	1	–	To December, 1953
1,200	4	1,192 (72.74)	Upright fan	1,2	A	To July, 1960
1,200	4	1,192 (72.74)	Upright fan	1,2	D	From August, 1960
1,300	4	1,285 (78.4)	Upright fan	1,2	F	From August, 1965
1,500	4	1,493 (91.1)	Upright fan	1,2	H	From August, 1967 ①
1,600	4	1,584 (96.6)	Upright fan	1,2	B	From August, 1969 ②
1,500	4	1,493 (91.1)	Upright fan	2	G	To July, 1965
1,500	4	1,493 (91.1)	Suitcase engine	3	K	To July, 1965 ③ From August, 1965 ④
1,500S	4	1,493 (91.1)	Suitcase engine	3 1500S	R	To July, 1965
1,600	4	1,584 (96.6)	Suitcase engine	3	T	From August, 1965
1,600	4	1,584 (96.6)	Suitcase engine	3 injected	U	From August, 1967
1,600	4	1,584 (96.6)	Upright fan	1,2	AD, AE	From August, 1970

① Type 2 from August, 1965
② Type 2 from August, 1967
③ High compression
④ Low compression

Type 1 Identification

Year	Chassis Numbers	Major Body Changes	Major Mechanical Changes
1971		Super Beetle introduced; flow through ventilation; increased luggage space; towing eyes front and rear; Super Beetle 3″ longer. Normal beetle continued.	Suspension strut front axle; 1600 cc. engine with 60 hp, dual port heads, relocated oil cooler with its own cooling air supply. Front brake size increased to 9¾″.
1970	11,0,2000001–	Louvers in rear hood; modified lights and reflectors; ignition lock buzzer warning.	1600 cc. 57 hp engine; vapor emission control system (California only).
1969	119,000,001–119,1,093,704	Electric rear window defroster; ignition lock combined with steering lock. Locking gas flap.	Double-jointed rear axle standard.
1968	118,000,000–118,1,016,098	Raised bumpers, front and rear; vertical bumper guards eliminated. Built-in headrest in front seats; extensive padding in front compartment and dashboard. Seat belts in rear standard; external gas filler.	Exhaust emission control; collapsible steering column; optional automatic stick shift.
1967	117,000,001–118,000,000	Back-up lights. Retractable seat belts. Armrest for driver. Locking buttons on doors. Parking light built into turn signals. Narrower chrome trim. Volkswagen nameplate on engine lid. Two-speed windshield wipers. Headlights now vertical in indented fenders.	Dual brake system. Increased horsepower, from 50 to 53. (SAE) Larger engine, from 1300 cc. to 1500 cc. 12-volt electrical system. Number of fuses increased from 8 to 10. More powerful starter motor. Equalizer spring rear axle.
1966	116,000,0001–116,1,021,298	Number "1300" on engine lid. Flat hub caps; ventilated wheel discs. Four-way flasher system. Dimmer switch on turn signal. Defroster outlet in center of dash. Front seat backs equipped with safety locks.	Increased engine size, from 1200 cc. to 1300 cc. Increased engine output, from 40 hp. to 50 hp. (SAE)
1965	115,000,0001–115,979,200	Larger windows, narrower window and door posts. Heater control levers now mounted on tunnel, formerly a twisting knob. Push-button handle on engine lid. Back of rear seat convertible to a flat platform.	No major changes.
1964	5,677,119–6,502,399	Steel sliding sunroof; crank operated. Wider license plate light. Non-porous leatherette upholstery replaced by porous vinyl material.	No major changes.
1963	4,846,836–5,677,118	Sunroof equipped with folding handle. Fresh air heating system. Nylon window guides. Introduction of leatherette headliner; formerly "mouse fuzz". Wolfsburg hood crest eliminated from front hood.	No major changes.
1962	4,010,995–4,846,835	Spring-loaded hood. Addition of seat belt mounting points. Gasoline gauge on dashboard; formerly only a reserve fuel tap. Size of tail lights increased. Sliding covers for front floor heating outlets. Windshield washer added; compressed air type.	Worm and roller steering; formerly worm and sector. Tie rod ends permanently lubricated.

Year	Chassis Numbers	Major Body Changes	Major Mechanical Changes
1961	3,192,507–4,010,994	Flatter gasoline tank. Increased front luggage space. Windshield washer; pump-type. Key slot in doors now vertical; formerly horizontal. Starter switch now non-repeat.	Increased engine output, from 36 hp. to 40 hp. (SAE). Automatic choke. Push-on electrical connectors. First gear now synchromesh; all forward speeds now synchromesh.
1960	2,528,668–3,192,506	"Dished" steering wheel. Push-button door handles; formerly lever-type. Foot rest for passenger. Padded sunvisor.	Front anti-sway bar added. Generator output increased to 180 watts, formerly 160. Steering damper added.
1959	2,007,616–2,528,667	No major changes.	Stronger clutch springs. Fan belt improved. Frame given additional reinforcement.
1958	1,600,440–2,007,615	Larger rear window and windshield. Front turn signal lights moved to top of fenders. Radio grill moved to far left of dashboard.	Wider brake drums and shoes.
1957	1,246,619–1,600,439	Doors fitted with adjustable striker plates. Front heater outlets moved rearward, to within five inches of door. Tubeless tires used; formerly tube-type.	No major changes.
1956	929,746–1,246,618	Tail light housings raised two inches. Steering wheel spoke moved lower and off-center. Heater knob moved forward. Adjustable front seat backs; formerly non-adjustable. Increased front luggage space.	Dual tail pipe; formerly single tail pipe.
1955	722,935–929,745	Flashing turn signal lights replace "semaphore"-type flappers. Indicators mounted near outside bottom of front fenders.	No major changes.
1954	575,415–722,934	Starter switch combined with ignition switch; formerly a separate button on dashboard. Interior courtesy light added.	Increased engine size, from 1131 cc. to 1192 cc. Addition of oil-bath air cleaner.
1953	428,157–575,414	Oval rear window replaces two-piece split rear window. Vent window handles now provided with a lock button.	No major changes.
1952	313,830–428,156	Vent windows added. Body vent flaps eliminated. Window crank geared down from 10½ to 3½ turns. Door added to glove compartment. Turn signal control to steering wheel; formerly on dashboard. 5.60 x 15 tires. Formerly 5.00 x16.	Top three gears synchromesh; formerly crashbox.
1951	220,472–313,829	Vent flaps in front quarter-panel of body. Wolfsburg crest above front hood handle.	No major changes.
1950	138,555–220,471	Ash tray added to dashboard.	Hydraulic brakes; formerly mechanical.
1949	91,922–138,554	Pull release for front hood; formerly locking handle.	Solex carburetor now standard equipment.

Vehicle Identification—Types 1, 2 and 3

Model	SAE Output	from Chassis No.	from Date	to Chassis No.	to Date
Vehicle, Type 1					
Standard Sedan	36bhp.	1-0575 415	December 1953	6 502 399	July 1964
Standard Sedan, Sedan A	36bhp.	115 000 001	August 1964	115 979 202	July 1965
Deluxe Sedan Karmann Ghia Models VW Convertible	36bhp.	1-0575 415	December 1953	3192 506	July 1960
	42bhp.	3192 507	August 1960	6 502 399	July 1964
		115 000 001	August 1964	115 979 202	July 1965
1200A	42bhp.	116 000 001	August 1965	1161 021 297	July 1966
VW 1200	42bhp.	117 483 306	January 1967	117 844 900	July 1967
		118 000 001	August 1967	1181 016 095	July 1968
		119 000 001	August 1968	1191 093 701	July 1969
		110 2000 001	August 1969		
VW 1300 Sedan Karmann Ghia Models VW Convertible	50bhp.	116 000 001	August 1965	1161 021 298	July 1966
VW 1300 A	50bhp.	117 000 001	August 1966	117 403 305	Jan. 1967
VW 1300 Sedan	50bhp.	117 000 001	August 1966	117 844 901	July 1967
		118 000 001	August 1967	1181 016 096	July 1968
		119 000 002	August 1968	1191 093 702	July 1969
		110 2000 002	August 1969		
VW 1500 Sedan Karmann Ghia Models VW Convertible	53bhp.	117 000 001	August 1966	117 844 902	July 1967
		118 000 001	August 1967	118 1016 097	July 1968
		119 000 003	August 1968	119 1093 703	July 1969
		110 2000 003	August 1969		
	57bhp.	110 2000 004	August 1969		
VW 1600 Sedan Karmann Ghia Models VW Convertible	57bhp.		1970		
VW 1600 Sedan Super Beetle Karmann Ghia Models VW Convertible	60bhp.		1971		

Vehicle Identification—Types 1, 2 and 3

Model		SAE Output	from Chassis No.	from Date	to Chassis No.	to Date
Vehicle, type 2						
		36bhp.	20-069 409	December 1953	614 455	May 1960
	1200	42bhp.	614 456	June 1960	1 328 271	July 1964
			215 000 001	August 1964	215 036 378	Sept. 1964
		51bhp.	1041 014	January 1963	1 328 271	July 1964
			215 000 001	August 1964	215 176 339	July 1965
Transporter	1500	53bhp.	216 000 001	August 1965	216 179 668	July 1966
			217 000 001	August 1966	217 148 459	July 1967
			218 000 001	August 1967	218 202 251	July 1968
	1600	57bhp.	219 000 001	August 1968	219 238 131	July 1969
			210 2000 001	August 1969		
		60bhp.		1971		
Vehicle, type 3						
			0 000 001	April 1961	0 483 592	July 1964
			315 000 001	August 1964	315 220 883	July 1965
			316 000 001	August 1965	316 316 237	July 1966
		54bhp.	317 000 001	August 1966	317 283 852	July 1967
Volkswagen 1500			318 000 001	August 1967	318 235 386	July 1968
			319 000 001	August 1968	319 264 031	July 1969
			310 2000 002	August 1969		
			0 221975	August 1963	0 483 592	July 1964
			315 000 001	August 1964	315 220 883	July 1965
			316 000 001	August 1965	316 316 238	July 1966
Volkswagen 1600		66bhp.	317 000 001	August 1966	317 233 853	July 1967
			318 000 002	August 1967	318 235 387	July 1968
			319 000 002	August 1968	319 264 032	July 1969
			310 2000 002	August 1969		

Ferdinand Porsche, father of the Volkswagen

LUBRICATION

Lubrication

The flow diagram represents the flow of lubricating oil through the Volkswagen engine.

After being sucked up through the suction tube at the bottom of the crankcase, oil flows through the oil pump to either the oil cooler or the oil pressure relief valve, depending on whether the oil is under high or low pressure. When the engine is cold, and the oil thick, the oil cooler is bypassed and the cold, high pressure, oil flows through the relief valve to the engine passageways. However, when the engine is warm and the oil thinner, oil travels through the oil cooler, which is directly in the path of the cooling air from the cooling fan. In this way, the oil is able to act as an even greater medium of engine cooling. After leaving the cooler or relief valve, the engine oil makes its way to critical lubrication points in the Volkswagen powerplant. The first route is to the crankshaft main bearings, where the oil is transferred to the crankshaft by means of drilled passageways. From the crankshaft, oil then flows to the connecting rod bearings, and is splashed onto the cylinder walls, pistons and piston rings. The force of oil hurled from the rotating parts to the cylinder walls is considerable. It is for this reason that the oil does a proper job of lubricating the cylinder walls and pistons.

A second route of the engine oil is to the camshaft bearings, while a third is through the hollow push rods to the rocker arm bearings and the valve stems.

The Volkswagen engine uses the geartype pump. In this method, two gears are en-

Aerial view of Volkswagen plant in Wolfsburg, Germany

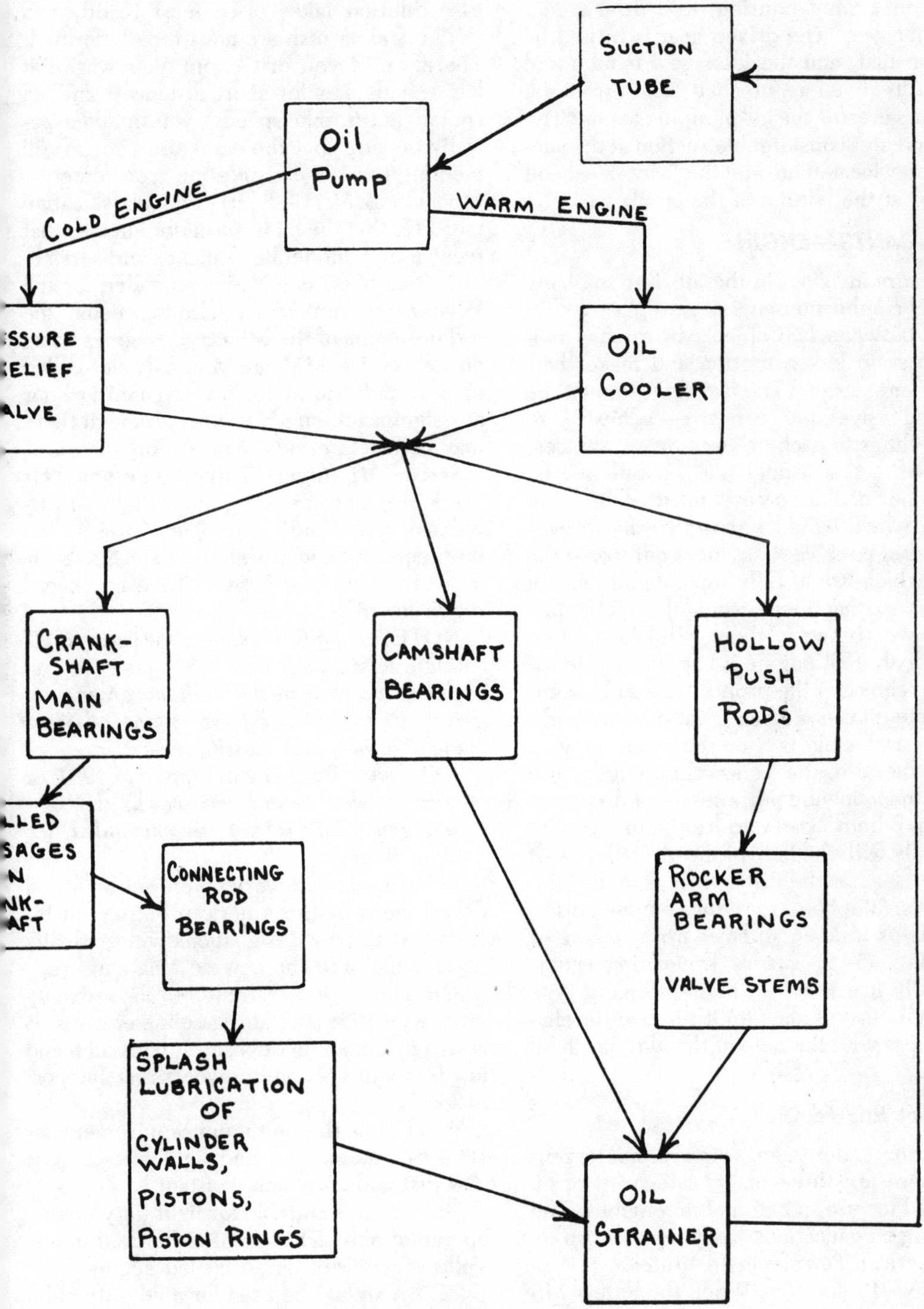
Suction Tube
Oil Pump
Cold Engine
Warm Engine
ssure
elief
alve
Oil Cooler
Crank-Shaft Main Bearings
Camshaft Bearings
Hollow Push Rods
lled
sages
n
nk-
aft
Connecting Rod Bearings
Rocker Arm Bearings
Valve Stems
Splash Lubrication of Cylinder Walls, Pistons, Piston Rings
Oil Strainer

Diagram of oil flow in the Volkswagen engine

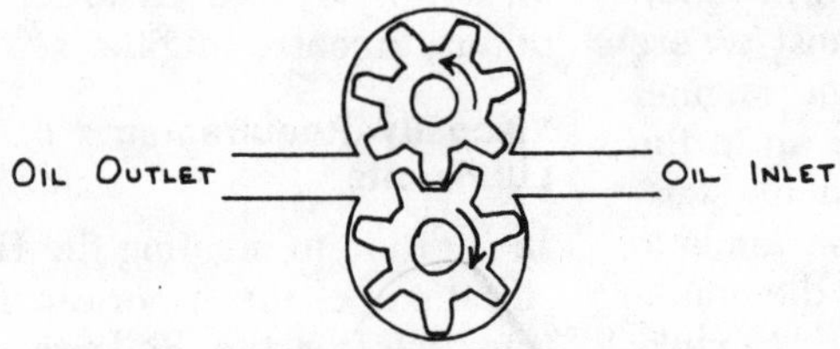
Oil Outlet
Oil Inlet

Gear-Type Oil Pump as used in Volkswagen

closed in a snug housing—the driven gear and idler gear. The driven gear is turned by the camshaft, and the idler gear is mounted to turn freely on a stub shaft. The turning of the gears creates the oil-pumping action. The pump creates considerable suction at the suction pipe located inside the wire mesh oil strainer at the bottom of the crankcase.

LUBRICANTS—ENGINE

The theory involved in the lubrication of any internal combustion engine is to place a substance between two objects in relative motion so as to lessen friction and make their movement easier. The substance must be both adhesive and cohesive—adhesive so that it clings to each of the moving surfaces, cohesive so that it does not separate and be driven out of the space it must occupy. An engine which would last practically forever would be possible if a lubricant could be found which would fully separate all moving surfaces so that there would be no contact whatsoever between them. Full lubrication is the goal of all engine lubrication systems, and the choice of the proper type and weight of engine oil can mean a great deal. In addition to reducing friction between moving parts, the oil in the Volkswagen engine also serves the following purposes: (1) it dissipates heat and helps parts to run more coolly, especially with the help of the oil cooler; (2) it acts as a seal for the pistons, rings, and cylinder walls; (3) it helps to reduce engine noises; (4) it helps to keep surfaces from rusting or corroding; (5) it acts as a cleaning agent, especially if it is of the high-detergent type commonly used today; (6) it removes foreign substances with the help of the wire mesh oil strainer.

Types of Engine Oil

In addition to detergent versus nondetergent oils, there are three major categories of oil designed for use in automobile engines. The following classifications have been set up by the American Petroleum Institute:

Service MS (*Severe*). When the letters MS appear on an oil container, they mean that the oil is refined and reinforced with additives so that it will satisfy the most severe demands made on it by a gasoline engine. Service MS oils are able to stand up to the especially hard demands imposed by start-stop driving in which condensation tends to build up on cylinder walls and in the crankcase. It is in this type of service that crankcase dilution takes place most readily and sludge and varnish are most rapidly formed. Therefore, if you drive your Volkswagen at low speeds and for short distances (and, of course, at turnpike speeds), you should especially be sure that the crankcase contains oil meeting the MS classification requirements.

Service MM (*Medium*). This classification indicates that the oil is meant for engines that receive only moderate demands and service. This type of oil is not recommended for the Volkswagen unless it also exceeds the requirements of the MS class. Engines using oil for service MM are generally not called upon to perform under severe conditions for any significant length of time, although there may be brief periods of severe operation.

Service ML (*Light*). This oil is designed for use in engines operating under light and favorable conditions, and which present no problems in the way of sludge deposits, bearing corrosion, or otherwise have no special requirements.

NOTE: *only oils displaying the ratings HD (high-detergency) and MS (motor severe) should be used in the Volkswagen engine. Ratings exceeded by the engine oil must include these two classifications.*

On some early engines (prior to 1954), a fiber camshaft timing gear was used. High-detergency oil is not recommended for these engines.

In 1970, new categories were set up for oil designations by the American Petroleum Institute. The new designations will gradually replace the old. The new designations are:

SD. This type oil is required for warranty service on 1968 and later gasoline engines. It resists formation of deposits at both high and low temperatures and prevents rust and corrosion.

SC. This is the minimum requirement for 1964–67 automobiles and light trucks. It is also rust and corrosion resistant.

SB. SB oil is suitable for light duty engine operation only. This is not to be used in any Volkswagen or other air cooled engine.

SA. SA should be used for mild duty only. It has no special protection capabilities. This oil is not to be used in any Volkswagen or other air cooled engine.

Viscosity Requirements of Engine Lubricants

In addition to meeting the HD and MS classifications of the American Petroleum Institute, oils for the Volkswagen engine must

Family portrait—from background to foreground: Fastback Sedan, Karmann Ghia Coupe, Station Wagon, Squareback Sunroof Sedan, Volkswagen 1500 Sunroof Sedan

also be of a certain viscosity, depending upon the outside temperature in which the car is operated. Viscosity is defined as resistance to flow, and oils with higher viscosity numbers (e.g. 30) are thicker than those of lower viscosity numbers (e.g. 10W). The "W" after the lower viscosity indices means that the oils are desirable for use in cold weather or winter periods.

SAE viscosity ratings presently run from 5 to 50, and reflect the flow ability of the oil at a definite temperature. It is most important that the correct viscosity oil be used in the Volkswagen engine. If the viscosity is too low, moving parts will tend to come into contact, thereby causing high friction and wear, and possible bearing failures. Just as oils must be able to separate moving parts properly, they must be thin enough to get between the parts in the first place. If an oil is too thick it will not be able to flow properly into tight and critical bearing areas, with the result that incomplete separation of moving parts leads to bearing failure or a high rate of wear. If an oil is either too thick or too thin it cannot provide full lubrication and separation of close-tolerance moving parts in the engine. In order to underscore the importance of the proper engine oil, consider the following example: the Volkswagen Squareback Sedan, while cruising at 70 miles per hour, will have its engine turning at approximately 3,000 revolutions per minute. This means that the crankshaft will turn 3,000 times each minute. Each point on the crankshaft number one main bearing surface is traveling in the same 2.16″ circle at a frequency of 58 times each *second!* The engine oil has only 1/3,000 of a second to get from the main bearing drilling into the crankshaft drilling; obviously not time enough for oil that flows too slowly. At this same time, the four pistons are sliding along the cylinder walls at a speed of 18 miles per hour. The choice of engine oil can mean the difference between sliding, gliding, rubbing, or galling in all of these parts. With the closely-machined surfaces and clearances in the Volkswagen engine, it is important that lubricating oil be of such a weight that it can separate moving parts effectively and still be able to flow at the proper rate. For maximum engine life and efficiency, the Volkswagen factory recommends the following selection process in choosing the oil for your car:

Viscosity of Oil	*Outside Temperature*
SAE 30	In the warm seasons and all year in countries with hot climates.
SAE 20 W/20	In the winter.
or SAE 10 W*	In areas where the average temperature is below −15° C (5° F).
SAE 5 W*	In countries with arctic climates and temperatures below −25° C (−13° F).

*Avoid driving at high speeds for long periods if using SAE 10 W oil and the outside temperature is above 0° C (32° F) or if using SAE 5 W oil when the temperature is above −15° C (5°F).

TRANSMISSION LUBRICANTS

The Volkswagen transmission and differential are combined in a single case, and lubricated by a common oil. The differential gears are of the hypoid (technically, a special type of skew bevel gearing) variety. Extreme-pressure hypoidgear lubricants must be used because of the high tooth pressures and high rubbing velocities encountered in this type of gearing. Care must be taken to see that straight mineral oil is not used in the Volkswagen transaxle assembly. Such a lubricant would lead to metal-to-metal contact, scoring, galling, and seizure of the gear teeth.

In the Volkswagen transaxle unit, use only good quality SAE 90 hypoid oil the year

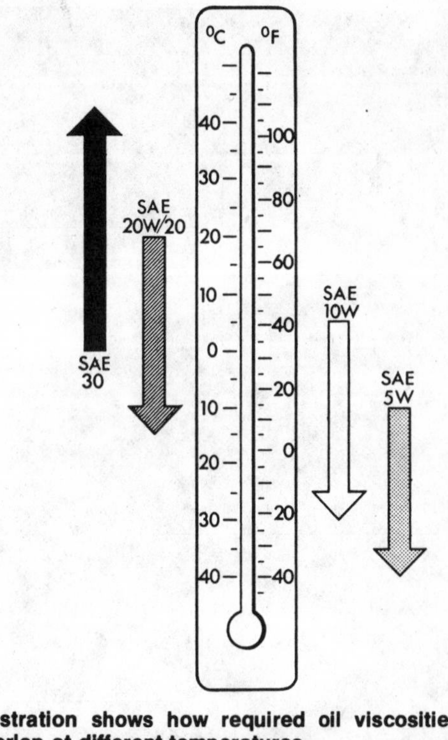

Illustration shows how required oil viscosities overlap at different temperatures.

'round. In countries with arctic climates, the thinner SAE 80 hypoid oil may be used.

Because hypoid oil can cause corrosion and premature hardening of the main drive shaft oil seal in a car that is stored for a long period, drain the transmission fluid and refill with an anti-corrosion oil before storing a car for the winter.

GREASE

Grease is a mineral oil thickened by compounding with soap and containing alkalis or metals such as calcium, sodium, lithium, barium and others to acquire various qualities. Because there are so many different varieties of grease, Volkswagen specifies them by chemical makeup and also by specifying the ASTM dropping point or melting point. Volkswagen transmission grease should be saponified with sodium and have a drip point above 284°F.

The multi-purpose greases specified for the lubrication of the front end, the front wheel bearings, and the breaker arm fiber block in the distributor are of the lithium base variety, and are to have a melting point of at least 330°F. With the temperatures generated and the shocks absorbed by the front wheel bearings, it is not surprising that the grease used must be of the highest quality.

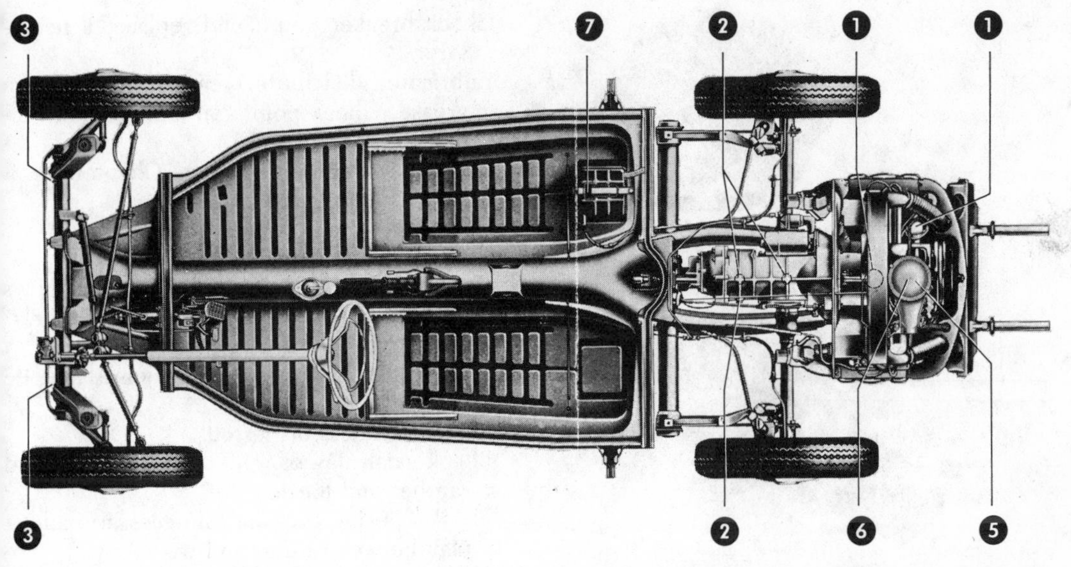

Maintenance points, 1500 models: (1) engine oil, (2) transmission oil, (3) front end, (4) door and hood locks, (5) carburetor linkages, (6) air cleaner, and (7) battery.

High-pressure universal grease is specified for the door and hood locks of the Volkswagen. This grease must be both cold-resistant and water-repellent and have a drip point above 230°F.

Greases: Summary

Lithium grease
(multi-purpose)

- Front end, front wheel bearings, breaker arm fiber block in distributor.

Universal grease

- Door and hood locks.

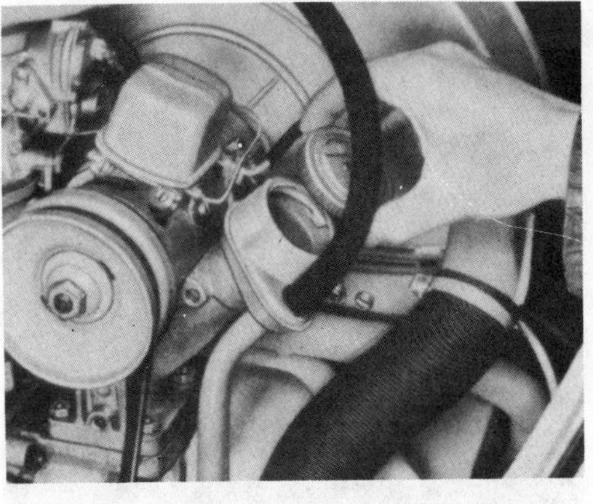

Oil filler, Type 1

ROUTINE MAINTENANCE

EVERY 600 MILES

Check tire pressures and tightness of wheel bolts.

EVERY 1,500 MILES

Lubricate tie rod ends on front end of 1961 and earlier models. Lubricate front axle tubes, king pins on 1965 and earlier models.

EVERY 3,000 MILES

Change engine oil, clean strainer.
Check for leaks from engine and transmission.
Lubricate carburetor controls and linkages.
Check battery, clean and grease terminals.
Examine the level of electrolyte in the cells and, if necessary, add distilled water via the plugs on top of the battery.

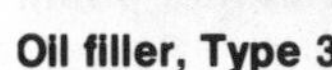

Oil filler, Type 3

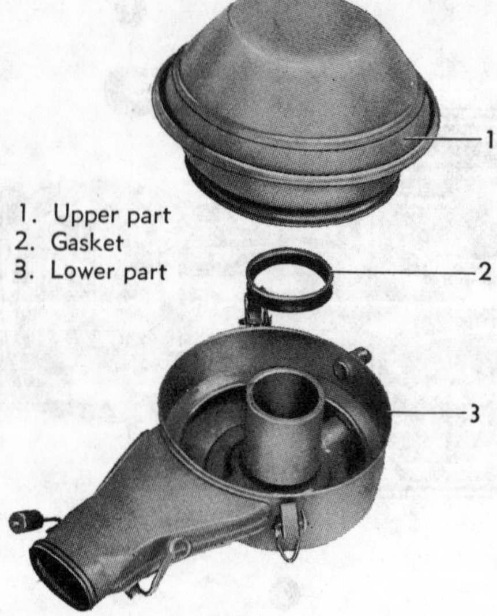

Oil bath air cleaner should be cleaned at regular intervals for best engine operation

Exploded view of oil strainer, which should be cleaned at each oil change

Bring the electrolyte level up to the top of the vertical separators.

Lubricate door and hood locks with cold-resistant, water-repellent universal grease.

Lubricate rear brake cable conduit tubes on earlier models which have fittings provided for this purpose. Universal grease should be applied to these fittings if they are present.

Lubricate pedal cluster grease nipple on earlier models having such a fitting.

EVERY 6,000 MILES

Check V-belt for tightness. Clean fuel pump filter.

Check breaker points and replace, if necessary.

Lubricate distributor cam with lithium grease. Check point gap and ignition timing. (See Chapter 2.)

Adjust valve clearances. (See Chapter 2.)

Clean and gap spark plugs.

Check compression pressures.

Check exhaust system for damage.

Check water drain flaps and cooling bellows on 1600 Fastback and Squareback models.

Adjust clutch pedal free play.

Check dust seals on steering joints and tie rod ends.

Check tightness of tie rods.

Check axial play of upper torsion arms; and camber and toe-in.

Check steering gear and, if necessary, adjust play between roller and worm.

Check for tire wear and damage.

Check braking system for leaks or damage.

Check brake fluid level; top up if necessary with Genuine VW Brake Fluid or Lockheed brake fluid. Do not use mineral oil.

Check for defective light bulbs and other possible breakdowns in the electrical system.

Check and clean air cleaner, top up if necessary.

Check rear axle oil level and inspect for leaks.

Lubricate front end.

Check automatic transmission level, fill up if necessary.

On automatic stickshift, check clutch servo rod clearance, clean control valve air filter, and clean and adjust shift lever contacts.

On Super Beetle, check suspension strut ball joint dust seals. This model requires no front end lubrication.

EVERY 12,000 MILES

Transporter—change oil in reduction gear cases.

Replace spark plugs and points.

Lubricate felt above cam bearing in distributor, earlier models.

EVERY 30,000 MILES

Clean, grease, and adjust front wheel bearings.

Renew transmission lubricant, clean two magnetic drain plugs, check for leaks.

On automatic stickshift, clean and lubricate rear wheel bearings.

On Super Beetle, check play of suspension strut ball joints.

MAINTENANCE PROCEDURES

Changing Engine Oil

The engine oil should be changed only after the engine has been warmed up to operating temperature. In this way, the oil holds in suspension many of the contaminants that would otherwise remain in the engine. As the oil drains, it carries dirt and sludge from the engine. After the initial oil change at 600 miles, the oil should be changed regularly at a period not to exceed 3,000 miles. If a Volkswagen is being operated mainly for short, slow-speed trips it may be advisable to change oil more often, say 1,500 or 2,000 miles, especially if cold temperatures prevail. In arctic climates, it is recommended that engine oil be changed every 750 miles.

When changing the oil, first unscrew the drain plug in the center of the crankcase and allow the dirty oil to drain into a suitable receptacle. During every oil change, the oil strainer should also be cleaned. This wire mesh strainer is held in place by six cap nuts, and should be cleaned thoroughly with a safe solvent. The strainer plate should also be cleaned. This lowest part of the crankcase collects a great deal of sludge in the course of 3,000 miles. Replace the assembly, using new gaskets (2) and the copper washers on the cap nuts in order to prevent leaking at the strainer plate. Before refilling the engine with oil, replace the drain plug and tighten to a torque not to exceed 22 foot-pounds (3mkg).

The proper amount of oil to put into the crankcase of any Volkswagen is 5.3 U.S. pints (2.5 liters). This quantity should be measured, possibly through use of a pint jar. Under no circumstances should a full 3

Carburetor linkage lubrication points, Type 1

Carburetor linkage lubrication points, type 3 dual carburetor engine

quarts be put into the engine. Overfilling will probably result in failure of various engine oil seals and severe leakage. It is not harmful if, upon refilling with this quantity, the oil level is either a few millimeters above or below the full mark on the dipstick. As long as the oil level is between the two marks, there is no danger of the oil level being too low. However, should the level fall below the lower mark at any time, approximately one quart should be added to the crankcase as soon as possible to assure proper lubrication.

It is recommended that the Volkswagen owner stay with the same brand of oil, because mixing different types of oils could possibly be detrimental to proper lubrication of the engine. If a Volkswagen has been run for many thousands of miles on a non-detergent oil (not recommended), it is advisable to be careful in switching to a high-detergency

Type 3 air cleaner is held to carburetor at each end by a wing nut which is built into the air cleaner housing

brand. When such a change is made, it is possible that the detergent oil will do its cleaning job too well, and clog up narrow oil passages with dirt or other foreign matter that has accumulated over the miles.

After the oil has been changed, the air cleaner should be inspected for possible cleaning and/or topping up with fresh oil. The refill requirement for the oil bath air cleaner is given in the Capacities and Pressures Chart. It is a welcome convenience that the total of the crankcase requirement and the oil cleaner requirement is approximately three quarts. In this way, there is no leftover or wasted oil. The air cleaner oil bath uses the same oil.

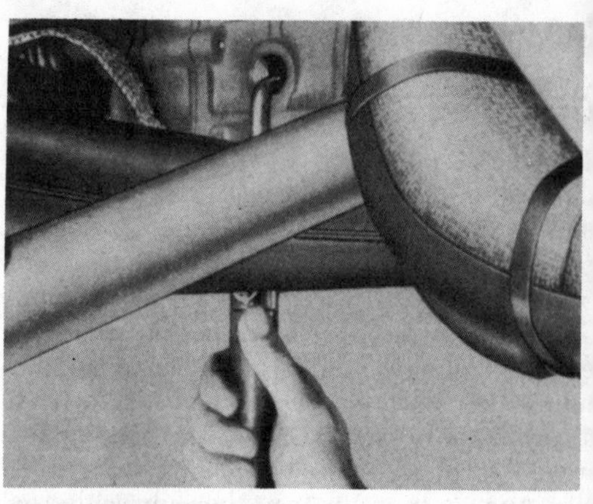

Transmission is refilled, and level inspected through this hole

Changing Transmission Oil

The oil in the transmission-differential unit should be changed approximately every 30,000 miles. As with the engine oil, the transmission lubricant should be changed only after it has reached operating temperature and carries in suspension the maximum quantity of unwanted particles of dirt and other matter. When draining the transmission oil, both magnetic drain plugs should be removed and cleaned. Because the magnetic tips of the drain plugs are little larger than a quarter of an inch, they can hold only a limited quantity of iron-based particles. If the oil is drained while the rear end is in an unloaded condition, it is possible that some oil will remain in the half axles. This may change the refill requirement slightly. However, the oil can be drained and renewed regardless of whether the rear end is loaded or unloaded.

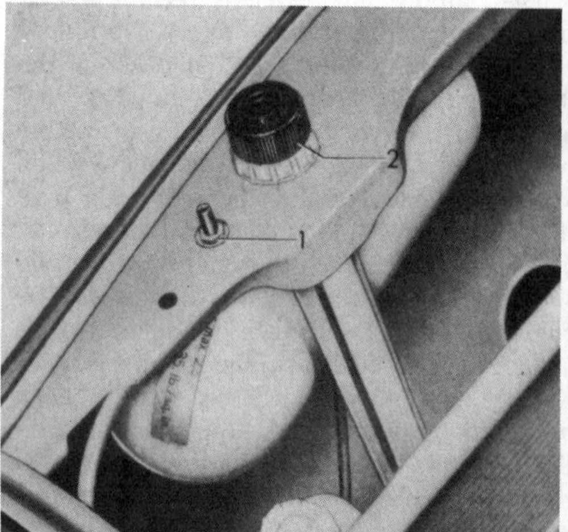

Window washer on pre-1968 models should be filled with air to no more than 35 psi

Transmission lubricant is drained via two magnetic plugs

There is one very important point of caution in refilling the Volkswagen transaxle unit with oil: if the oil has been put in too quickly it may overflow from the filler hole and give the impression that the unit has been filled when, in fact, it has not. The Volkswagenwerke, therefore, suggests that it is good practice to pour in two or three pints, wait a few minutes, and then pour the rest in.

On automatic stickshift type 1 models, draining the transmission oil requires removing, cleaning, and replacing the transmission oil pan. The refill capacity of each model is given in the Capacities and Pressures Chart.

Greasing Front Axle

It is important to the proper functioning of the front end that all moving parts be thoroughly lubricated at the correct intervals. Most important, the front axle should be raised during the entire operation. This will ensure that grease will be able to reach all points requiring service.

On 1966 and later models, it is recommended that the front axle be greased only every 6,000 miles. However, on models preceding 1966, service should be carried out more frequently; the torsion bar nipples should be greased at least once every 3,000 miles and preferably every 1,500 miles to eliminate any doubt. The front suspension on 1971 Super Beetles requires no lubrication.

Before lubricating the front end, all grease nipples should be wiped clean with a suitable rag, and the nipples should be inspected for damage. If a body-point high lift is not used, the car may be jacked up one side at a time so that the fittings on that side can be lubricated. Raising the car in this manner should be done on a level surface, with the wheels chocked on the side not being raised. After letting the car down, the handbrake should be released and reset before raising the other side. This is a good way to keep the car from moving in the fore-and-aft direction while you are jacking up the second side. Because the Volkswagen jack is applied to the midpoint of the car's weight at the side supports, it is relatively easy for the car to move slightly and twist the jacking support if care is not taken to avoid this.

NOTE: *never do any work on or under a jacked-up car unless the weight of the vehicle is supported by heavy wooden blocks or jackstands.*

Owners of 1962 and earlier models must see that the tie rod ends are lubricated via the grease nipples provided for this purpose. Owners of 1965 and earlier models should lubricate the four grease nipples that serve the king pins and the torsion arm link pins.

When greasing, continue to apply grease until fresh grease can be seen emerging from the extremities of the lubrication points. Care should be taken to see that no grease or oil comes into contact with rubber parts, especially the tires and brake hoses. If grease should accidentally contact these parts it should be wiped off immediately.

Lubricating Steering Gear

The Volkswagen steering gear is filled with transmission oil and does not need topping up or regular changing. However, on earlier models, it had been recommended that the

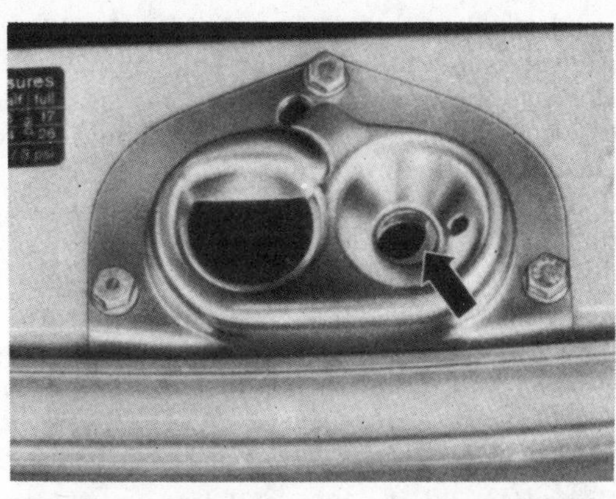

When lubricating, attention should be paid to hood lock, shown

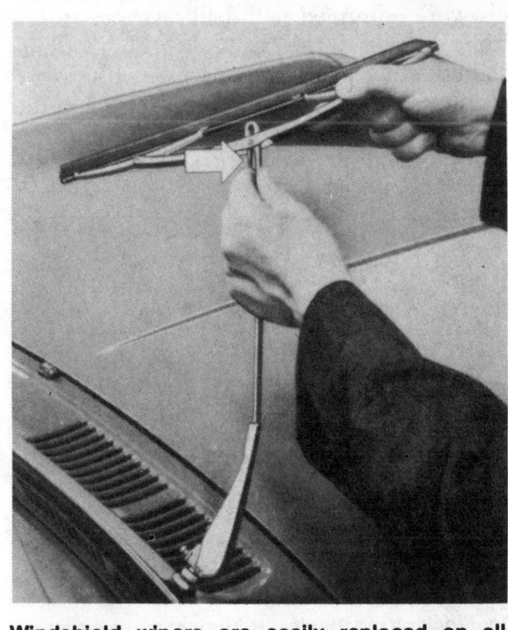

Windshield wipers are easily replaced on all Volkswagens

Door lock striker plates require occasional treatment with universal grease

level of oil in the steering gearbox be kept slightly below the filler plug hole. While periodic topping up and changing are not necessary, the steering gearbox should be checked for the proper oil level at intervals of 3,000 miles in order to ensure that there has been no extensive leakage which might otherwise be overlooked. The steering gear should be lubricated only with SAE 90 hypoid oil and under no circumstance should any other lubricant be used.

Greasing Front Wheel Bearings

Beginning with the 1966 models, tapered roller bearings were used in the front wheels of all model Volkswagens. Previously, all models were equipped with ball bearings in the front wheels. The front wheel bearings should be cleaned and repacked with grease at intervals of 30,000 miles. In servicing the front wheel bearings, the following procedures should be followed:

BALL-BEARING EQUIPPED MODELS

1. Jack up the side of the car; remove hub cap from wheel; remove wheel.
2. Remove small dust cap that covers locking nuts at tip of axle.
3. Unscrew the hexagonal lock nut, remove the locking plate, inner hexagonal nut, and the thrust washer. Nuts on left axle have left-hand thread; those on the right have right-hand thread.
4. Pull the brake drum off the axle stub, while at the same time being careful to keep the inner raceway and the cage of the outer bearing from falling in the dirt. If brake drum resists being removed, it may be necessary to back off the brake adjustment slightly and also bolt the wheel back onto the brake drum so as to have more leverage in pulling on the drum.
5. Remove plastic grease seal from hub and take out cage of inner bearing.
6. Leaving inner raceway in place on axle,

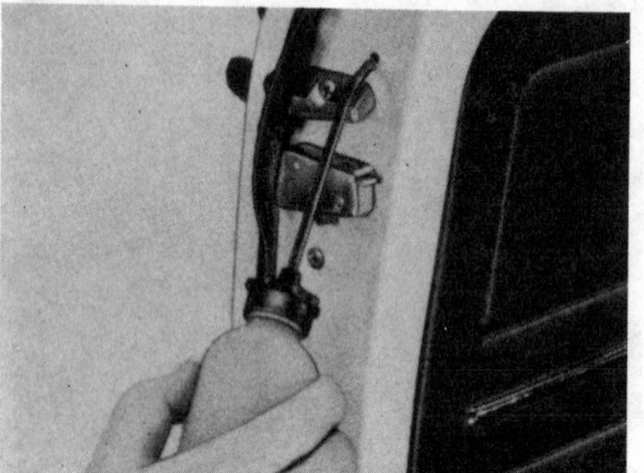

Door locking mechanism is lubricated via small oil hole

Two of the four lubrication points at the end of the type 3. The torsion bars should be lubricated only with the weight off the front wheels

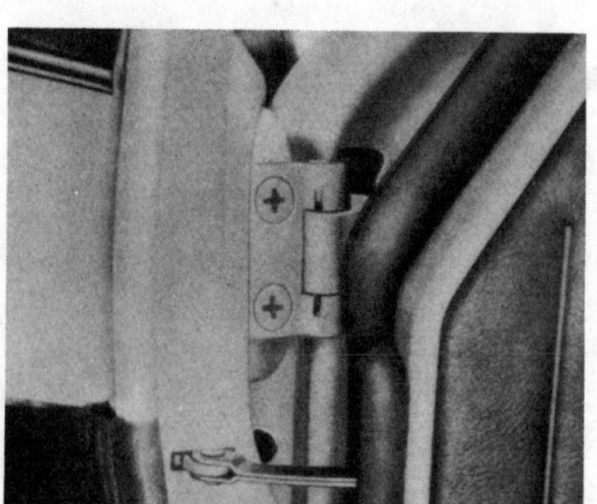

Door hinges should be lubricated regularly, especially during winter months

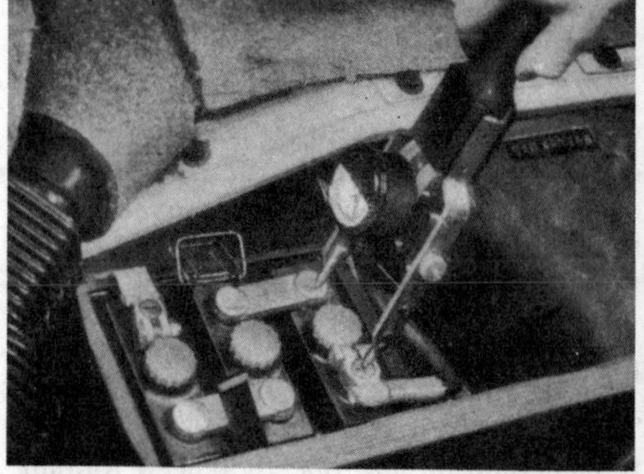

Except for Karmann Ghia and Transporter, Volkswagen batteries are under the rear seat

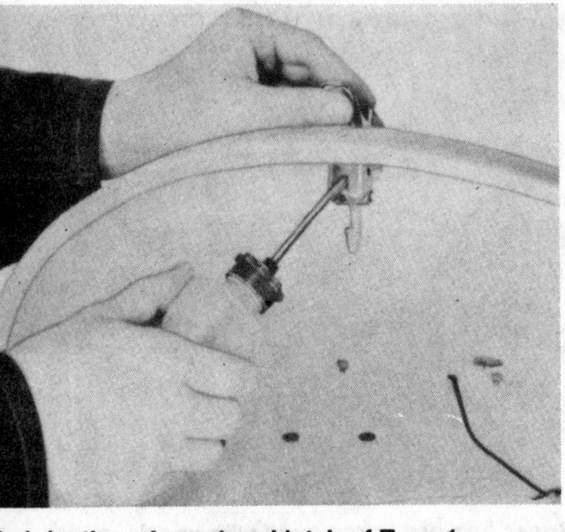

Lubrication of rear hood latch of Type 1

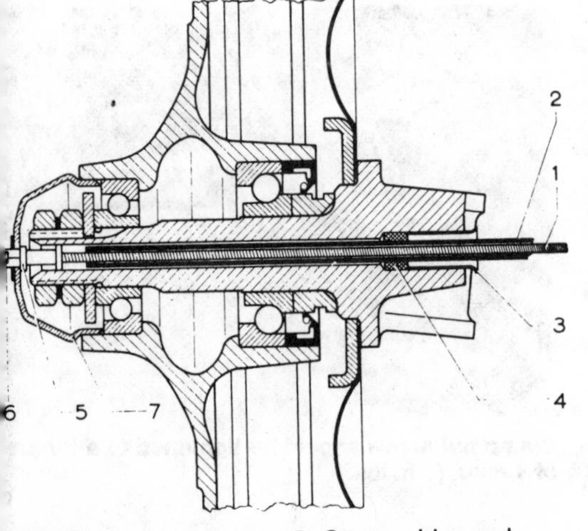

1. Cable
2. Plastic sheath
3. Metal sleeve
4. Rubber sleeve
5. Square drive end
6. Cotter pin
7. Hub cap with square hole

Cross-sectional view of front wheel bearings. Wheel shown is left front, for cotter pin and speedometer drive cable are visible

and outer raceway in place in hub, clean all components in solvent and also clean the inside of the brake drum, being careful to keep any grease or oil from touching the interior surface of the drum. Caution should also be exercised in order that the brake shoes themselves will remain free of grease.

7. Repack the inner bearing cage with grease and place within the hub. Now the plastic seal can be reinstalled by tapping it in lightly until it achieves a flush position. A flat piece of wood placed atop the seal may prove helpful in this operation.

8. The inner raceway on the axle should now be greased and the wheel replaced. After repacking the outer bearing cage, this part can now be inserted in the hub. Bearing installation is completed with the installation of the inner race, thrust washer and hexagonal nut.

9. Tighten the hexagonal nut until the thrust washer can just be moved sideways with a screwdriver. Replace the locking plate (renew if unusable) and the lock nut. The locking plate tabs should be bent over, and the hexagonal nut tightened down.

NOTE: *it is always a good idea to use new plastic seals and locking plates. When working on the left front wheel, take note that this wheel drives the speedometer cable. After removing the cotter pin and the dirving end of the cable, proceed normally.*

ROLLER-BEARING EQUIPPED MODELS

Roller-bearing equipped models include the type 3 and the type 1 Karmann Ghia and beetle models of 1966 and later.

On beetle models, equipped with drum brakes, the procedure is much the same as that listed for roller-bearing equipped models except that the final adjustment will be more exacting. Adjustment requires that the following procedure be followed:

1. Loosen clamp nut screw.
2. Tighten clamp nut to a torque of 11 ft. lbs. while at the same time turning the wheel.
3. Loosen clamp nut until the axial play of the wheel is between .03 and .12 mm. (.001–.005").
4. Tighten clamp nut screw to a torque of 7 ft. lbs. and recheck axial play.
5. Install hub cap.

The following directions apply to type 3 and 1971 and later type 2 models, and the 1500 and 1600 Karmann Ghia, supplied with disc brakes:

1. After removing front wheel and disc cap, bend up the lock plates on the caliper securing screws and remove both the screws and the caliper assembly.
2. Secure caliper to the brake hose bracket by means of a piece of wire or rope. The caliper should not be allowed to hang by the brake hose.
3. Loosen the socket head screw of the clamp nut. Unscrew clamp nut.
4. Remove the wheel bearing thrust washer.
5. Remove disc.
6. The parts removed should be cleaned

Left front wheel contains the speedometer drive shaft tip, which can be removed after taking out cotter pin

Removing brake drum. If brakes drag slightly, removal can be impeded. If difficulty is experienced, back off brake adjustment two or three notches

Loosening pinch bolt in nut. The nut at the left front wheel has a left-hand thread

Inner hub cap is removed with special puller

Clamp nut screw should be tightened to a torque of 1 mkg. (7 ft. lbs.)

thoroughly in a cleaning solvent solution. Because dirt and lining dust can act as abrasives, these particles should be kept out of the bearings for obvious reasons. Check all parts for wear, damage, and proper size.

7. Lubricate bearings with a lithium grease of the proper type, pressing grease into the cages and fill the grease cavity of the disc. Grease should not be put into the disc cap.

8. Press in outer race of inner bearing.

9. Fit the inner race and cage and insert grease seal. When fitting grease seal, drive in by tapping lightly with a rubber hammer; avoid tilting seal.

10. Press in outer race of outer bearing.

11. Install thrust washer and ensure that it is not tilted.

12. Adjust bearings so that axial play is between .03 and .12 mm. (.001 and .005"). The adjustment process is as described in the preceding section on adjusting front wheel bear-

ings on beetle models equipped with roller bearings.

Greasing Door Hinges and Hood Locks

The door hold-open rods and hood locks should be greased lightly with universal grease. Hinges of the doors and hoods should be oiled at each lubrication service after they have been cleaned. Late type 1 models have a plastic plug in each external door hinge. To lubricate the hinge, pry out the plug and insert two or three drops of engine oil. Molybdenum disulphide-based paste should be used in lightly greasing the striker plates on their friction surfaces. Excess grease in this area should always be cleaned off. A graphite lubricant should be used for the door lock cylinders. It is especially advisable to lubricate the door lock cylinders in the winter months to help prevent moisture from accumulating and freezing the mechanism. Dip the key in graphite, insert in the lock and turn several times to ensure full lubrication.

Greasing Carburetor Linkages

Ball joints on the carburetors (type 3 dual carburetors) should be lubricated with a molybdenum disulphide-based paste. In the type 3, three ball joints are on each of the two carburetors, and two additional ball joints on the center three-arm lever. While the molybdenum-based paste is desirable, chassis grease can also be used on these ball joints if the molybdenum variety is not available.

Other parts of the carburetor(s) that should be given periodic lubrication are the choke valve shaft, the throttle valve shaft, the accelerator cable swivel pin, and the connecting rod and lever that operate the accelerator pump. Use a few drops of oil in each location.

Servicing Air Cleaner

The Volkswagen air cleaner, of the oil-bath type, collects dirt in the oil bath section and must be serviced periodically in order to remove the accumulated dirt and to renew or top up the oil. If inspection reveals that there is very little oil above the sludge layer, the bottom section should be removed and cleaned thoroughly prior to renewing the oil. If, however, inspection shows that there is little sludge, but the oil level is low, the oil may simply be topped up to the specified level. Ordinarily, the top section of the Volkswagen air cleaner does not require cleaning. The upper section should never be set down with the opening upwards.

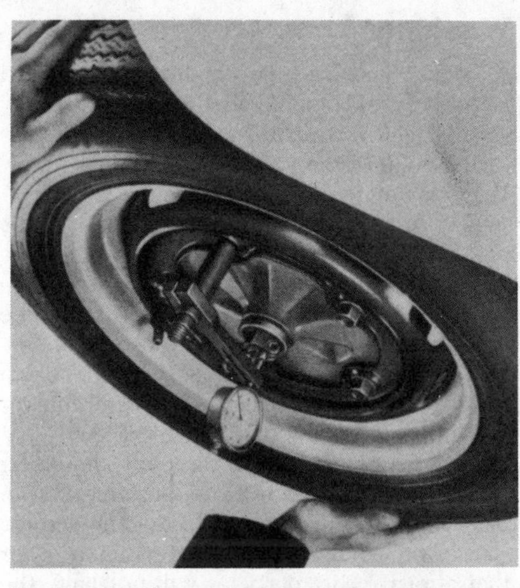

Checking axial play of front wheel bearings. If the play is not between .001–.005", bearings must be readjusted

Protecting Battery Terminals

Cover with petroleum jelly whenever the battery is serviced or replaced.

Servicing Ignition Distributor

If necessary, multi-purpose grease should be applied to the breaker arm fiber block whenever the points are inspected. Use enough to do the job—but avoid excess grease that could come into contact with the breaker points and cause misfiring of the ignition system. On older Volkswagens there is a felt wick in the center of the distributor cam shaft which requires a few drops of light oil every 15,000 miles. If the indentation in the top of the cam shaft is entirely metallic, no lubrication is required. On models that have a felt ring in the contact breaker base plate, this point should receive a few drops of light oil every 3,000 miles.

CARE OF THE BODY

Besides being a constant source of pride for the owner, a well-preserved Volkswagen will be worth many more dollars at trade-in time.

Washing

A new Volkswagen should be washed frequently during the first weeks of ownership. This will contribute to the best possible final drying of the paint. The paint on a new Volkswagen is not really *wet*, but it is still relatively soft and has not yet hardened to the point where it should be waxed or polished. In washing the Volkswagen, it is well to have a soft sponge for the body, a soft brush for the wheels, a long-handled brush for the underside of the chassis, and a good supply of clean water. A chamois leather will be desirable for drying the car after it has been washed.

Dirt on the exterior of the body should be sprayed evenly with water, after which it can be removed with a soft sponge. The sponge should be cleaned at short intervals in order that abrasive dirt particles will not have the chance to scratch the polished surfaces. After washing, the body should be rinsed thoroughly and dried. The washing process may be made easier with various auto soaps and wash-and-wax preparations. After using any such detergent, it is very important to rinse the body thoroughly with clean water. A powerful jet of water should never be allowed to hit the painted surface of the car.

Waxing

The paint of a new Volkswagen should not be waxed until after the first 8–10 weeks. Before applying a coat of wax preservative, the car must be washed and completely dried with a chamois. When water on the painted surfaces tends to remain in large patches instead of forming small beads and running off, it is time for an application of wax. Wax can be applied in the form of wash-and-wax preparations if the interval between washings is not too great. This method is not nearly as long-lasting as those involving the harder-to-apply paste waxes. In general, it can be stated that the harder a wax is to apply, the longer it will protect the finish. While there are exceptions to every rule, this is a good one to remember. The car should never be waxed in open sunshine. A preservative specially produced for the paint of the Volkswagen is available at Volkswagen dealers and is known as "L 190" preservative. When applying the L 190, one spreads a thin film on the finish and then rubs it down when it is dry, using a soft polishing cloth.

Polishing

After years of exposure to the elements, any paint will have its appearance adversely affected by dust, sunlight and rain. In this event, it is possible to renew much of the original luster of the paint with the use of a polishing compound. One made especially for the synthetic-resin enamel finish of the Volkswagen is available at most Volkswagen dealerships, and is known by the designation "L 170". This specially-formulated polish seems to be one of the best possible compounds for restoring both the original color and brightness of the Volkswagen finish. It is recommended that the paint be waxed after every application of polish so that the renewed luster can be maintained for as long as possible. When polishing the Volkswagen one should be careful not to polish too large an area at one time, and, in any event, to observe the instructions given on the label by the manufacturer.

Chrome Care

Chrome parts can be best preserved by being periodically washed, dried, and treated with a chrome preservative such as that available at Volkswagen dealers—"VW Chromlin."

Removing Spots

Because water alone will not always be able to remove tar, oil, insects, etc., this type of foreign matter must be removed as soon as possible by other means. Tar splashes in particular have a tendency to corrode the finish in a short time, and should be removed with a soft cloth soaked with fuel, kerosene, or turpentine oil. After removing the tar spots the treated areas must be washed with mild, lukewarm soap solution, and the area rinsed in order to remove the cleansing agent. Preservatives such as the VW L 190 and L 170 can also be used for this purpose. Baked-on insects can be removed with either a soap solution or with the previously-mentioned preservatives. Tree droppings and industrial dirt should, like all foreign matter on the paint, be removed as soon as possible. Special cleaners containing acid can be used for the purpose of removing industrial grime that adheres to the paint, and can be obtained from automobile accessory dealers.

Care of Windows

Windows are best cleaned with an ammonia solution in which ammonia is combined with uke-warm water. Because silicone is present n many liquid and paste cleaners, the windshield should not be exposed to any such preparations. When silicone comes into contact with the windshield, the result is severe streaking by the wiper blades and subsequent poor visibility and danger. When cleaning the windshield with ammonia, the blades should also be wiped off with the same solution. It is advisable to move the wiper arms forward where they will be out of the way and less likely to become bent or otherwise abused. Care should be taken to see that ammonia solutions do not come into contact with the paint.

Weatherstripping

Doors and windows will not seal properly if weatherstripping becomes brittle or damaged. For this reason, all weatherstripping on the Volkswagen should be given a light treatment with talcum powder from time to time. If the movement of rubber weatherstripping causes squeaking or groaning noises, apply talcum powder or glycerine to the surface of the rubber. If the weatherstripping around the windshield or rear window is not leakproof, apply a good quality window cement between the rubber seal and the metal frame.

Upholstery

The leatherette upholstery of U.S. Volkswagens is cleaned by means of either a mild soap solution or a solution of water and leatherette cleaner. The use of a soft brush will facilitate the cleaning process. After the leatherette is cleaned, it should be rubbed with a soft rag until dry.

Capacities and Pressures

Model	Crankcase Refill After Draining (pts.)	Transmission Refill After Draining (pts.) Standard	Auto. Stick Shift	Fully Auto.	Reduction Gears	Final Drive (pts.)	Air Cleaner (pts.) ⑧	Fuel Tank (gals.)	Normal Fuel Pressure (psi)
Type 1	5.3	6.3	6.3 ①	N/A	N/A	②	.5 ③	10.5 ⑨	⑩
Type 2	5.3	7.4	N/A	N/A	.5 each	②	.63 ④	15.8	⑩
Type 3	5.3	6.3	N/A	6.3-8.4 ⑥	N/A	2.1 ⑦	.85 ⑤	10.5	⑩

N/A - Not applicable to this vehicle.

① The total capacity of the Automatic Stickshift torque converter circuit is 7.6 pts. ATF. The refill capacity is somewhat less.

② in unit with transmission

③ 1,300 cc. Karmann Ghia - .63 pts., 1,500 cc. Karmann Ghia - .96 pts., 1,500 cc. sedan and convertible - .85 pts.

④ 1,200 cc. - .44 pts., Late 1,500 and 1,600 cc. -.95 pts.

⑤ Single carburetor engine; .44 pts, fuel injected engine .53 pts.

⑥ Total capacity - 12.6 pts. ATF.

⑦ Only with automatic transmission; otherwise, note ② applies.

⑧ Since so many different air cleaners have been used in production, it is best to rely on the full mark on the air cleaner body. If there is no such mark, these figures may be used.

⑨ Super Beetle - 11.1 gals.

⑩

Pump Marking	Pressure @ RPM
Unmarked (36 hp and earlier)	1.3-1.8 @ 1,000 - 3.000
Unmarked	2.5 @ 3,000 - 3,400
VW 2	5.0 @ 3,800
VW 3	3.5 @ 3,400-3,800
VW 4	3.5 @ 3,800
VW 6	5.0 @ 3,800
VW 7	3.5 @ 3,800
VW 8	3.5 @ 3,800

Tune-Up

TUNE-UP PROCEDURES

As any car including the Volkswagen covers the miles between tune-ups, changes occur in the engine and elsewhere. The clearances between engine parts and the adjustments in other systems of the car become slowly less efficient. Mechanical wear, high temperatures and engine vibration all play a part in causing engine performance to fall off. Loss of power becomes almost impossible for the driver to notice.

One reason why the VW engine should be tuned at periodic intervals is that a small, four-cylinder engine can't really afford to be running inefficiently. Unlike big American cars, the Volkswagen is designed to operate with a small, economical engine and give reasonable performance. However, when the engine is out of tune, it can't do either. While an American V-8, with 300-plus horsepower, can afford to have 100 of these horses sleeping, the Volkswagen can ill afford to have even 20 horsepower going to waste. When a V-8 is running on only seven cylinders, it's only a 12% drop. However, when one cylinder in a Volkswagen fails to produce, the drop is twice as great—25%.

Apart from power and efficiency considerations, there is one other major reason for giving the Volkswagen engine periodic tuning attention—money. This is one incentive that should appeal to practically everyone. An engine that is kept in perfect tune will last longer because it's running exactly the way its manufacturers intended it to. And the Volkswagenwerke are by no means going to ruin their reputation of Teutonic efficiency by recommending tuning specs which do not contribute to the maximum life of their engines. Besides lasting longer, a consistently-tuned engine will get more miles per gallon over its entire life. Tuning is not expensive, either. The most expensive component of a tune-up, new spark plugs, will pay for itself in gas mileage alone even if replaced every 10,000 miles. So there you have it: more miles per gallon, more miles per engine, and most important, more miles per dollar.

Steps in a Tune-Up

1. Battery service
2. Compression check
3. Electrical and mechanical checks
4. Air cleaner and fuel filter service
5. Fan belt deflection check
6. Spark plug service
7. Point adjustment and ignition timing
8. Carburetor or fuel injection adjustment

9. Valve clearance adjustment
10. Throttle regulator adjustment

With these steps accomplished, the Volkswagen engine will have been given a very thorough tuning. If, after tuning, the engine should still not perform up to par, the next chapter (Troubleshooting) should be consulted.

BATTERY SERVICE

Without a battery strong enough to crank it, even the best of engines can't go anywhere. Make sure that the battery is filled to the level of the plates with electrolyte. If it is not up to the proper level (just above the vertical plates) add distilled water, which is available at any auto supply store. The average battery lasts something like two years, but with periodic attention to the electrolyte level most would last much longer.

COMPRESSION CHECK

Before going to the trouble of trying to tune an engine, it is a good idea to first check and see if it is possible to tune the engine satisfactorily. If compression is much below par in any or all of the cylinders it will be impossible to tune the engine without first having the cause of the low compression remedied. If any Volkswagen is found to have a compression lower than 65 pounds per square inch in one or more cylinders, it will be difficult to put the engine in proper running condition through tuning alone.

The first step in checking the compression is to warm the engine to operating temperature so that all moving parts will expand to their normal functioning sizes. Next, remove all four spark plugs and call on an assistant to turn the starter over while you are checking the compression of each cylinder. In measuring the compression in a cylinder, the starter motor should be turned over for roughly three seconds—perhaps a second longer if the starter is particularly slow. The compression gauge must be inserted firmly into the spark plug opening and held there during the cranking of the engine. During the first one or two cranks of the engine it is a good idea to place the gauge loosely against the spark plug hole in order that any dirt or other particles will be blown from between the gauge and the plug opening. If foreign particles are able to disturb the seal between the compression gauge and the spark plug opening, the result will be a too low reading for that cylinder.

It is important to have the throttle wide

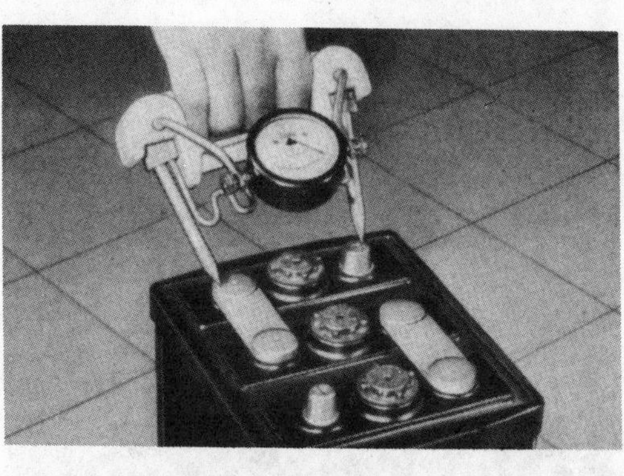

Each battery cell can be tested separately by placing the voltmeter between the three different sets of plus and minus poles

open so that the piston will have a chance to develop its full potential of compression pressure. Care must also be taken to ensure that the choke valve is also fully open. The resulting compression pressure should be in the neighborhood of that specified for each of the Volkswagen engines. Compression differences between cylinders should be no greater than fifteen pounds per square inch (15 psi), and any cylinder that is even ten pounds less than the others should be given particularly close attention during subsequent compression checks.

When compression is low in one cylinder, it is due either to worn piston rings or to valve leakage in that cylinder. While troubleshooting is left largely to the next chapter, it is sufficient to mention here that squirting about a tablespoon of heavy lubricating oil into the spark plug hole will reveal the cause of the low compression. If, after squirting the oil into the cylinder, compression increases, the low compression is due to worn piston rings. If, on the other hand, squirting the oil does not result in a higher compression reading, the problem is most likely to be leaking valves. With regard to leaking valves, a valve may leak slightly in a compression test due to the presence of a particle of dirt on the seat of that valve. In this case, subsequent compression checks will probably reveal that the reading involving the dirt particle was unusually low.

It is an excellent idea to check and record compression readings in all cylinders at periodic intervals, especially if one is interested in keeping a close eye on engine wear and also wants to be forewarned of problems which might otherwise come as a surprise at an inconvenient time. Although compression readings on any particular engine will vary

Water drain hole in air cleaner of type 3 must be kept free of obstructions

widely from one compression check to the next (due to oil temperature, viscosity, outside temperature, method of measurement, etc.) cylinders will generally show the same relative readings. For example cylinder number one may always be 3–4 lbs. higher than cylinder two, and cylinder three may usually be 5–6 lbs. higher than number four.

ELECTRICAL AND MECHANICAL CHECKS

Every engine tune-up should include a visual check of major electrical and mechanical systems, including the following: (1) coil primary wiring and connections, (2) battery connections, (3) starter, generator, and voltage regulator connections. Electrical connections must be tight to ensure trouble-free operation. Wiring that is frayed or cracked should be replaced.

Visual checking of mechanical components should include inspection of the following: fuel-line and vacuum-line connections, tightness of carburetor attaching nuts, and freedom of operation of the choke and carburetor linkages.

AIR CLEANER AND FUEL FILTER SERVICE

The air cleaner should be serviced as described in the preceding chapter, and the fuel filter (built into the fuel pump) should be cleaned and re-installed. The fuel pump filter on recent Volkswagen models is removed by unscrewing the hexagonal head plug from th side of the fuel pump assembly.

FAN BELT DEFLECTION CHECK

On all Volkswagens except the type 3 and 4 the V-belt drives both the generator and th blower which cools the engine. On the type 3 and 4 the V-belt drives the generator only the blower fan being mounted directly on th crankshaft of the engine rotates at the sam speed as the engine. In all Volkswagen models, the fan belt should deflect approximatel 15 mm. (.6″) when pressed firmly at its midpoint with one's thumb. The quality and adjustment of the fan belt is especially important on the smaller Volkswagens, in which i drives the cooling fan. If the fan belt goes bac in one of the beetle models, all is lost and th car can be driven no further without causing severe damage to the engine. However, in the type 3 and 4, it is possible to drive without the fan belt for fairly long distances, especially in the daytime. An average battery wil power a car's ignition for some distance before running out of sparks. However, if th headlights must also be used, the distanc that can be covered will be much shorter. In short, if the fan belt fails in a VW, stop righ then and there without further delay. (Whe you see the red light in the speedometer dial, the generator is no longer charging.) But i the belt fails in a Squareback, Fastback, o 411, you can drive to the nearest servic area. Regardless of the model you drive, it i a good idea to carry an extra V-belt.

ADJUSTING FAN BELT TENSION

If belt tension is too great, the result will be a shortening of the life of the generator bear-

When pressed firmly at mid-point, fan belt shoul yield approximately 15mm. (.6″)

ngs due to unnecessary stress. If the belt is oo loose, the result will be a loss of cooling fficiency in beetles and a loss of generating ower in both the small and large Volks-vagens. The following steps should be fol-owed in adjusting the fan belt tension on all Volkswagens, regardless of year:

1. Remove holding nut from the generator pulley shaft. In type 3 models, the pulley must be held from turning by using a suitable wrench. In the smaller Volkswagens the pul-ey is held by a screwdriver wedged between he notch in the generator pulley and the upper generator housing bolt.

2. Remove the outer half of the generator pulley and adjust the fan belt tension by fit-ing the proper number of spacer washers be-ween the halves of the pulley. Each washer added or removed changes the play in the belt about ¼″.

3. If the fan belt is too loose, one or more spacer washers will have to be removed from between the pulley halves. If the belt is too ight one or more washers will have to be added between the pulley halves.

4. When correct adjustment has been achieved, the belt will deflect approximately 6 in. (15 mm.) when pressed by thumb pres-sure at its midpoint.

5. When adjustment is correct, install the outer half of the generator pulley, and insert all left-over washers between the pulley nut and the outer pulley half. In this way, all spacer washers will remain on the pulley shaft and will be readily available whenever subsequent belt adjustments are required.

6. Tighten pulley nut.

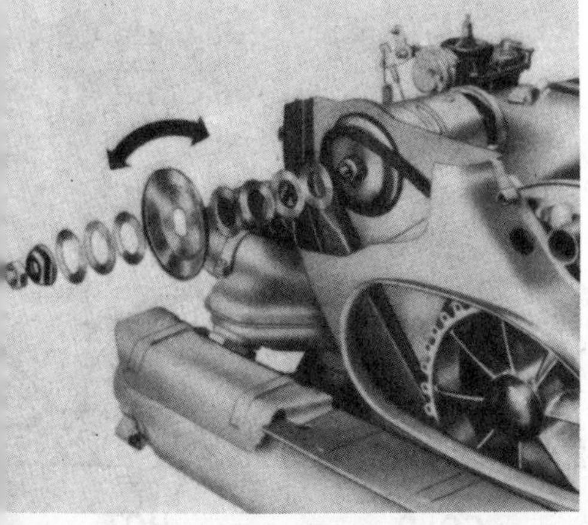

Exploded view of type 3 generator pulley and spacers. Putting more spacers inside pulley makes belt more slack

Exploded view of the Type 1 and 2 generator pulley and adjusting shims which are at the end of the shaft and also between the pulley halves

Loosening of the generator pulley nut of the Type 1 and 2 engine involves a counterclockwise torque (wrench) along with a clockwise torque to keep the pulley from turning (screwdriver wedged as shown)

If the belt has stretched to the extent that correct adjustment can no longer be achieved by removing spacers from between the pulley halves, the belt should be replaced. Also, if a belt has frayed edges or cracks, it should be replaced. Fan belts should be kept free from grease and oil.

It is recommended that a new belt be inspected regularly during the first several hundred miles of use, since new belts have a tendency to stretch slightly.

SPARK PLUG SERVICE

Spark plugs should be cleaned and gapped at 6,000 mile intervals and replaced every 12,000 miles.

See the Tune-Up Specifications Chart for recommended spark plugs.

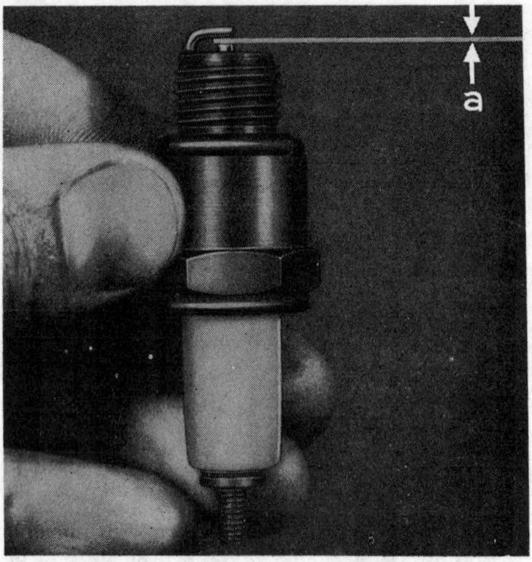

Spark plug gap between .024–.028″ for all models

After the spark plugs are removed from the engine, they should be inspected for outside appearance which gives valuable information on the running condition and mixture adjustment of the engine.

See the "Color Insert" for further details.

In the dual-carburetor type 3 engine, each carburetor feeds two cylinders. It is not unusual to discover that one bank of cylinders is running either richer or leaner than the other bank. When this situation occurs, the carburetors should be adjusted properly.

The spark plugs in the Volkswagen should be gapped to between .024″ and .028″ (.6 to .7 mm.). In general, the best idling will result from a wide spacing of the spark plug gap, but a wide gap will also cause starting to be slightly harder. A wide gap at high speeds will also lead to missing. On the other hand, a plug with a smaller gap will miss less at high speeds, give easier starting, but will cause poor idling. In order to improve starting ability when outside temperatures are very low, the plug gap may *temporarily* be reduced to .020″ (.5 mm). Because of the wide range of conditions under which the Volkswagen operates, it is probably best to gap plugs in the middle of the .024″–.028″ range, in other words .026″. However, if one places more emphasis on good idling than on good high-speed performance, or vice-versa, he may wish to choose gaps in either the higher or the lower portion of the recommended range. The Volkswagen will operate equally well at any setting in the recommended range, and any differences would probably be so slight as to be unnoticeable.

It is advisable to adjust only the side electrode by bending it either toward or away from the center electrode with a special spark plug gapping tool. In the normal operation of the engine, spark plug gaps increase due to natural burning, so used plugs must have their gaps reduced in order to achieve the correct adjustment.

Volkswagen, like most car manufacturers, specifies plugs intended for *average* driving conditions. Because of this, the individual owner may decide to use slightly different plugs for his particular type of driving. If a great deal of high-speed driving is done, it may be desired to change to plugs of a cooler heat range. If mostly slow-speed driving is commonplace for another Volkswagen, its

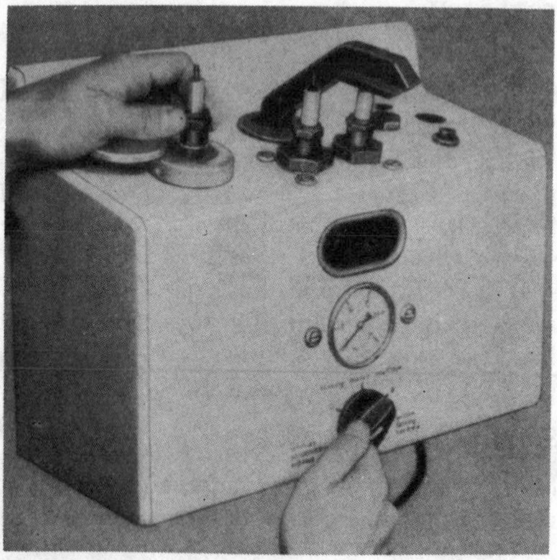

Spark plugs are tested under operating conditions in a compression box like this one

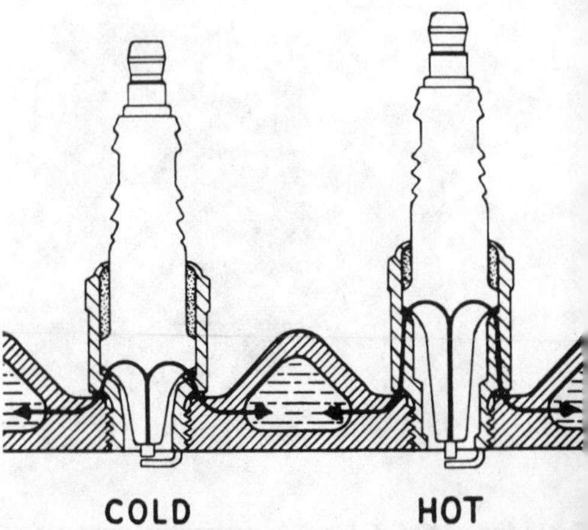

Illustration shows the different lengths of the heat travel-paths in hot and cold-running spark plugs

owner may wish to change to hotter plugs in order to prevent fouling. The length of the porcelain insulator in the nose of the plug determines the heat range of the plug. The longer the porcelain nose, the longer the time required to dissipate heat from the insulator to the cylinder head. Hence, a longer-nosed insulator means a hotter-running spark plug.

When installing spark plugs, care should be taken not to overtighten them. The Volkswagen cylinder head are made of a relatively light alloy and can be cross-threaded more easily than the more common cast iron heads in domestic automobiles. For this reason, a few drops of light oil should be placed on each plug before it is inserted by hand (using the extension holder supplied with the VW tool kit) and turned cautiously for several turns before tightening down to a torque of roughly 22–29 ft. lbs. New gaskets should be used. When the proper torque is used in tightening the plugs, only the compression ring of the new gaskets will be crushed—this is the desirable condition

CONTACT POINT ADJUSTMENT AND IGNITION TIMING

The breaker points are the heart of the Volkswagen ignition system, and must be given their share of attention. All Volkswagens ever made require a breaker point gap of .016″ (COLD) and a dwell angle of 50 degrees. It is best if the engine is cold from sitting overnight or for several hours. If you are not able to rest your hand comfortably on any part of the engine, it is too warm to set the breaker point gap and the ignition timing. In adjusting the contact points, the following steps are taken:

1. Remove distributor cap and rotor.
2. Turn the engine by hand until the fiber block on the movable breaker point rests on a high point of the cam lobe.
3. With a screwdriver, loosen the locking screw of the stationary breaker point.
4. Manipulate the stationary point plate so that the clearance between the points is .016″.
5. Tighten the locking screw of the stationary point.
6. Recheck gap, correct if it has changed from step (4) due to the tightening of the locking screw.

When replacing points, the same steps as above are followed, except that in between steps (3) and (4), the old points are taken out

Right-hand mark is 10 degrees BTDC, one on left is 7.5 degrees BTDC on early engines. See text for details of markings on other engines

1. Spring for breaker arm
2. Breaker arm
3. Distributor with cam
4. Connection for contact
5. Breaker plate
6. Vacuum unit
7. Condenser
8. Insulator
9. Securing screw
10. Pins on breaker plate
11. Breaker point
12. Eccentrics for return springs
13. Return springs
14. Pull rod

Interior of a typical Volkswagen distributor

and the new points inserted. Points should be replaced when they have been badly burned or have been in use so long that correct adjustment is no longer possible. When checking the gap of points which have been in use for some time, it is advisable to use a round gauge rather than a flat feeler gauge. In the case of points that have a peak in one point and a valley in the other, the flat-type gauge will result in a reading which is smaller than the actual gap between the two points.

It is only after adjusting the breaker points properly that the ignition timing should be adjusted. It is most important that the ignition timing adjustment be carried out only when the engine is dead cold, because rising engine temperature causes the setting to become different.

If, in exceptional cases, it is necessary to adjust the timing with a warm engine, not exceeding 122°F, the timing should be advanced about 2.5° beyond the normal setting. The timing must then be rechecked at the first opportunity with the engine cold.

VW engines have had several different arrangements of crankshaft pulley timing marks. On early type 1 engines, the pulley bore two timing marks, 7.5° before top dead center and 10° before top dead center, reading clockwise. Later, with the introduction of emission controls, a 0° top dead center mark was added. The 7.5° and 10° marks were subsequently removed, leaving only the 0° mark. Current engines have only a 5° after top dead center mark. Type 2 engines are generally the same as type 1 models. Early type 3 engines have marks at 7.5° and 10° before top dead center; later engines have marks at 7.5°, 10°, and 12.5° before top dead center. Fuel injected type 3 engines have marks corresponding to 0°, 7.5°, 10°, and 12.5° before top dead center. Refer to the Tune-Up Specifications Chart and the sticker on the particular engine for the correct timing setting.

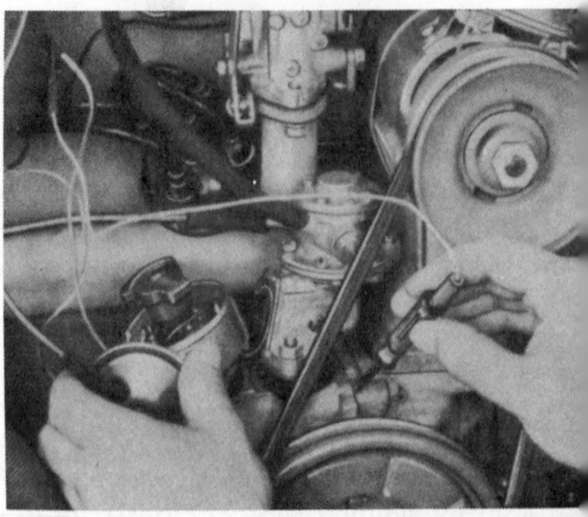

A 6/12-volt test lamp is used in setting the ignitio timing of all pre-1968 Volkswagens. One lead the test lamp is connected to terminal 1 of the co the other to the ground

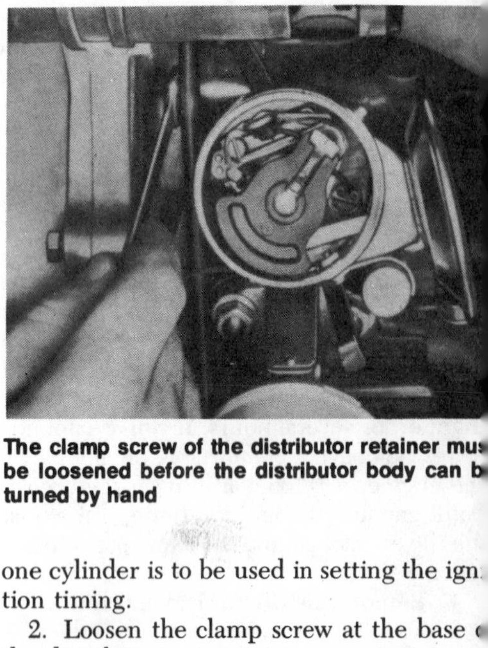

The clamp screw of the distributor retainer mu be loosened before the distributor body can b turned by hand

SETTING THE TIMING

1. Turn the engine by hand until the appropriate mark on the crankshaft pulley is lined up with the crankcase dividing line. (On type 3 models, the mark is to be lined up with the timing setting surface, or pointer, on the fan housing. At the same time that the appropriate mark is opposite the dividing line the rotor must be pointing to the lead wire of cylinder number one (the cylinder toward the front of the car on the passenger [right] side). Number one position is indicated by a mark on the rim of the distributor. See Chapter 8 for an illustration showing cylinder numbering. If the rotor is not pointed toward number one cylinder, the crankshaft must be turned one more revolution clockwise until it is. On recent models, number three cylinder is retarded about 4° compared with number one cylinder and only number one cylinder is to be used in setting the ign tion timing.

2. Loosen the clamp screw at the base the distributor.

3. Attach the lead of a test lamp (6 volt f 1966 and earlier models, 12 volt for 1967 an later) to terminal 1 of the ignition coil an ground the test lamp.

4. With the ignition switched on, rotat the distributor body clockwise until the co tact points close, and then rotate it slowl counter-clockwise until the contact poin close, and then rotate it slowly counte clockwise until the points begin to open an the lamp lights.

5. Without moving the distributor body tighten the clamp screw at the base of th distributor.

urning the distributor body in the clockwise di-ection retards the ignition timing. Turning coun-erclockwise advances

6. Recheck adjustment by turning the rankshaft pulley counter-clockwise one-half urn, and then turning clockwise until the nark is within one inch of the dividing line. t this point, proceed more slowly by tap-ing the right side of the fan belt with your and. Such tapping will cause the fan belt to nove in either moderate or very small umps, depending on the strength of the tap. light taps toward the end of the check will nsure the finest possible check on the accu-acy of the adjustment. If, upon rechecking, he lamp lights before the mark gets to the ividing line, the timing will have to be re-arded slightly by loosening the clamp screw nd rotating the distributor body in the lockwise direction. Rotating the distributor lockwise retards the timing, while rotation the counter-clockwise direction advances he timing.

NOTE: *adjustment of ignition timing on 1967 and earlier engines must always be done with a test lamp. A stroboscopic timing light should not be used, as it will alter the entire setting range. However, it is recommended that exhaust emission controlled engines (1968 and later) and type 3 fuel injected engines be timed with a stroboscopic light. These engines should be timed at idle speed, with the distributor vacuum line disconnected and the engine at normal operating temperature.*

ARBURETOR ADJUSTMENT

s a part of a routine tune-up it is necessary nly to adjust the idling speed and mixture rews on the carburetors of most single car-

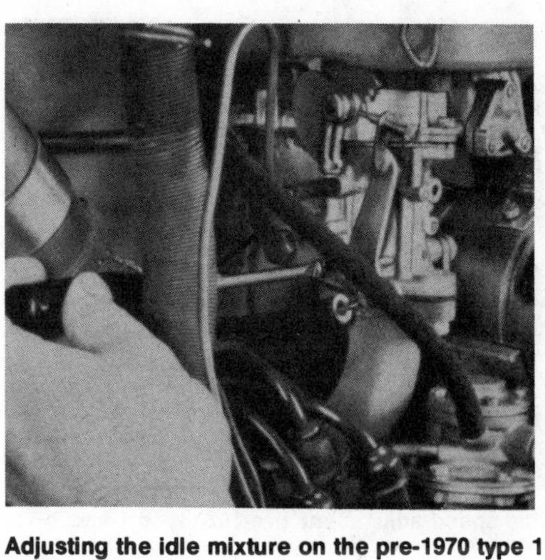

Adjusting the idle mixture on the pre-1970 type 1 and 2 carburetor

buretor Volkswagens. On 1970 and later type 1 and 2 engines, the volume control screw is factory set and the throttle valve remains closed during idling. Idling speed adjustments are made with the air bypass screw. On the 30 PICT-3 carburetor (1970), the air bypass screw is below the volume control screw. On the 34 PICT-3 carburetor (1971), the air bypass screw is above the volume control screw. Before adjustment is begun, the engine should be at normal operating temperature and the idle adjusting screw must not be resting on the fast idle cam of the automatic choke. The following steps should be followed in setting the idle speed and mixture adjustments on single-carburetor Volkswagen engines:

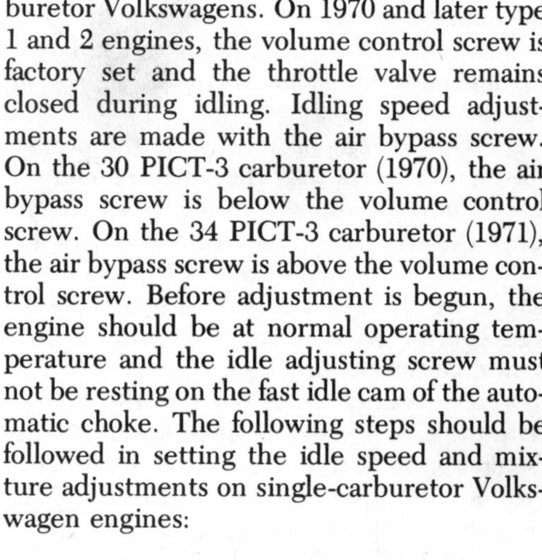

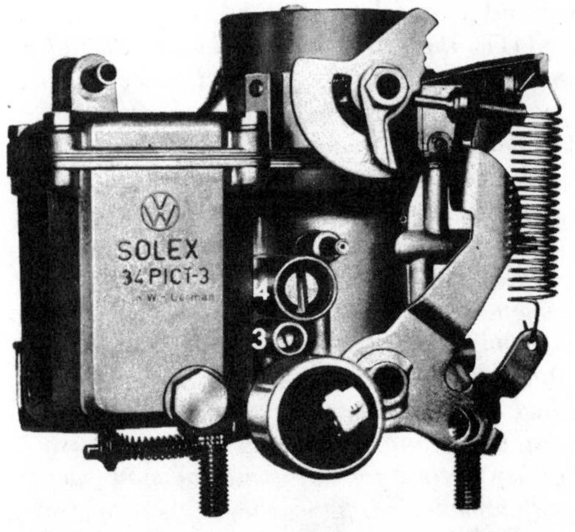

Adjustment screws on Solex 34 PICT-3 carburetor, 1971 type 1 and 2. 3 is the volume screw. 4 is the air bypass screw

Idle speed adjustment, pre-1970 type 1 and 2

1. With the engine warm and running, turn the idling speed adjusting screw in or out until the proper idling speed is attained. The correct speed can be found in the Tune-Up Specifications Chart and on the sticker on the engine.

2. With the engine running at the proper idle speed, turn the idle mixture control screw slowly clockwise until the engine speed begins to drop, then turn slowly in the counterclockwise direction until the engine is running smoothly again. Now turn the mixture control screw another ¼ turn in the counterclockwise direction.

3. If necessary, re-adjust the idle speed. With the clutch pedal depressed, the engine should continue to run after the accelerator has been quickly depressed and released. If the engine stalls, either the mixture adjustment or the idle speed adjustment is incorrect and should be remedied.

NOTE: *the setting of the slow-speed (idle) mixture will have a great influence on the performance and economy of the Volkswagen at speeds as great as fifty or sixty miles per hour. If the mixture is too rich, the result will be excess fuel consumption, stalling when the accelerator pedal is suddenly released, and possible "running on" when the ignition switch is turned off. If the mixture is too lean (too much air, not enough gasoline), the result will be better fuel consumption, but exhaust valves may suffer burning or warping. The previously-given method for adjusting the slow-speed adjustment will give the proper mixture setting. Turning the mixture screw clockwise will lean the mixture, while turning counterclockwise will enrich it.*

CARBURETOR ADJUSTMENT—DUAL CARBURETOR MODELS

On certain type 3 models, there are two carburetors—one for each bank of two cylinders. While the current models are equipped with a fuel injection system, type 3 vehicles sold in the U.S.A. in 1966 and 1967 have dual carburetors and require slightly more sophistication in the tune-up operation. Adjusting the carburetors on the dual-carb models requires the use of a special instrument to measure air flow. A commonly-used product is that known as the Uni-Syn, available for under $10 from most mail-order auto accessory sources. This device measures the vacuum created by carburetor suction by means of a red piston which rides up and down inside a graded glass tube. The higher the vacuum, the higher the piston is raised.

Besides the synchronizing device mentioned above, a small frozen-juice can will also be required in order that the device will fit on the air horns of the carburetors. Because of the screws that stick straight up from the air horn for the purpose of holding the air cleaner, the small can (open on both ends) is needed. By mounting it on top of the can, the test device will clear the screws without losing vacuum. Before attempting adjustment the engine must be at operating temperature.

Adjustment Steps

1. Remove the right-hand connecting rod of the carburetor linkage system. This is the rod which connects the center bell crank with the right-hand carburetor throttle.

2. Remove the air cleaner. It is held on

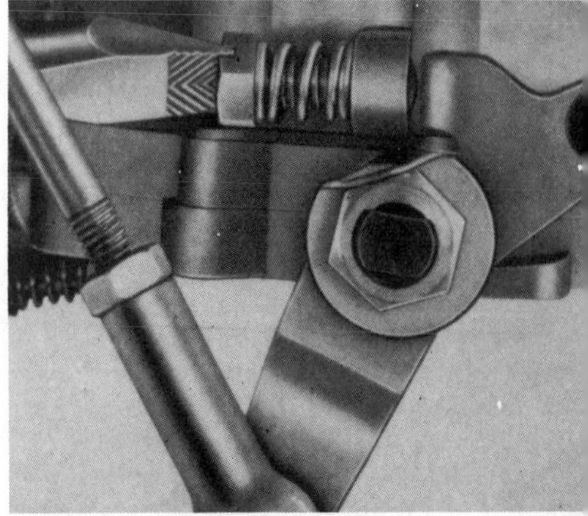

Close-up of idle speed adjusting screw, which is just about to contact throttle lever

The dual-carburetor type 3 engine's air cleaner is fastened down at three points. The center wing nut should always be the first one loosened and the last one to be tightened

by two wing nuts on each carburetor and one wing nut in the center. The connections to the air intake and to the crankcase ventilation system must also be removed.

3. With the engine running, adjust the idle speed adjusting screw of each carburetor until the correct idling speed is attained. Each carburetor should then be sucking the same amount of air. When the test device is moved from one carburetor to the other, the height of the red piston should not change more than one inch, preferably less. Because of the fine adjustment possible with the use of the idle speed adjusting screws there is no

1. Accelerator cable
2. Connecting rod, right
3. Connecting rod, left
4. Carburetor pull rod with return spring

The type 3 dual carburetor linkage

excuse for not being able to adjust the carburetor idle speeds so that the maximum variation is less than one-quarter of an inch. When checking the air flow through each carburetor, the disc on the device should be turned clockwise or counterclockwise until the piston rides approximately in the center of the range.

4. In adjusting the volume control screw of each carburetor, slowly turn the screw clockwise until the engine speed begins to drop, then turn counterclockwise until the engine runs smoothly once again, then a further ¼ of a turn in the counterclockwise direction.

5. Recheck the idle speed adjustment, and if necessary increase or decrease the idle speed of each carburetor so that the correct speed is maintained and the test device shows the same reading when it is moved from one carburetor to the other without moving the disc on the device.

6. Recheck the adjustment on the mixture control screws. On the 1600 models, there is present on each screw a raised portion on the outside perimeter. This will enable one to feel the position of the screw when he cannot see it. The correct position for the mixture control screw will be approximately 1½ turns from the screwed-in position. When turning the screw fully in the closed position, care should be taken not to apply too much torque, for the seat or needle of the screw could be damaged in this way.

7. After the mixture adjustment has been rechecked the idle speed and balance should also be checked again and corrected if necessary.

8. In checking the balance of the carburetors at an increased speed, it is necessary to install once again the right-hand connecting rod which was removed in step (1). By means of a suitable object (e.g. a tool box) wedged against the accelerator pedal, the engine speed should be maintained at approximately 1,200–1,500 RPM in order to check the higher-speed balance of the two carburetors.

9. Apply the test device to the left-hand carburetor and adjust the disc until the red piston rides in the center of the range. Now move the device over to the right-hand carburetor and, without moving the disc, compare the height of the piston here with the height achieved at the left carburetor. If the height of the piston is higher on the right side, the length of the right-hand connecting rod must be increased slightly. If the height

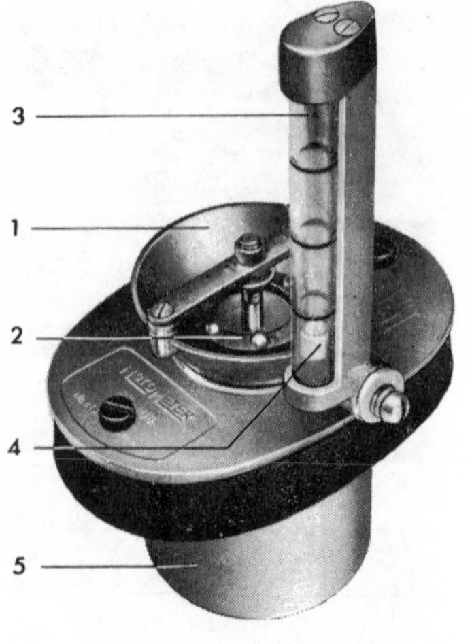

1. Funnel shaped opening
2. Adjustable throttle disc
3. Measuring glass
4. Piston in measuring glass
5. Distance piece

Device used to balance the dual carburetors by equalizing the airflow through them at idle and moderate speeds. The more air being sucked in by the carburetor, the higher the piston rises in the measuring glass

Carburetor balancing device in use. Distance piece is necessary because of screws protruding from mouth of carburetors

of the piston is lower on the right side, the length of the right-hand connecting rod will have to be decreased. Changing the length of the right-hand control rod is accomplished by loosening the nuts on both ends and twisting the rod while leaving the ends stationary. The opposite ends have threads which tighten in opposite directions. The length of the right control rod must be adjusted until there is little or no difference between the

A special three-arm lever operating device can be used in checking the carburetor balance at increased speed

Fan housing cover on type 3 dual carburetor engine is held down firmly by two clips at extreme ends and can be removed for turning engine by hand as is done in ignition and valve adjustment operations

readings of the test device when it is moved from one carburetor to the other.

(Hint: for a really fine adjustment, it is possible to loosen only one of the control rod ends and turn it slightly in the desired direction. If loosening and moving this end is not sufficient to effect the adjustment needed, then the opposite end must also be loosened and moved slightly after the first end has been tightened. This is a step-by-step method which is guaranteed to be more accurate than simply loosening both ends and tightening them up again at the same time. It is quite impossible to avoid changing the setting when tightening the ends. Ordinarily the ends are offset by 90 degrees, but the step-by-step method takes into consideration that the ends may be offset slightly more or less if it will contribute to a more accurate balance.

10. After low-speed and high-speed balance has been checked, the connecting rods should be lubricated at their ends with lithium grease and the carburetor's moving parts lubricated with a light oil.

11. Reinstall the oil bath air cleaner, being careful to tighten the two outer wing nuts first, and then the center wing nut. If the center wing nut is tightened first, it is possible that the adjustment of the right-hand carburetor will be altered when the air cleaner is fastened tightly to the screw protruding from its air horn. Replace the crankcase ventilation hose and air intake connections. In order to install the air cleaner it will be necessary to remove the right-hand carburetor connecting rod temporarily. Take care not to bend this rod.

FUEL INJECTION IDLE SPEED ADJUSTMENT

The only tune-up adjustment possible on the Bosch electronic fuel injection system is that for idle speed. The adjusting screw is located on the left side of the intake air distributor. Early models have a knurled screw with a lockspring; current models have a locknut on the adjusting screw. After adjusting idle speed to specifications, make sure that the throttle valve is completely closed at idle. See Chapter 5 for further information on fuel injection.

Adjusting idle speed on fuel injected engine. Turn screw toward a to increase speed. Turn locknut toward c to tighten

ADJUSTING VALVE CLEARANCE

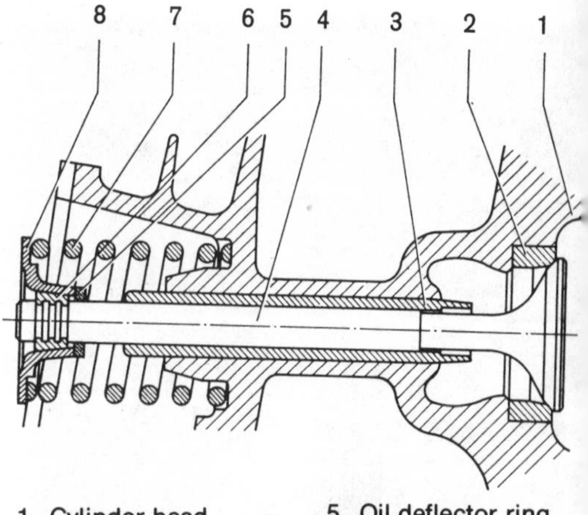

1. Cylinder head
2. Valve seat insert
3. Valve guide
4. Valve
5. Oil deflector ring
6. Valve cotter
7. Valve spring
8. Valve spring cap

Cross-sectional view of valve and associated hardware

Valve clearances given by sticker on fan housing should be adhered to. Stickers are on most Volkswagens manufactured since late 1964

If valve clearances in the Volkswagen engine are too small, the valves can be seriously damaged by warping or burning, and compression will eventually suffer from lack of proper valve sealing. Valves are cooled by resting against the valve seat—if the valves are opened for too long, they have insufficient time to rest against their seats, and hence to transfer their heat to the cylinder head. On the other hand, if the valve clearance is too great, the result will be rough running, loss of power, and excessive wear of the valve train components. However, if error is necessary, it is best to err in the direction of too large a clearance. A few thousandths of an inch of excess clearance will be much less harmful than the same error in the opposite direction. As long as you can hear the valves clicking, you are at least assured that they are not burning.

Before the valves can be adjusted in any Volkswagen, the engine must be stone cold, preferably after sitting overnight. Volkswagen valve clearances vary somewhat between models of different years. To determine the correct setting, refer to both the Tune-Up Specifications Chart and the engine sticker.

Preference is to be given to the valve clearance specified on the engine fan housing sticker, if one is present. On models built after late 1964, such a sticker will be on the fan housing. Such stickers will also be present on all factory rebuilt engines, regardless of horsepower output, and the clearances specified should be followed closely.

Steps in Adjustment

1. Remove distributor cap and turn engine until rotor points to notch in distributor rim and the crankshaft pulley timing mark is aligned with the crankcase split or pointer. #1 cylinder is now at top dead center of its compression stroke. See Chapter 8 for an illustration showing cylinder numbering. (In the type 3 engines, the belt housing cover must be removed so that the engine can be turned by hand.)
2. Remove the rocker arm cover of cylinders #1 and #2.
3. With the proper feeler gauge, check the clearance between the adjusting screw and the valve stem of both valves for #1 cylinder. If the feeler gauge slides in snugly without being forced, the clearance is correct. It would be well to use the "go—no go" gauge system in which the proper leaf slides in but one which is .002" thicker will not.
4. If the clearance is incorrect, the lock nut must be loosened and the adjusting screw turned until the proper clearance is attained. After tightening down the lock nut it is then advisable to recheck the clearance, because it is possible to alter the adjustment when tightening the lock nut.
5. Turn engine one-half revolution in the counterclockwise direction. This will turn the distributor rotor 90 degrees in the counterclockwise direction so that it will now point to the lead wire for cylinder #2. #2 cylinder is now at top dead center.

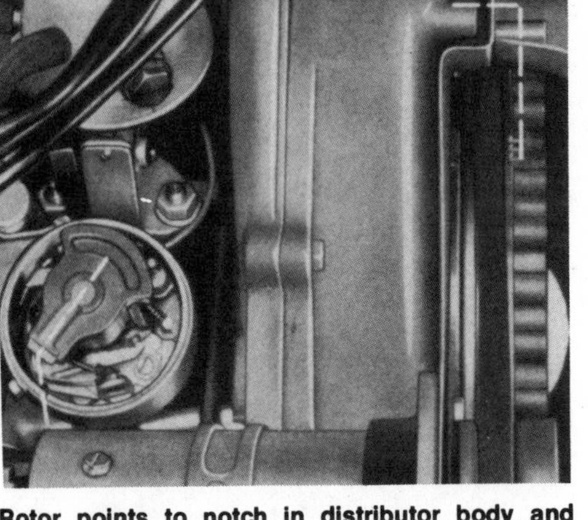

Rotor points to notch in distributor body and crankshaft pulley has notch facing pointer (type 3 engine). Cylinder #1 is now at TDC and its valve can be adjusted

Volkswagen firing order is 1-4-3-2 and rotor turns clockwise. If engine is turned backwards one-half revolution, rotor will turn ¼ revolution backwards, and valves can be adjusted in numerical order

6. Repeat adjustment process for cylinder #2.

7. Replace valve rocker arm cover on cylinders #1 and 2, using a new gasket and cleaning off the seating surfaces to guard against leakage.

8. Remove valve rocker arm cover on cylinders #3 and 4.

9. Turn the engine another one-half turn in the counterclockwise direction so that the distributor rotor now points to the lead wire of cylinder #3. #3 cylinder is now at top dead center.

10. Adjust the clearances on cylinder #3. NOTE: *on pre-1971 type 1 and 2 engines, #3 cylinder runs hotter than the other three cylinders because its cooling air flow is partially blocked by the oil cooler. To counter a tendency for this cylinder to burn exhaust valves, some mechanics set the #3 exhaust valve clearance .001 to .002″ wider than specified.*

11. Turn the engine a further one-half turn counterclockwise and adjust the clearances of the valves in cylinder #4.

12. Replace the rocker arm cover of cylinders #3 and 4, cleaning the sealing surfaces and using a new gasket.

13. Replace distributor cap. Replace belt housing cover in type 3 models.

While correct valve clearance is important to all Volkswagen engines, it is especially important in those having a specified clearance of .008″ and .012″ (intake and exhaust). In these engines the valve clearance actually decreases as the engine warms up, so too little initial clearance, or a clearance obtained

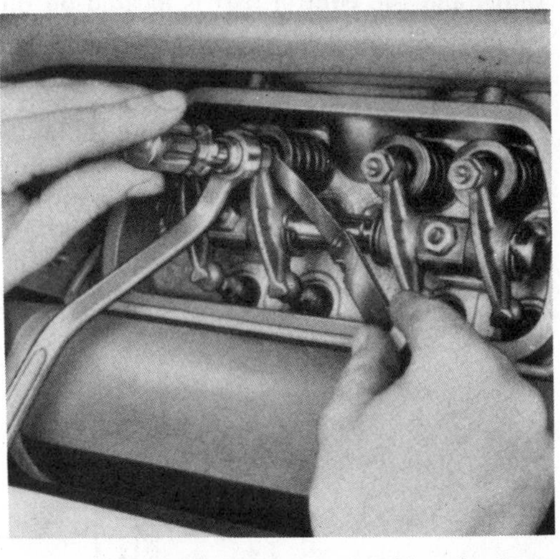

Turning adjusting screw while checking clearance with feeler gauge. Valves should be adjusted only when engine is cold

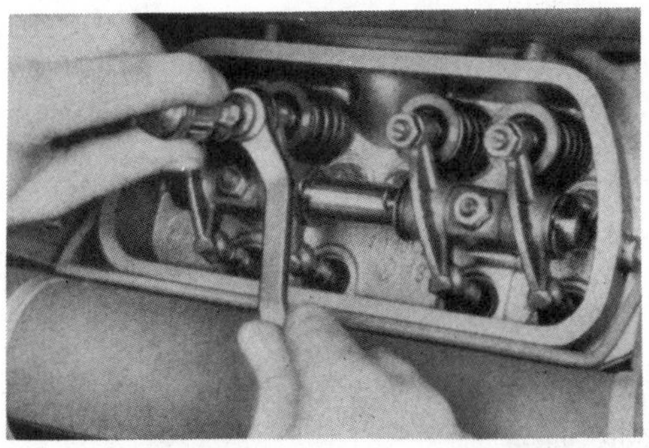

Tightening locknut while holding adjusting screw steady with screwdriver. Clearance should be rechecked after nut is tightened

with a warm engine, can lead to trouble within a short time. On engines with .004″ clearance, the clearance increases as the engine temperature increases.

It is also possible to adjust valves in normal firing order sequence, 1-4-3-2, rotating the engine clockwise. It is helpful to mark the crankshaft pulley directly opposite the 0° mark in order to determine precisely when the engine is turned one-half revolution.

THROTTLE REGULATOR ADJUSTMENT

The exhaust emission control device used on type 1 and 2 vehicles, 1968–72, is the throttle valve regulator. This device holds the throttle open slightly on deceleration to prevent an excessively rich mixture.

On 1970–72 models, the throttle regulator consists of two parts, connected by a hose. The operating part is mounted at the carburetor, and the control part is located on the left sidewall of the engine compartment. The 1968–1969 unit is one piece, mounted at the carburetor.

1. Engine must be at operating temperature, with automatic choke fully open.
2. Start engine. Turn regulator adjusting screw clockwise until control rod just starts to move throttle valve lever. The stop collar on the control rod will be against the regulator body. Engine speed should be 1,700–1,800 rpm.
3. If speed is too high, shorten control rod.
4. After adjustment, tighten lock nuts on control rod.
5. Turn regulator adjusting screw counterclockwise until an idle speed of 850 rpm is obtained.
6. Increase engine speed to 3,000 rpm, then release throttle valve lever. Engine should take 3–4 seconds to return to idle.

Incorrect throttle regulator adjustment may cause erratic idle, excessively high idle speed, and backfiring on deceleration.

CONCLUSION

With the completion of the preceding tune-up operations, the Volkswagen engine will have received a rather complete renewal of the efficiency designed into its electrical, mechanical, and fuel systems. However, should these operations fail to restore the operation of the Volkswagen to a satisfactory condition, it may be necessary to track down the causes of poor performance using the methods described in the "Troubleshooting" (9) chapter.

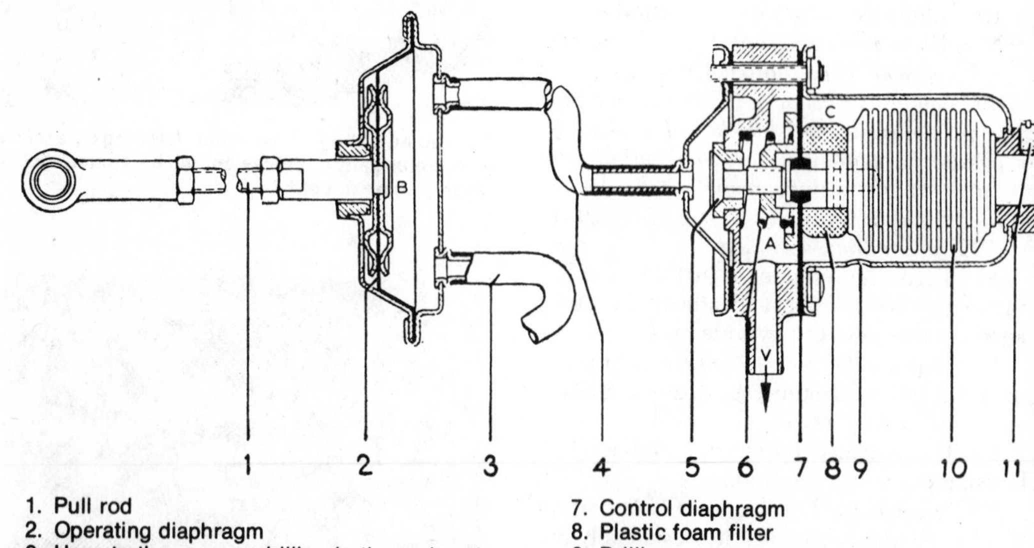

1. Pull rod
2. Operating diaphragm
3. Hose to the vacuum drilling in the carburetor
4. Hose between operating and control part
5. Valve
6. Spring
7. Control diaphragm
8. Plastic foam filter
9. Drilling
10. Altitude corrector
11. Lock screw
12. Adjusting screw

Throttle regulator, 1970–72 Type 1 and 2 vehicles

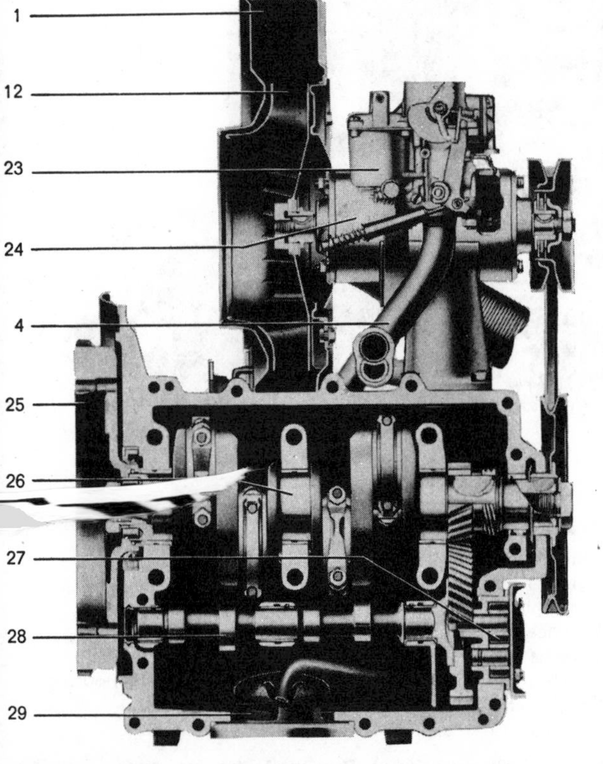

1. Fan housing
2. Ignition coil
3. Oil cooler
4. Intake manifold
5. Fuel pump
6. Ignition distributor
7. Oil pressure switch
8. Valve
9. Cylinder
10. Piston
11. Oil pressure relief valve
12. Fan
13. Oil filter and breather
14. Pre-heating pipe
15. Connecting rod
16. Spark plug
17. Cylinder head
18. Thermostat
19. Rocker arm
20. Push rod
21. Heat exchanger
22. Cam follower
23. Carburetor
24. Generator
25. Flywheel
26. Crankshaft
27. Oil pump
28. Camshaft
29. Oil strainer

Cross-sectional view, type 1 and 2 engine. Note compact size, presence of numerous cooling fins on cylinders and cylinder heads

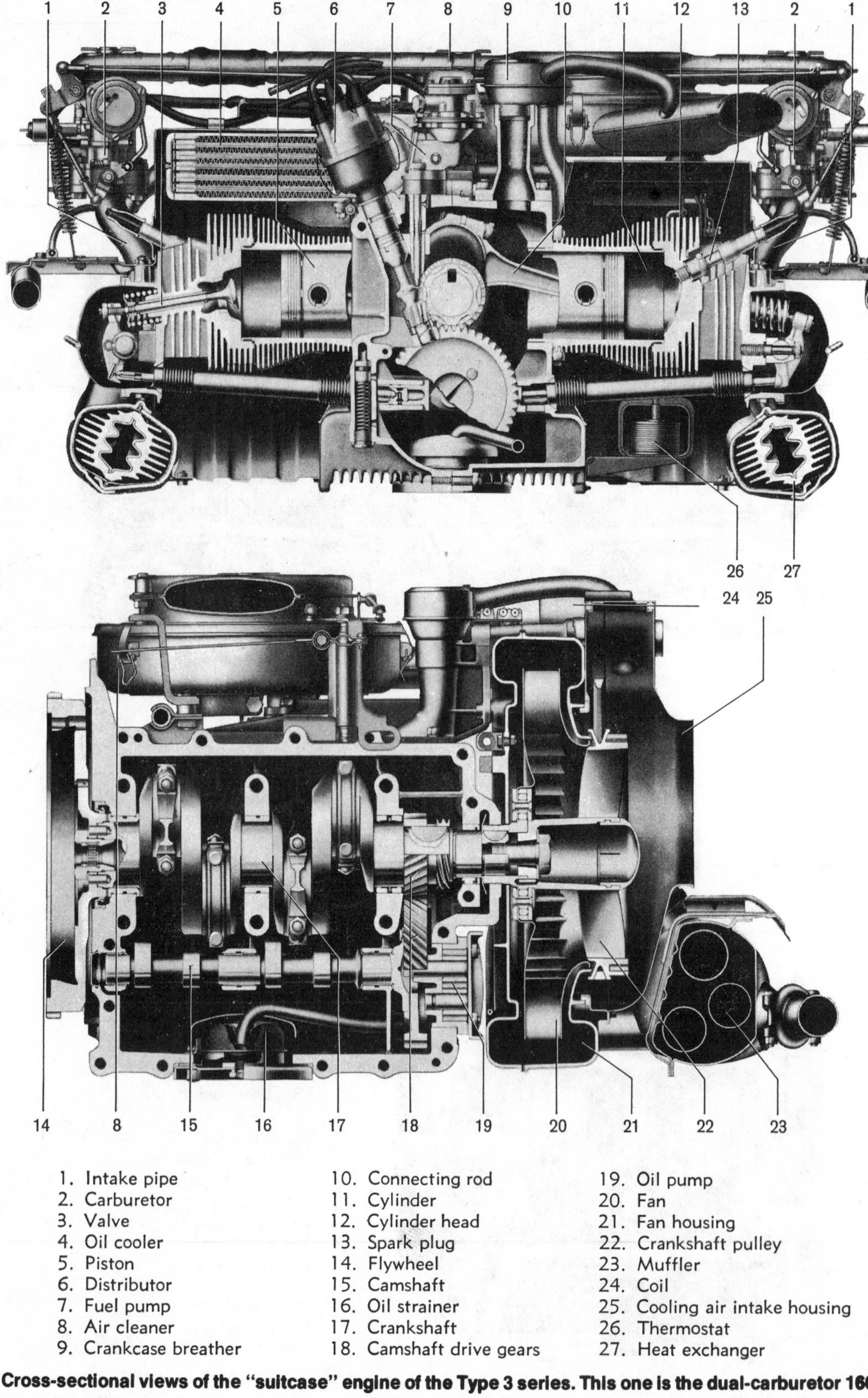

1. Intake pipe
2. Carburetor
3. Valve
4. Oil cooler
5. Piston
6. Distributor
7. Fuel pump
8. Air cleaner
9. Crankcase breather
10. Connecting rod
11. Cylinder
12. Cylinder head
13. Spark plug
14. Flywheel
15. Camshaft
16. Oil strainer
17. Crankshaft
18. Camshaft drive gears
19. Oil pump
20. Fan
21. Fan housing
22. Crankshaft pulley
23. Muffler
24. Coil
25. Cooling air intake housing
26. Thermostat
27. Heat exchanger

Cross-sectional views of the "suitcase" engine of the Type 3 series. This one is the dual-carburetor 1600

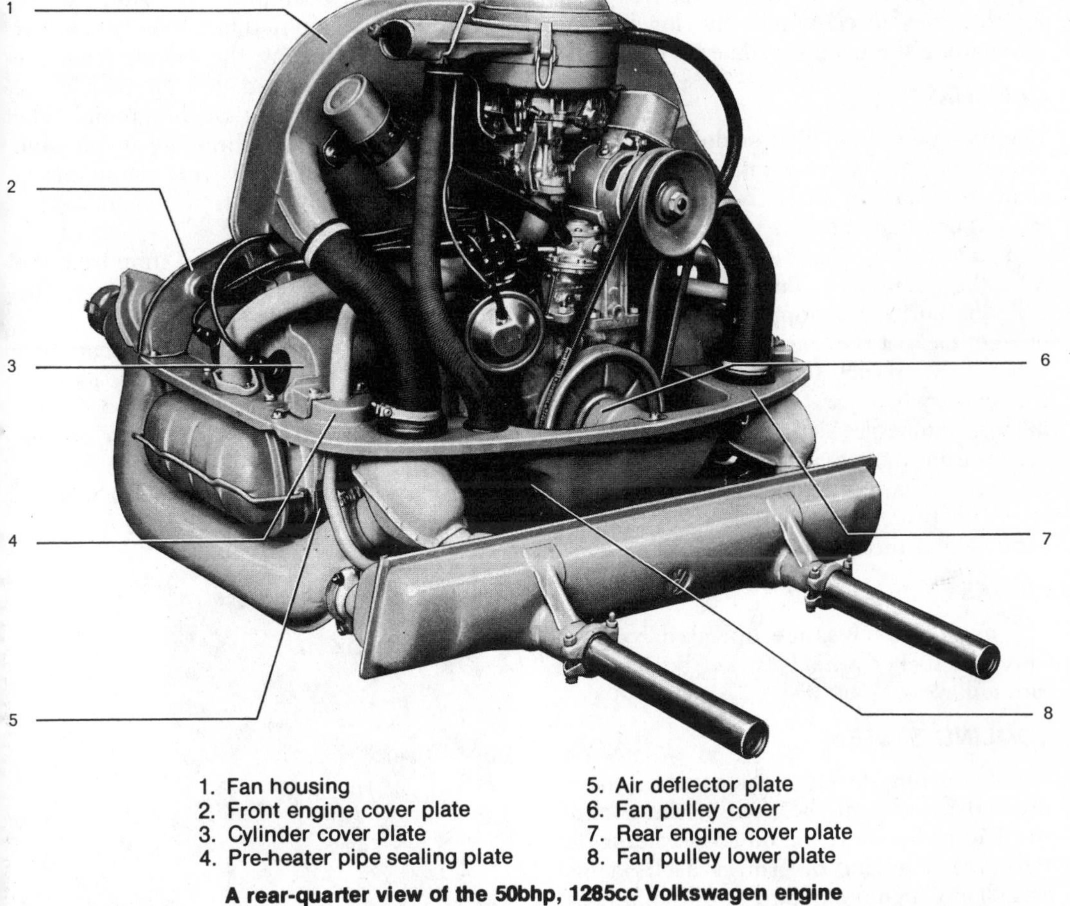

1. Fan housing
2. Front engine cover plate
3. Cylinder cover plate
4. Pre-heater pipe sealing plate
5. Air deflector plate
6. Fan pulley cover
7. Rear engine cover plate
8. Fan pulley lower plate

A rear-quarter view of the 50bhp, 1285cc Volkswagen engine

CRANKSHAFT

The crankshaft runs in four main bearings, and is heat-treated at all bearing points. The main bearings are of light alloy and are lead coated. The end thrust of the crankshaft is taken up by No. 1 main bearing (as seen from the clutch). No. 2 main bearing is of the split type—the other 3 bearings are the one-piece type. In the engine of the beetle, the generator-fan pulley is bolted onto the crankshaft, while in the type 3 "suitcase" engine, the cooling fan is attached directly to the crankshaft. The clutch side of the crankshaft is provided with an oil seal, the fan side with an oil thrower and oil return thread. Drive gears for the camshaft and the distributor are secured to the crankshaft by means of woodruff keys.

PISTONS AND CYLINDERS

The four pistons are made of light alloy and have three rings—two compression and one oil-scraping. Each piston is provided with a fully-floating piston pin secured by means of circlips. The cylinders in the Volkswagen engine are interchangeable, and can be easily replaced along with their corresponding pistons. Fins on the cylinders ensure efficient cooling of the engine.

CYLINDER HEADS

Each pair of cylinders shares a detachable cylinder head made of light alloy casting. The cylinder head contains the overhead valves of both cylinders, and is also provided with cooling fins to further improve cooling efficiency. Shrunk-in valve guides and inserts are used, and there is no gasket between the cylinders and the cylinder head on 1963 and later engines.

CONNECTING RODS

The four connecting rods are steel forgings and have lead-bronze bearings at the crankshaft end, while the piston pin ends are equipped with bronze bushes. The connecting rod caps are held to the rods by bolts which screw directly into the lower caps, eliminating the need for separate bolt nuts.

CAMSHAFT

Beginning with the 1966 model year, Volkswagen engines were equipped with camshafts running in three replaceable steel-backed bearings. Prior to this time, the camshaft ran in three bearings which were built into the crankcase. Because of the four-cylinder horizontally-opposed design of the engine, each of the four camlobes drives two valves, one on each side of the crankshaft. It is necessary to separate the crankcase halves in order to replace the camshaft, which is driven from the crankshaft by means of helical gears. The end thrust of the camshaft is taken up by a special shoulder on the left-hand side of the crankcase.

VALVES

The overhead valves are operated by push rods and rocker arms actuated by flat base cam followers.

COOLING SYSTEM

The air cooling system includes an oil cooler situated directly in the path of the cooling air. The presence of the oil cooler helps the Volkswagen engine to protect itself against excessively high temperatures of the internal engine parts served by the lubricating oil. The cooling fan moves a very large quantity of air in performing its very important function. For example, the cooling fan of the type 3 moves approximately 20 cubic feet of air each second when operating at 4000 engine rpm. When operating at cruising speed (approx. 84 mph.), the fan forces the equivalent of a roomful of cooling air through the engine each minute. This flow is regulated by thermostat in order to ensure quick warm-up as well as efficient high-speed cooling.

ENGINE REMOVAL

The Volkswagen engine is mounted on the transmission, which in turn is attached to the frame. In the beetle models, there are four attaching points—two bolts and two studs—while on the type 3 there is an extra mounting point at the rear of the engine. Type 3 vehicles with automatic transmission have front and rear engine and transmission mounts. At the front, the gearbox is supported by the rear tubular crossmember; at the rear, a crossmember is bolted to the crankcase and mounted to the body at either end. When removing the engine from the car, it is recommended that the rear of the car be about three feet off the ground. The engine is removed by bringing it out from underneath the car. However, before raising the car, the following steps should be followed:

1. Disconnect the ground strap from the battery, cables from generator (and, in beetle models, regulator).
2. Remove air cleaner from engine, and the rear engine cover plate on beetle models. Remove throttle positioner.
3. Rotate the distributor of beetle models so that this part will be able to clear the rear cover plate. (NOTE: *on 1967 and later models, the rear cover plate need not be removed,*

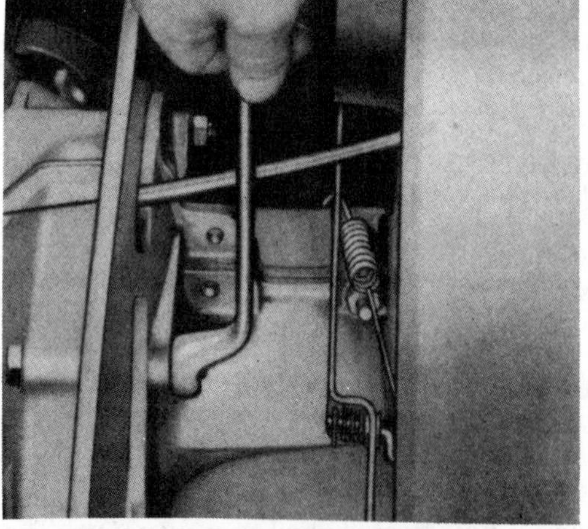

Removing the upper engine mounting bolts. The engine is in a Type 1 vehicle, and an assistant is necessary in this operation

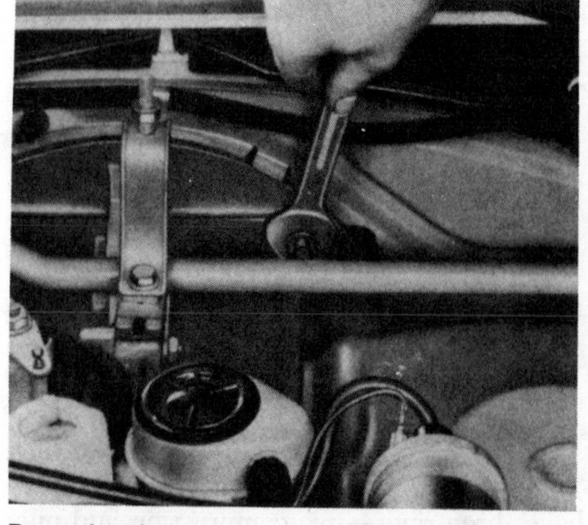

Removing the upper engine mounting bolts from a Type 3

since the redesigned rear deck and compartment allow sufficient room for engine withdrawal from the car.)

4. Disconnect throttle cable from carburetor(s), and remove electrical connections to automatic choke, coil, electromagnetic cut-off jet, and oil pressure sending unit.

5. Disconnect the fuel hose at the front engine cover plate and seal it to prevent leakage.

6. On type 3 models, remove the oil dipstick and the rubber boot between the oil filler and body.

7. Remove the cooling air intake bellows on type 3 models after loosening the clip that secures the unit.

8. Remove the warm air hose on the type 3 models.

9. After disconnecting the appropriate electrical and control cables, remove the rear engine support (type 3) and raise the car off the ground.

10. After removing the flexible air hoses between the engine and heat exchangers, disconnect the heater flap cables, unscrew the two lower engine mounting nuts and slide a jack under the engine. Be sure that it is suitable for supporting the weight of the engine without placing undue strain on the components.

On type 1 Automatic Stickshift models, disconnect the control valve cable and manifold vacuum hoses. Disconnect the ATF suction line and plug it with a 16 x 1.5 mm. cap. On type 3 fully automatic models, disconnect the vacuum hose and kickdown cable. On either model, remove the four 8 mm. bolts from the converter drive plate through the holes in the transmission case. After removing the engine, hold the torque converter in place on the transmission with a strap. On fuel injected type 3 models, the fuel pressure and return lines must be clamped off and disconnected, and the injection unit wiring disconnected.

11. Raise the jack until it just contacts the engine, and have an assistant hold the bolts of the two upper engine mounts so that you will be able to unscrew the nuts. If an assistant is not available at this stage, it is possible to wedge sockets into the proper places so that one man can do the job without having four hands.

12. When the engine mounts are disconnected and there are no remaining cables or controls linking the engine with the car, roll the engine backwards slightly so that the release plate will be able to clear the main drive shaft.

13. Lower the engine very slowly, and be sure that the clutch release plate does not contact the main drive shaft of the transmission.

ENGINE INSTALLATION

Roughly speaking, engine installation is the reverse of the preceding operation, although it is important that some special precautions be taken. Before replacing the engine, the clutch plate must be centered, the clutch release bearing and release plate checked for wear, and a number of components greased or cleaned. The starter shaft bush should be lubricated with lithium grease, the needle bearing in the gland nut supplied with 1 gram of universal grease, and the main drive shaft splines lubricated with molydenum-disulphide powder applied with a clean cloth or brush. Before installing the engine, care must also be taken to ensure that the mating surfaces of the engine and transmission are cleaned thoroughly.

The engine is then lifted into position and the engine rotated via the generator pulley so that the clutch plate hub will engage the transmission shaft splines. In pushing the engine home, care must be taken to see that the gland nut needle bearing, clutch release bearing, and main drive shaft are not damaged. After the engine is in position, put the lower engine mounting bolts through the holes in the flange of the transmission case and press the engine against the flange so that proper and even contact is made. Tighten the upper nuts first, then the lower ones. After this initial tightening, tighten all nuts evenly in this same sequence.

To avoid interference with the function of the automatic stickshift clutch, take care to route the connecting hoses so that they are not kinked or jammed when installing the engine. This applies particularly to the small diameter pipe from the control valve to the carburetor venturi, which will work properly only if routed in the original production manner.

On the type 3 reinstallation, synthetic washers are used to raise the engine about 2–3 mm. when the rear engine mounting is attached and tightened. Use only enough washers in the rear mount so that the engine is lifted no more than 3 mm. when the mounting is tightened down. Care should be used when installing the rear air intake housing bellows of the type 3 engine, for this unit can be easily damaged through careless handling. Reconnect cables and controls. Attach the thick lead to terminal D+ of the generator. Adjust the accelerator cable with the engine at full throttle, and set the ignition timing.

ENGINE DISASSEMBLY AND ASSEMBLY OPERATIONS

The disassembly of the type 3 engines is different from that of the other VW engines mainly in the removal of the engine cover plates and cooling ductwork. In tearing down a Volkswagen engine, the following is the recommended sequence of operations:

1. Drain engine oil.
2. Remove hoses between engine and heat exchangers.
3. Remove front engine cover plate.
4. Remove muffler and intake manifold, including carburetor(s).
5. Remove fan belt, cooling air intake housing, generator and crankshaft pulley.
6. Remove rear half of fan housing, fan, and front half of fan housing.
7. Remove distributor and fuel pump and take out distributor drive pinion.
8. Remove cooling air ductwork from cylinder area.
9. Remove oil cooler.
10. Remove rocker arm shaft and cylinder heads.
11. Remove cylinders and pistons.
12. Remove clutch assembly and flywheel.
13. Remove oil pump and oil strainer.
14. Disassemble crankcase and remove camshaft, crankshaft and connecting rods.

Assembly, generally speaking, is the reverse of the foregoing procedure. Detailed R and R instructions follow.

Major Engine Components Removal and Replacement

NOTE: *the torque, capacity, tune-up, and clearance figures given in the text apply, generally, to the most common engines. However, since there are so many variations in production, it is always best to consult the applicable chart for the figure in question.*

R & R, CYLINDER HEAD

In order to remove the cylinder head of either pair of cylinders, it is first necessary that the rocker arm assembly be removed. The cylinder head is held in place by eight studs. Since the cylinder head also holds the cylinders in place in the VW engine, if it is not desired that the cylinders be removed, they should be held in place with an appropriate holding clamp. After the rocker arm cover, the rocker arm retaining nuts and rocker arm assembly have been removed, the cylinder head nuts can be removed and the cylinder head lifted off.

When reinstalling the cylinder head, several points must be remembered. The cylinder head should be checked for cracks both in the combustion chamber and in the intake and exhaust ports. Cracked cylinder heads should be replaced. Spark plug threads should be checked at this time for tightness. If the threads are stripped, they can be corrected by means of Heli-coil threaded inserts. On 1963 and later engines, no gasket is necessary between the cylinder head and the cylinders. However, on earlier models, which do not have a fresh air heating system, a gasket should be fitted. New seals should be used on the push rod tube ends, and should be checked for proper seating.

The push rod tubes should be turned so that the seam faces upwards. In order to ensure perfect sealing, used tubes should be stretched to the correct length of 190–191 mm. before they are installed. (Note: in the 40 hp. engine, the correct length is 180.5–181.5 mm. On the 40 hp. engine, the sealing ring between the outer shoulder of the cylinder and the cylinder head should be renewed, placing the slotted side of the ring toward the cylinder head. On the 50 hp. engine of 1966 and subsequent engines, no sealing ring is needed.)

After inserting the cylinder head nut washers, the cylinder head nuts should be tightened slightly, and then to a torque of 7 ft. lbs. before fully tightening them to a torque of 23 ft. lbs. (27 ft. lbs. in 1959 and earlier models). The sequences of tightening shown in the accompanying diagram should be followed. (Note the different sequences for the initial and final tightening procedures.)

R & R, CYLINDERS

Before removing the cylinders, the cylinder head, valve push rods, push rod tubes, and deflector plate below the cylinders must be taken out. The cylinders may then be pulled off.

Reinstall the cylinders as follows:

Engine Rebuilding Specifications—Pistons, Cylinders and Rings

Engine	Cylinders									Pistons									Wrist Pin ② Diameter (in.)		Rings				
	Cylinder Diameter (mm.)									Piston Diameter (mm.)											Side Clearance (in.)			End Gap (in.)	
	Std.			1st O/S			2nd O/S			Std.			1st O/S			2nd O/S					Top	2nd	Oil Scraper	Top 2nd	Oil Scraper
	B	P	G	B	P	G	B	P	G	B	P	G	B	P	G	B	P	G	No Mark	Green					
1,131, 1,200, and 1,300 cc.	76.99	77.00	77.01	77.49	77.50	77.51	77.99	78.00	78.01	76.95	76.96	76.97	77.45	77.46	77.47	77.95	77.96	77.97	19.996-20.00①	20.001-20.004 ①	.002-.0027	.002-.0027	.001-.002	.012-.018	.010-.016
1,500 cc.	82.99	83.00	83.01	83.49	83.50	83.51	83.99	84.00	84.01	82.96	82.96	82.97	83.45	83.46	83.47	83.95	83.96	83.97	21.996-22.000	22.001-22.004	.0027-.0035	.002-.0027	.001-.002	.012-.018	.010-.016
1,600 cc.	85.49	85.50	85.51	85.99	86.00	86.01	86.49	86.50	86.51	85.45	85.46	85.47	85.95	85.96	85.97	86.45	86.46	86.47	21.996-22.000	22.001-22.004	.0027-.0035	.002-.0027	.001-.002	.012-.018	.010-.016

O/S - Oversize

Color coding of cylinders and matching pistons: B - blue
P - pink
G - green

① Pin diameter given applies to 1,131 and 1,200 cc. engines only. Pins for the 1,300 cc. engine are the same as for the 1,500 and 1,600.

② Pin should be light push fit in piston. Piston pin to connecting rod clearance: .0004 - .001 in. - maximum - .002 in.

Engine Rebuilding Specifications—Valves

Engine	Seat Angle Deg.	Valve Seat Width (in.) Intake	Valve Seat Width (in.) Exhaust	Spring Pressure (lbs. @in.)	Stem (in.) Diameter Intake	Stem (in.) Diameter Exhaust	Stem to Guide Rock (in.) Intake	Stem to Guide Rock (in.) Exhaust	Valve Guide Remove-able
25 hp., 36 hp., A engine - Type 1, and Type 2 engine before May, 1959	45	.05 -.09	.05- .09	73.5± 3.7@ 1.1	.2739- .2736	.2736- .2732	.011- .012	.011- .012	With Special Equipment
All Later Engines	45	.05- .09	.05- :09	①	.3130- .3126	.3118- .3114	.008- .009	.011- .012	With Special Equipment

① Engine Code	To Engine No.	Spring Pressure
G	0627578	96.4± 6.6 @ 1.32 in.
K, R, T	0663330	
D	6805938 (type 2) 6850939 (type 1)	102.0± 5.0 @ 1.35 in.
K	0042987	
Engines with progressively wound springs		126.0± 8.8 @ 1.22 in.

NOTE: Cylinder head combustion chamber volumes are are as follows:

Engine	Volume (cc.)
A	45.5 - 47.0
D	43.0 - 45.0
F	44.0 - 46.0
All 1,500 and 1,600 cc.	48.0 - 50.0

Cylinders should be checked for wear, and if necessary replaced with another matched cylinder and piston assembly of the same size. Also check the cylinder seating surface on the crankcase, cylinder shoulder, and gasket, for cleanliness. Foreign matter here could cause leaks due to distortion of the mating parts. When reinstalling the cylinders, a new gasket should be used between each cylinder and the crankcase.

The piston rings, and piston pin should be liberally oiled (a MoS_2 based lubricant is suitable). Compress rings with compression tool.

Be sure that ring gaps are adequate and staggered on the piston with the oil ring inserted into the cylinder so that its gap is positioned UP when the pistons are in their horizontal position in the engine.

Lubricate the cylinder wall and slide cylinder over piston. Crankcase studs should not contact cylinder cooling fins. Install the deflector plates under the cylinders, bending slightly if necessary to make them seat tightly on the cylinder head studs.

Install push rod tubes and push rods, ensuring that the tubes are inserted with the seam facing upwards and are of the proper length.

R & R, PISTONS

Following the removal of the cylinder head and the cylinder, the pistons should be marked with a number (cylinder number) and an arrow (pointing to clutch side of engine) if they are to be reinstalled in the engine. The pistons are removed as follows:

Using piston circlip pliers, remove the circlips used to retain the piston wrist pin. Heat the piston to 80°C. (176°F.), remove the piston pin and take the piston off the end of the connecting rod. If it is necessary to remove the piston rings, use piston ring pliers in order to avoid damage.

Install the piston as follows: First, clean the piston and the ring grooves, taking care to see that the ring grooves are not scratched or otherwise damaged. The piston should then be checked for wear and, if necessary, replaced by one of corresponding size and

Engine Rebuilding Specifications—Crankshaft

Engine	Main Bearing Journals (in.)												Connecting Rod Journals (in.)						Max. Journal Out-of-Round (in.)
	Journal Diameter								Oil Clearance		Shaft End-Play	Thrust On No.	Journal Diameter				Oil Clearance	End-Play	
	Journal 1, 2, 3				Journal 4														
	Std.	1st U/S	2nd U/S	3rd U/S	Std.	1st U/S	2nd U/S	3rd U/S	Journal 1, 2, 3	Journal 4			Std.	1st U/S	2nd U/S	3rd U/S			
36 hp, A engine - type 1, and Type 2 Engine-before May, 1959 ③	1.9681, 1.9675	1.9583, 1.9577	1.9484, 1.9478	1.9386, 1.9380	1.5748, 1.5742	1.5650, 1.5643	1.5551, 1.5545	1.5453, 1.5446	.002-.004	.002-.004	.0027-.005	1 (at flywheel)	1.9861, 1.9675	1.9583. 1.9577	1.9484, 1.9478	1.9386, 1.9380	.0008-.0024	.0067-.016	.001
All later engines ①	2.1648. 2.1642	2.1551, 2.1544	2.1453, 2.1445	2.1353, 2.1347	1.5748, 1.5742	1.5650, 1.5643	1.5551, 1.5545	1.5452, 1.5446	②	.002-.004	.0027-.005	1 (at flywheel)	2.1650, 2.1645	2.1553, 2.1544	2.1455, 2.1448	2.1355, 2.1350	.0008-.003 ④	.004-.016	.001

NOTE: The crankshaft of type 1/1,200 cc, engines may be reground only twice.

U/S - undersize

① *Including modified 36 hp. type 2 engine from May, 1959 (chassis 469477, engine 3400000)*

② *Bearings No. 1 and 3 from August, 1965: .0016 - .004 in..*
Bearings No. 1, 2, 3; to engine 3520332: .0016 - .0035 in. ① *to engine 3472699: .001 - .0035 in.* ①
Steel backed bearing No. 2 from August, 1965 and all other steel backed bearings (used in cold countries): .001 - .0035 in.

③ *Also 25 hp.*

④ *All 1,500 and 1,600 cc : .0008 in.*

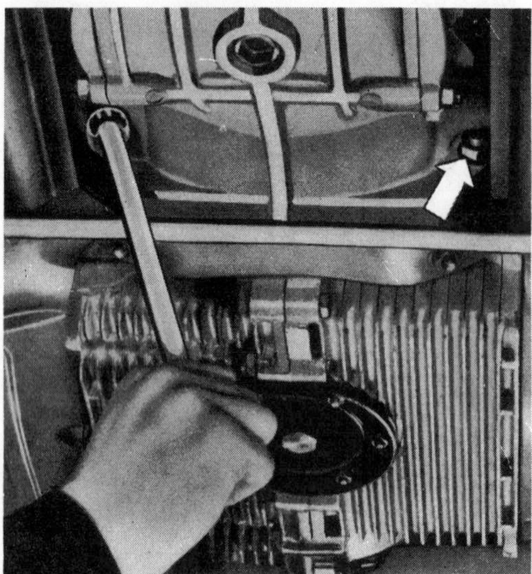

Unscrewing the two nuts of the lower engine mounting points

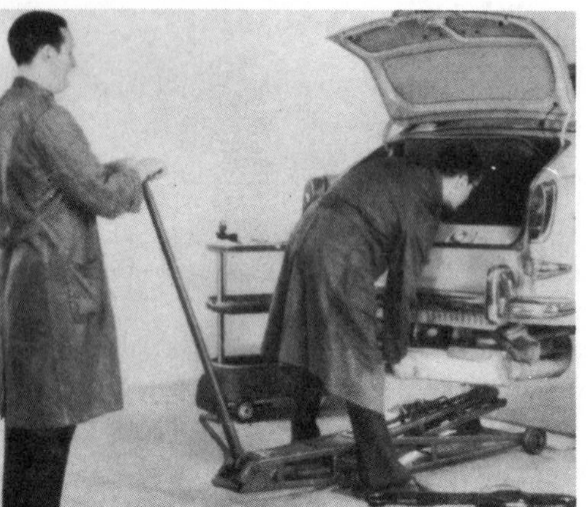

When lowering the engine, care should be taken that the clutch release plate or the main drive shaft is not bent or damaged

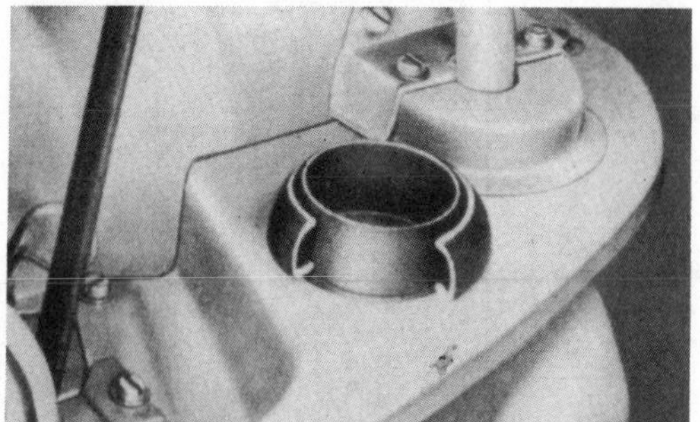

When the rear cover plate of the Type 1 engine is installed, the rubber seal must be situated in such a way that both edges of the cover plate are covered

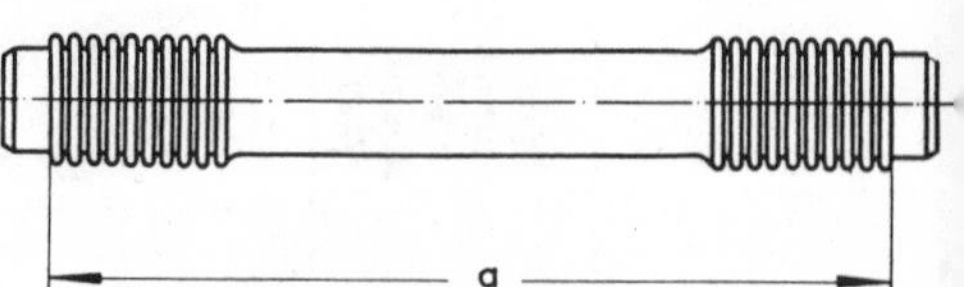

Push rod tube length (distance "a") is 190–191mm. for the 1,300, 1,500 and 1,600 cc. engines, and 180.5–181.5 for the 40 hp. 1,200 cc. engine

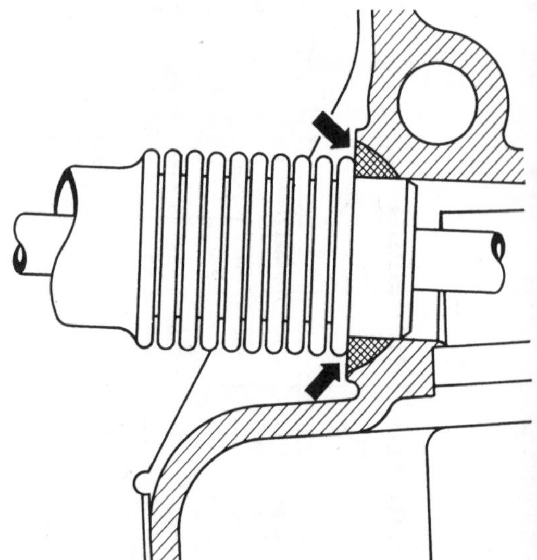

When cylinder head is installed, care should be taken to ensure that the oil seals at the ends of the pushrod tubes are properly seated

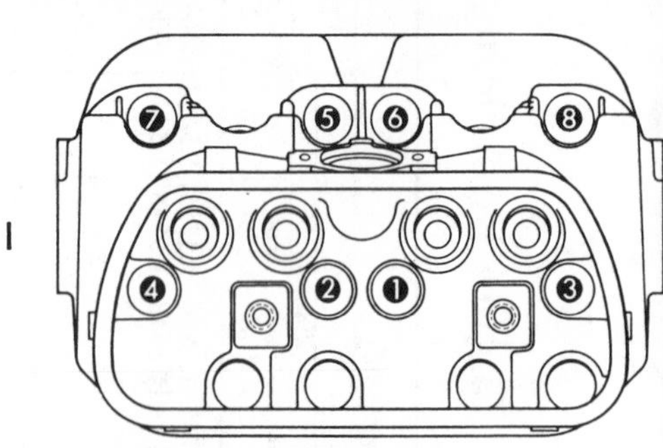

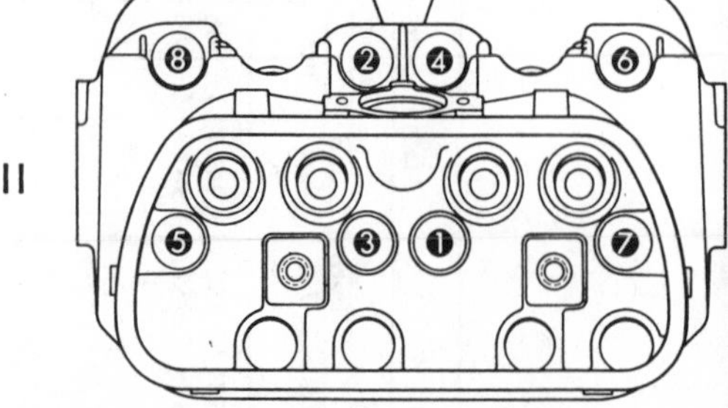

The cylinder head nuts should initially be tightened to 7 ft. lbs. in order I, then tightened to the recommended torque (See Engine Torque Specifications Chart) in order II

When sliding the cylinder over the piston, the crankcase studs must not be allowed to contact the cooling fins of the cylinder

The deflector plates under the cylinders must be tight up against the cylinder head studs so they do not rattle or work loose after installation

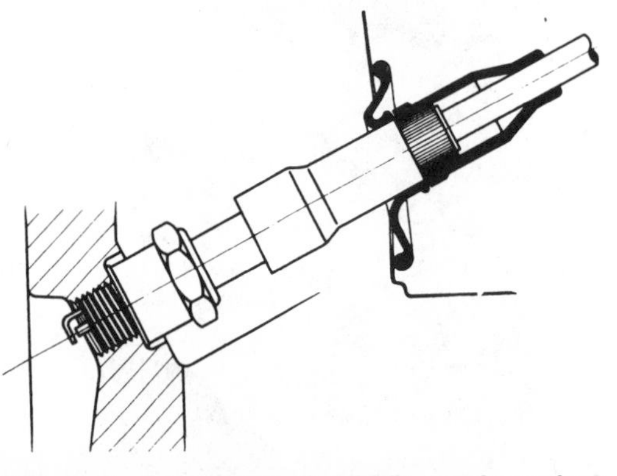

The spark plug rubbers should fit snugly against the cylinder cover plate so that valuable cooling air is not lost

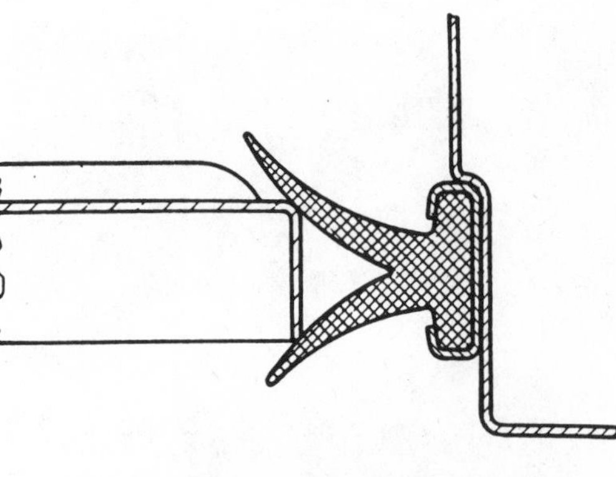

The weatherstripping around the exterior of the Type 1 engine should contact the sheet metal of the engine compartment in the manner shown

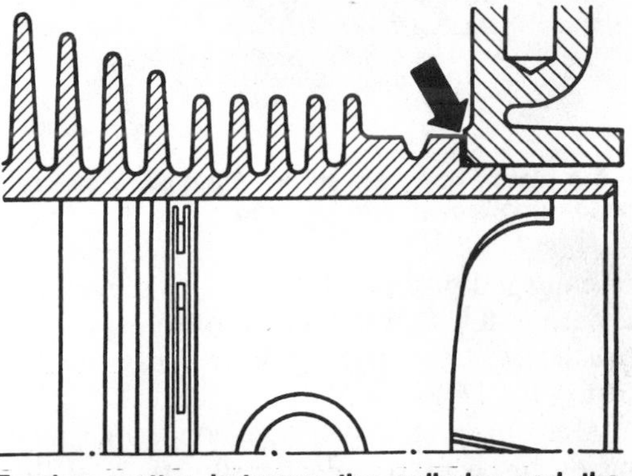

Foreign matter between the cylinder and the crankcase could cause distortion of the cylinder. Gaskets between crankcase and cylinders should never be re-used.

If the pistons are to be replaced, they should be marked to ensure their return to original positions

weight. Weight between pistons must not be greater than 10 grams. If the running clearance between the piston and cylinder is .2 mm. (.008″) or more, the piston and cylinder should be replaced by a set of the same size grading. If, however, the cylinder of a worn

If the piston rings are to be removed, a special piston ring tool should be used

or damaged piston shows no signs of wear, it is permissible to install a new piston of appropriate size. See accompanying diagram for piston markings.

After making a decision concerning the piston to be used, select piston rings of the correct size. After the ring has been inserted in the cylinder and pushed down about .2" by the piston, check the gap with a feeler gauge. After using a piston ring tool to install the rings, check the side clearance of the rings in their grooves with a feeler gauge. Ring side clearance and end gap should be as specified in the Engine Rebuilding Specifications Chart for Pistons, Cylinders, and Rings in this chapter.

Because the compression rings are slightly tapered, they should be installed with the marking "Top" or "Oben" toward the top of the piston. Insert the piston pin circlip which faces toward the flywheel. Because piston pin holes are offset, make sure that the arrow (or word "vorn") points toward the flywheel. This offset is to help accommodate thrust loads which amplify and lead to objectionable piston slap.

Check and fit piston pin. The pin may be found to be a light finger-push fit in the piston, even when the piston is cold. However, this condition is normal, even to the extent of the pin sliding out of the piston under its own weight. Clearance between the piston pin and the connecting rod bushing should be as

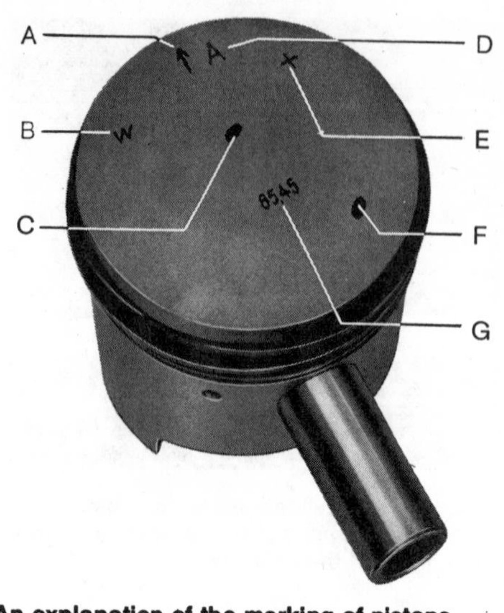

An explanation of the marking of pistons

A. Arrow (indented or stamped on) which must point toward the flywheel when piston is installed
B. Details of piston pin bore size indented or stamped on (s = black, w = white)
C. Paint spot indicating matching size (blue, pink, green)
D. The letter near the arrow corresponds to the index of the part number of the piston concerned. It serves as an identification mark
E. Details of weight grading (+ or –) indented or stamped on
F. Paint spot indicating weight grading (brown = – weight, grey = + weight)
G. Details of piston size in mm

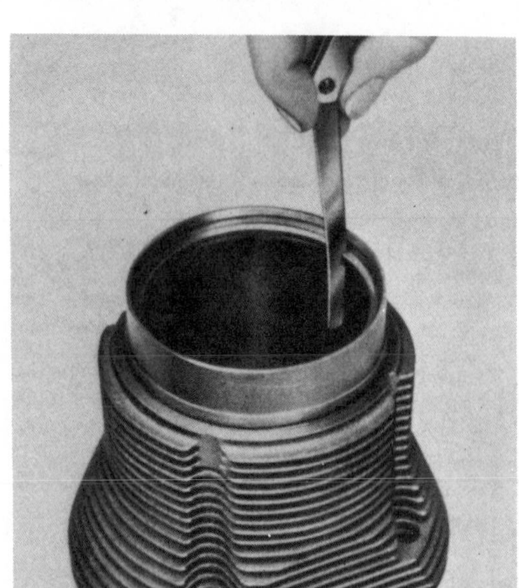

Using a reliable feeler gauge to measure ring end gap

Checking the piston ring side clearance with a feeler gauge

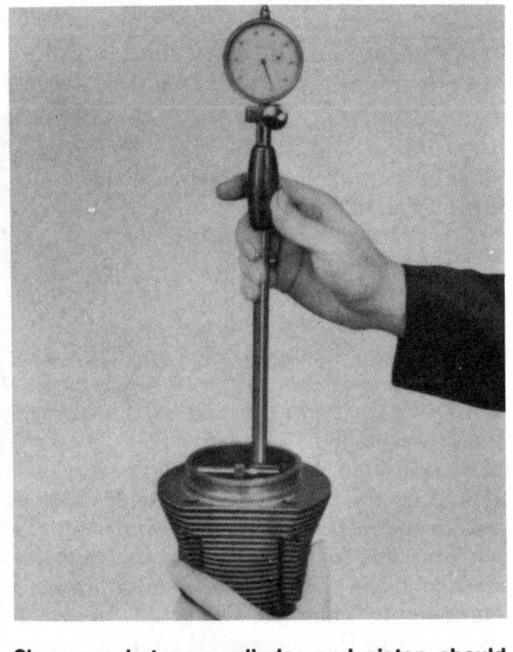

Clearance between cylinder and piston should not exceed .20mm (.008"), and should be measured by measuring both the piston and the cylinder (shown). The cylinder is measured 10–15mm below the upper edge

specified in the Engine Rebuilding Specifications Chart. If the clearance is near the wear limit, renew the piston pin and the rod bushing. It is not advisable to install an oversize pin in this case. In all cases where the pin is not a light finger push fit in the cold piston, heat the piston in oil to about 176°F. Insert the second circlip and make sure that the circlips fit perfectly in their grooves. A good barometer in deciding whether or not a new cylinder and piston should be installed is oil consumption. If the engine uses more than one quart of oil each 600 miles, it is quite likely that the engine is in need of reconditioning.

DISASSEMBLY AND ASSEMBLY OF THE CRANKCASE

With the cylinders, pistons, and other outer parts removed, the crankcase is split as follows:

1. Remove the oil strainer, oil pressure switch, and crankcase nuts.
2. Keep the cam followers of the right crankcase half in position by using the retaining springs.
3. Use a rubber hammer to break the seal between the crankcase halves. Under no circumstances insert sharp tools, wedges, etc. between the crankcase halves, for this will surely lead to serious leakage of lubricant.

After being loosened with a rubber hammer, the right half of the crankcase can be lifted off. Because there is no gasket between the joining faces, leakage will result if prying tools are used

Before the 12 mm. nuts are fully tightened, the 8 mm. nut near the #1 crankshaft bearing must be tightened (see arrow). Then the 12 mm. nuts can be tightened fully

With the engine assembled and flywheel fitted, the crankshaft end play should be .06–.12 mm. (.003″–.005″) with a war limit of .15 mm. (.006″)

4. After the seal between the mating surfaces has been broken, remove the right-hand crankcase half, the crankshaft oil seal and camshaft end plug, and lift out the camshaft and the crankshaft.

5. Remove cam followers, bearing shells and oil pressure relief valve.

Assembly is generally the reverse of the foregoing procedure, but includes the following:

1. Before reassembling crankcase, check it for damage and cracks after cleaning thoroughly. Mating and sealing surfaces should be cleaned especially well. A solvent should be used to remove traces of the old sealant from mating surfaces.

2. Flush and blow out all ducts and oil passages.

3. Check the oil suction pipe for leaks.

4. Check studs for tightness. If tapped holes are worn, correction involves the installation of Helicoil inserts.

5. Insert cam followers after checking both the followers and their bores in the crankcase.

6. Install crankshaft bearing dowel pins and bearing shells for crankshaft and camshaft.

7. Install crankshaft and camshaft after bearings have been well lubricated. (When installing crankshaft, note position of timing marks on timing gears.)

8. Install camshaft end plug, using sealing compound.

9. Install thrust washers and crankshaft oil seal. The oil seal must rest squarely on the bottom of its recess in the crankcase.

10. Check and install oil pressure switch.

11. Spread a thin film of sealing compound on the crankcase joining faces. Use care so that no sealing compound enters the oil passages of the crankshaft or the camshaft bearings.

12. Keep cam followers of right crankcase half in place by using retaining springs.

13. Join the crankcase halves and evenly torque the fasteners to the torque specified in the Engine Torque Specifications Chart.

(NOTE: *first tighten the 8 mm. nut which is beside the 12 mm. stud of the #1 crankshaft bearing. Only then should the 12 mm. nuts be tightened fully.*)

14. Turn the crankshaft to check for ease of movement, and check the end play of the crankshaft. The crankshaft end play is measured with the engine assembled and the flywheel installed.

R & R, CAMSHAFT

Removal of the camshaft requires that the crankcase be split. The camshaft and camshaft bearing shells are then easily removed. Before reinstalling the camshaft, it should be checked for wear of the bearing faces and bearing points. In addition, the riveted joint between the camshaft timing gear and the camshaft should be examined for security. If there is slight damage to the camshaft, it may be smoothed with a silicon carbide oilstone. A 100–120 grit stone is first used to smooth the damaged area, and then a 280–320 stone may be used for final polishing. The camshaft should be checked for runout, which should not exceed .0008″. The timing gear should be checked for correct tooth contact and for wear, and the edges of the camshaft bearing bores lightly chamfered to avoid seizure. If the camshaft shells removed are either worn or damaged, new shells should be fitted. The camshaft bearing shells should be installed with the tabs engaging the notches in the crankcase. Before installing camshaft, the bearing journals and cams should be generously coated with oil. When the camshaft is installed, care should be taken to ensure that the timing gear tooth marked "O" is located between the two teeth of the crankshaft timing gear marked by a center punch. The end play at the thrust bearing (bearing number 3) is .06–.11 mm. (.002″–.004″) and the wear limit is .14 mm. (.006″).

R & R, CRANKSHAFT AND CONNECTING RODS

Removal of the crankshaft requires the removal of the cylinder heads, cylinders, pis-

Camshaft in recent engines runs in three shell-type bearings, shown here. End thrust of the camshaft is taken by the bearing nearest the timing gear (bearing #3)

Installation of camshaft bearing shells. Note flange on bearing #3 (foreground)

Checking run-out of camshaft

tons, the splitting of the crankcase halves, and the withdrawal of the camshaft. When installing the crankshaft, check to see that the crankcase does not have sharp edges at points of junction. If foreign matter has become lodged in the main bearings, it will be necessary to remove it with a scraper, taking care not to remove material from the bearing shell itself. Check the dowel pins for tightness. Place one half of #2 crankshaft bearing in the crankcase. Slide on crankshaft bearing #1 so that the dowel pin hole is toward the flywheel. Install crankshaft, making sure that the dowel pins are correctly seated in the crankshaft bearings. When installing camshaft, note the marks on the timing gears.

After the crankshaft has been removed and clamped into position, remove the connecting rod clamping bolts and the connecting rods and caps. When installing, check the connecting rods for external damage and for weight. The difference in weight of the connecting rods in an engine must not be in excess of 10 grams in order that proper engine balance can be maintained. If necessary, metal should be removed from the hea-

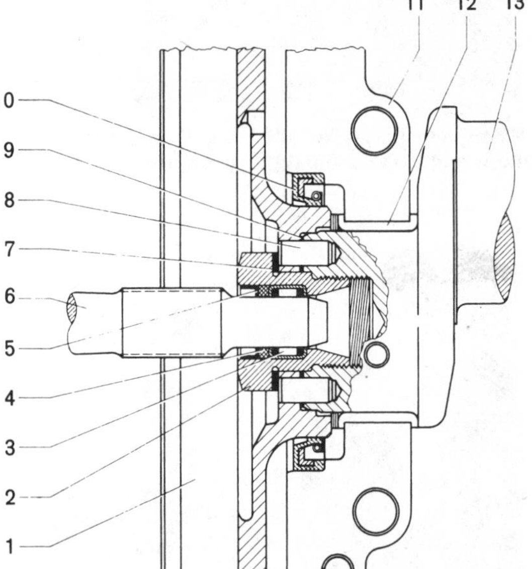

1. Flywheel
2. Gland nut
3. Needle bearing
4. Felt ring
5. Retaining ring
6. Main drive shaft
7. Lock washer
8. Dowel pin
9. Paper or metal gasket
10. Oil seal
11. Crankcase
12. Crankshaft bearing
13. Crankshaft

A cross-sectional view of the flywheel end of the crankshaft

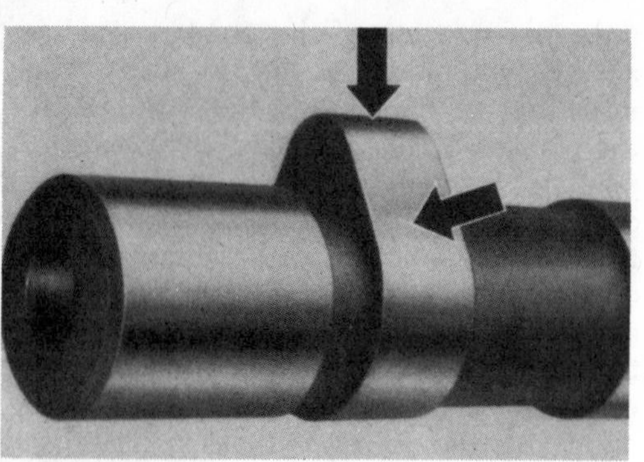

Cam faces should be smooth and square. If scored slightly, they can be smoothed and polished

When camshaft is installed, the illustrated timing mark relationship should be observed

Note that the marks of the connecting rods are pointing upward. The con rods are pointing toward their respective cylinders

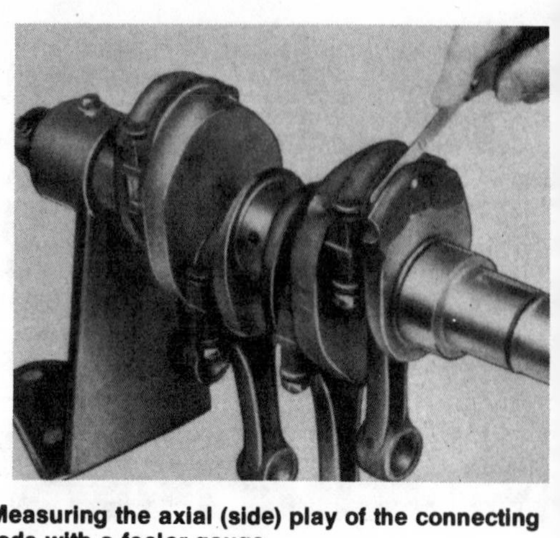

Measuring the axial (side) play of the connecting rods with a feeler gauge

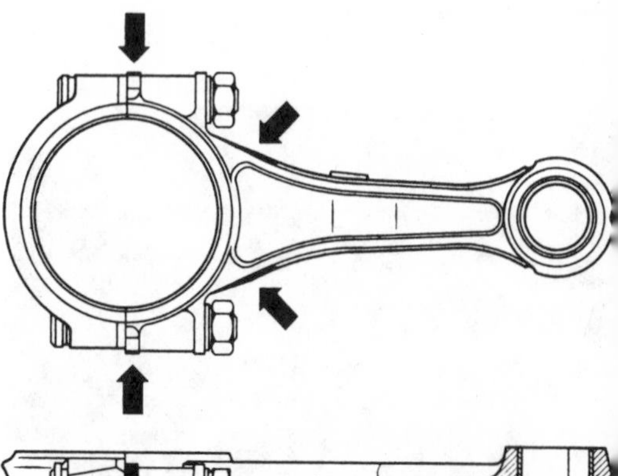

Maximum weight difference between connecting rods in one engine is 10 grams. Metal can be removed from the arrowed portions of the connecting rod

The connecting rod bolts should be tightened to the proper torque

vier connecting rods at the points indicated on the accompanying drawing. Inspect the piston pin bushing. With a new bushing, the correct clearance is indicated by a light finger push fit of the pin at room temperature. Check and, if necessary, correct connecting rod alignment. Reinsert connecting rod bearing shells after all parts have been thoroughly cleaned and assemble connecting rods on crankshaft. The identification numbers stamped on connecting rods and bearing caps must both be on one side.

NOTE: *new connecting rod screws should always be used, and the wax removed from the screws before they are installed.*

Tighten connecting rod bolts to the specified torque. A slight pretension between the bearing halves, which is likely to occur when tightening connecting rod bolts, can be eliminated by light hammer taps. The connecting rods, lubricated with engine oil prior to assembly, must slide on the crank pin by their own weight. The connecting rod bushings must not be scraped, reamed or filed during assembly. Using a peening chisel, secure the connecting rod bolts in place.

CRANKSHAFT END PLAY

With engine installed, the crankshaft end play can be read with a dial indicator mounted at the pulley side of the engine. End play should be as specified with an upper wear limit of .15 mm. (.006"). When the engine is not installed, crankshaft end play can be measured at the flywheel end with an indicator mounted on the flywheel. Desirable end play is obtained by adding or subtracting shims at the outer end of the main bearings. Shims for this purpose are available in various thicknesses. Never use more than one gasket.

R & R, FLYWHEEL

The flywheel is attached to the crankshaft with a gland nut, and is located by 4 dowels. Some models have a paper gasket between the flywheel and the crankshaft; others have a metal gasket. Beginning with the 1967 model year, a metal sealing gasket is no longer present between the flywheel and crankshaft. An oil seal is recessed in the crankcase casting at#1 main bearing. A needle bearing, which supports the main drive shaft, is located in the gland nut. Prior to removing the flywheel, it is necessary to remove the clutch pressure plate and the clutch driven plate. Loosen gland nut and

The flywheel gland nut is tightened to a torque of 30 mkg (217 ft. lbs.)

remove, using 36 mm. special wrench and flywheel retainer. Remove guide plate of special wrench. Remove gland nut and withdraw flywheel.

Installation is the reverse of the foregoing procedure, plus the following: check flywheel teeth for wear and damage. Check dowel holes in flywheel and crankshaft and renew dowels if necessary. Adjust crankshaft end play and check needle bearing in gland nut for wear. Lubricate needle bearing with about 1 gram of universal grease. Insert flywheel gasket, if one is used in the engine. (Note: to minimize engine imbalance, the crankshaft, flywheel, and clutch are marked at their heaviest points. Upon assembly, be sure that the marks on these units are offset by 120°. If but two of these parts are marked, the marks should be offset by 180°. Tighten flywheel gland nut to 217 ft. lbs. torque and check flywheel run-out, which should be a maximum of .3 mm. (.012").

R & R, CRANKSHAFT OIL SEAL (ENGINE ASSEMBLED)

Oil losses at the flywheel could well be the result of a leaky crankshaft oil seal. This seal is removed after removing the flywheel. After the flywheel is removed, inspect the surface on the flywheel joining flange where the oil seal makes contact. Remove old oil seal by prying it out of its counterbore. Before installing new crankshaft oil seal, clean the crankcase oil seal recess and coat it thinly with sealing compound. The sharp edges should be slightly chamfered so that the outer edge of the seal is not damaged. Using VW tool 204b, press in the new seal, being sure that it rests squarely on the bottom of its

Crankshaft oil seal is installed with special tool. Seal must fit squarely into its recess

The rocker arm assembly can be removed after the rocker arm support nuts have been taken off

recess. Remove tool and reinstall flywheel after coating the oil seal contact surface with oil.

VALVE SYSTEM SERVICE

R & R, ROCKER ARM MECHANISM

Before the valve rocker assembly can be reached, it is necessary to undo the clip that retains the cover plate. Prior to removing the cover plate, however, it is advisable to dust off and clean the cylinder head and cover plate. This will prevent dirt from entering the assembly. Remove the cover plate after taking off the retaining clip with a screwdriver or other suitable lever. Remove the rocker arm retaining nuts, the rocker arm shaft and the rocker arms. Remove the stud seals.

Before installing the rocker arm mechanism, be sure that the parts are as clean as possible, including the inside of the cover plate. Install the stud seals and the rocker shaft, making sure that the chamfered edges of the supports are pointing outward and the slots, upward. Tighten the retaining nuts to a torque of 14–18 ft. lbs. The only type of retaining nuts which should be used are 8 mm. nuts of the 8 G grade. These nuts are distinguishable by their copper color. Ball ends of the push rods must be centered in the sockets of the rocker arms. In addition, the help valves rotate during operation, the rocker arm adjusting screws should contact the tip of the valve slightly off center. It should be neither in the center nor all the way to one side, but exactly in the middle of the two extremes. After adjusting valves to their proper clearance, reinstall the cover plate with a new gasket. Be sure that the proper cover plate gasket is used. There are two types of gaskets, early and late. The late type is straight across the top edge, while the early type has a tab in the center of the top edge. After the engine has been run for a brief period, check the cover plates for oil leakage.

DISASSEMBLY AND ASSEMBLY OF ROCKER ARM MECHANISM

Remove the spring clips from the rocker arm shaft. Remove washers, rocker arms, and bearing supports. Before installation, check the rocker arm shaft for wear, and the seats and ball sockets of the rocker arm adjusting screws. Loosen adjusting screws before installing rocker arms. Otherwise, installation is the reverse of the disassembly procedure.

R & R, VALVES

In order to remove the valves, the cylinder head must first be taken off. With the cylinder head removed, compress the valve springs with a special tool and remove valve keys, valve spring caps, valve springs, and oil deflector rings. Remove valves from cylinder head after removing any burrs that may be present near the seating surface of the keys on the valve stem. While the valve springs are out, they should be tested. Proper valve spring pressures are given in the Engine Rebuilding Specifications Chart for Valves. Valve keys should be checked prior to in-

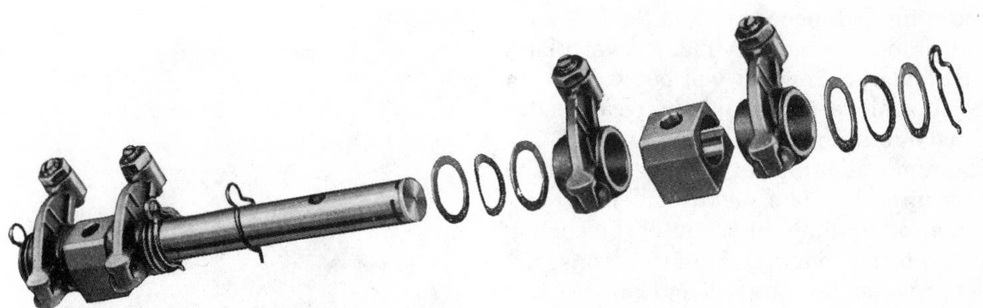

Exploded view, rocker arm mechanism

stallation, and new and worn keys ground at the joining faces until it is still possible to turn the valve when the key halves are pressed together. Valve stems should be checked for run-out and valve guides for wear. Valves should be checked for leaks and for wear. Because exhaust valves generally do heavy-duty work in the air-cooled engine of the Volkswagen, it is good practice to replace them since their cost is not great and the engine is already apart. If the stems of the valves are hammered in, the valves can still be used again after valve caps have been installed. Polish rough valve stems carefully with emery cloth. After coating the valve stems with a moly paste, insert them into their guides and fit oil deflector rings. Install valve springs with the close-wound coils facing the cylinder head. Used valves must be refaced before being reinstalled. Damaged seats must also be reconditioned.

VALVES, ADJUSTMENT

Valve clearances must be adjusted with the engine *cold,* and adjustment is carried out in accordance with the method described in Chapter Two.

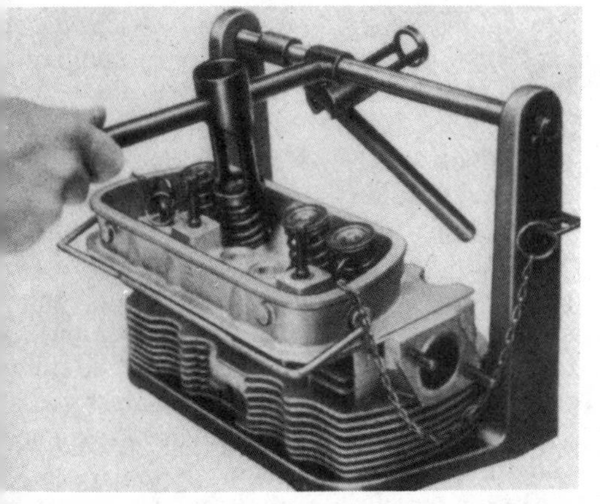

This special fixture facilitates the removal of valves

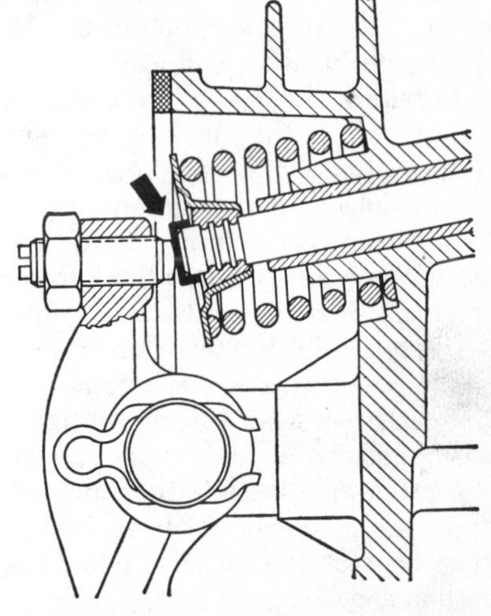

Valves that have a damaged stem end are still usable, via a small cap fitted onto the stem prior to fitting the rocker arm

COOLING SYSTEM SERVICE

R & R, FAN HOUSING

Removal of the type 1 and 2 fan housing is as follows: Remove two heater hoses and generator strap. Pull out the lead wire of the ignition coil. Remove distributor cap and take off spark plug connectors. Remove the retaining screws on both sides of the fan housing. Remove outer half of generator pulley and remove fan belt. Remove the thermostat securing screw and take out the thermostat. Remove lower part of carburetor preheater duct. Fan housing can now be removed with the generator. After removal, check fan housing for damage and for loose air-deflector plates. Accumulated dirt should be removed at this time.

Installation is the reverse sequence, and involves installation of fan housing flap assemblies, and the insertion of the thermostat actuating rod in the cylinder head and lower fan housing. It is necessary that the fan housing fit properly on the cylinder cover plates so that loss of cooling air will be avoided. In order to achieve proper fit, the cover plates may have to be bent slightly.

The removal of the fan housing of the type 3 is accomplished in a slightly different manner due to the different layout of the cooling system of this engine. Remove crankshaft pulley, rear fan housing half and fan. Unhook the linkage and spring at the right-hand air control flap. Remove the attaching screws of the front half of the fan housing. Prior to installation, the front half of the fan housing should be checked for damage.

In installing the fan housing, first install the front half of the fan housing, ensuring correct sealing with the cylinder cover plates. Replace and tighten two lower mounting screws slightly. Turn the two halves of the fan housing to the left until the left crankcase half is contacted by the front lug. Tighten fully the two lower mounting screws. Loosen nuts at the breather support until it can be moved. Insert and tighten the mounting screws of the upper fan housing half. Tighten fully the breather support nuts. Connect the linkage and spring to the right-hand air control flap. Install fan and rear half of fan housing.

R & R, FAN

The cooling fan of the type 1 and 2 models is removed as follows: using a T-wrench, remove the four retaining screws on the fan cover. Remove the generator and fan. While holding fan from rotating, unscrew the fan retaining nut and take off the fan, spacer washers, and hub.

Installation of the fan is as follows: place the hub on the generator shaft, making sure that the woodruff key is securely positioned. Insert the spacer washers. (Note: the distance between the fan and the fan cover should be between 1.5–1.8 mm. (.06″–.07″). Place the fan into position and tighten its retaining nut with a torque wrench and socket to 40–47 ft. lbs. Check the distance from fan to cover. Correct spacing is achieved by inserting the proper number of spacer washers between the hub and the thrust washer. When only one washer is used, the other two should be positioned between the lock washer and the fan. Insert the generator in the fan housing and tighten the retaining screws on the fan housing cover. (With 1967 and more recent models, be sure that the

The Type 1 fan housing is removed along with th generator and fan

cooling air intake slot is at the bottom whe the retaining plate is screwed onto the fa housing.)

On the type 3, fan removal begins with th removal of the crankshaft pulley, coil, an the rear half of the fan housing. The fan ca then be removed.

On installation of the fan, check the condi tion of the oil return thread on the fan hub and install rear half of fan housing, coil an crankshaft pulley.

R & R, CRANKSHAFT PULLEY

On the type 1 and 2, the crankshaft pulle can be removed while the engine is still i the car. However, in this instance it is neces sary for the rear cover plate of the engine t be removed. Remove cover plate after takin out screws in the cover plate below th crankshaft pulley. Remove fan belt, an crankshaft pulley securing screw. Using puller tool, remove the crankshaft pulley The crankshaft pulley should be checked fo proper seating and for proper belt contac surface. The oil return thread should b cleaned and lubricated with a molybdenum disulphide based oil. The crankshaft pulle should be installed in the reverse sequence and should have no runout.

On the type 3, the crankshaft pulley can b removed only when the engine is out of th

Removing the cooling air intake housing from a type 3 engine

The type 3 crankshaft pulley is taken off after the pulley bolt has been removed

The plastic cap on the type 3 fan pulley can be removed by prying with a screwdriver

Using a special puller to remove the fan from the type 3 crankshaft end

car and the muffler, generator, and cooling air intake housing are removed. After these parts have been removed, take out the plastic cap on the pulley. This can be done easily with a screwdriver. Remove the crankshaft pulley retaining bolt and remove the pulley.

Installation is the reverse of the foregoing but the following should be noted: when installing use a new paper gasket between the fan and the crankshaft pulley. If shims are used, do not forget them. No more than two shims may be used. When inserting the pulley, make sure that the pin engages the hole in the fan. The crankshaft pulley retaining bolt should be tightened to a torque of 94–108 ft. lbs. Ensure that the clearance between the generator belt and the intake housing is at least 4 mm. and that the belt is parallel to the housing. Check the seal on the cooling air intake housing and if damaged, cement a new seal into place.

LUBRICATING SYSTEM SERVICE

R & R, OIL STRAINER

All Volkswagen models are equipped with the same type of oil strainer, a view of which is shown in the accompanying diagram. The oil strainer can be easily removed simply by removing the restraining nuts, washers, oil strainer plate, strainer and gaskets. Once taken out, the strainer must be thoroughly cleaned and all traces of old gaskets removed prior to fitting new ones. The suction pipe should be checked for tightness and proper position. When the strainer is installed, be

1. Gasket
2. Oil strainer
3. Gasket
4. Cover plate
5. Cap nut with washer
6. Plug with washer

Exploded view of crankcase oil strainer and components. New gaskets should be used when replacing strainer after cleaning

sure that the suction pipe is correctly seated in the strainer. If necessary, the strainer may be bent slightly. The measurement from the strainer flange to the tip of the suction pipe should be 10 mm., plus or minus 1 mm. The measurement from the flange to the bottom of the strainer should be 6 mm. plus or minus 1 mm. The cap nuts at the bottom of the strainer should not be overtightened, for the bottom plate may become distorted and lead to leakage of engine lubricant. If it is desired, the strainer can be equipped with a permanent magnet designed to retain metal particles that are circulating in the oil. This magnet is held in place by means of a spring clip, and should be removed and cleaned whenever the strainer is removed for the same purpose. Magnetic drain plugs are also available.

R & R, OIL COOLER

The Volkswagen oil cooler is mounted on the crankcase and is positioned in the path of the cooling air. The oil cooler in the type 1 can be removed with the engine in the car, but it is first necessary that the fan housing be removed. The oil cooler can be removed after the three oil cooler retaining nuts have been

Oil cooler of type 3 engine is positioned horizontally, and fastened with retaining nuts, shown

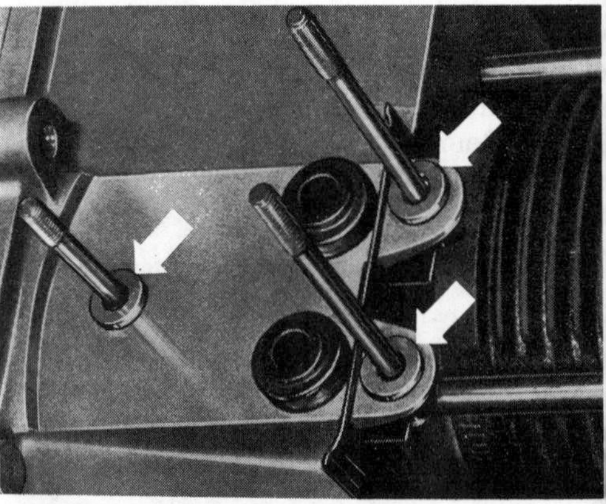

Purpose of spacer rings (arrows) is to prevent the oil cooler seals from being squeezed together too much, thereby stopping the flow of oil

taken off. The gaskets should be removed along with the oil cooler and replaced with new ones when the cooler in installed. Before installation, the oil cooler should be checked for leaks at a pressure of 85 psi. If the cooler is found to leak, the oil pressure relief valve should also be checked. The studs and bracket on the cooler should be checked for tightness. See that the hollow ribs of the oil cooler do not touch one another. Clean the contact surfaces on the crankcase, install new gaskets, and attach oil cooler. Tighten retaining nuts. On the type 3, be sure that a spacer ring is present between the crankcase and the cooler at each securing screw. If these rings are omitted, the seals may be squeezed too tightly, resulting in a stoppage of oil flow and consequent damage to the engine. The type 3 oil cooler is similar in design to that of the type 1 and 2, except that it lies horizontally cross-wise in the path of the air, while that of the other models is in a vertical position.

Beginning 1971, the type 1 and 2 oil cooler is mounted farther forward on an intermediate flange and has its own cooling air supply through the fan housing. This prevents the oil cooler from blocking off the cooling air to No. 3 cylinder and causing that cylinder to run hot.

R & R, OIL PUMP

An exploded view of the Volkswagen oil pump is given in the accompanying illustration. In the type 3, the oil pump can be taken out only after the engine is removed from the car and the air intake housing, the belt pulley fan housing, and the fan are dismantled. On the type 1 and 2, the pump can be removed with the engine in the car, but it is first necessary to remove the cover plate, the crankshaft pulley, and the cover plate under the pulley. Removal on all model Volkswagens is similar. On Automatic Stickshift models, the torque converter oil pump is driven by the engine oil pump.

Remove the nuts from the oil pump cover and remove the cover and its gasket. Remove the gears and take out the pump body with a special extractor. Care should be taken not to damage the inside of the pump housing.

Prior to assembly, check the oil pump body for wear, especially the gear seating surface. If the pump body is worn, the result will be loss of oil pressure and possible damage to the engine. Check driven gear shaft for tightness, and if necessary peen it tightly into place or replace the pump housing. The dimension *a* in the accompanying diagram should be .5–1.0 mm. (.02–.04"). The gears should be checked for wear, backlash and end play. Backlash may be from .03–.08 mm. (.0012–.0031") and the maximum end play, without gasket, .1 mm. (.004"). The end play can be checked using a T-square and a feeler gauge. Check the mating surfaces of the pump body and the crankcase for damage and clean them. Install pump body with gasket, but without sealing compound. Insert oil pump pilot instead of oil pump drive shaft into pump body. Then turn the camshaft by 360° (one complete turn of the camshaft requires two complete turns of the crankshaft.) This will ensure the centering of the pump body opposite the slot in the camshaft. Mark the pump body so that the correct fit of the oil pump can be checked after the cover has been installed. Remove the oil pump pilot and install the gears. Check the cover for wear—worn covers should be either machined or replaced. Before installing cover, new gaskets should be fitted and secured with sealing compound. Install cover and tighten nuts without disturbing the position of the pump housing.

R & R, OIL BREATHER

The Volkswagen crankcase is ventilated by a hose which carries oil fumes from the crankcase into the air cleaner where they are burned with the fuel-air mixture. In order to remove the oil breather, the connecting hose must be pulled off, the threaded ring removed, and the oil filler and drain pipe taken out.

Installation involves putting a rubber cap on the water drain pipe and the sliding of the rubber valve properly onto the drain pipe (until the button on the valve engages the hole in the pipe). When installing the oil filler, do not omit the gasket between the generator support and the oil filler.

On the pre-1968 type 3 engine, the oil breather serves the same function as in the other models, and the procedure is much the same. However, since the oil filler tube serves as the dipstick tube, it is necessary to use a setting jig to ensure dipstick accuracy if the filler pipe is removed and then replaced. Otherwise, the procedure is similar to that just described. After 1968, type 3 engines have a closed ventilation system with a separate dipstick tube.

R & R, OIL PRESSURE RELIEF VALVE

The function of the oil pressure relief valve is as indicated on the diagram in Chapter 1. When the oil is cold and thick, and oil pressure is very high, the plunger is in its lowest position and oil flows directly to the lubrication points and some of it back to the crankcase. When the oil warms up and thins out, the oil pressure drops, the plunger covers the by-pass port and oil flows to the lubrication points both directly and via the oil cooler. After the oil has warmed up to normal operating temperature and is thin, oil pressure is low, the plunger of the relief valve is in its highest position, and the oil goes to the lubrication points only after it has passed through the oil cooler.

The oil pressure relief valve should be checked whenever there is any disturbance in oil circulation, and especially when the oil cooler is found to be leaky. If the plunger

1. Gasket
2. Oil pump body
3. Gears
4. Gasket
5. Oil pump cover
6. Nut and spring washer

Exploded view of oil pump and components

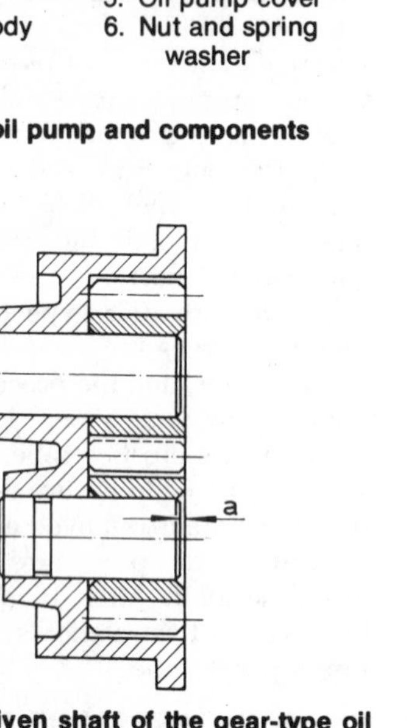

Arrow points to driven shaft of the gear-type oil pump. Dimension "a" should be between .02 and .04"

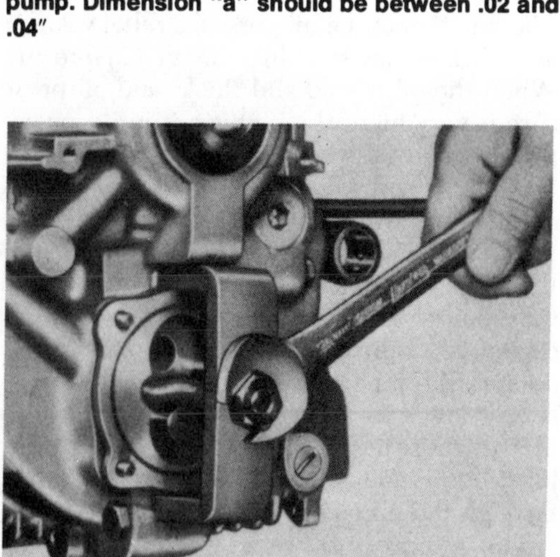

The body of the oil pump is removed via a special extractor

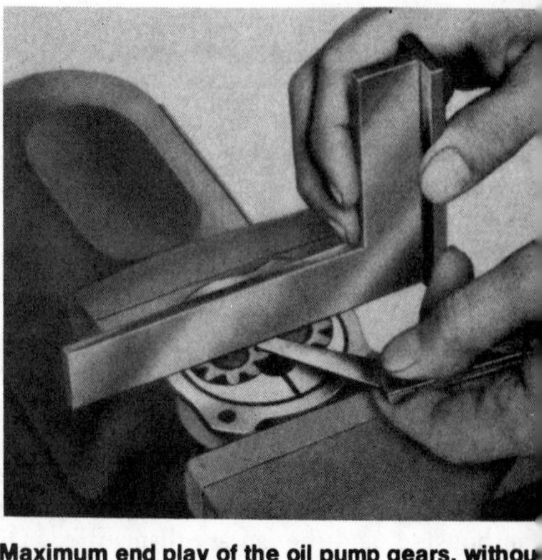

Maximum end play of the oil pump gears, without gasket, is .1mm. Shown are tools required for measurement—a square and a feeler gauge.

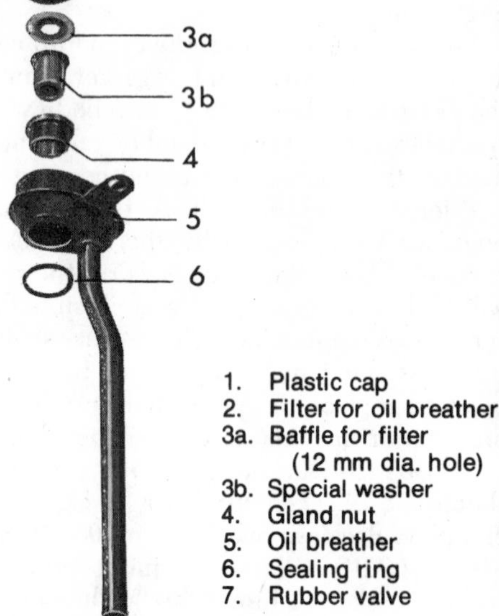

1. Plastic cap
2. Filter for oil breather
3a. Baffle for filter (12 mm dia. hole)
3b. Special washer
4. Gland nut
5. Oil breather
6. Sealing ring
7. Rubber valve

Exploded view of oil breather components, on pre-1968 type 3 engine.

should stick at its highest point when the oil is thick, there is danger of the oil cooler leaking from excess pressure. If, on the other hand, the plunger sticks in the bottom of its travel, the oil will tend to flow directly back to the sump and lubrication will be lacking when the engine is warm.

1. Plunger
2. Spring
3. Gasket
4. Plug

Exploded view, oil pressure relief valve. If oil cooler is leaky, this may be the cause

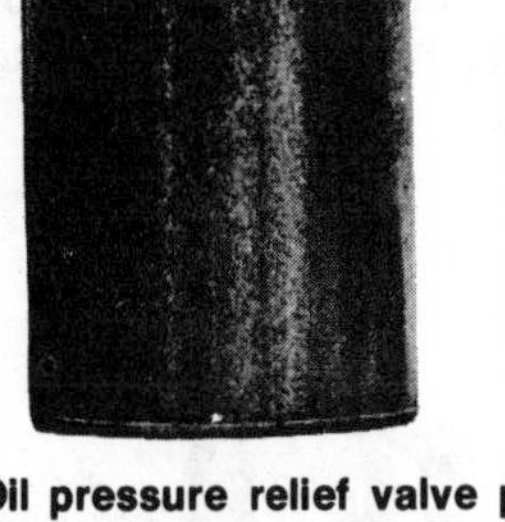

Oil pressure relief valve plungers; the grooved type gives increased oil cooling

The oil pressure relief valve is removed by unscrewing the end plug and removing the gasket ring, spring and plunger. If the plunger is stuck, it can be removed by screwing a 10 mm. tap into it. Prior to installation, check the plunger and the bore in the crankcase for signs of seizure. If necessary, the plunger should be renewed. The spring should be checked to assure that it conforms to the following specifications:

Condition	*Length*	*Load in lbs.*
Unloaded	2.44–2.52″	0
Loaded	.93″	17.1 lbs.

When installing the relief valve, care should be taken to ensure that the upper end of the spring does not scratch the wall of the bore. The gasket should be removed and the end plug tightened securely.

There are two types of oil pressure relief valve plungers available. The first is the plain type normally found in type 1 and 2 engines. The second type is longer and has an annular groove. This is used in some type 3 engines. It has been found that, if the grooved plunger is substituted for the plain plunger, the result will be more oil flow through the cooler and a drop in oil temperature of about 15°F. This, as all other engine modifications, is discouraged by the VW factory.

1970 and later type 1 and 2 engines have two oil pressure relief valves. The second valve is located at the flywheel side of the oil sump and is identical to the first.

EXHAUST SYSTEM SERVICE

R & R, MUFFLER

To remove the muffler from all Volkswagen models, first remove the clamps from the muffler and heat exchangers. (Early 1963 and earlier models do not have exchangers.) Remove clips connecting warm air channels. Loosen clamps on tail pipe(s) and remove tail pipe(s). Remove nuts from muffler flange and remove pre-heater adaptor pipe. Remove four screws from manifold preheater pipe and take muffler off, including gaskets. Check muffler to be installed and exhaust pipes for leaks or damage. If necessary, exhaust pipes can be re-used. However, in practice it is often difficult to remove tail pipes from old muffler without damaging them extensively. This generally occurs with old mufflers that have become rusty, and in such cases it is advisable to install new tail pipes. Type 1 tail pipes should protrude about 7.5″ on pre-1968 models; 8.3″ on later models. New gaskets should be used in installing the muffler.

R & R, HEAT EXCHANGERS

To remove the heat exchangers remove exhaust pipe clamps, the clamps between heat exchanger and exhaust pipe, and the rear engine cover plate (type 1 and 2). Remove nuts on cylinder head and warm air pipe connecting clips. The heat exchanger can now be removed. Check outer shell and exhaust pipes for damage and leakage. If the heat exchangers leak, there could be a possibility of poisonous gases entering the heating system. Sealing surfaces must be clean and smooth, and flanges that are distorted or bent through excessive tightening should be

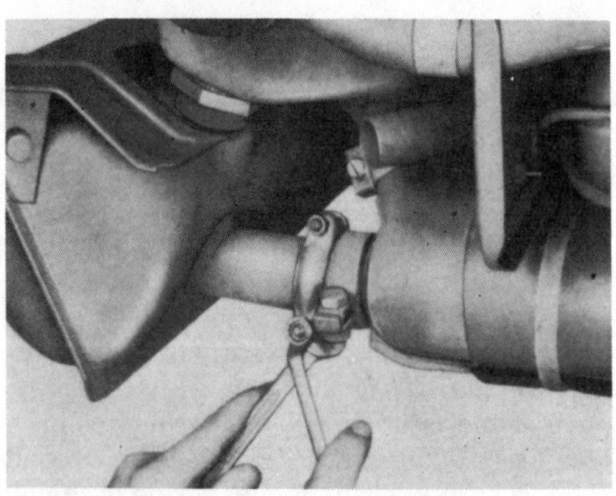

Two wrenches are required to remove the clamps between the muffler and the front heat exchangers

Removing screws that help support front heat exchangers

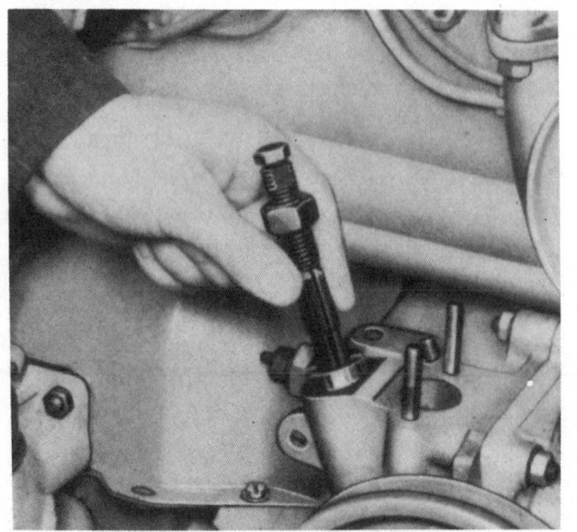

Removal tool is used to extract distributor drive shaft

straightened or machined. Use new gaskets and ensure that all connections are gastight. Heat exchangers must be attached at the cylinder heads with self-locking 8 mm. hexagon nuts. It is not permissible for any other types of nuts to be used, even with lockwashers.

ACCESSORY EXHAUST SYSTEMS

Accessory exhaust systems are not approved by the VW factory and are not generally sold by dealers. Further, some states with outdated inspection codes disapprove of any exhaust system that is not an original factory equipment type. However, accessory systems do usually give a power boost (up to 10%) and a satisfying sound.

There are two basic types of accessory exhaust systems currently available. The first, the header type, has a separate muffler on each side, one for cylinders 1 and 2, and one for cylinders 3 and 4. This type of system does not allow the use of the heater and will not fit on sedans and buses, unless the rear body panels have been cut away. The header system is rather loud and rough sounding, because it is actually two completely separate two cylinder systems. It is most often seen on dune buggies, where a large ground clearance is necessary.

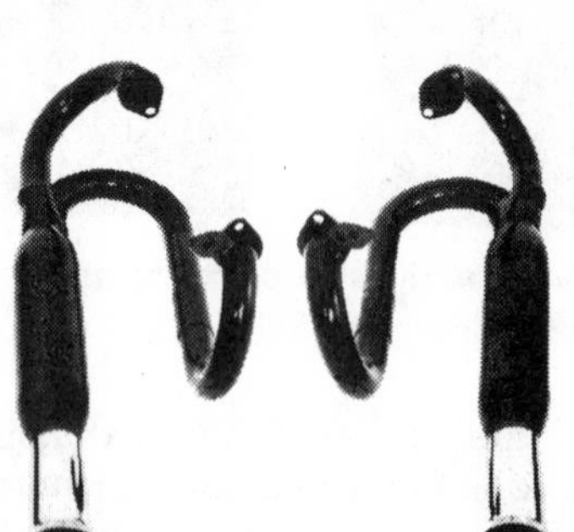

Header exhaust system, as used on VW-based dune buggies

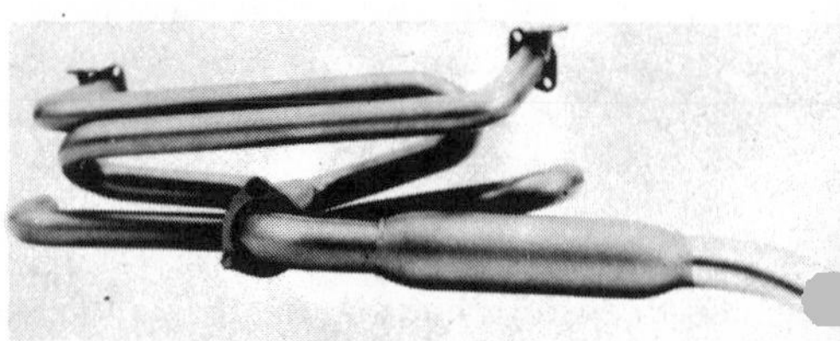

180° tuned, or extractor, exhaust system for VW engines

The second type of accessory exhaust system is known as the 180° tuned, or extractor system. In most such systems, equal length pipes are run from each cylinder, the pipes from each cylinder 180° apart in the firing order are run together, and then both these pipes are run together into a single outlet. The effect is a small horsepower boost and a smooth exhaust note. These systems are installed in much the same way as the stock muffler, and are available in models which utilize the original heater. Some extractor exhaust kits furnish canvas tubing to connect the heat exchangers to the fan housing tubing. The canvas tubing will rot out quickly, and should be replaced with stanless steel flexible tubing held with screw type hose clamps.

When fitting any low restriction exhaust system, it is advisable to rejet the carburetor to prevent an excessively lean mixture and resultant valve burning. Normally a main jet one or two sizes larger will be sufficient. It may also be necessary to replace the air correction, or air bleed, jet. The spark plugs and the inside of the tailpipe will give evidence of changes in mixture.

NOTE: *the results of rejetting, or of any other engine modifications, must be checked with suitable testing equipment to make sure that exhaust emissions remain within legal limits.*

DISTRIBUTOR SERVICE

R & R, DISTRIBUTOR DRIVE PINION

To remove the distributor drive shaft loosen the distributor clamp bolt, turn the engine so that the rotor is pointing to number one cylinder (the notch on the distributor housing), lift out the distributor. Remove fuel pump and intermediate flange, gaskets, and fuel pump push rod. Remove the distance spring on the distributor drive shaft. Be sure that number one cylinder is at its firing point, and withdraw the drive shaft via a removal tool by pulling with the extractor and turning the drive shaft to the left at the same time.

Remove the washer(s) under the drive shaft, being careful not to drop a washer into the crankcase. When the engine is installed, a magnet is handy for removing these washers.

When installing, the reverse of the previous procedure applies. The fuel pump push rod drive eccentric and the pinion teeth should be checked for wear. If the teeth are badly worn, the teeth on the crankshaft should also be examined. Check the washer under the drive shaft for wear and replace if necessary. Position number one cylinder at its firing point and insert the distributor drive shaft.

The slot in the top of the distributor driveshaft has an offset slot which divides the top of the driveshaft into two unequal segments.

The driveshaft is installed as follows:

Engine	*Distributor Driveshaft Installation (No. 1 Cylinder in Firing Position)*
Type 1 and 2 (except early 1968 models with throttle positioner)	Slot at right angles to crankcase split, small segment toward crankshaft pulley.
Type 3	Slot at about 60° to crankcase split, small segment toward oil cooler.

Insert the distance spring, install the distributor, set the ignition timing, and install the fuel pump. (Note: When the engine has been completely disassembled, it is necessary that the oil pump, the fan housing, the fan, and the crankshaft pulley be installed before the distributor drive shaft is inserted.) See Chapter 8 for distributor installation.

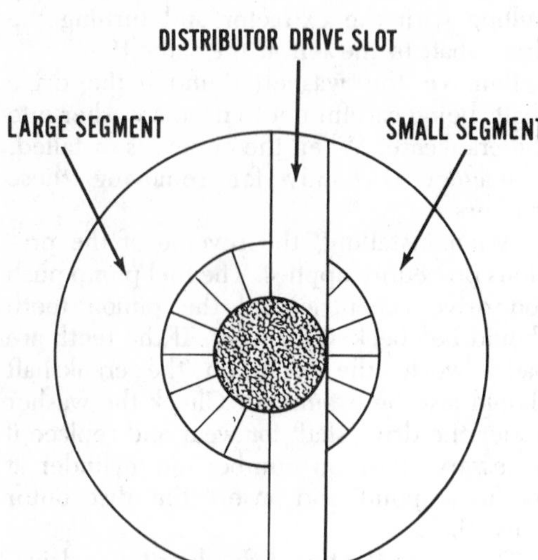

Detail of top of distributor driveshaft, showing off-set slot referred to in text

Type 1 and 2 distributor driveshaft is installed wit the number 1 cylinder at firing point

When number 1 cylinder of the type 3 is at its firing point, the slot of the distributor driveshaft mus form an angle of approximately 60 degrees, a shown, with the smaller segment pointing towar the oil cooler

Torque Specifications—Engine

Fastener	*Thread Size*	*Torque (ft. lbs.)*
All Engines		
1-Nuts for crankcase halves	M12x1.5	25 ①
2-Screws and nuts for crankcase halves	M8	14
3-Cylinder head nuts ②	M10	23
4-Rocker shaft nuts	M8	14-18
5-Flywheel gland nut	M 28x1.5	217
6-Connecting rod bolts and nuts	M9x1	22-25 ④
7-Special nut for fan	M12x1.5	40-47
8-Generator pulley nut	M12x1.5	40-47
9-Crankshaft pulley bolt	M20x1.5	29-36
10-Spark plugs	M14x1.25	22-29
11-Oil drain plug	M14x1.5	25
12-Clutch to flywheel	M8x1.5	18
13-Self-locking nuts for engine carrier to the crankcase	M8	18 ⑤
14-Nuts for oil pump	M8	14
15-Cap nut for oil filter cover	M6	5
16-Nuts for engine mounting	M10	22
17-Screws for converter to drive plate	M8	18
25 and 36 hp. - exceptions		
1-Nuts for crankcase halves	M10	22
3-Cylinder head nuts ②	M10	26-27
11-Oil drain plug ③	M18x1.5	22-29
13-Insert for spark plug	M18x1.5	50-54
Type 3 - exceptions		
8-Generator pulley nut	M12x1.5	40-47
9-Special bolt for fan and crankshaft pulley	M20x1.5	94-108
17-Screws for converter to drive plate	M8	14
19-Self locking nuts for engine carrier to body	M8	18 ⑤

① *For cap nuts: 18 ft. lbs.*

② *Tightening sequences are given in Chapter 4.*

③ *As above from August 1959.*

④ *Contact surfaces oiled. 1,300 cc. and earlier - 28 - 36 ft. lbs.*

⑤ *Renew.*

Fuel System

THE VOLKSWAGEN FUEL SYSTEM

The fuel system of the Volkswagen begins at the front of the automobile, where the fuel tank is situated behind the spare tire. On type 2 vehicles, the tank is at the rear, ahead of the engine. From the tank the fuel is drawn through fuel lines to the mechanically-operated fuel pump located on the crankcase of the engine. From the pump, fuel goes to either a single down-draft Solex carburetor (type 1 and 2) or to a pair of Solex down-draft carburetors (type 3).

Since 1968, the type 3 has used an electronic fuel injection system. This system is discussed at the end of this chapter.

Volkswagens have used a variety of carburetors over the years, but all have a great deal in common. First, all are Solex; second, all operate under the same conditions in practically identical ways. On the following pages will be found detailed diagrams of the most popular Solex carburetors used in Volkswagens. Where one type is vastly different from others, this will be noted accordingly. Tuning of Volkswagen carburetors is found in Chapter 2.

Choking System

Every carburetor must have a way of enriching the mixture in order that a cold engine can be easily started. On Volkswagens produced through the 1960 model year, the choke was of the manual variety. In this set-up the butterfly valve in the carburetor horn was turned to restrict incoming air as the knob on the dashboard was pulled out. As the engine warmed up and ran smoother, thoughtful drivers gradually pushed the choke home again.

The Volkswagen automatic choke is a simple, trouble-free unit. All the driver must do is fully depress the accelerator pedal and let it up again before starting a cold engine, even on the coldest mornings. The construction of the automatic choke is illustrated in the accompanying diagrams and photographs.

The automatic choke is located at the upper half of the carburetor on most Volkswagen models. Inside the cover of the choke control housing is a bi-metallic spring which is curled up with a slight hook at its outer end. When the temperature is low, the coil tends to uncurl, thereby causing the butterfly valve to close off the air horn from incoming air. When the temperature is high, or the

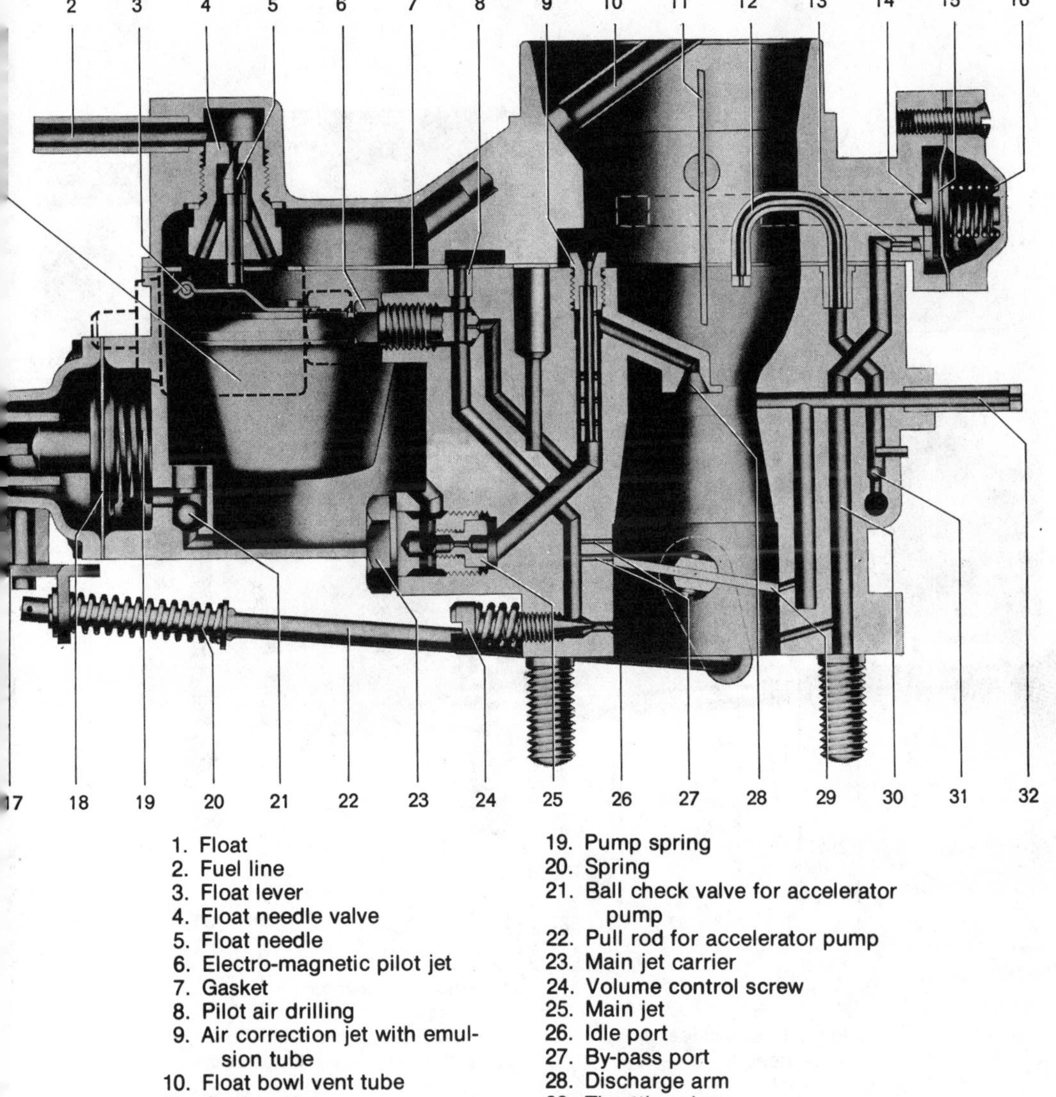

1. Float
2. Fuel line
3. Float lever
4. Float needle valve
5. Float needle
6. Electro-magnetic pilot jet
7. Gasket
8. Pilot air drilling
9. Air correction jet with emulsion tube
10. Float bowl vent tube
11. Choke valve
12. Accelerator pump discharge tube
13. Jet in vacuum drilling
14. Diaphragm rod
15. Vacuum diaphragm
16. Spring for vacuum diaphragm
17. Pump lever
18. Pump diaphragm
19. Pump spring
20. Spring
21. Ball check valve for accelerator pump
22. Pull rod for accelerator pump
23. Main jet carrier
24. Volume control screw
25. Main jet
26. Idle port
27. By-pass port
28. Discharge arm
29. Throttle valve
30. Vacuum drilling
31. Ball check valve in accelerator pump drilling
32. Vacuum connection

The carburetors on the Karmann Ghia models are fitted with a power fuel system

Cross-section of the Solex 30 PICT-1 used on the 1300 and 1500 type 1 and 2 (up to 1968) models

engine warm, the bi-metal coil tends to coil up tighter, and the hooked end acts upon the intermediate lever and butterfly valve shaft to open the valve fully. Also, a fast-idle cam makes the engine idle more quickly when it is cold, thereby avoiding stalling the engine. There are several "steps" on the fast idle cam. As the engine warms up, and the bi-metallic spring curls up, the fast-idle cam is turned so that the throttle stop screw or lever rests on a lower step. When the engine is completely warm, the cam will be turned to its lowest step and idle speed will be normal. For this reason, idle speed should not be adjusted unless the engine is warm.

Because the choke valve is off-center (i.e. the shaft does not run through the center of the valve), incoming air tends to open the

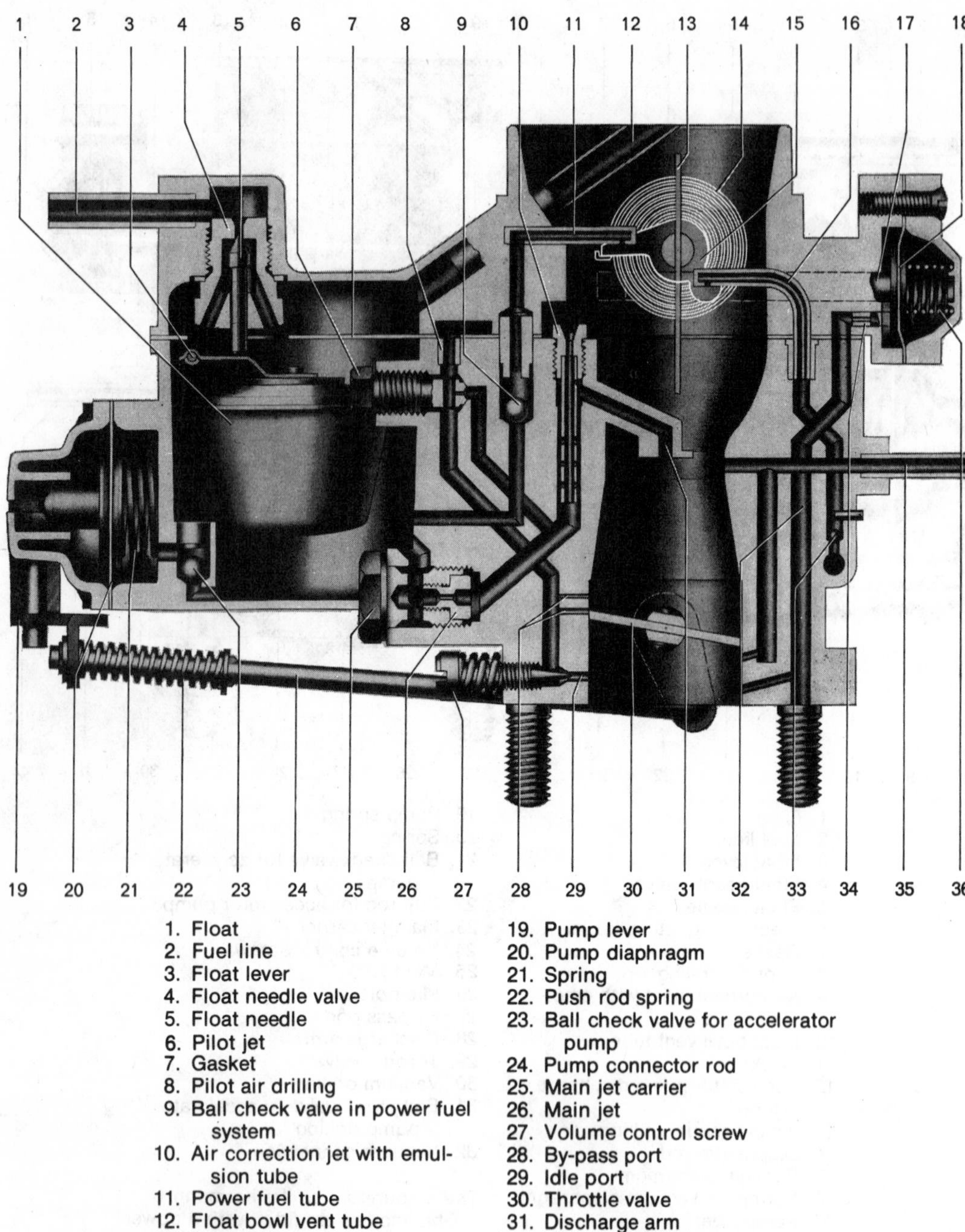

1. Float
2. Fuel line
3. Float lever
4. Float needle valve
5. Float needle
6. Pilot jet
7. Gasket
8. Pilot air drilling
9. Ball check valve in power fuel system
10. Air correction jet with emulsion tube
11. Power fuel tube
12. Float bowl vent tube
13. Choke valve
14. Bi-metal spring
15. Operating lever
16. Accelerator pump discharge tube
17. Diaphragm rod
18. Vacuum diaphragm
19. Pump lever
20. Pump diaphragm
21. Spring
22. Push rod spring
23. Ball check valve for accelerator pump
24. Pump connector rod
25. Main jet carrier
26. Main jet
27. Volume control screw
28. By-pass port
29. Idle port
30. Throttle valve
31. Discharge arm
32. Vacuum drilling
33. Ball check valve in accelerator pump drilling
34. Jet in vacuum drilling
35. Vacuum connection
36. Diaphragm spring

Solex 28 PICT-1, used on 1200 cc. engines, a cross-sectional view

butterfly and make the mixture less rich. Opposing the force of the incoming air is the tension of the bi-metal spring. However, as the spring heats up, it loses its closing power and even ends up holding the butterfly valve wide open.

The heating of the coil is accomplished both through the heating of the engine and through electricity supplied to the choke heating element when the ignition is turned on. The current to the heating coil is supplied by a wire from terminal #15 of the ignition coil. After only a few minutes, the heating coil will cause the bi-metal spring to curl up and release its closing force on the choke valve. Because most of the warming-up is the result of the current to the heating element of the choke, it is wise to drive off as soon as the engine is started on cold days. If the key is turned on and the engine is not started until minutes later, the choke will be "warm", but the engine will still be cold, hence difficult starting.

On the 32PDSIT carburetors used in the type 3, there is a vacuum piston which automatically modifies the choke valve position to better suit engine operating conditions. When the throttle is slightly open, a vacuum is set up in the vaccum cylinder, causing the piston to move and transmit a rotational force to the operating lever which in turn weakens the mixture by opening the choke valve.

The Solex carburetors used in the Volkswagen meet the engine's differing requirements under different conditions by utilizing four systems: (1) idling, or low speed, (2) normal operating, (3) accelerating, and (4) the power fuel system. The type 1 1200A and the Karmann Ghia 1300 and 1500 models have the power fuel system. In addition, the 1966 1600 type 3 also incorporated it, along with the 1500 type 3 "notch-back" and other 1500 type 3 models which were never officially imported and sold by Volkswagen of America. The presence of four different systems tends to make the Volkswagen carburetor similar to four carburetors in one. Each system operates under its own conditions, as well as overlapping with other systems as the need arises.

Idle (Low-Speed) System

When the engine is idling or running at a very slow speed, the formation of the fuel-air mixture takes place mainly through the idling system. At idle speed, the throttle valve is practically closed, so there is not enough vacuum in the venturi to cause the fuel to be drawn out of the discharge arm (see diagram). In this case the fuel coming from the float chamber passes through the main jet and is mixed with air which has been drawn in by the pilot air bleed jet (above the pilot jet in the 32PDSIT). The combination of air and fuel flows through a drilling slightly below the nearly-horizontal throttle valve. The degree of opening of the end of this drilling is controlled by the volume (mixture) control screw. If the screw is turned in the clockwise direction, the idle mixture will be lean because the air coming past the slightly-open throttle valve will have less fuel to mix with. On the other hand, if the volume control screw is turned in the counter-clockwise direction, the result will be a richer mixture, for the incoming air in the air horn will have more fuel to mix with.

On the carburetors used in 1970 and later type 1 and 2 models, the throttle valve is completely closed during idle. These carburetors have an air bypass passage which allows the air necessary for idling to bypass the throttle valve. The idling mixture is factory set with the volume control screw. An air bypass screw is used to regulate idle speed. Adjusting the air bypass screw has no effect on mixture strength, since an increase in volume of bypass air causes more fuel to be drawn from the idling system.

For the engine to make a smooth transition from the idle speed to normal running, it is necessary to incorporate what are known as "by-pass ports." These are small drillings near the throttle valve, and they may have different positions in different engines. If a new carburetor has a flat spot in acceleration (transfer from slow speed to normal), the cause may be the lack of a by-pass drilling or the presence of a by-pass drilling which is in the wrong position.

NORMAL RUNNING

When the car is running normally, under partial load, the mixture for the combustion chamber is supplied by the discharge arm (see diagram). The vacuum in the venturi area of the carburetor is great enough so that fuel is forced from the float bowl, through the main jet, to the emulsion (mixing) tube, and finally to the discharge arm. As the fuel first enters the discharge arm, it is mixed with air which has come in through the air correction jet.

The nozzle of the discharge arm is placed in the narrowest part of the venturi (the constricted section of the carburetor "pipe"), where the incoming air suddenly accelerates on its way to the engine. As a result of this air acceleration, the discharge nozzle, depending on the position of the throttle valve, is in the center of a varying amount of vacuum.

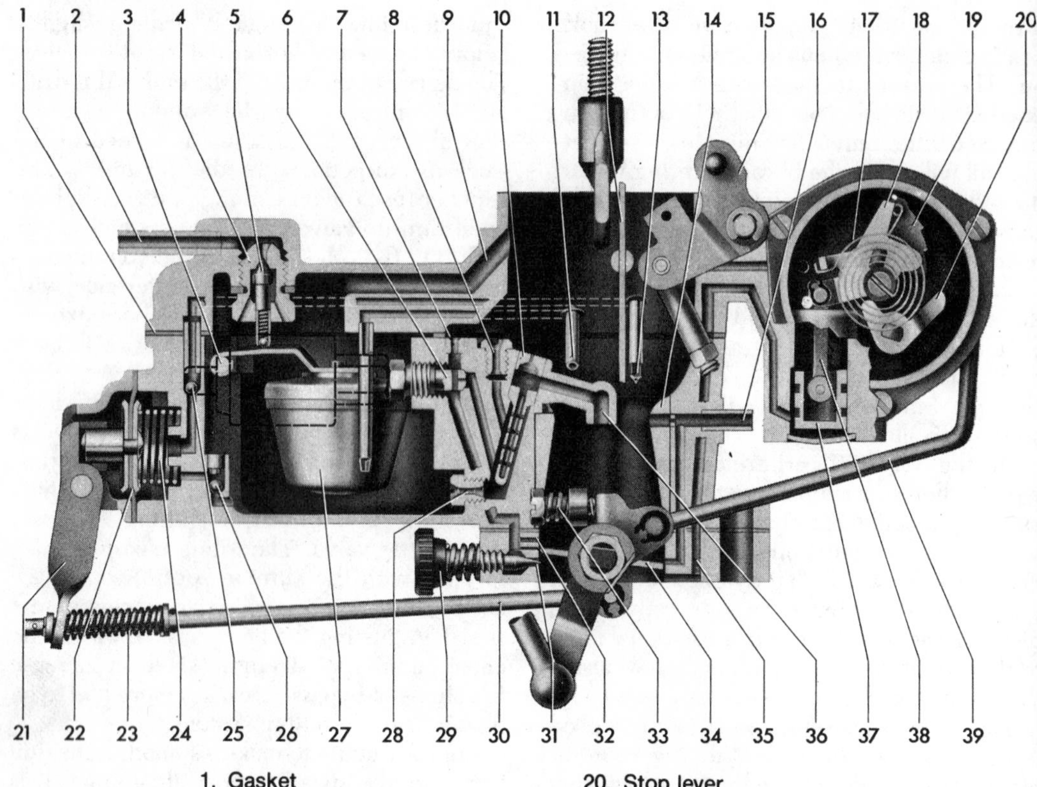

1. Gasket
2. Fuel pipe
3. Float pin
4. Float needle valve
5. Float needle
6. Pilot jet
7. Pilot air bleed drilling
8. Air correction jet
9. Vent passage for float chamber
10. Emulsion tube with ventilation jet
11. Power fuel pipe
12. Choke valve
13. Injector tube accelerator pump
14. Venturi
15. Relay lever
16. Vacuum connection
17. Bi-metal coil
18. Intermediate lever
19. Fast idle cam
20. Stop lever
21. Pump lever
22. Pump diaphragm
23. Connecting rod spring
24. Diaphragm spring
25. Ball pressure valve
26. Ball suction valve
27. 'Float
28. Main jet
29. Volume control screw
30. Connecting rod
31. Idling mixture port
32. By-pass port
33. Idle adjustment screw
34. Throttle valve
35. Vacuum drilling
36. Discharge arm
37. Vacuum piston
38. Piston rod
39. Operating rod

The Solex 32 PDSIT-2 used on the dual-carb type 3 engine. The 32 PDSIT-2 is the left-hand carburetor, and contains a double vacuum drilling for the distributor advance mechanism

The more open the throttle valve, the higher the vacuum will be at the center of the venturi. The normal running circuit is set up so that the air correction jet acts to weaken the mixture as the engine speed increases, thereby eliminating a tendency toward rich mixtures at these speeds. In the Volkswagen carburetor, there are two sources of air for the fuel-air mixture: (1) the so-called "primary" air which flows directly from the air horn to the engine, and (2) the air which goes to the engine only after it has passed through the air correction jet.

Accelerating System

The accelerating system of the Volkswagen is centered around a mechanical accelerator pump positioned at the side of the carburetor body. When the throttle is suddenly opened, motion is transmitted via the throttle shaft to a connecting rod, pump lever and a dia-

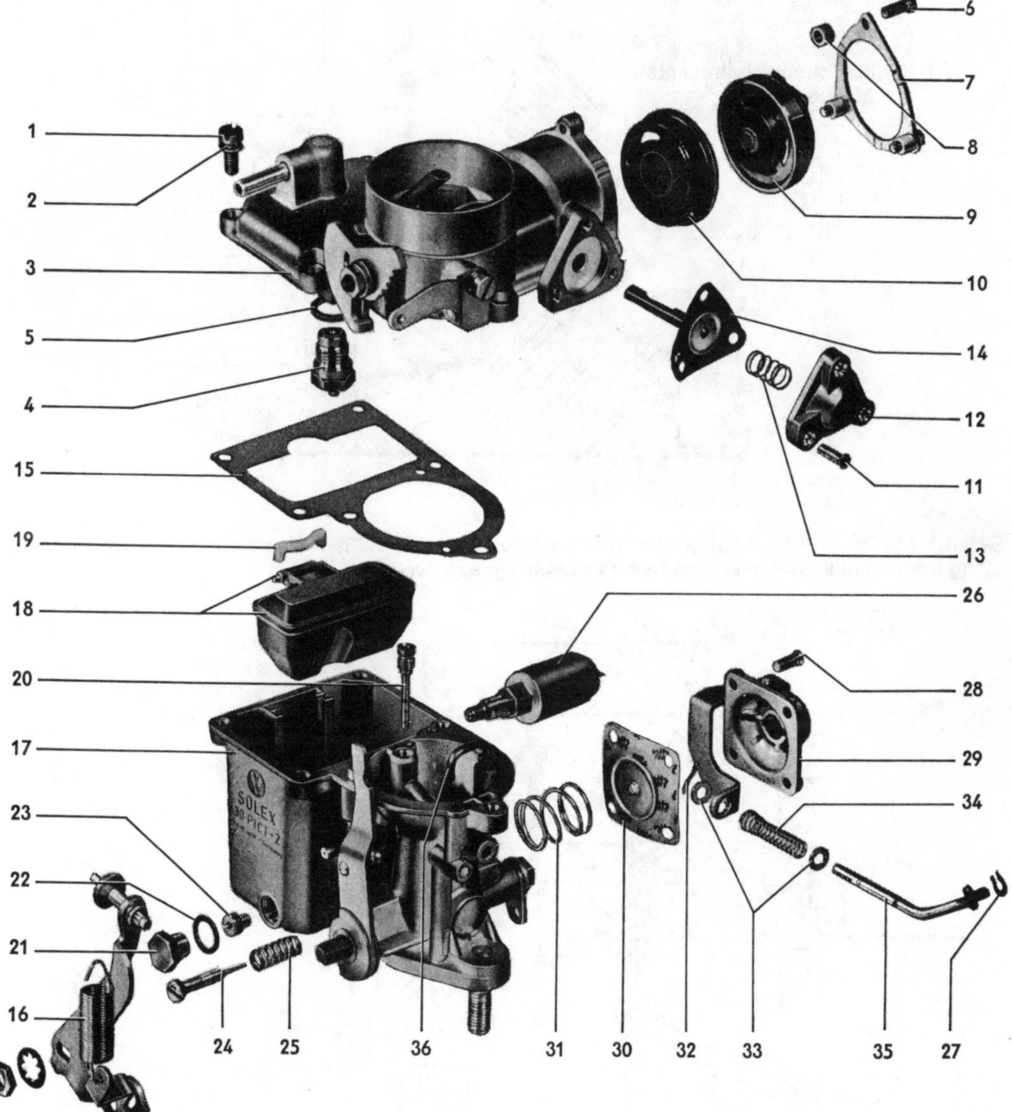

1. Screw for carburetor upper part
2. Spring washer
3. Carburetor upper part
4. Float needle valve 1.5 mm diameter
5. Washer 15 x 12 x 1 mm for float needle valve
6. Screw for retaining ring
7. Retaining ring for cap
8. Spacer for retaining ring
9. Choke unit with spring and heater element
10. Plastic cap
11. Fillister head screw
12. Cover for vacuum ciaphragm
13. Diaphragm spring
14. Vacuum diaphragm
15. Gasket
16. Return spring for accelerator cable
17. Carburetor lower part
18. Float and pin
19. Bracket for float pin
20. Air correction jet
21. Plug for main jet
22. Plug seal
23. Main jet
24. Volume control screw (designation 1, 2 and 3)
25. Spring
26. Pilot jet cut-off valve "A"
27. Circlip
28. Fillister head screw
29. Cover for pump
30. Pump diaphragm
31. Spring for diaphragm
32. Cotter pin 1.5 x 15 mm
33. Washer 4.2 mm
34. Spring for connecting rod
35. Connecting rod
36. Injector tube for accelerator pump

Exploded view, Solex 30 PICT-2 carburetor, standard equipment on 1968–69 VW 1500 type 1 and 2

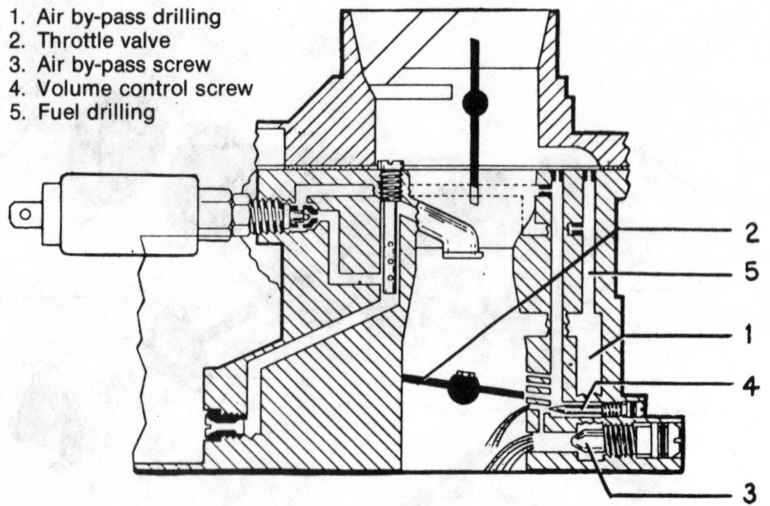

Details of Solex 30 PICT-3 carburetor used on 1970 type 1 and 2. The volume control screw is factory set. Idling speed adjustments are made with the air bypass screw

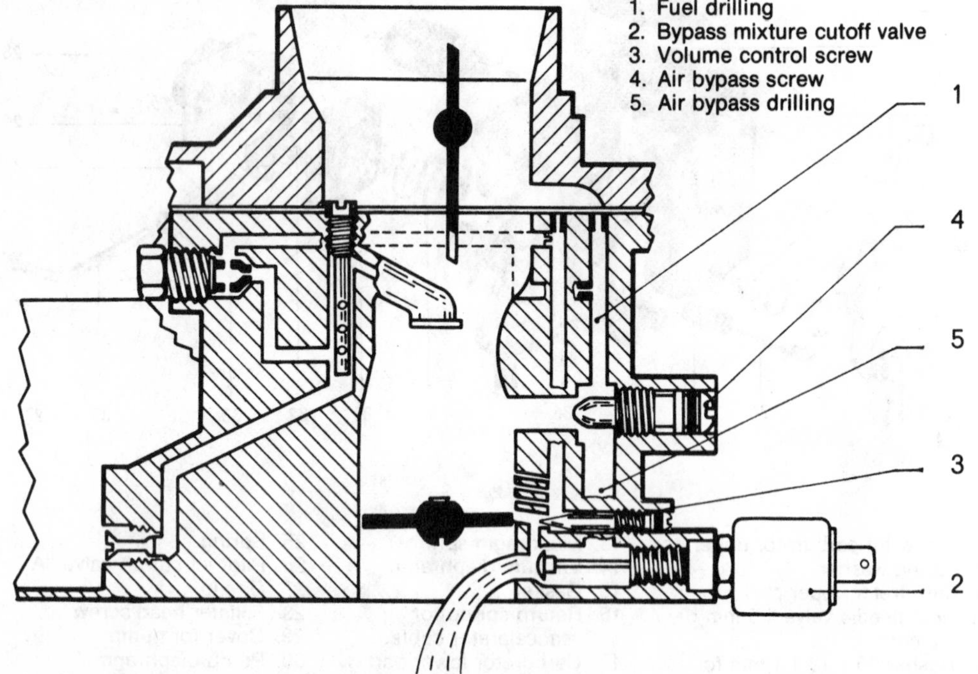

Details of Solex 34 PICT-3 carburetor used on 1971 type 1 and 2. The volume control screw is factory set. Idling speed adjustments are made with the air bypass screw

phragm which pumps additional fuel into the mixing chamber.

The presence of ball check valves in the accelerating system serves to help regulate the quantity of raw fuel which is squirted into the mixing chamber. As the throttle is first pushed open, the diaphragm moves forward and fuel is forced out of a calibrated drilling into the accelerator pump discharge arm. When the fuel is forced out, the upper ball check valve is pushed upward toward the outlet of the drilling. When the upper ball reaches the outlet, fuel flow is cut off. When the throttle is once again closed, the diaphragm relaxes and the lower ball check valve is drawn inward, allowing more fuel to

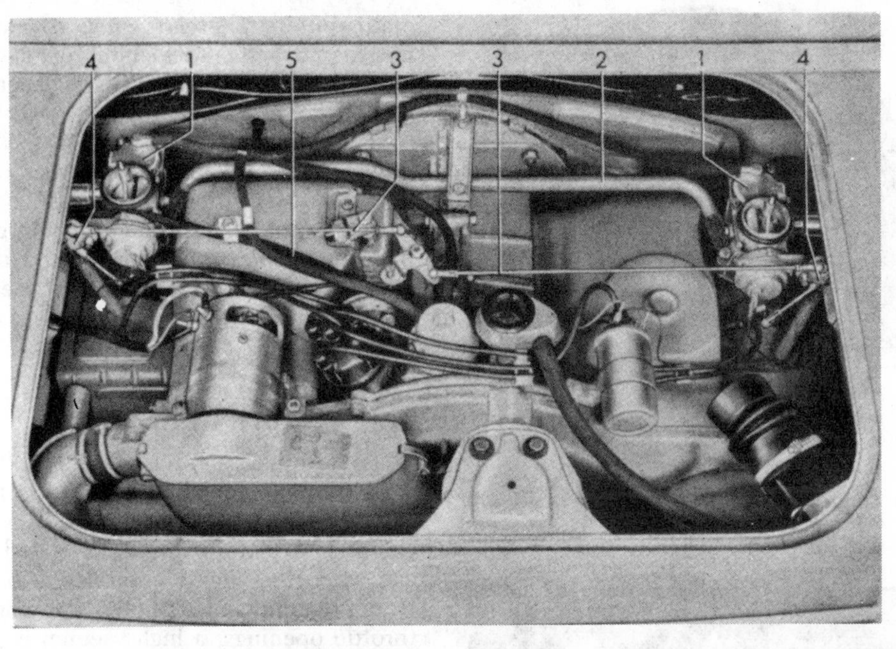

The linkage set-up of the dual carburetor type 3 engine: (1) carburetor, (2) balance pipe, (3) rods with ball joints, (4) relay levers. The left and right carburetors cannot be interchanged

The type 3 engine with the air cleaner attached; (6) is the common air cleaner, and (7) are the distribution ducts to the left and right carburetors

enter the diaphragm chamber for use the next time the throttle is opened.

The accelerator pump system operates only in the lower and medium speed ranges. When the throttle is almost open, the diaphragm is already fully depressed and therefore has no movement left when the throttle is opened further. The injection of fuel begins when the throttle first begins to open and ends when the throttle valve reaches an angle of about 30°.

During normal running, every downward movement of the accelerator pedal tends to cause enriching of the mixture via the accel-

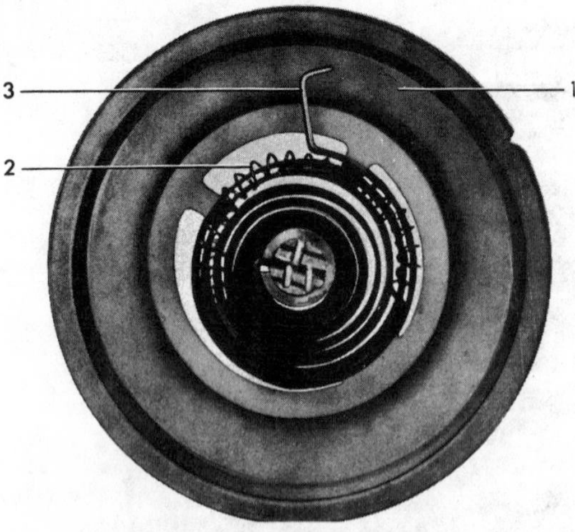

Choke control housing: (1) ceramic insert with heater element, (2) bi-metallic coil, (3) hook at end of bi-metal coil

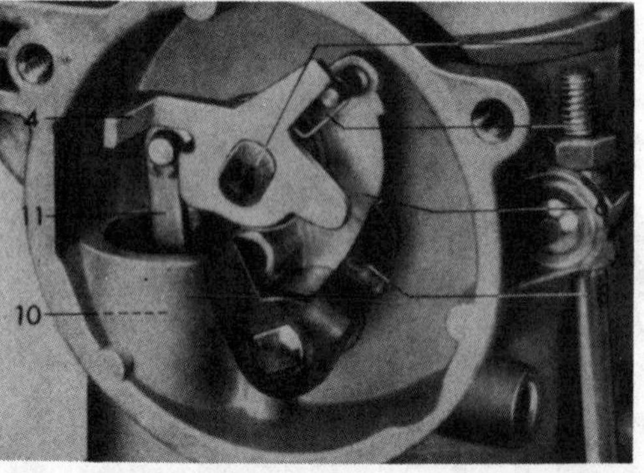

Choke valve shaft and linkages: (4) intermediate lever, (5) choke valve shaft, (6) fast idle cam, (7) return spring, (8) stop lever, (9) operating rod, (10) vacuum piston cylinder

erator pump. Therefore, it is advantageous not to move the accelerator up and down more than absolutely necessary if maximum fuel economy is to be attained. With the excellent economy capability of the Volkswagen, it is a shame to see so many drivers unwittingly motoring along using the accelerator as a foot-exerciser and wasting gasoline through needless acceleration and deceleration. Constant, slowly-changed, speeds are best both for the life of the engine and for economy.

The Power Fuel Circuit

The power fuel system is present on 1966 and earlier type 3, as well as on the type 1 1200A and Karmann Ghia 1300 models. This system comes into play in the upper speed ranges and when the engine is pulling at full load. Under conditions of high RPM and large throttle openings, a high vacuum is present near the outlet of the power fuel discharge tube. This causes additional fuel to be drawn out of the tube under the vacuum present at higher speeds. When the engine is operating at maximum speed, fuel is also drawn through the accelerator pump, thereby enriching the mixture further.

Oil Bath Air Cleaner

Volkswagen carburetors are equipped with the very efficient oil bath type of air cleaner.

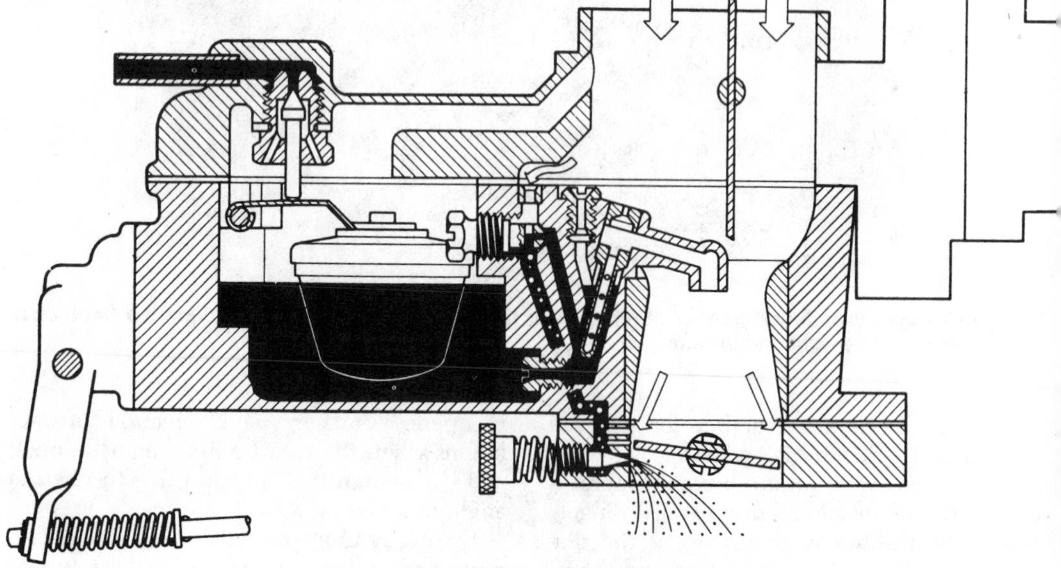

32 PDSIT–2/3 carburetor idling system in operation

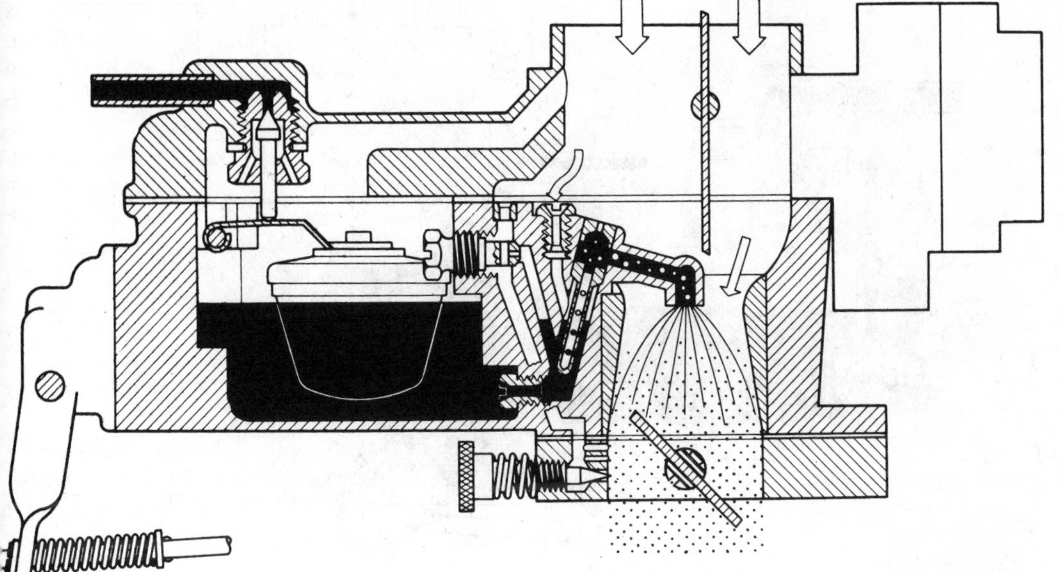

Normal operation of Solex 32 PDSIT-2/3

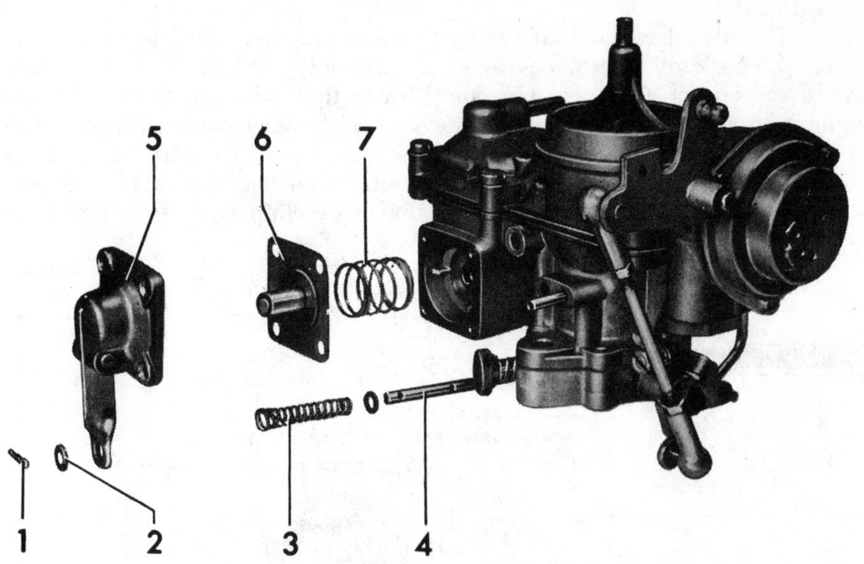

1. Cotter pin
2. Washer
3. Connecting rod spring
4. Connecting rod
5. Pump cover
6. Diaphragm
7. Diaphragm spring

Exploded view of accelerator pump of Solex 32 PDSIT-2 (note holes in connecting rod)

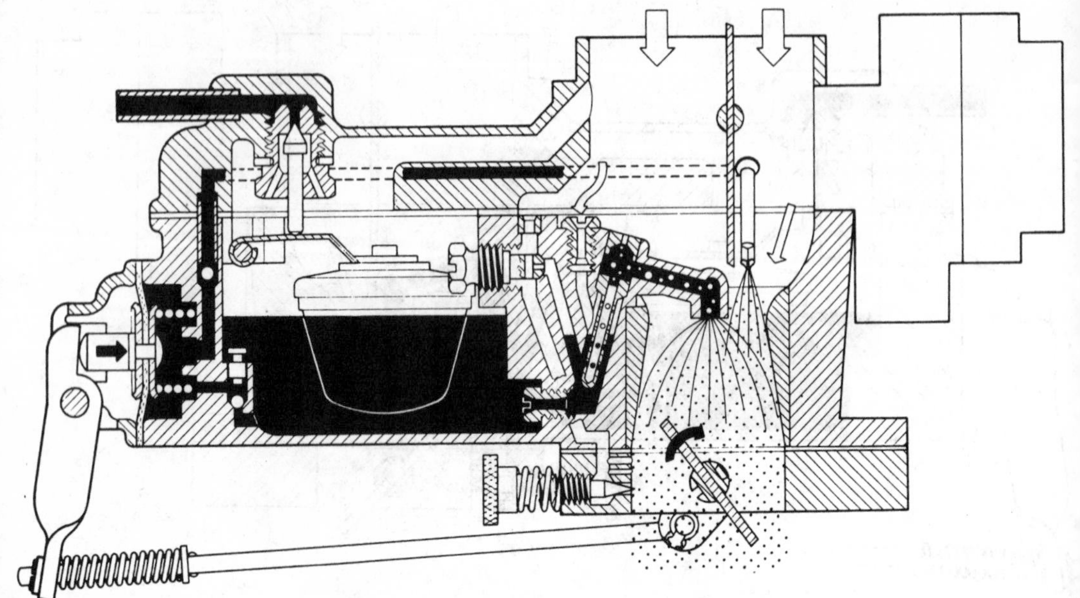

32 PDSIT–2/3 carburetor acceleration system

In this type of cleaner, the incoming air is directed over the surface of the oil bath, causing a large portion of the dust contained to be retained in the oil bath.

Type 1 and 2 models have had numerous variations on the basic oil bath air cleaner. Most have some sort of an intake pipe or pipes, equipped with one or two warm air hoses. At low speeds, a weighted flap in the intake portion of the air cleaner is closed, causing pre-heated air from the cylinder head to enter the carburetor. At higher speeds, the flap is forced open by the force of the air, and pre-heated air is kept from entering. This arrangement makes it possible to have smoother idling and faster warm-up in extremely cold temperatures while at the same time allowing all of the needed air to enter the air cleaner at higher speeds. For summertime or higher-temperature operation, it is recommended that the flaps be held open by clipping their weight levers to the

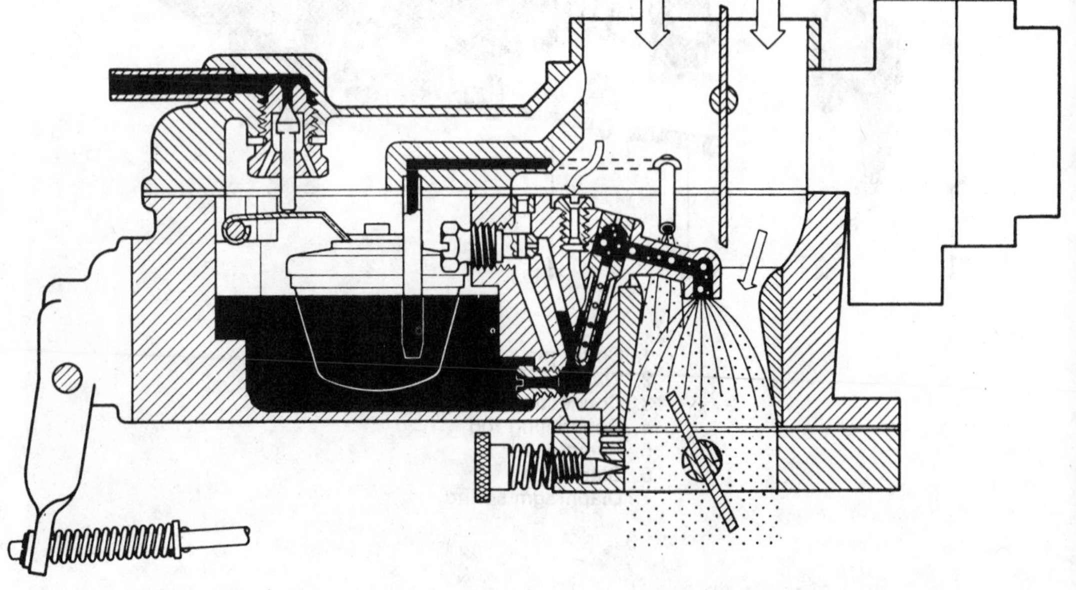

Power fuel system of 32 PDSIT–2/3, present in models up to 1967 model year

side of the intake pipe. In wintertime it is necessary that these flaps be allowed to rotate freely, because this helps to prevent the formation of carburetor icing.

On later models, the adjustable flap is replaced by a thermostatically controlled flap. On some units, the flap is regulated through a Bowden cable by a thermostatic unit mounted on the engine. On others, the thermostatic unit is located on the body of the air cleaner.

The oil bath air cleaner on the type 3 models is similar to that of the type 1 models, except for the presence of more extensive ductwork, needed because the same air cleaner serves both of the 32PDSIT carburetors of this engine. Also, the type 3 air cleaner is equipped with a second flap which allows air from the engine compartment to enter the air cleaner. Otherwise, air comes in from the slits on each side of the rear fender position. The fuel-injected type 3 has a similar air cleaner.

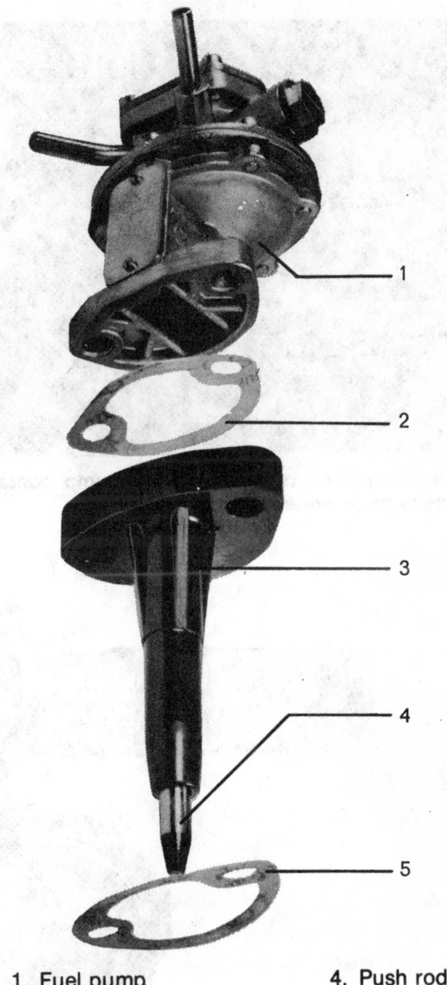

1. Fuel pump
2. Gasket
3. Plastic intermediate flange
4. Push rod
5. Gasket

Exploded view, lower portion of fuel pump

Fuel Pump

The Volkswagen fuel pump, except on fuel injected engines, is mechanical, and of the diaphragm type, being push-rod operated from a cam on the distributor drive gear. The fuel flow is regulated automatically as the fuel is used up from the float bowl. The fuel pump consists of the top cover, containing the suction valve and the delivery valve, and the lower half, which contains the rocker mechanism.

As the distributor shaft turns, the cam on the distributor drive gear pushes the push rod against the rocker arm, which in turn pulls the diaphragm downward against the diaphragm spring. In this way a vacuum is created above the diaphragm, causing the lifting of the suction valve off its seat so that fuel can be drawn in. After the push rod moves away, the loaded diaphragm spring pushes the diaphragm upward, forcing the fuel in the pump through the delivery valve and to the carburetor. This process is repeated each time the distributor drive gear turns, which is once each two turns of the engine.

The pump pressure is determined by the amount the diaphragm spring is compressed during the suction stroke of the pump. The pressure of the spring is balanced by the upward force of the carburetor float on the needle valve. The higher the fuel level in the

Fuel pump is secured by two retaining nuts

Measuring push rod stroke from pump contact surface on intermediate flange

carburetor, the greater is the upward force on the needle valve. Under normal engine operation, the diaphragm of the fuel pump is moved only a fraction of an inch.

Other than cleaning the filter of the pump at regular intervals, no other maintenance is necessary. The push rod and pump rocker arm are lubricated by the lubricant in the lower part of the pump.

FUEL SYSTEM SERVICE

R & R, AIR CLEANER

On type 1 models, the air cleaner is removed by taking the preheater pipe(s) from the in-

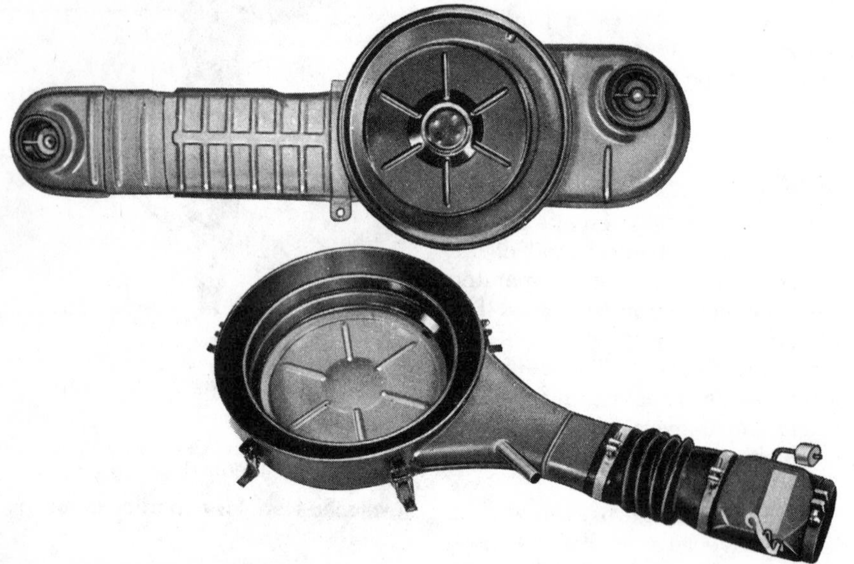

Air cleaner of dual-carb type 3 engine

On type 3 engine, clip should be loosened before intake hose is pulled off

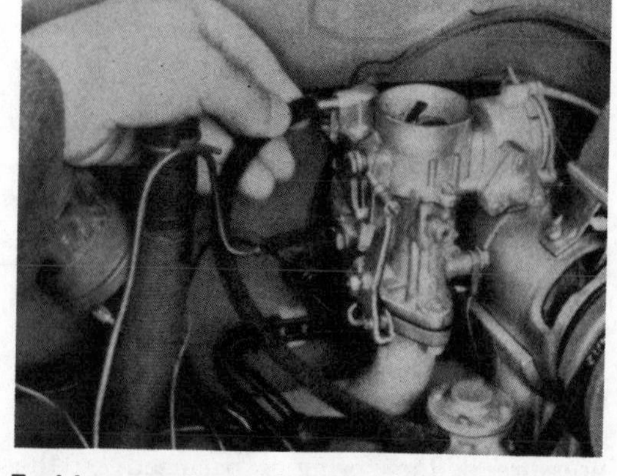

Fuel hose and vacuum hose are removed from carburetor before it is removed from intake manifold

take tube of the air cleaner, disconnecting the thermostatic flap control wire, pulling the crankcase breather hose from the cleaner, and loosening the clamp screw that holds the cleaner onto the carburetor throat. After the air cleaner has been removed, the top part can be separated from the lower part by removing the clips that hold the halves together.

When the cleaner has been taken apart, the dirty oil should be poured out and the lower part cleaned. The upper part does not generally require cleaning. The bottom part of the air cleaner should then be filled to the mark with new engine oil of the same viscosity as that used in the engine. If there is no mark, refill with the quantity of oil specified in the Capacities and Pressures Chart.

Removal of the air cleaner in the type 3 dual carburetor engine is slightly more complex, but accomplished in much the same manner. The right-hand connecting rod must be removed from between the rotating lever and the carburetor, the cables removed from the automatic choke and electromagnetic pilot jet, the crankcase ventilation hose taken off the air cleaner, and the three wing nuts unscrewed. The center wing nut is removed before removing the air cleaner; those at each of the carburetors remain in place. After the center wing nut is removed, the air cleaner can be lifted from its position and the upper and lower parts separated.

When installing the air cleaner of the type 3 engine, care should be taken to see that the oil is up to the mark, that the rubber sealing ring on each carburetor is secure, that the water drain hole is free in the lower part of the air cleaner, and that the marks are lined up when the upper and lower halves are put back together. If the marks do not line up exactly, the intake pipe will point in the wrong direction and be either difficult or impossible to connect to the intake extension. When tightening the wing nuts of the air cleaner, it is very important that the outer wing nuts are tightened down first. There is an expansion-contraction joint between the left outer wing nut and the center wing nut which makes these not quite so critical. However, there is no such joint between the center and right-hand wing nuts. Subsequently, if the center nut is tightened first, and then the right-hand nut, the result could be a slight movement on the part of the right-hand carburetor, thus causing an alteration in a very sensitive adjustment. Tighten down the center wing nut only after the two outer wing nuts have been fully tightened.

R & R, CARBURETOR

On the type 1, remove the pre-heat hose from the air cleaner intake pipe. Disconnect the thermostatic flap control wire. Disconnect the crankcase breather hose from the air cleaner intake. Loosen the air cleaner holding clamp and remove the air cleaner. Disconnect the fuel and vacuum hoses from the carburetor. Disconnect the wires from the automatic choke and the electromagnetic pilot jet. Disconnect the throttle cable at the carburetor and take off the spring, pin and spring retaining plate. Take off the two carburetor retaining nuts and remove the carburetor from the intake manifold. The throttle positioner may be removed in unit with the carburetor. It would, at this point, be a good idea to stuff part of a clean rag into the intake manifold hole in order to ensure that dirt and other foreign matter will not find its way into the manifold and cause damage to the engine.

Installation of the carburetor is the reverse of the previous operation. When installing the carburetor, it is advisable that a new intake manifold gasket be used. The retaining nuts should be tightened evenly, but not too tightly. The accelerator cable should be adjusted so that there is very little play (about 1 mm.) between the throttle lever and the stop point on the carburetor body when the pedal is fully depressed. The idle speed should be checked with the engine at operating temperature.

On the type 3, remove the air cleaner as described earlier. Be sure that the electrical connections are removed from the automatic chokes and the electromagnetic pilot jets. Remove the connecting rods from between the center lever and the left- and right-hand carburetors. Disconnect the carburetor return springs and pull off the spark plug connecting caps. Remove the balance tube from between the carburetors by pulling it out of the connecting hoses on either side. Remove the nuts that hold the intake manifolds to the cylinder heads. Remove intake pipes, cylinder head gaskets, and take carburetors off of intake pipes.

Installation of the type 3 carburetors is the reverse of the preceding. New gaskets should be used on the cylinder head intake, and the carburetor gaskets should be inspected for damage and replaced if need be.

On type 3 engine, the nuts holding the intake manifold to the cylinder head are removed

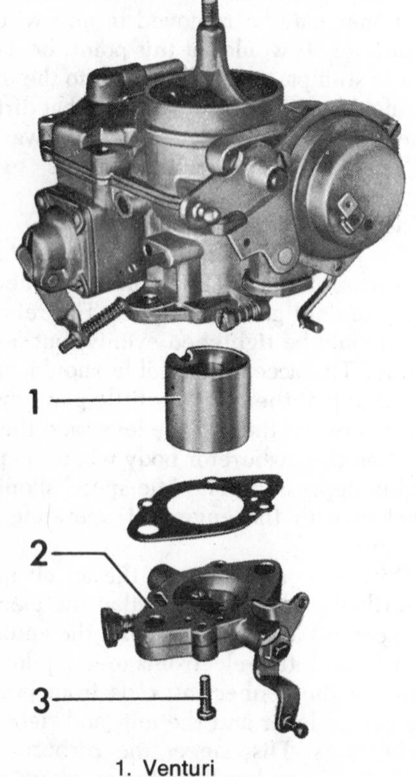

1. Venturi
2. Throttle valve part
3. Screw

Exploded view of removable venturi, gasket and throttle valve section of carburetor

CARBURETOR, DISASSEMBLY AND ASSEMBLY

Disassembly of all Volkswagen carburetors is covered by much the same procedure. After removing the five screws that retain the top part of the carburetor, take off the upper part. Remove the float, needle valve, and

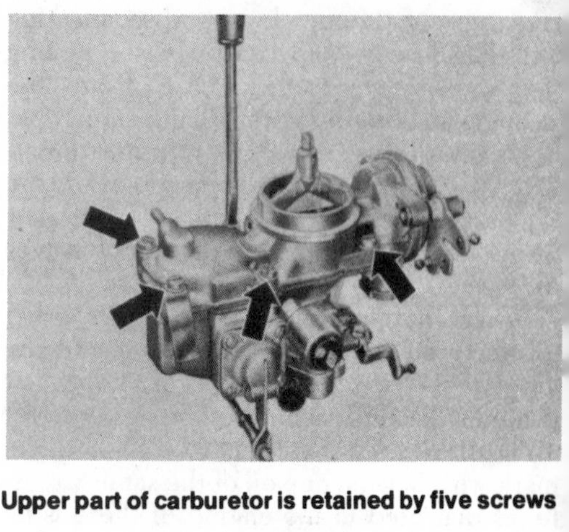

Upper part of carburetor is retained by five screws

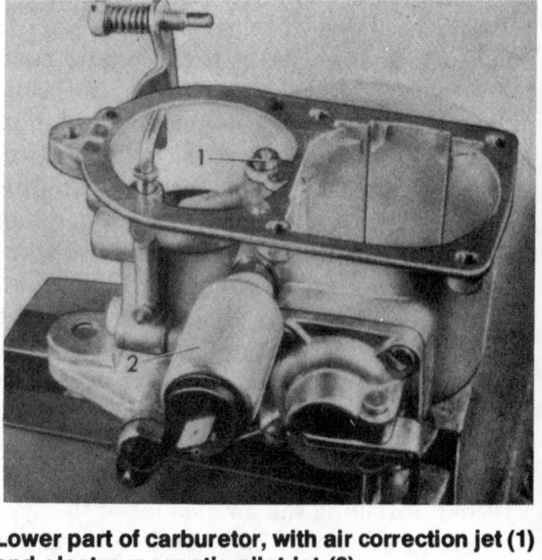

Lower part of carburetor, with air correction jet (1) and electro-magnetic pilot jet (2)

Float needle valve should be checked for freedom of movement and for leakage

Main jet is removed after unscrewing plug (1); volume control screw (2) determines low-speed mixture and is removable. Volume control screw should not be turned in too tightly because its seat could become damaged

Height of power fuel tube opening from upper part of carburetor should be 15 mm. on type 3 carburetors equipped with power fuel system

The height of the injector tube opening from the upper part of the 32 PDSIT–2/3 carburetor should be 12mm for engines up to number T 0244544, 9mm thereafter

Measuring throttle valve gap of 32 PDSIT–2/3. Gap should be between .60–.65mm (.024–.026″)

Left carburetor Right carburetor

Choke operating controls are not the same on the left- and right-hand carburetors

Alignment of choke housing cover with upper part of carburetor is as shown

needle valve gasket. Remove automatic choke housing, retaining ring, and bi-metallic spring. The choke unit is attached by three retaining screws. Remove the accelerator pump cotter pin (connects pump lever to connecting rod). Remove the four screws from pump housing, and remove the pump diaphragm and spring. The main jet and the volume control screws should be removed, along with the plug that allows access to the main jet.

After disassembly, clean all parts in a suitable solvent, except for the cover of the automatic choke unit. After cleaning through soaking and rubbing with soft cloth, all jets, valves and drillings should be blown out with compressed air. Mouth pressure or the pressure from a simple tire pump is not enough. If necessary, pack the pieces into a box and head for the place where you usually buy gasoline. It is highly probable that the attendant will be glad to lend you the use of his compressed air hose. Especially important in the compressed air cleaning process is the cleaning of the needle valve. When cleaning the carburetor passageways and jets, do not use pins, pipe cleaners, or other pieces of wire. The drillings are finely calibrated and might be damaged or enlarged through such mistreatment.

When taking the carburetor apart for cleaning, it is not necessary that every single part be dismantled. It is sufficient for most purposes to remove only the major components, along with the needle valve, float, main jet and accelerator pump diaphragm. The most important part of the entire operation is probably the blowing out with compressed air of all passageways.

On reassembly, check the needle valve for proper operation. On the type 3, the height of the accelerator pump injector tube opening should be 12 mm. (.47″) from the upper part of the carburetor (9 mm. for engine nos. T0244544 and onward). When the carburetor is assembled, the injector tube should squirt gasoline directly into the gap between the throttle valve and the carburetor throat when the accelerator pump is displaced. The power fuel tube opening of the type 3 dual carburetor models should be 15 mm. (.59″) from the upper part of the carburetor. When the carburetor is assembled this tube should point roughly in the center of the gap between the discharge arm and the venturi. When replacing the cover of the automatic choke, be sure that the hooked end of the bimetallic spring engages the operating lever. The mark on the cover of the choke should line up with the center lug on the upper part of the carburetor. When fastening down the automatic choke cover, care should be taken not to over-tighten the retaining screws. Be sure to put the proper choke on the proper carburetor. They are not interchangeable.

The diaphragm of the accelerator pump should be checked for leakage, and replaced if defective. The diaphragm should be tightened down while pressed in the pressure stroke position. On the type 3, the length of the operating rod should be adjusted so that a gap of .60–.65 mm. (.024–.026″) exists at the throttle valve when the choke valve is closed. This gap should be measured with a wire feeler gauge while the throttle valve is pushed lightly in the closing direction. After tightening the two nuts on the operating rod, be sure that the parts have sufficient freedom of movement.

Alignment of choke housing cover with upper carburetor part, Type 1 single carburetor

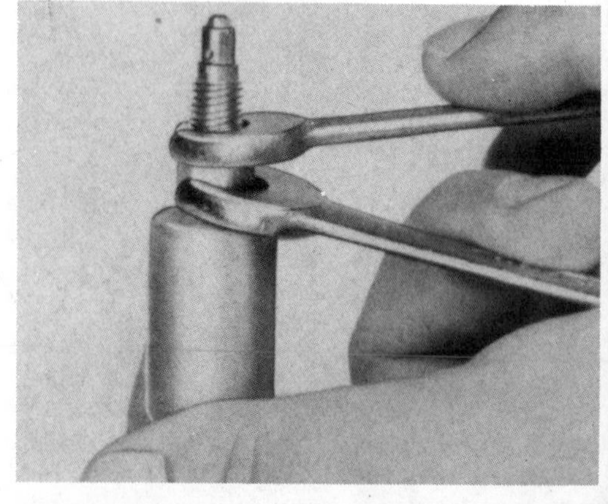

Two wrenches are used in screwing the pilot jet from the cut-off valve. Electro-magnetic operation keeps engine from running on when ignition is shut off

CHECKING ELECTROMAGNETIC PILOT JET

If the engine is equipped with an electromagnetic pilot jet in the carburetor, and still shows a tendency to "run-on" after being shut off, chances are that the electromagnetic jet is defective. Operation can be checked by turning on the ignition and touching the slip-on connector against the terminal of the jet. If the jet is operating properly, a clicking sound will be heard each time the connector touches the terminal. When the current is off, the needle of this jet moves so as to block off the fuel supply, so when the connector is removed while the engine is running, it should stop the engine.

On 1971 type 1 and 2 engines with the Solex 34 PICT-3 carburetor, the pilot jet cut-off valve has been replaced by an idle bypass mixture cutoff valve. The new unit performs the same function.

ADJUSTMENT AND SYNCHRONIZATION

After reassembly, the carburetor should be adjusted as described in the "Tuning" chapter. If the car is equipped with dual carburetors, these should be synchronized at idle and at 1,500 RPM by the method shown in the same chapter.

ADJUSTING ACCELERATOR PUMP INJECTION

In the type 3, the amount of fuel injected by the accelerator pump can be adjusted by altering the position of the cotter pin on the connecting rod. Moving the cotter pin from the center to either the outer or the inner hole of the connecting rod will result in either less or more fuel injected when the throttle valve is moved from the fully closed to the fully opened position:

Hole in Rod	*Quantity of Fuel*
inner	larger (by .3 cc)
center	normal (.35–.55 cc)
outer	smaller (by .3 cc)

R & R, ACCELERATOR CABLE

The Volkswagen accelerator cable runs from the accelerator pedal to the carburetor by means of the central tunnel, the fan housing and the throttle valve lever. Guide tubes are used in both the central frame tunnel and the fan housing, while a plastic hose is present between the tunnel and the front engine cover plate.

To remove the accelerator cable, disconnect the cable from the throttle lever pin, raise the rear of the car, and pull the cable through from the front of the car after disconnecting the rod from the accelerator pedal.

Installation is the reverse of the removal. Grease the cable well before inserting from the front of the car. Be sure that the rear rubber boot and hose are properly seated, so that water will not enter the guide tubes. In order to avoid excessive strain of the throttle cable and assembly, there should be about 1 mm. (.04") clearance between the throttle stop and the carburetor body when the throttle is in the wide-open position. For this reason, it is advisable that the cable be tightened down at the carburetor end only when the accelerator pedal is at the fully-floored position.

Measuring accelerator pump injection quantity

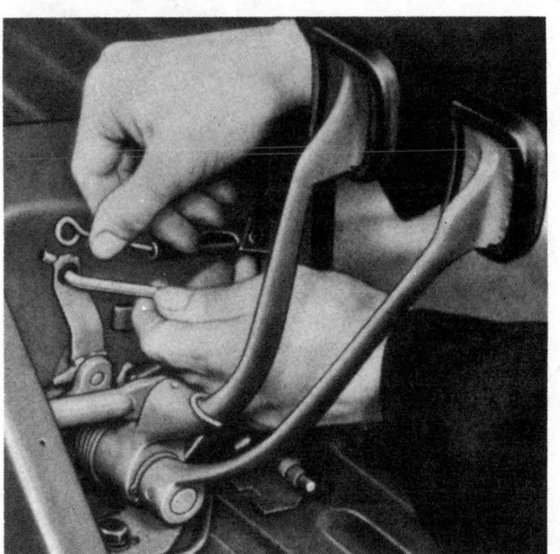

Attachment of accelerator cable to pedal linkage. Cable is removed to the front

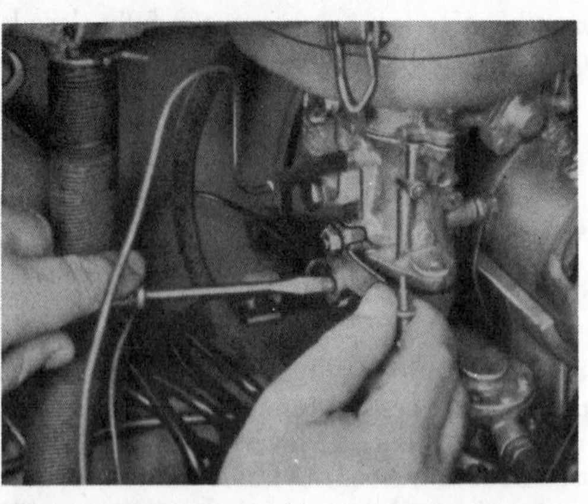

When throttle valve is open, pedal floored, there should be a slight clearance (about 1 mm) between the throttle lever and the stop on the carburetor body

R & R, FUEL PUMP

The fuel pump is removed by taking off the fuel line, disconnecting the hose from the pump, and removing the retaining nuts from the mounting studs. After the pump has been removed, the intermediate flange, push rod and gaskets can be removed. Be careful in handling the push rod, as it could be inconvenient to have to fish it out of the crankcase.

Once removed, the stroke of the fuel pump is adjusted by the insertion or removal of the proper number of flange gaskets. Adjustment is checked after installing the intermediate flange with two gaskets and push rod, and nuts are tightened to the same tightness as if the entire pump were being installed. Normal full-stroke is approximately 4

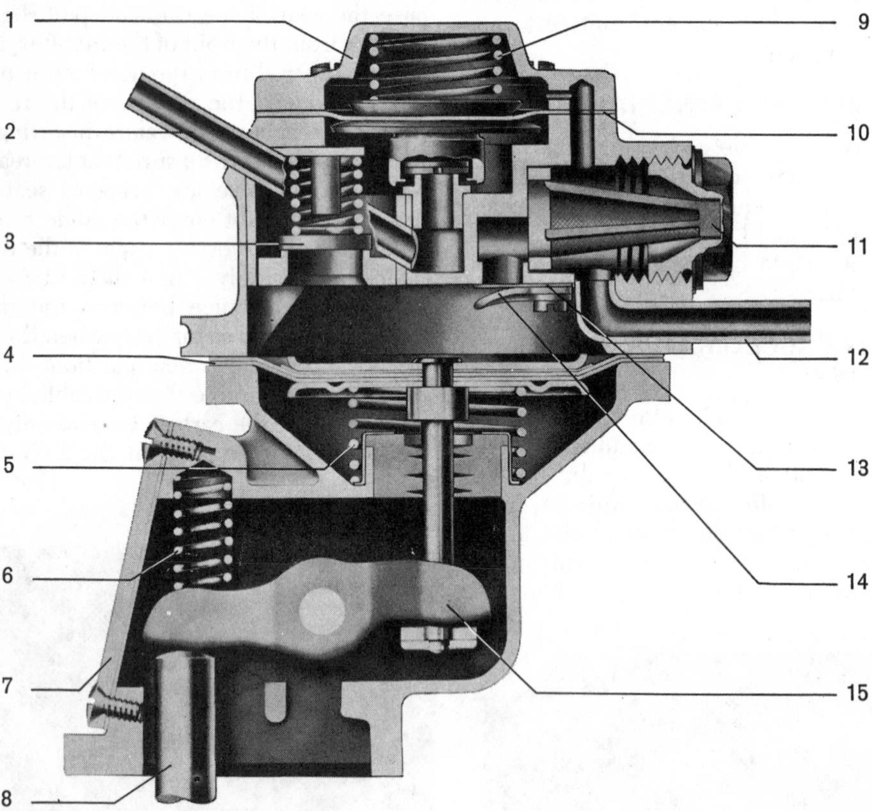

1. Cover
2. Fuel outlet
3. Pressure valve
4. Diaphragm
5. Diaphragm spring
6. Pump leverl spring
7. Sealing plate
8. Push rod
9. Spring for cut-off diaphragm
10. Cut-off diaphragm
11. Strainer
12. Suction pipe
13. Suction valve
14. Suction valve retainer
15. Pump lever

Cross-sectional view, fuel pump. Fuel injected type 3 models have an electrical pump

mm. The length of the push rod stroke is measured from the pump contact surface on the intermediate flange, including gaskets.

When installing the fuel pump, care must be taken to install the intermediate flange before the push rod, otherwise the rod may fall through into the crankcase. Before installing the fuel pump, the lower chamber should be filled with universal grease. Tighten nuts to mounting studs, taking care not to overtighten. (Nuts should be retightened when the engine has reached operating temperature.) Connect the fuel line and hose, and check for correct seating of the fuel line rubber grommet in the panel of the engine compartment.

Fuel pump pressure can be checked by the insertion of a suitable gauge between the pump and the carburetor. Correct fuel pump pressure for various models is given in the Capacities and Pressures Chart.

CARBURETOR AND FUEL PUMP REBUILDING KITS

Carburetor and fuel pump repair and rebuilding kits are available at authorized Volkswagen dealers and various other sources. These kits contain the critical parts of the units to be rebuilt or repaired, and are well worth the money compared to the trading in of the old unit on a new one. Such kits are also handy to have on hand during long trips through low-population areas, because even the ultra-reliable Volkswagen sometimes (though rarely) becomes incapacitated due to unexpected failures in these two most important elements of the fuel system.

FUEL INJECTION SYSTEM

One advantage of the Volkswagen fuel injection system is the reduction of unburnt fuel, carbon monoxide and hydrocarbons in the exhaust gas. The engine receives the proper air-fuel mixture under all conditions as the result of the sophisticated controls designed into the system. The fuel injection system is made up of three sub-systems—the fuel system, the air system and the control unit.

FUEL INJECTION—THE FUEL SYSTEM

Fuel is drawn from the front-mounted tank through a filter by an electric fuel pump. The pump pushes the fuel through the pressure line into the fuel loop line, to which the electro-magnetic injectors are connected by distributor pipes. A pressure regulator is present to keep the fuel at a constant pressure of 28 psi. Excess fuel flows back to the tank via a return line.

FUEL INJECTION—THE AIR SYSTEM

Four pipes are used to transfer air into the four cylinders. Connected to the pipes is the intake air distributor, which is in turn connected to the pressure switch and pressure sensor. The intake side of the air distributor

The type 3 fuel-injected engine

Fuel system of the fuel-injected engine: (1) electric fuel pump, (2) filter, (3) pressure line, (4) fuel loop line, (5) electro-magnetic fuel injectors, (6) distributor pipes, (7) pressure regulator, and (8) return line

contains a throttle valve attached to the accelerator pedal via a cable. When the engine is idling, the throttle valve is fully closed and the air must pass through an idling air circuit. An idling air screw controls the amount of air for idling. An auxiliary air regulator is used to vary the quantity of air to suit the engine temperature when the engine is idling.

FUEL INJECTION—THE CONTROL SYSTEM

The central brain of the fuel injection system is the control unit which controls the amount of fuel injected according to various inputs, such as the engine speed, the intake manifold pressure, and the engine temperature. The main relay supplies current to the control unit when the ignition is turned on. The control unit controls the fuel pump via the pump relay.

The control unit "masterminds" the operation by electrically opening the injector valves in pairs. No. 1 and 4, and No. 2 and 3 injector valves open simultaneously. It keeps the injector valves open for exactly the right length of time to suit the requirements of the engine. Because the fuel is under constant pressure (28 psi), the amount of fuel injected

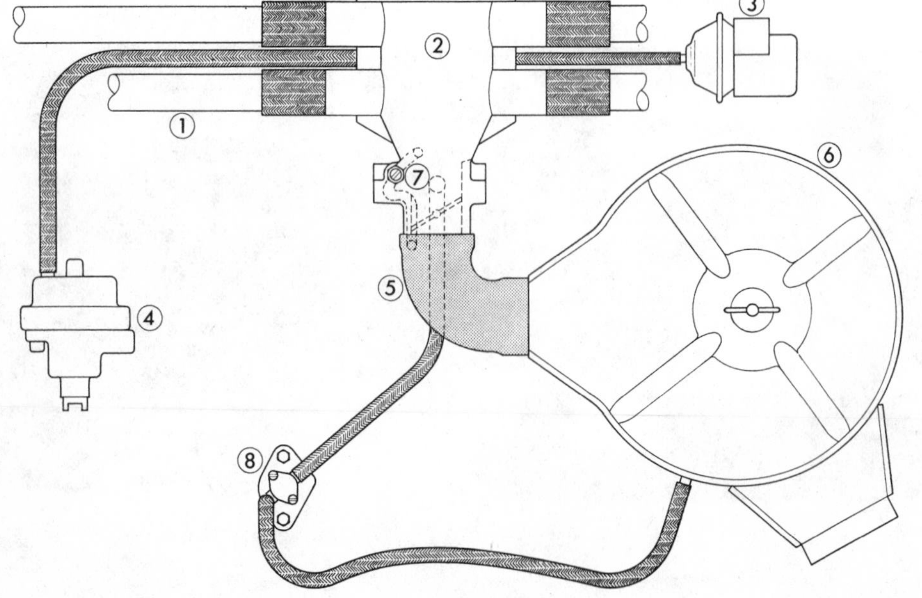

Air system of the fuel-injected engine: (1) intake pipes, (2) intake air distributor, (3) pressure switch, (4) pressure sensor, (5) idle air circuit, (6) air cleaner, (7) idling air screw, (8) auxiliary air regulator

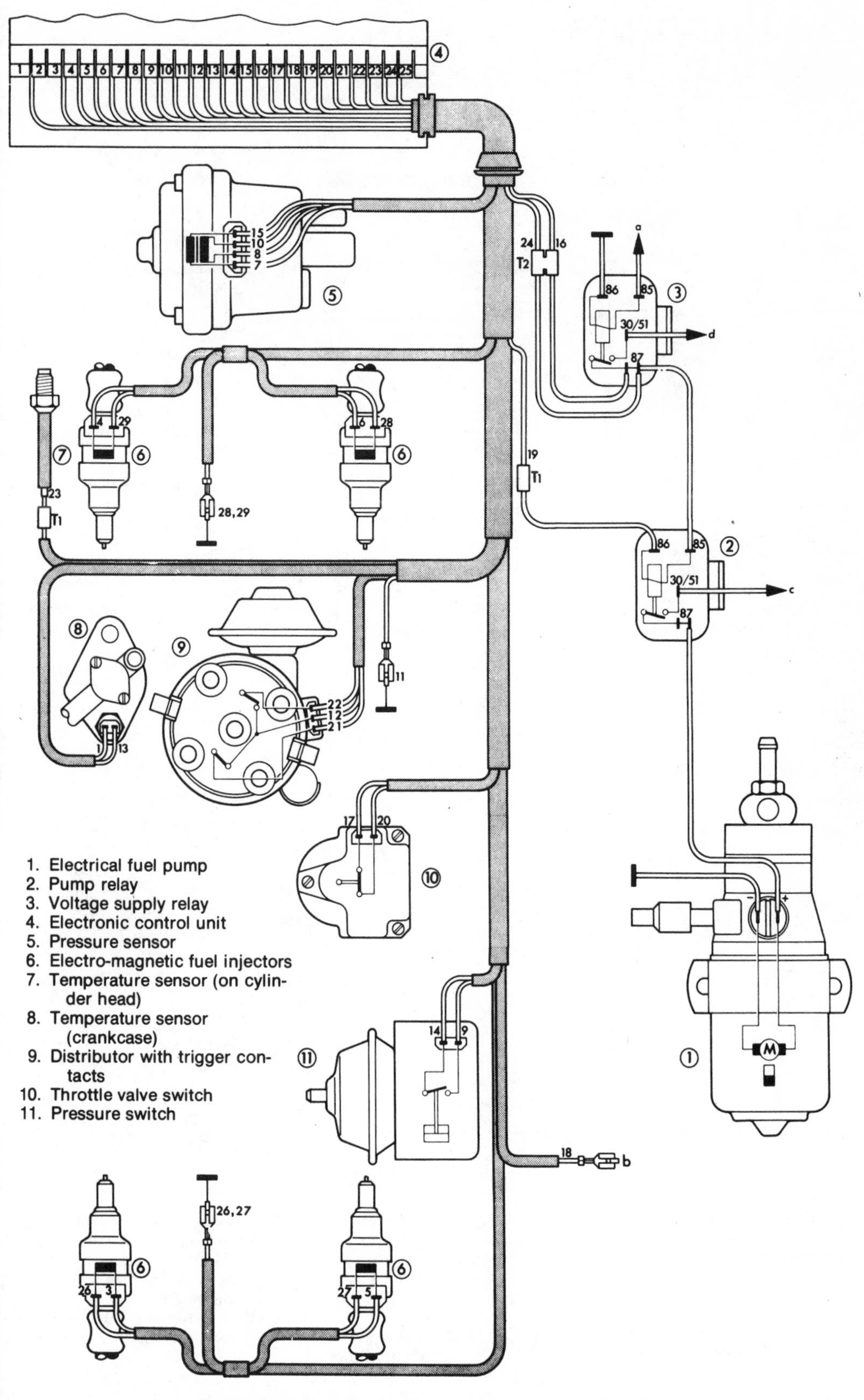

Fuel injected engine control system and components

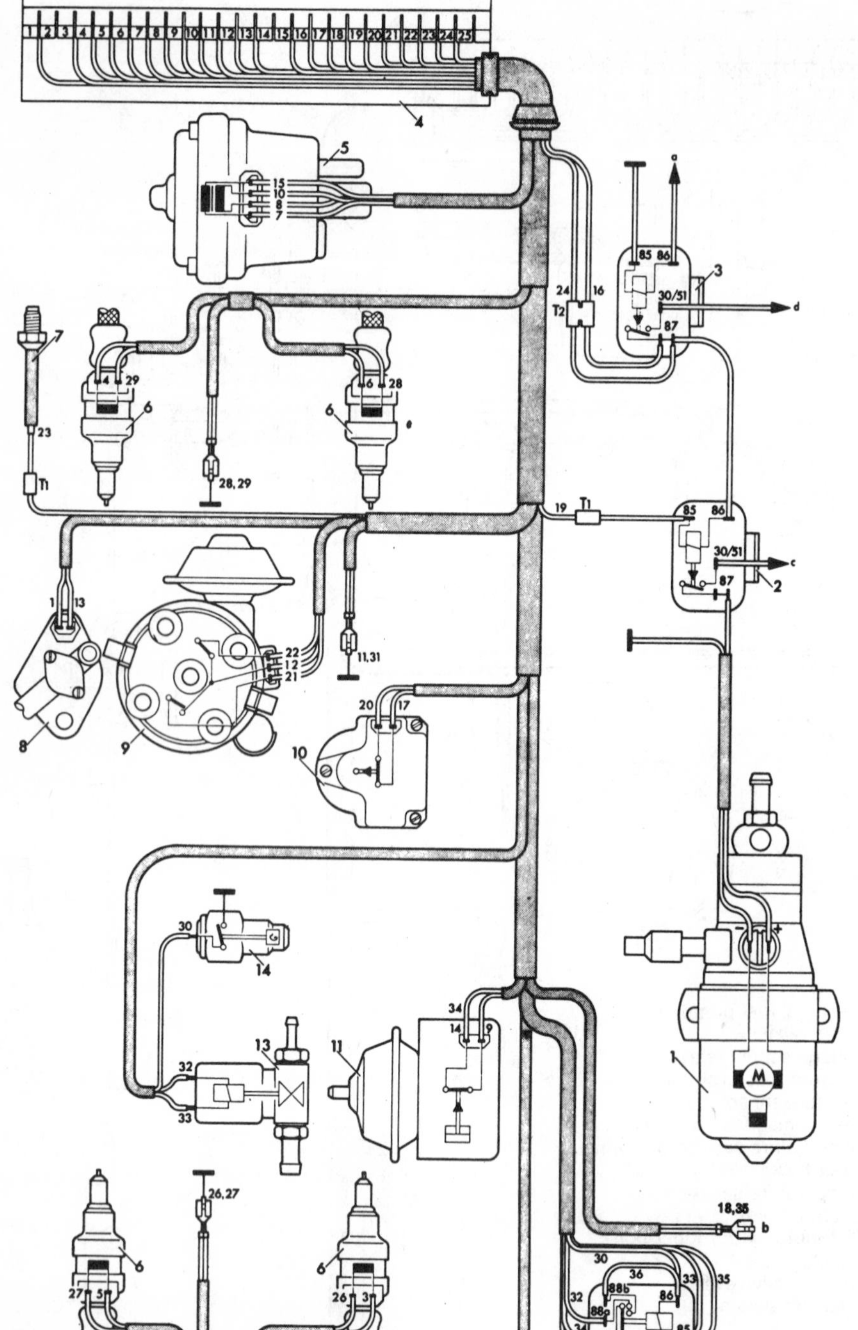

1. Electric fuel pump
2. Pump relay (relay I)
3. Voltage supply relay (relay II)
4. Electronic control unit
5. Pressure sensor
6. Elec. magnetic fuel injectors
7. Temp. sensor (cyl. head)
8. Temp. sensor (crankcase)
9. Ign. distr. with trigger contacts
10. Throttle valve switch
11. Pressure switch (no longer used)
12. Relay (cold starting jet)
13. Elec. magnetic cutoff (cold starting jet)
14. Thermo switch (cold starting)

a. Wire to ign. switch (terminal 15)
b. Wire to starter solenoid (term. 50)
c. Wire to terminal 30
d. Wire to pos. battery terminal

Control system and components of fuel injection system with cold starting device

into the cylinders is directly proportional to the length of time that the injectors are held open by the control unit. In "deciding" how long to keep the injectors open, the control unit processes information received from the following sources: pressure sensor, pressure switch, two temperature sensors, trigger contacts in the distributor, and the throttle valve switch. The pressure sensor senses the load condition of the engine by measuring the pressure in the intake manifold. The pressure switch controls fuel enriching at full load, and is actuated by the difference in pressure between the air in the intake manifold and the air in the surrounding atmosphere. Two temperature sensors in the crankcase and cylinder head control the mixture enrichment both during starting and warming up of the engine. On later units, one sensor is fitted in the intake air distributor and the other to the cylinder head. Trigger contacts in the distributor "tell" the control unit into which set of cylinders to inject the fuel. The contacts also regulate injection timing. The function of the throttle valve switch is to cut off the supply of fuel when the engine is decelerating. In later models, the throttle valve switch also controls mixture enrichment on acceleration.

A cold starting device is present in later units. This device consists of a fuel jet fitted to the intake air distributor and a thermostatic switch. The switch actuates at 5°5F. The cold starting device is available as a kit for installation in earlier models. In current production, a new cold starting device is used, consisting of a thermostatic switch, which operates between 32°F and 50°F and a fuel jet combined into a single unit, fitted under and between the intake manifolds on the right side. The new cold starting device cannot be used to replace the earlier unit.

FUEL INJECTION SYSTEM SERVICE

Testing and troubleshooting of the fuel injection system requires special Bosch electronic testing apparatus. For this reason, these operations are best left to qualified personnel at an authorized dealer's shop. Removal and replacement of components, and adjustments that can be made without special equipment are covered in this section. Refer to Chapter 2 for ignition timing and idle speed adjustments.

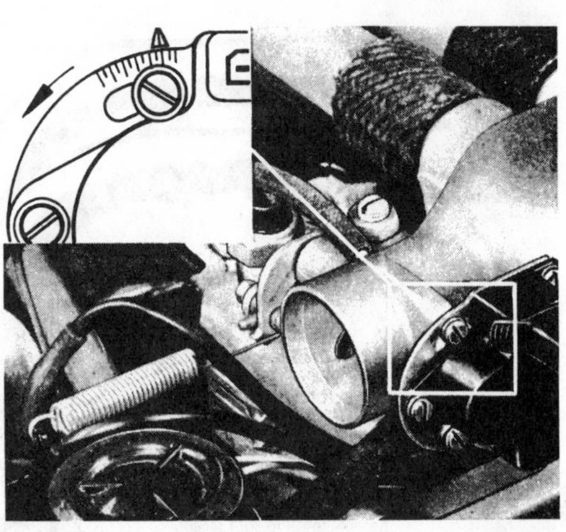

Throttle valve switch details. Each graduation indicates 2°

THROTTLE VALVE SWITCH ADJUSTMENT

The throttle valve switch is mounted to a base plate with graduated markings secured to the intake air distributor inlet. An alignment mark is located on the air distributor housing. The switch is affixed by two mounting screws and an electrical plug. To adjust the switch:

1. Remove air cleaner for access.
2. Close throttle valve completely.
3. Loosen base plate mounting screws. Slowly rotate switch and plate assembly counterclockwise until a click is heard.
4. Continue rotating switch and plate assembly counterclockwise one more graduation. (Each graduation indicates 2°.)
5. Tighten base plate mounting screw.

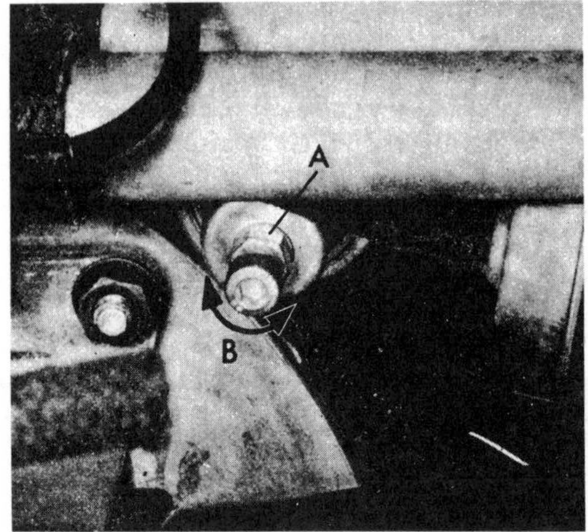

Pressure regulator, located under the right side of the intake manifold. A is the locknut, B is the adjusting nut

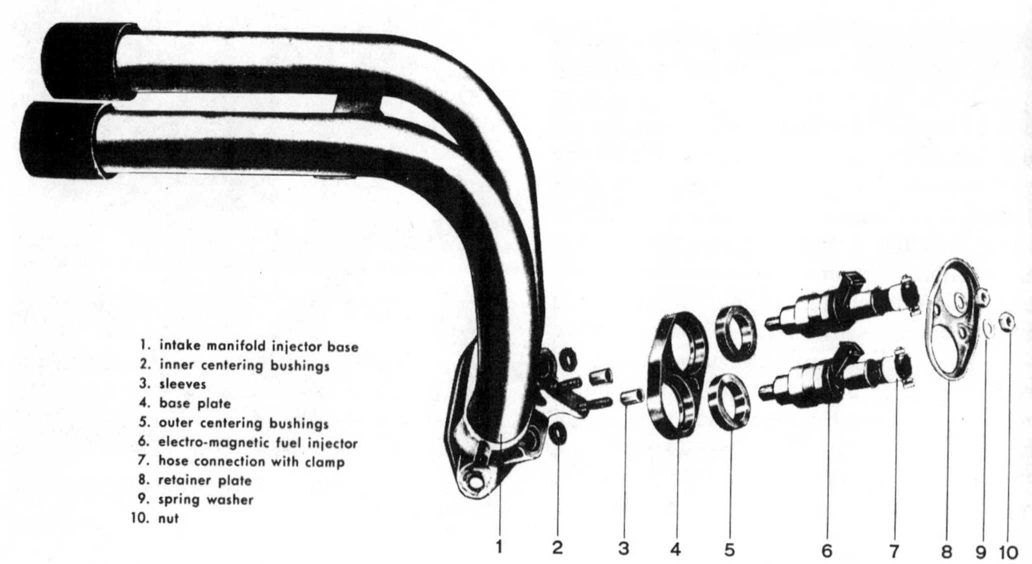

Details of injectors and right side of intake manifold

6. Throttle valve switch should come into operation when throttle has moved 4° from the closed position. Unhook throttle return spring and check that throttle is not binding.

7. Replace throttle spring and air cleaner.

PRESSURE REGULATOR ADJUSTMENT

The pressure regulator is located on the front engine cover plate beneath the right side of the intake manifold. It is fitted with an adjusting nut and a locknut. There is a T-fitting for a pressure gauge in the fuel loop line between the takeoff points for the right side injector units. This fitting is normally plugged with a stop screw.

NOTE: *before making any adjustment, be absolutely certain that the pressure gauge being used is accurate.*

To adjust the pressure regulator:

1. Remove the air cleaner for access.
2. Attach the pressure gauge securely to the T-fitting.
3. Start the engine and allow it to idle. Make sure that the idle speed is correct. Adjustment of idling speed is explained in Chapter 2.
4. If the pressure reading is not 28 psi (2 atmospheres), loosen the locknut and regulate the pressure with the adjusting nut.
5. Tighten the locknut. Check that pressure is still correct.
6. Stop engine. Disconnect pressure gauge and plug T-fitting with stop screw. Replace air cleaner.

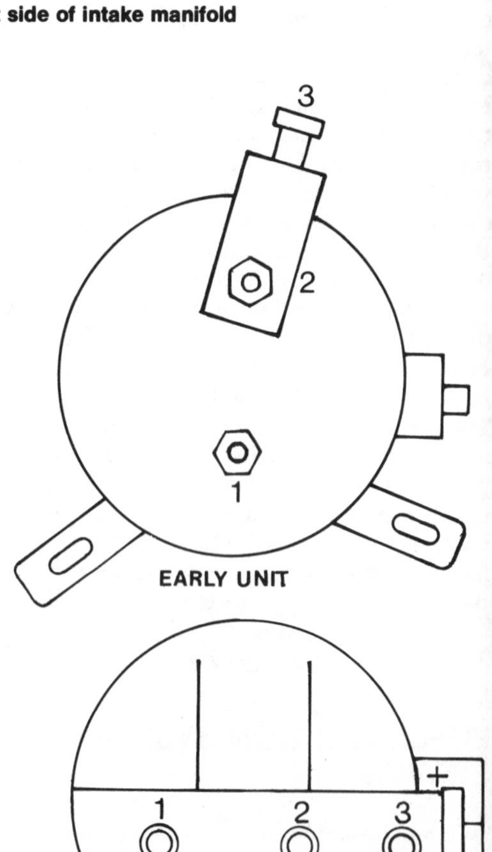

Front view of electric fuel pumps, showing suction (1), pressure (2), and return (3) connections

Fuel filter, which must be replaced periodically. The arrow shown must point to the pump

Distributor used with fuel injected engines. The two screws pointed out hold the fuel injection trigger contact plate in place

AIR CLEANER R & R

To remove the air cleaner:

1. Detach crankcase and auxiliary air regulator hoses.
2. Loosen hose clamps at either end of air cleaner. Pull off rubber hoses.
3. Remove wingnut and air cleaner.

To clean, refill, and replace air cleaner:

1. Release three clips. Remove top section.
2. Clean filter assembly out and refill with SAE 30 oil to the red mark. SAE 10 may be used in arctic climates.
3. Be sure that red arrows on top and bottom sections are aligned when reassembling.
4. Reconnect hoses, tighten clamps and wingnut.

INJECTOR R & R

To remove the injectors on either side of the engine:

1. Remove both cable plugs.
2. Unscrew both retainer plate nuts.
3. Pull out both injectors with retainer plate, centering bushings, base plate, and stud sleeves. Be sure to remove the inner bushings from the intake manifold base.
4. Loosen the hose clamps and pull out the injectors. Be careful not to damage the needles.
5. Reverse the procedure to replace the injectors. Use lockwashers under the retaining nuts. Torque them to 4.3 ft. lbs. Install cable plug with gray protective cap toward rear of car, and plug with black cap at front.

FUEL PUMP R & R

The electric fuel pump is mounted at the front of the chassis. There are three fuel lines, suction, pressure, and return.

To remove the pump:

1. Pinch clamp the fuel lines shut to prevent leakage.
2. Unplug the electrical cable plug.
3. Cut off original hose clamps. Pull off the hoses and catch the fuel which drains out.
4. Raise the pressure hose to prevent draining the fuel loop line.
5. Unbolt and remove the pump.

To replace the pump:

1. Connect the three fuel hoses. Install screw type hose clamps at all three connections.
2. Bolt the pump to the mounting supports.
3. Remove the pinch clamps from the hoses.
4. Install the cable plug. The brown negative ground wire must be to the bottom and the half circular cavity toward the right. Install the protective plug cap.

FILTER R & R

The fuel filter is in the pump suction line, either near to, or mounted on the fuel pump. It should be replaced every 6,000 miles. To replace the filter:

1. Pinch clamp the fuel lines shut on either side of the filter.
2. Remove the pin holding the filter bracket to the pump. Remove the filter.
3. Install the new filter making sure that

the arrow points to the pump. Replace the bracket and pin.

4. Install screw type hose clamps on the fuel lines.

5. Remove the pinch clamps.

DISTRIBUTOR TRIGGER CONTACT R & R

The distributor on fuel injected engines has two breaker plates. The first is the normal breaker point plate for the ignition system. The second plate, mounted in the base of the distributor head, carries two similar breaker assemblies which regulate fuel injection. There is no adjustment provided for the injection trigger contact breakers. To replace the trigger contacts:

1. Remove the distributor cap. Pull out the triple plug and disconnect the flat plug at terminal 1 of the coil. Loosen the clamp and remove the distributor after noting the rotor position and marking the relationship between the engine block and the distributor body.

2. Remove the two contact plate holding screws.

3. Pull out the plate holder.

4. Reverse the procedure to install the new plate holder. If ignition timing is correct, the injection timing will also be correct.

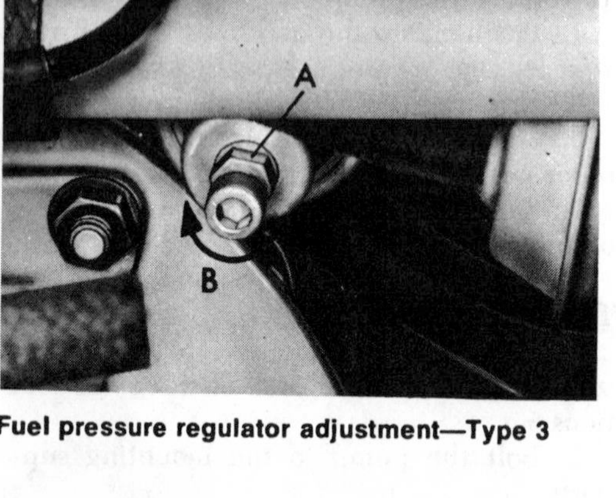

Fuel pressure regulator adjustment—Type 3

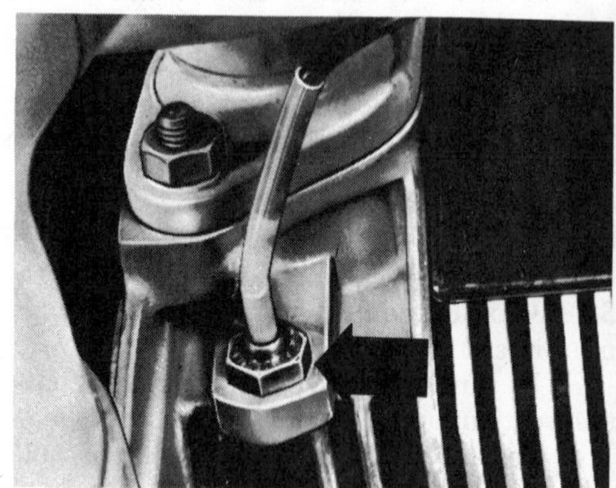

Cylinder head temperature sensing switch

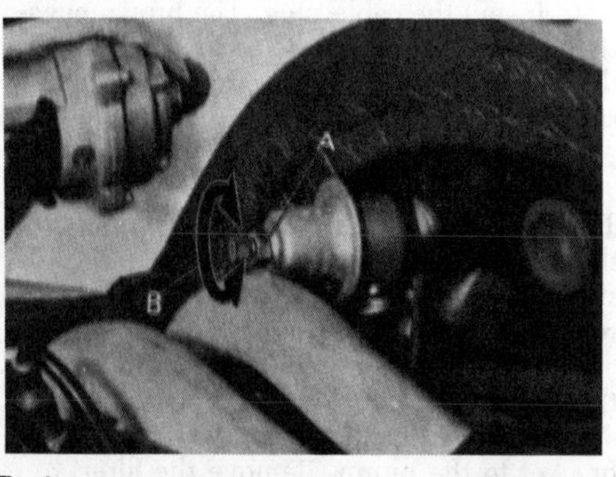

Fuel pressure regulator adjustment—Type 4

Thermo (air temperature) switch location—Type 1

Carburetor Specifications — Types 1 and 2

Vehicle	Engine	Carburetor	Venturi (mm dia.)	Main Jet	Air Correction Jet	Pilot Jet	Pilot Jet Air Bleed or Pilot Air Jet (mm. dia.)	Pump Fuel Jet	Pump Air Correction Jet	Power Fuel Jet (mm.dia.)	Emulsion Tube	Emulsion Tube Carrier (mm.dia.)	Float Needle Valve (mm.dia.)	Float Needle Valve Washer (mm.)	Float Weight (gms.)	Accel. Pump Cap. (cc./Stroke)	By Pass Mixture Cutoff Valve
Type 1	1,131 cc. 25 hp.	Solex 28 PCI	20	105	190	50	.8	50	2.0	–	10	–	1.5	–	12.5	–	–
Type 1	1,200 cc. 36 hp. from No. 695282	Solex 28 PCI	21.5	122.5	200	g50	.8	50	2.0	–	29	5.0	1.5	–	5.7	.4 -.6	–
Type 1	1,200 cc. 36 hp. from No. 849905	Solex 28 PCI	21.5	117.5	195	g50	.8	50	2.0	–	29	5.0	1.5	–	5.7	.4 -.6	–
Karmann Ghia-Type 1	1,200 cc. 36 hp. from No. 1118403	Solex 28 PCI	21.5	117.5	180	g50	.8	50	2.0	–	29	5.0	1.5	–	5.7	.4 -.6	–
Type 2	1,200 cc. 36 hp. from No. 991590	Solex 28 PCI															
Type 1 & 2	1,200 cc. 42 hp. from No. 5000 001	Solex 28 PICT(1)	22.5	122.5	130Y/ 140Z/ 135Z/	g55	2.0	.5	–	1.0/75	①	–	1.5	–	5.7	1.1-1.4/ .8-1.0	–
Type 2	1,500 cc. 51 hp. from No. 0143543	Solex 28 PICT-2	22.5	115	145Y/ 150Z/	g45	1.55	.5	–	.7	①	–	1.5	–	5.7	1.1-1.4/ 1.2-1.3	–
Type 1	1,300 cc. 50 hp. from No. F0 000 001	Solex 30 PICT-1	24.0	125	125Z ②	g55	150	50	–	– ③	①	–	1.5	–	5.7	1.3-1.6	–

Carburetor Specifications—Types 1 and 2

Vehicle	Engine	Carburetor	Venturi (mm dia.)	Main Jet	Air Correction Jet	Pilot Jet	Pilot Jet Air Bleed or Pilot Air Jet (mm. dia.)	Pump Fuel Jet	Pump Air Correction Jet	Power Fuel Jet (mm. dia.)	Emulsion Tube	Emulsion Tube Carrier (mm. dia.)	Float Needle Valve (mm. dia.)	Float Needle Valve Washer (mm.)	Float Weight (gms.)	Accel. Pump Cap. (cc./Stroke)	By Pass Mixture Cutoff Valve
Type 1	1,131 cc. 25 hp.	Solex 28 PCI	20	105	190	50	.8	50	2.0	–	10	–	1.5	–	12.5	–	–
Type 1	1,200 cc. 36 hp. from No. 695282	Solex 28 PCI	21.5	122.5	200	g50	.8	50	2.0	–	29	5.0	1.5	–	5.7	.4 -.6	–
Type 1	1,200 cc. 36 hp. from No. 849905	Solex 28 PCI	21.5	117.5	195	g50	.8	50	2.0	–	29	5.0	1.5	–	5.7	.4 -.6	–
Karmann Ghia-Type 1	1,200 cc. 36 hp. from No. 1118403	Solex 28 PCI	21.5	117.5	180	g50	.8	50	2.0	–	29	5.0	1.5	–	5.7	.4 -.6	–
Type 2	1,200 cc. 36 hp. from No. 991590	Solex 28 PCI															
Type 1 & 2	1,200 cc. 42 hp. from No. 5000 001	Solex 28 PICT(1)	22.5	122.5	130Y/ 140Z/ 135Z/	g55	2.0	.5	–	1.0/75	①	–	1.5	–	5.7	1.1- 1.4/ .8-1.0	–
Type 2	1,500 cc. 51 hp. from No. 0143543	Solex 28 PICT-2	22.5	115	145Y/ 150Z/	g45	1.55	.5	–	.7	①	–	1.5	–	5.7	1.1-1.4/ 1.2-1.3	–
Type 1	1,300 cc. 50 hp.	Solex 30	24.0	125	125Z ②	g55	150	50	–	– ③	①	–	1.5	–	5.7	1.3- 1.6	–

55 WAYS
TO IMPROVE
FUEL ECONOMY

CHILTON'S FUEL ECONOMY & TUNE-UP TIPS

une-up • Spark Plug Diagnosis • Emission Controls

uel System • Cooling System • Tires and Wheels

ieneral Maintenance

CHILTON'S FUEL ECONOMY & TUNE-UP TIPS

Fuel economy is important to everyone, no matter what kind of vehicle you drive. The maintenance-minded motorist can save both money and fuel using these tips and the periodic maintenance and tune-up procedures in this Repair and Tune-Up Guide.

There are more than 130,000,000 cars and trucks registered for private use in the United States. Each travels an average of 10-12,000 miles per year, and, and in total they consume close to 70 billion gallons of fuel each year. This represents nearly ⅔ of the oil imported by the United States each year. The Federal government's goal is to reduce consumption 10% by 1985. A variety of methods are either already in use or under serious consideration, and they all affect you driving and the cars you will drive. In addition to "down-sizing", the auto industry is using or investigating the use of electronic fuel delivery, electronic engine controls and alternative engines for use in smaller and lighter vehicles, among other alternatives to meet the federally mandated Corporate Average Fuel Economy (CAFE) of 27.5 mpg by 1985. The government, for its part, is considering rationing, mandatory driving curtailments and tax increases on motor vehicle fuel in an effort to reduce consumption. The government's goal of a 10% reduction could be realized — and further government regulation avoided — if every private vehicle could use just 1 less gallon of fuel per week.

How Much Can You Save?

Tests have proven that almost anyone can make at least a 10% reduction in fuel consumption through regular maintenance and tune-ups. When a major manufacturer of spark plugs sur-

TUNE-UP

1. Check the cylinder compression to be sure the engine will really benefit from a tune-up and that it is capable of producing good fuel economy. A tune-up will be wasted on an engine in poor mechanical condition.

2. Replace spark plugs regularly. New spark plugs alone can increase fuel economy 3%.

3. Be sure the spark plugs are the correct type (heat range) for your vehicle. See the Tune-Up Specifications.

Heat range refers to the spark plug's ability to conduct heat away from the firing end. It must conduct the heat away in an even pattern to avoid becoming a source of pre-ignition, yet it must also operate hot enough to burn off conductive deposits that could cause misfiring.

The heat range is usually indicated by a number on the spark plug, part of the manufacturer's designation for each individual spark plug. The numbers in bold-face indicate the heat range in each manufacturer's identification system.

Manufacturer	**Typical Designation**
AC	R **45** TS
Bosch (old)	WA **145** T30
Bosch (new)	HR **8** Y
Champion	RBL **15** Y
Fram/Autolite	41**5**
Mopar	P-**62** PR
Motorcraft	BRF-**42**
NGK	BP **5** ES-15
Nippondenso	W **16** EP
Prestolite	14GR **5** 2A

Periodically, check the spark plugs to be sure they are firing efficiently. They are excellent indicators of the internal condition of your engine.

On AC, Bosch (new), Champion, Fram/Autolite, Mopar, Motorcraft and Prestolite, a higher number indicates a hotter plug. On Bosch (old), NGK and Nippondenso, a higher number indicates a colder plug.

4. Make sure the spark plugs are properly gapped. See the Tune-Up Specifications in this book.

5. Be sure the spark plugs are firing efficiently. The illustrations on the next 2 pages show you how to "read" the firing end of the spark plug.

6. Check the ignition timing and set it to specifications. Tests show that almost all cars have incorrect ignition timing by more than 2°.

veyed over 6,000 cars nationwide, they found that a tune-up, on cars that needed one, increased fuel economy over 11%. Replacing worn plugs alone, accounted for a 3% increase. The same test also revealed that 8 out of every 10 vehicles will have some maintenance deficiency that will directly affect fuel economy, emissions or performance. Most of this mileage-robbing neglect could be prevented with regular maintenance.

Modern engines require that all of the functioning systems operate properly for maximum efficiency. A malfunction anywhere wastes fuel. You can keep your vehicle running as efficiently and economically as possible, by being aware of your vehicle's operating and performance characteristics. If your vehicle suddenly develops performance or fuel economy problems it could be due to one or more of the following:

PROBLEM	POSSIBLE CAUSE
Engine Idles Rough	Ignition timing, idle mixture, vacuum leak or something amiss in the emission control system.
Hesitates on Acceleration	Dirty carburetor or fuel filter, improper accelerator pump setting, ignition timing or fouled spark plugs.
Starts Hard or Fails to Start	Worn spark plugs, improperly set automatic choke, ice (or water) in fuel system.
Stalls Frequently	Automatic choke improperly adjusted and possible dirty air filter or fuel filter.
Performs Sluggishly	Worn spark plugs, dirty fuel or air filter, ignition timing or automatic choke out of adjustment.

Check spark plug wires on conventional point type ignition for cracks by bending them in a loop around your finger.

Be sure that spark plug wires leading to adjacent cylinders do not run too close together. (Photo courtesy Champion Spark Plug Co.)

7. If your vehicle does not have electronic ignition, check the points, rotor and cap as specified.

8. Check the spark plug wires (used with conventional point-type ignitions) for cracks and burned or broken insulation by bending them in a loop around your finger. Cracked wires decrease fuel efficiency by failing to deliver full voltage to the spark plugs. One misfiring spark plug can cost you as much as 2 mpg.

9. Check the routing of the plug wires. Misfiring can be the result of spark plug leads to adjacent cylinders running parallel to each other and too close together. One wire tends to pick up voltage from the other causing it to fire "out of time".

10. Check all electrical and ignition circuits for voltage drop and resistance.

11. Check the distributor mechanical and/or vacuum advance mechanisms for proper functioning. The vacuum advance can be checked by twisting the distributor plate in the opposite direction of rotation. It should spring back when released.

12. Check and adjust the valve clearance on engines with mechanical lifters. The clearance should be slightly loose rather than too tight.

SPARK PLUG DIAGNOSIS

Normal

APPEARANCE: This plug is typical of one operating normally. The insulator nose varies from a light tan to grayish color with slight electrode wear. The presence of slight deposits is normal on used plugs and will have no adverse effect on engine performance. The spark plug heat range is correct for the engine and the engine is running normally.
CAUSE: Properly running engine.
RECOMMENDATION: Before reinstalling this plug, the electrodes should be cleaned and filed square. Set the gap to specifications. If the plug has been in service for more than 10-12,000 miles, the entire set should probably be replaced with a fresh set of the same heat range.

Oil Deposits

APPEARANCE: The firing end of the plug is covered with a wet, oily coating.
CAUSE: The problem is poor oil control. On high mileage engines, oil is leaking past the rings or valve guides into the combustion chamber. A common cause is also a plugged PCV valve, and a ruptured fuel pump diaphragm can also cause this condition. Oil fouled plugs such as these are often found in new or recently overhauled engines, before normal oil control is achieved, and can be cleaned and reinstalled.
RECOMMENDATION: A hotter spark plug may temporarily relieve the problem, but the engine is probably in need of work.

Incorrect Heat Range

APPEARANCE: The effects of high temperature on a spark plug are indicated by clean white, often blistered insulator. This can also be accompanied by excessive wear of the electrode, and the absence of deposits.
CAUSE: Check for the correct spark plug heat range. A plug which is too hot for the engine can result in overheating. A car operated mostly at high speeds can require a colder plug. Also check ignition timing, cooling system level, fuel mixture and leaking intake manifold.
RECOMMENDATION: If all ignition and engine adjustments are known to be correct, and no other malfunction exists, install spark plugs one heat range colder.

Carbon Deposits

APPEARANCE: Carbon fouling is easily identified by the presence of dry, soft, black, sooty deposits.
CAUSE: Changing the heat range can often lead to carbon fouling, as can prolonged slow, stop-and-start driving. If the heat range is correct, carbon fouling can be attributed to a rich fuel mixture, sticking choke, clogged air cleaner, worn breaker points, retarded timing or low compression. If only one or two plugs are carbon fouled, check for corroded or cracked wires on the affected plugs. Also look for cracks in the distributor cap between the towers of affected cylinders.
RECOMMENDATION: After the problem is corrected, these plugs can be cleaned and reinstalled if not worn severely.

Photos Courtesy Fram Corporation

MMT Fouled

APPEARANCE: Spark plugs fouled by MMT (Methycyclopentadienyl Maganese Tricarbonyl) have reddish, rusty appearance on the insulator and side electrode.
CAUSE: MMT is an anti-knock additive in gasoline used to replace lead. During the combustion process, the MMT leaves a reddish deposit on the insulator and side electrode.
RECOMMENDATION: No engine malfunction is indicated and the deposits will not affect plug performance any more than lead deposits (see Ash Deposits). MMT fouled plugs can be cleaned, regapped and reinstalled.

High Speed Glazing

APPEARANCE: Glazing appears as shiny coating on the plug, either yellow or tan in color.
CAUSE: During hard, fast acceleration, plug temperatures rise suddenly. Deposits from normal combustion have no chance to fluff-off; instead, they melt on the insulator forming an electrically conductive coating which causes misfiring.
RECOMMENDATION: Glazed plugs are not easily cleaned. They should be replaced with a fresh set of plugs of the correct heat range. If the condition recurs, using plugs with a heat range one step colder may cure the problem.

Ash (Lead) Deposits

APPEARANCE: Ash deposits are characterized by light brown or white colored deposits crusted on the side or center electrodes. In some cases it may give the plug a rusty appearance.
CAUSE: Ash deposits are normally derived from oil or fuel additives burned during normal combustion. Normally they are harmless, though excessive amounts can cause misfiring. If deposits are excessive in short mileage, the valve guides may be worn.
RECOMMENDATION: Ash-fouled plugs can be cleaned, gapped and reinstalled.

Detonation

APPEARANCE: Detonation is usually characterized by a broken plug insulator.
CAUSE: A portion of the fuel charge will begin to burn spontaneously, from the increased heat following ignition. The explosion that results applies extreme pressure to engine components, frequently damaging spark plugs and pistons.

Detonation can result by over-advanced ignition timing, inferior gasoline (low octane) lean air/fuel mixture, poor carburetion, engine lugging or an increase in compression ratio due to combustion chamber deposits or engine modification.
RECOMMENDATION: Replace the plugs after correcting the problem.

Photos Courtesy Champion Spark Plug Co.

EMISSION CONTROLS

13. Be aware of the general condition of the emission control system. It contributes to reduced pollution and should be serviced regularly to maintain efficient engine operation.

14. Check all vacuum lines for dried, cracked or brittle conditions. Something as simple as a leaking vacuum hose can cause poor performance and loss of economy.

15. Avoid tampering with the emission control system. Attempting to improve fuel econ-

FUEL SYSTEM

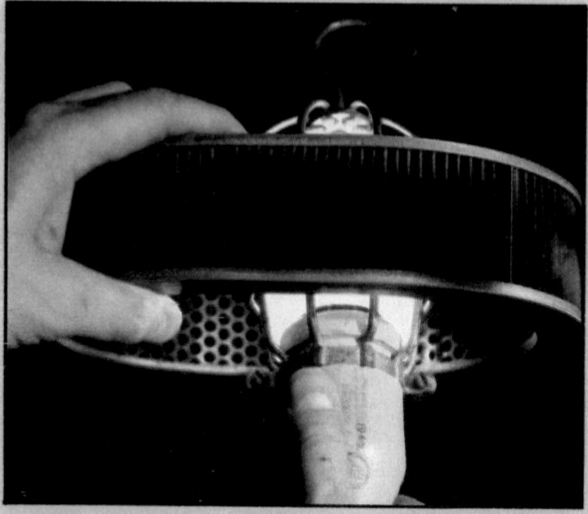

Check the air filter with a light behind it. If you can see light through the filter it can be reused.

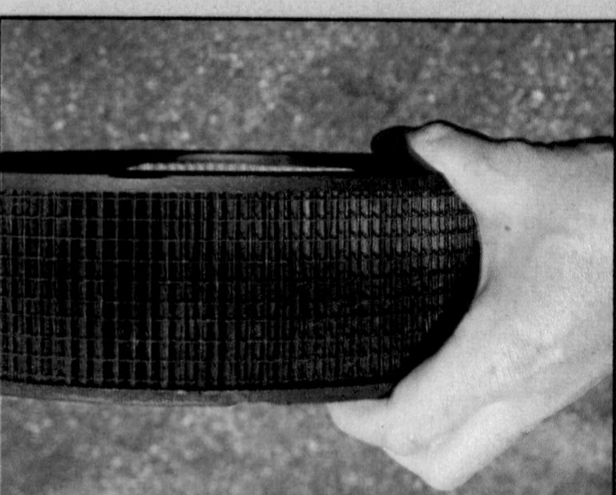

Extremely clogged filters should be discarded and replaced with a new one.

18. Replace the air filter regularly. A dirty air filter richens the air/fuel mixture and can increase fuel consumption as much as 10%. Tests show that ⅓ of all vehicles have air filters in need of replacement.

19. Replace the fuel filter at least as often as recommended.

20. Set the idle speed and carburetor mixture to specifications.

21. Check the automatic choke. A sticking or malfunctioning choke wastes gas.

22. During the summer months, adjust the automatic choke for a leaner mixture which will produce faster engine warm-ups.

COOLING SYSTEM

29. Be sure all accessory drive belts are in good condition. Check for cracks or wear.

30. Adjust all accessory drive belts to proper tension.

31. Check all hoses for swollen areas, worn spots, or loose clamps.

32. Check coolant level in the radiator or expansion tank.

33. Be sure the thermostat is operating properly. A stuck thermostat delays engine warm-up and a cold engine uses nearly twice as much fuel as a warm engine.

34. Drain and replace the engine coolant at least as often as recommended. Rust and scale

TIRES & WHEELS

38. Check the tire pressure often with a pencil type gauge. Tests by a major tire manufacturer show that 90% of all vehicles have at least 1 tire improperly inflated. Better mileage can be achieved by over-inflating tires, but never exceed the maximum inflation pressure on the side of the tire.

39. If possible, install radial tires. Radial tires deliver as much as ½ mpg more than bias belted tires.

40. Avoid installing super-wide tires. They only create extra rolling resistance and decrease fuel mileage. Stick to the manufacturer's recommendations.

41. Have the wheels properly balanced.

omy by tampering with emission controls is more likely to worsen fuel economy than improve it. Emission control changes on modern engines are not readily reversible.

16. Clean (or replace) the EGR valve and lines as recommended.

17. Be sure that all vacuum lines and hoses are reconnected properly after working under the hood. An unconnected or misrouted vacuum line can wreak havoc with engine performance.

23. Check for fuel leaks at the carburetor, fuel pump, fuel lines and fuel tank. Be sure all lines and connections are tight.

24. Periodically check the tightness of the carburetor and intake manifold attaching nuts and bolts. These are a common place for vacuum leaks to occur.

25. Clean the carburetor periodically and lubricate the linkage.

26. The condition of the tailpipe can be an excellent indicator of proper engine combustion. After a long drive at highway speeds, the inside of the tailpipe should be a light grey in color. Black or soot on the insides indicates an overly rich mixture.

27. Check the fuel pump pressure. The fuel pump may be supplying more fuel than the engine needs.

28. Use the proper grade of gasoline for your engine. Don't try to compensate for knocking or "pinging" by advancing the ignition timing. This practice will only increase plug temperature and the chances of detonation or pre-ignition with relatively little performance gain.

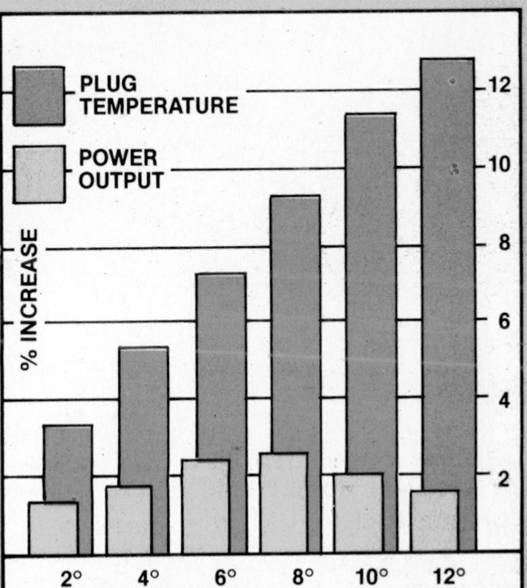

Increasing ignition timing past the specified setting results in a drastic increase in spark plug temperature with increased chance of detonation or preignition. Performance increase is considerably less. (Photo courtesy Champion Spark Plug Co.)

that form in the engine should be flushed out to allow the engine to operate at peak efficiency.

35. Clean the radiator of debris that can decrease cooling efficiency.

36. Install a flex-type or electric cooling fan, if you don't have a clutch type fan. Flex fans use curved plastic blades to push more air at low speeds when more cooling is needed; at high speeds the blades flatten out for less resistance. Electric fans only run when the engine temperature reaches a predetermined level.

37. Check the radiator cap for a worn or cracked gasket. If the cap does not seal properly, the cooling system will not function properly.

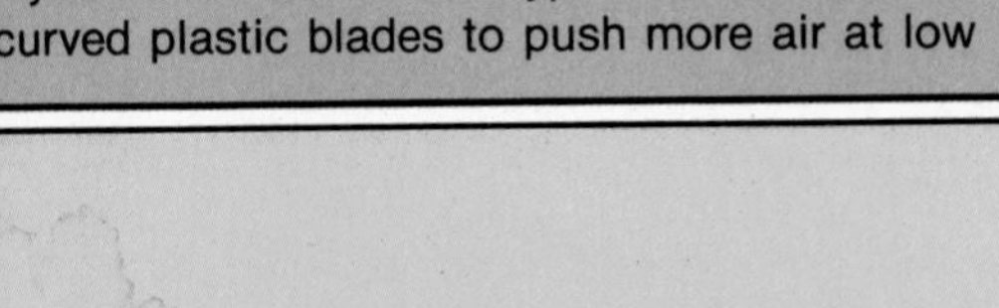

42. Be sure the front end is correctly aligned. A misaligned front end actually has wheels going in differed directions. The increased drag can reduce fuel economy by .3 mpg.

43. Correctly adjust the wheel bearings. Wheel bearings that are adjusted too tight increase rolling resistance.

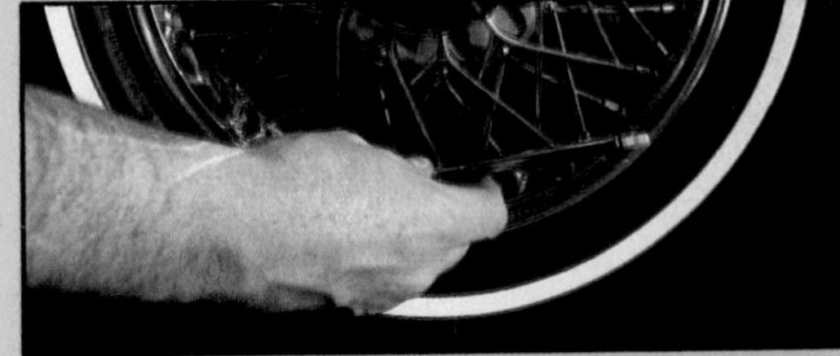

Check tire pressures regularly with a reliable pocket type gauge. Be sure to check the pressure on a cold tire.

GENERAL MAINTENANCE

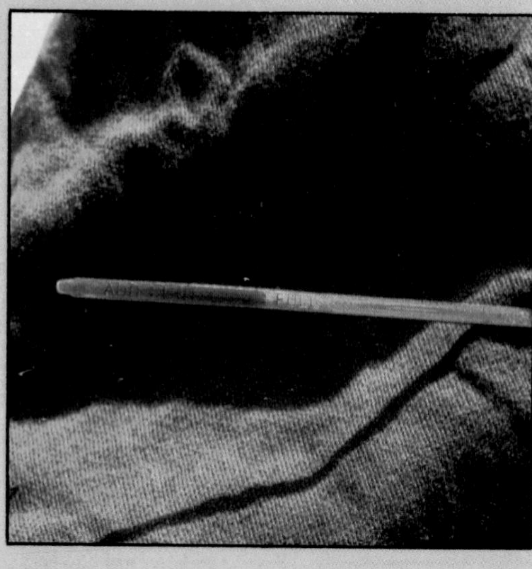

Check the fluid levels (particularly engine oil) on a regular basis. Be sure to check the oil for grit, water or other contamination.

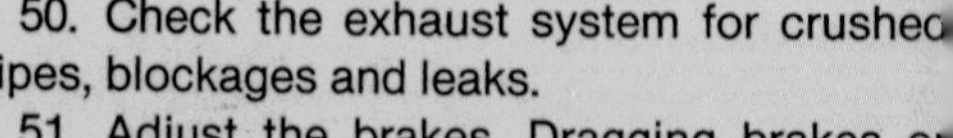

A vacuum gauge is another excellent indicator of internal engine condition and can also be installed in the dash as a mileage indicator.

44. Periodically check the fluid levels in the engine, power steering pump, master cylinder, automatic transmission and drive axle.

45. Change the oil at the recommended interval and change the filter at every oil change. Dirty oil is thick and causes extra friction between moving parts, cutting efficiency and increasing wear. A worn engine requires more frequent tune-ups and gets progressively worse fuel economy. In general, use the lightest viscosity oil for the driving conditions you will encounter.

46. Use the recommended viscosity fluids in the transmission and axle.

47. Be sure the battery is fully charged for fast starts. A slow starting engine wastes fuel.

48. Be sure battery terminals are clean and tight.

49. Check the battery electrolyte level and add distilled water if necessary.

50. Check the exhaust system for crushed pipes, blockages and leaks.

51. Adjust the brakes. Dragging brakes or brakes that are not releasing create increased drag on the engine.

52. Install a vacuum gauge or miles-per-gallon gauge. These gauges visually indicate engine vacuum in the intake manifold. High vacuum = good mileage and low vacuum = poorer mileage. The gauge can also be an excellent indicator of internal engine conditions.

53. Be sure the clutch is properly adjusted. A slipping clutch wastes fuel.

54. Check and periodically lubricate the heat control valve in the exhaust manifold. A sticking or inoperative valve prevents engine warm-up and wastes gas.

55. Keep accurate records to check fuel economy over a period of time. A sudden drop in fuel economy may signal a need for tune-up or other maintenance.

Carburetor Specifications—Types 1 and 2

Vehicle	Engine	Carb-uretor	Venturi (mm. dia.)	Main Jet	Air Correction Jet	Pilot Jet	Pilot Jet Air Bleed or Pilot Air Jet (mm. dia.)	Pump Fuel Jet	Pump Air Correction Jet	Power Fuel Jet (mm. dia.)	Emulsion Tube	Emulsion Tube Carrier (mm.dia.)	Float Needle Valve (mm.dia.)	Float Needle Valve Washer (mm.)	Float Weight (gms.)	Accel. Pump Cap. (cc./ Stroke)	By Pass Mixture Cutoff Valve
Type 1	1,600 cc. 57 hp. from No. B6000001	Solex 30 PICT-3	24.0	x122.5	125Z	65	135	–	–	100	①	–	1.5	1.5	8.5	1.2-1.35	–
Type 1	1,600 cc. 57 hp. Automatic from No. B6000002	Solex 30 PICT-3	24.0	x112.5	125Z	65	135	–	–	100	①	–	1.5	1.5	8.5	1.2-1.35	–
Type 2	1,600 cc. 57 hp. from No. B5116437	Solex 30 PICT-3															
Type 1 & 2	1,600 cc. 60 hp. 1971 Models	Solex 34 PICT-3	26	130	75Z	60	147.5	–	–	100	–	–	1.5	.5	8.5	–	–

① *Fixed to air correction jet.*
② *Karmann Ghia - 170Z*
③ *Karmann Ghia - 75*
④ *Karmann Ghia - 135Z*
⑤ *From engine No. H0874200 - 140*
⑥ *From No. H0874200 - 8.5*
⑦ *With emission control.*

Carburetor Specifications—Type 3

Vehicle	Engine	Carburetor	Venturi (mm.dia.)	Main Jet	Air Correction Jet	Pilot Jet	Idling Air Drilling	Pump Injector Tube (mm. dia.)	Pump Air Correction Jet	Power Fuel Jet (mm. dia.)	Emulsion Tube (No.)	Emulsion Tube Carrier (mm. dia.)	Float Needle Valve (mm. dia.)	Float Needle Valve Washer (mm.)	Float Weight (gms.)	Accel. Pump Cap. (cc./ Stroke)	Throttle Valve Gap (mm.)
Type 3 Single Carbur-etor	From No. 0 000 001	Solex 32 PHN	23.5	137.5	125	g45 g50	–	.8	–	1.05	48	–	1.5	–	12.5	.9-1.2 /1.2-1.5	.8-.9
	From No. 0 084 752 -	Solex 32 PHN -1	23.5	132.5	115	g45	–	.8	–	.7	48	–	1.5	–	12.5	.9-1.2	.8-.9
	From No. 0220137	Solex 32 PHN -1	23.5	127.5	115	g45	–	.8	–	.7	48	–	1.5	–	12.5	.9-1.2	.8-.9
	From No. 0319841	Solex 32 PHN	23.5	130.0	115	g50	–	.7	–	.7	48	–	1.5	–	12.5	.8-1.0	.8-.9
	From No. K0150001	Solex 32 PHN	23.5	01300	115	–	1.4	.7	–	.7	48	–	1.5	–	12.5	.8-1.0	.8
Type 3 Dual Carbur-etors	1,500cc. From No. 0255001	Solex ① 32 PDSIT-2(-3)	21.5	x125	180	g45	–	.5 (12 mm.)	–	.9 (9.5 mm.)	–	–	1.2	–	7.3	.35-.55	.60 -.65
	1,500cc. From No. 0633331	Solex 32 PDSIT-2(-3) ①	23	x135	180	g45	–	.5 (15 mm.)	–	.8 (10.5mm.)	–	–	1.2	1.5	7.3	.35 -.55	.60 -.65
	1,600cc. From No. T0000001	Solex ① 32 PDSIT -2(-3)	23	x130	240	g45	–	50 (12 mm.)	–	80 (15 mm.)	–	–	1.2	1.5	7.3	.35-.55	.60 -.65
	1,600cc. From No. T0244544	Solex 32 PDSIT-2 (Left)	24	x132.5	150	g50	–	.5 (9 mm.)	–	–	–	–	1.2	.5	7.3	.35-.55	.60-.65

Carburetor Specifications—Type 3

Vehicle	*Engine*	*Carburetor*	*Venturi (mm.dia.)*	*Main Jet*	*Air Correction Jet*	*Pilot Jet*	*Idling Air Drilling*	*Pump Injector Tube (mm. dia.)*	*Pump Air Correction Jet*	*Power Fuel Jet (mm. dia.)*	*Emulsion Tube (No.)*	*Emulsion Tube Carrier (mm. dia.)*	*Float Needle Valve (mm. dia.)*	*Float Needle Valve Washer (mm.)*	*Float Weight (gms.)*	*Accel. Pump Cap. (cc./Stroke)*	*Throttle Valve Gap (mm.)*
		Solex 32 PDSIT-3 (Right)	24	x130	120	g50	–	.5 (9 mm.)	–	–	–	–	1.2	.5	7.3	.35-.55	.60-.65
	1,600cc. From No. T0576724	Solex 32 PDSIT-2 (Left)	24	x132.5	150	50	–	.5	–	–	–	–	1.2	.5	7.0	.35-.55	.60-.65
		Solex 32 PDSIT-3 (Right)	24	x130	120	50	–	.5	–	–	–	–	1.2	.5	7.0	.35-.55	.60-.65
Type 3 Dual Carbur-etors –Auto-matic	1,600cc. From No. T0690001	Solex 32 PDSIT-2 (Left)	24	x130	155	–	135	–		–	–	–	1.2	.5	7.0	.3-.45	.7
		Solex 32 PDSIT-3 Right	24	x127.5	120	–	135	–		–	–	–	1.2	.5	7.0	.3-.45	.7
	1,600cc. From No. T0463930	Solex 32 PDSIT-2 (Left)	24	130	155	50	–	.5 (9 mm.)		–	–	–	1.2	.5	7.0	.25-.4	.60-.65
		Solex 32 PDSIT-3 (Right)	24	127.5	120	50	–	.5 (9 mm.)		–	–	–	1.2	.5	7.0	.25-.4	.60-.65
	1,600cc. From No. T069000	Solex 32 PDSIT-2 (Left)	24	130	155	–	135	–		–	–	–	1.2	.5	7.0	.23-.4 ②	.9
		Solex 32 PDSIT-3 (Right)	24	127.5	120	–	135	–		–	–	–	1.2	.5	7.0	.25-.4 ②	.9

① 2 - Left carburetor, with distributor vacuum connection
3- Right carburetor

② Return valve for accelerator pump - .3

Power Train

VW AUTOMATIC STICKSHIFT

Since 1968, Volkswagen has offered an automatic clutch control three speed transmission. This unit is called the Automatic Stickshift.

It consists of a three speed gear box connected to the engine through a hydrodynamic torque converter. Between the converter and gearbox is a vacuum-operated clutch, which automatically separates the power flow from the torque converter while in the process of changing gear ratios.

While the torque converter components are illustrated here, the picture is for familiarization purposes only. The unit cannot be serviced. It is a welded unit, and must be replaced as a complete assembly.

The power flow passes from the engine via converter, clutch and gearbox to the final drive, which, as with the conventional gearbox, is located in the center of the transmission housing.

Converter and clutch components for Automatic Stickshift

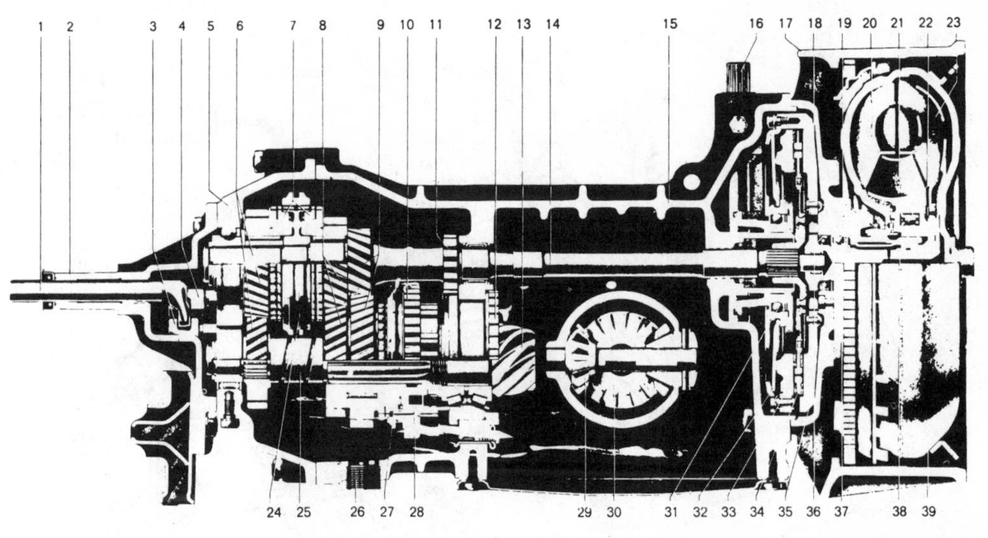

1. Inner transmission shift lever
2. Gear shift housing
3. Selector shaft for 1st and driving range
4. Selector shaft for 2nd and 3rd driving range
5. Gear carrier
6. Gear train, 3rd driving range
7. Synchronizing rings, 3rd and 4th driving range
8. Gear train, 2nd driving range
9. Gear train, 1st driving range
10. Operating sleeve, 1st and reverse driving range
11. Drive, driving range
12. Tension nut for driving pinion
13. Drive pinion
14. Drive shaft
15. Transmission housing
16. Release shaft for separator clutch
17. Converter housing
18. Support tube for converter freewheel
19. Shaft sealing ring for torque converter
20. Impeller
21. Stator
22. Freewheel
23. Turbine
24. Operating sleeve, 2nd and 3rd driving range
25. Axial spring, 2nd and 3rd driving range
26. Magnetic oil drain plug
27. Synchronizing ring, 1st driving range
28. Clutch gear, 1st and reverse driving range
29. Differential pinion
30. Differential side gear
31. Release bearing for separator clutch
32. Cup spring
33. Pressure plate
34. Drive plate
35. Clutch carrier plate
36. Shaft sealing ring for converter housing
37. Grooved ball bearing for turbine shaft
38. Turbine shaft
39. Torque converter

Power transmission components of Automatic Stickshift

The converter functions as a conventional clutch for starting and stopping. The shift clutch serves only for engaging and changing the speed ranges. Friction-wise, it is very lightly loaded.

There is an independent oil supply for the converter provided by an engine driven pump and a reservoir. The converter oil pump, driven off the engine oil pump, draws fluid from the reservoir and drives it around a circuit leading through the converter and back to the reservoir.

This circuit also furnishes cooling for the converter fluid.

Operation

The control valve is activated by a very light touch to the top of the shift selector knob which, in turn, is connected to an electromagnet. It has two functions.

At the beginning of the selection process, it has to conduct the vacuum promptly from the intake manifold to the clutch servo, so that the shift clutch disengages at once, and thus interrupts the power flow between converter and transmission. At the end of the selection process, it must, according to driving conditions, automatically ensure that the shift clutch engages at the proper speed. It may neither slip nor engage too harshly. The control valve can be adjusted for this purpose.

As soon as the selector lever is moved to the engaged position, the two contacts in the lever close the circuit. The electromagnet is then under voltage and operates the main valve. By this means the clutch servo is connected to the engine intake manifold, and at the same time the connection to the atmosphere is closed. In the vacuum space of the servo system, a vacuum is built up, the dia-

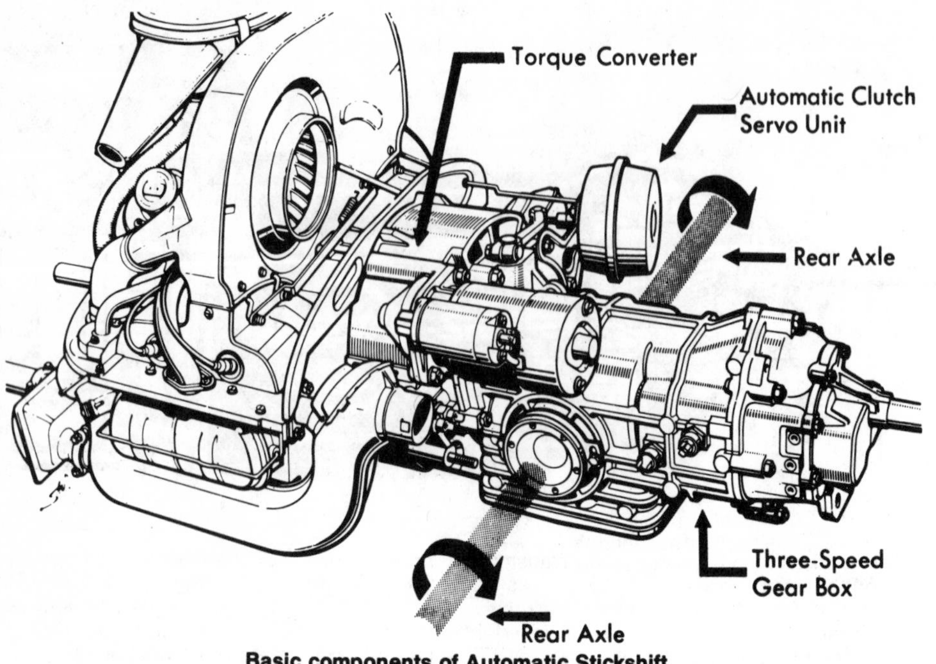

Basic components of Automatic Stickshift

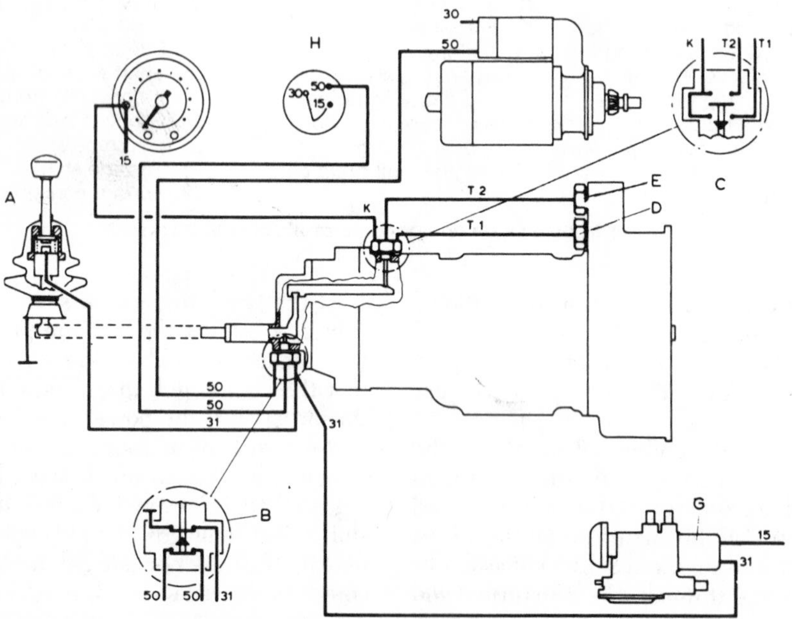

A. Selector lever with switch
B. Starter locking switch with bridging switch
C. Selector switch
D. Temperature switch for 3rd speed range
E. Temperature switch for 2nd speed range
F. Warning light
G. Electro-magnet for control valve
H. Ignition switch
J. Starter F

Automatic Stickshift electrical circuit

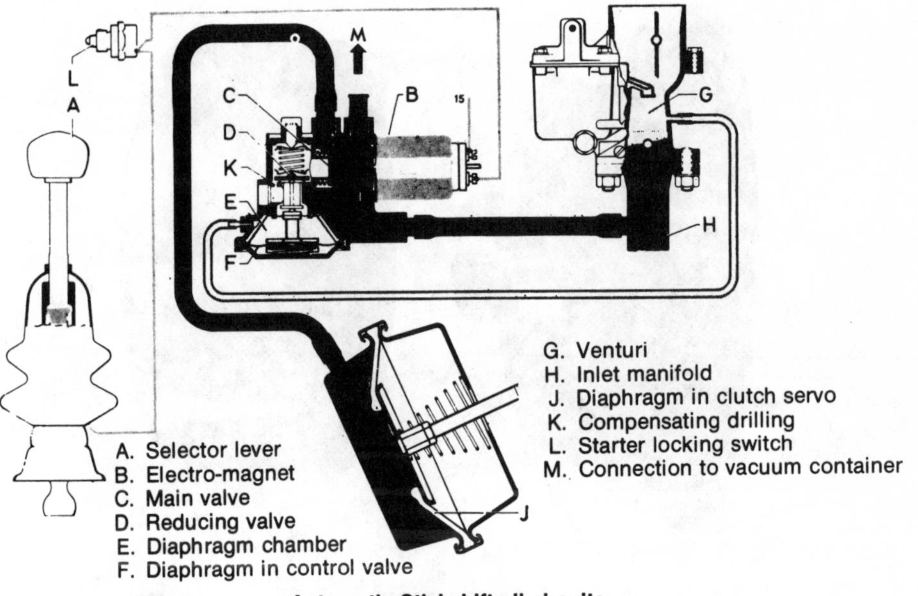

Automatic Stickshift oil circuits

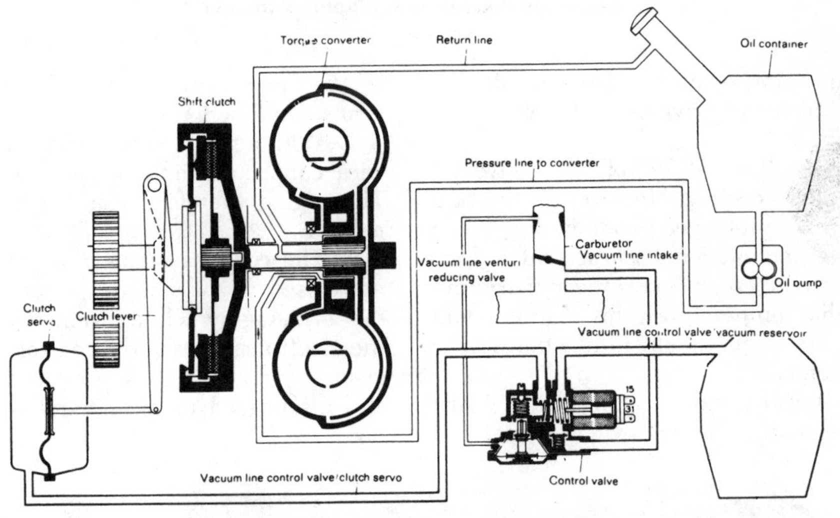

Automatic Stickshift vacuum circuits

phragm of the clutch servo is moved by the difference with atmospheric pressure and the shift clutch is disengaged via its linkage. The power flow to the gearbox is interrupted and the required speed range can be engaged. The process of declutching, from movement of the selector lever up to full separation of the clutch, lasts about 1/10 sec. The automatic can, therefore, declutch faster than would be possible by means of a foot-operated clutch pedal.

When the selector lever is released after changing the speed range, the switch interrupts the current flow to the electro-magnet, which then returns to its rest position and closes the main valve. The vacuum is reduced by the reducing valve and the shift clutch re-engages.

Clutch engagement takes place, quickly or slowly, according to engine loading. The clutch will engage suddenly, for example, at full throttle, and can transform the full drive moment into acceleration of the car. Or, this can be effected slowly and gently if the braking force of the engine is to be used on overrun. In the part-load range, too, the duration of clutch re-engagement depends on the throttle opening, and thus the depression in

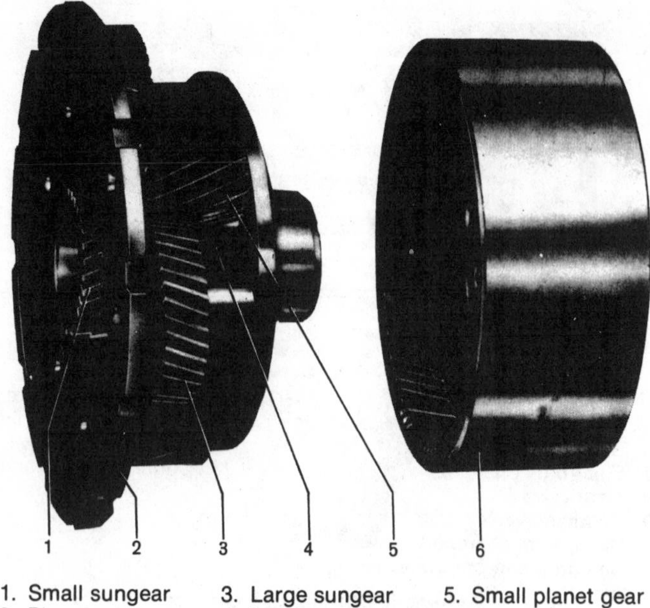

1. Small sungear
2. Planet carrier
3. Large sungear
4. Large sungear
5. Small planet gear
6. Ring gear

Automatic transmission planetary gear unit

the carburetor venturi. This results in smooth, pleasant driving under all conditions.

Vanes on the outside of the converter housing aid in cooling. However, in the case of abnormal prolonged loading (lugging a trailer over mountain roads in second or third speed), converter heat may exceed maximum permissible temperature. This condition will cause a red warning light to function in the speedometer.

There is also a starter locking switch. This, combined with a bridging switch, is operated by the inner transmission shift lever. It performs two functions:

1. With a speed range engaged, the electrical connection to the starter is interrupted. The engine, therefore, can only be started in neutral.

2. The contacts in the selector lever are not closed in the neutral position. Instead, the bridging switch transmits a voltage to the electromagnets of the control valve. This ensures that the separator clutch is also disengaged in the neutral shifter position.

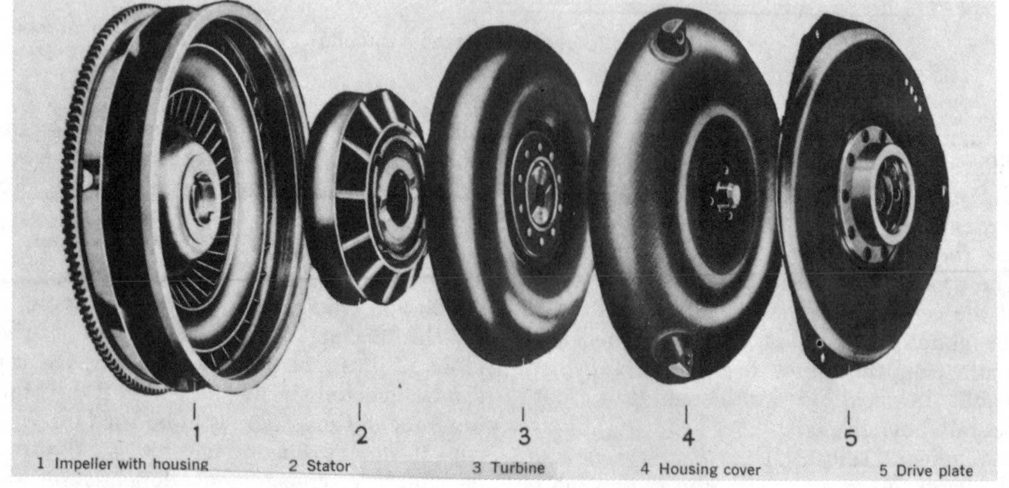

Torque converter for automatic transmission

FULLY AUTOMATIC TRANSMISSION

The fully automatic transmission, consisting of an automatically shifted three speed planetary transmission and a torque converter, was introduced in 1969.

The torque converter is a conventional three element design. The three elements are an impeller (driving member), a stator (reaction member), and the turbine (driven member). Maximum torque multiplication, with the vehicle starting from rest, is two and one-half to one. Maximum converter efficiency is about 96 per cent.

The automatic transmission is a planetary unit with three forward speeds which engage automatically, depending on engine loading and road speed. The converter, planetary unit, and control system are incorporated together with the final drive in a single housing. The final drive is located between the converter and the planetary gearbox. Driving and driven shafts fit one inside the other in contrast to the manual transmission in which they are located one below the other. The planetary gear unit is controlled by two multi-plate clutches which make up the third-reverse and forward clutch, a first gear band, a second gear band, and a roller clutch which permits the planetary ring gear to rotate only in the direction of drive.

The transmission control system includes a gear type oil pump, a centrifugal governor which regulates shift points, a throttle modulator valve which evaluates engine loading according to intake manifold pressure, and numerous other regulating components assembled in the transmission valve body.

Automatic transmission oil pump

1. Manual valve
2. Solenoid for kickdown valve
3. Oil strainer
4. Transfer plate
5. Valve body
6. Vacuum unit for primary throttle modulator valve

Automatic transmission valve body (© Volkswagen)

Automatic transmission centrifugal governor

Power flow passes through the torque converter to the turbine shaft, then to the clutch drum attached to the turbine shaft, through a clutch to a sungear. The output planet carrier then drives the rear axle shafts via the final drive.

Transmission ranges are Park, Reverse, Neutral, Drive (3), Second (2), and First (1).

THE CLUTCH

CLUTCH ADJUSTMENT—MANUAL TRANSMISSION

The Volkswagen clutch is a dry, single-plate unit fitted to the flywheel. Earlier models had a carbon throw-out bearing, while the later models are equipped with the ball-bearing type. With the carbon type bearing, wear on the bearing was significant when the clutch pedal was depressed for any length of time, although in normal and proper use the carbon bearings generally lasted for the life of the clutch lining. Neither the carbon bearing nor the ball-type bearing requires periodic maintenance.

Routine clutch maintenance is limited to adjusting the free play present at the clutch pedal. As the clutch lining wears, clearance between the release bearing and release plate is reduced until these parts touch. Such a condition can lead to damage or excessive wear, as well as clutch slipping and burning of the lining. The proper clutch pedal free play is 10–20 mm. (.4–8″) measured at the pedal.

Adjustment is carried out at the rear of the car, at the cable end of the clutch. First loosen the locking nut, and then the adjusting nut. On 1966 and subsequent models, a single wing nut serves both purposes. The adjusting nut is turned until the proper amount of free play is evident at the pedal. Then the lock nut, if present, is tightened, after which the pedal should be depressed several times and the free play rechecked. After the clutch is adjusted, the thread on the cable end should be greased.

CLUTCH ADJUSTMENTS—AUTOMATIC STICKSHIFT

Checking Clutch Play

A minimum clutch play is required to prevent slippage and excessive wear. The adjustment is made on the linkage between the clutch arm and the vacuum servo unit. To check the clutch play:

1. Pull off servo vacuum hose.
2. Measure clearance between upper edge of servo unit mounting bracket and lower edge of adjusting turnbuckle. If the clearance is .16″ or more, the clutch needs adjustment.
3. Replace vacuum hose.

Adjusting Clutch Play

To adjust the clutch:

1. Pull off servo vacuum hose. Loosen turnbuckle locknut slightly. Turn turnbuckle 5–5½ turns away from the locknut. There should now be .25″ clearance between the locknut and the turnbuckle.
2. Tighten locknut against turnbuckle.
3. Replace vacuum hose.
4. The clutch adjustment is correct when there is no slippage and reverse can be engaged silently. If the clutch arm contacts the clutch housing, there is no more adjustment possible and the clutch plate must be replaced.

Adjusting Speed of Engagement

The clutch should normally take a full second to engage after shifting down from 2 to 1, at 44 mph without accelerating. Engagement speed may be adjusted to suit personal preference, within certain limits. However, excessively fast clutch action may cause transmission damage, while excessively slow action may cause overheating and rapid lining wear. Speed of clutch engagement is adjusted at the reducing valve, to the left of the ignition coil. The adjusting screw is on top of the unit, under a cap. In the normal position, the adjusting screw has two threads protruding from the unit.

To adjust the speed of clutch engagement:

1. Remove the reducing valve cap.
2. To slow engagement, turn adjusting screw ¼–½ turn clockwise. To speed engagement, turn screw ¼–½ turn counterclockwise.
3. Replace cap.
4. Test operation by shifting from 2 to 1 at 44 mph without depressing accelerator.

R & R, CLUTCH

Manual Transmission

To remove the clutch, first remove the engine; then remove the clutch-to-flywheel attaching bolts by gradually and alternately backing the bolts out of the flywheel; and finally take off the clutch cover and lift out the clutch driven plate.

Installation of the clutch is the reverse of the preceding. Before installing, inspect and resurface the pressure plate if it is worn in excess of .008″. The friction surface should be polished. Inspect the driven plate and renew it if there is any doubt as to its reliability. Examine the release plate, release levers, and springs for damage. Check release bearing for damage and replace if necessary. If the release bearing has a plastic ring, it must be roughed up with emery cloth and lubricated sparingly with molybdenum disulphide paste. This prevents an annoying whistling sound which sometimes comes from the re-

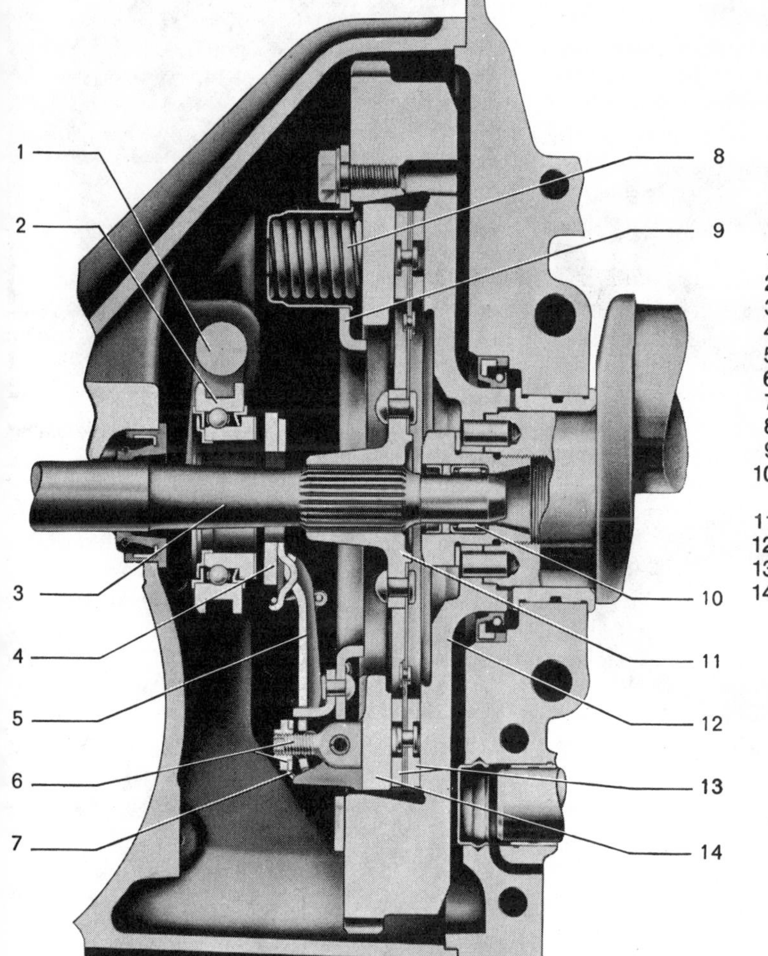

1. Operating shaft
2. Relase bearing
3. Main drive shaft
4. Release plate
5. Release lever
6. Bolt and special nut
7. Release lever spring
8. Thrust pring
9. Cover
10. Needle bearing for gland nut
11. Driven plate
12. Flywheel
13. Lining
14. Pressure plate

Cross-sectional view of clutch assembly

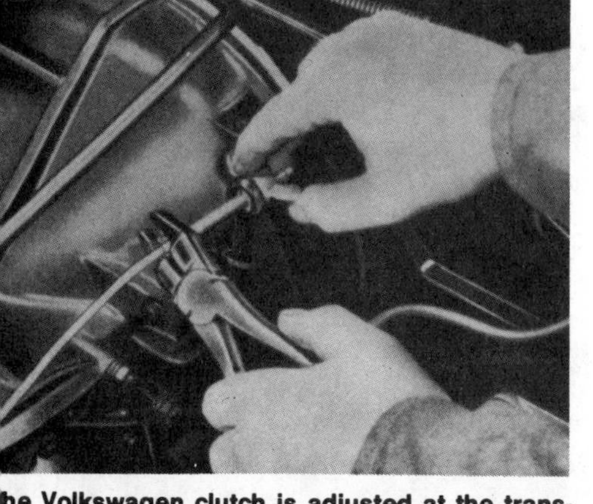

he Volkswagen clutch is adjusted at the trans- ission end via a wing nut. On earlier models an djusting nut was used along with a lock nut.

Free play at the clutch pedal should be between 10–20mm (.4–.8″)

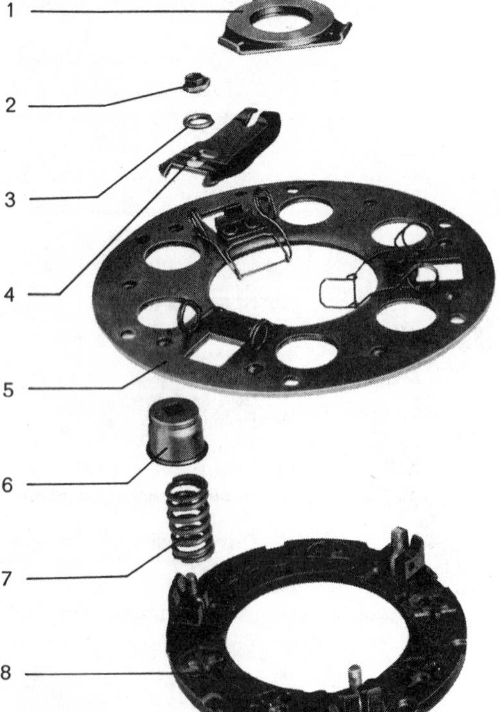

1. Release plate
2. Nut
3. Washer
4. Release lever
5. Clutch cover
6. Spring cap
7. Spring
8. Pressure plate

Exploded view, clutch assembly

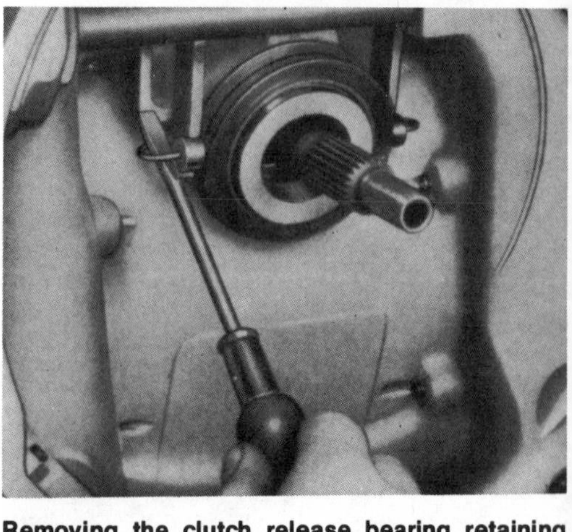

Removing the clutch release bearing retaining springs

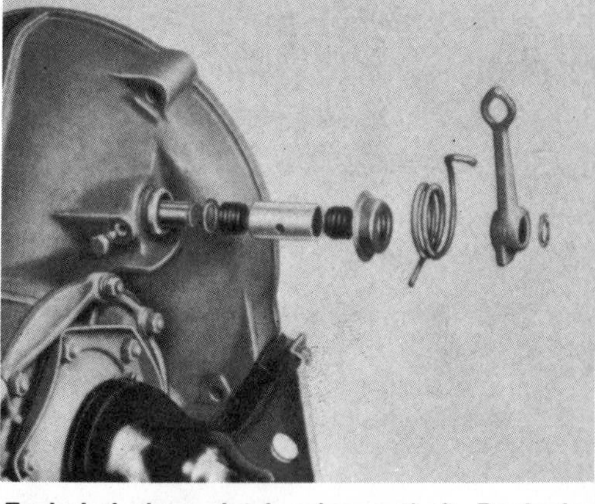

Exploded view, clutch release shaft. Beginning with the 1966 models, a plastic bushing is used

Pressure plate bolts should be loosened gradually and diagonally in order not to distort the pressure plate

Pedal end of clutch cable

lease bearing. Inspect the bearing points of the clutch operating shaft for wear. Lubricate the needle bearing in the flywheel gland nut with approximately 10 grams of universal grease. Then, reinstall the driven (lined) plate, using a pilot mandrel to ensure correct centering alignment. Evenly and alternately tighten the clutch-to-flywheel bolts. Check proper distance and parallelism between clutch cover contact face at flywheel and the clutch release plate with a clutch adjustment gauge. Adjust free play at the clutch pedal to .4–.8″.

Automatic stickshift

To remove the clutch, the engine and then the transmission must be removed. Engine removal is covered in Chapter 4. Transmission removal is covered later in this Chapter.

To remove the clutch:

1. Pull off the torque converter. Seal off the hub opening.
2. Mount transmission in a repair stand or on a suitable bench.
3. Loosen clamp screw and pull off clutch operating lever. Remove transmission cover. Remove hex nuts between clutch housing and transmission case (two inside the differential housing).
4. The oil need not be drained if the clutch is removed with the cover opening up and the gearshift housing breather blocked.
5. Pull transmission off clutch housing studs.
6. Turn clutch lever shaft to disengage release bearing.
7. Remove both lower engine mounting bolts.
8. Loosen clutch retaining bolts gradually and alternately to prevent distortion. Remove bolts, diaphragm clutch, clutch plate, and release bearing.
9. Do not wash the release bearing. Wipe dry only.

To replace the clutch:

10. Check clutch plate, pressure plate, and release bearing for wear and damage. Check clutch carrier plate, needle bearing, and seat for wear. Replace all parts as necessary.
11. If clutch is wet with ATF, replace clutch carrier plate seal and clutch. If clutch is wet with transmission oil, replace transmission case seal and clutch.
12. Coat release bearing guide on transmission case neck and both lugs on release bearing with lithium grease containing a molybdenum disulphide additive. Insert bearing into clutch.
13. Apply lithium grease to carrier plate needle bearing. Install clutch plate and clutch, centering the plate with an old main drive shaft or a suitable dummy shaft.
14. Tighten clutch retaining bolts evenly and alternately. Make sure that release bearing is correctly located in diaphragm spring.
15. Insert lower engine mounting bolts from front. Replace sealing rings if necessary. Some units have aluminum sealing rings and capnuts.
16. Push transmission onto converter housing studs. Insert clutch lever shaft behind rlease bearing lugs. Push release bearing onto transmission case neck. Tighten hex bolts holding clutch housing to transmission case.
17. Install clutch operating lever.

To adjust new clutch:

18. Clutch operating lever should contact clutch housing. Tighten lever clamp screw slightly.
19. Refer to the adjustment illustration. Adjust dimension to a .335″, b to 3.03″, and c to 1.6″. Tighten the clutch lever clamp screw fully.
20. Push torque converter onto support tube. Insert into turbine shaft by turning.
21. Check clutch play after installing transmission and engine.

R & R, CLUTCH CABLE—STANDARD TRANSMISSION

The clutch cable runs from the pedal to the release bearing, which in turn presses against the release plate and moves it axially. To remove the cable, first remove the left rear wheel. Disconnect the cable from its operating lever on the transmission. Pull the rubber boot from the guide tube and cable. Disconnect the brake master cylinder push rod and unbolt the pedal assembly. Unhook the cable from the pedal cluster and pull it forward through the hole from which the pedal cluster was removed.

Installation is the reverse of the above. The cable should be lubricated thoroughly with universal grease. While the pedal assembly is out of the frame tunnel, it is a good idea to lubricate this part well also. The cable guide should be bent slightly by inserting a suitable number of washers between the transmission case bracket and the end of the cable guide (A). (See illustration.) Adjust pedal free play.

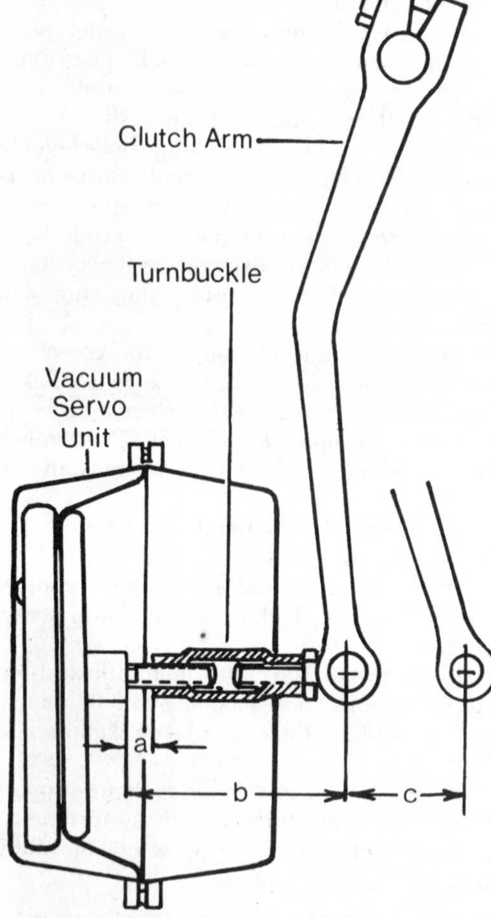

Adjustment dimensions required after installing new clutch in Automatic Stickshift unit. a should be .335 in., b should be 3.03 in., and c should be 1.6 in.

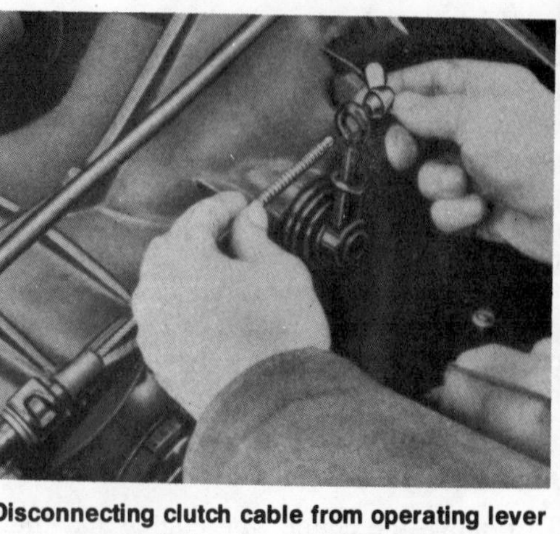

Disconnecting clutch cable from operating lever

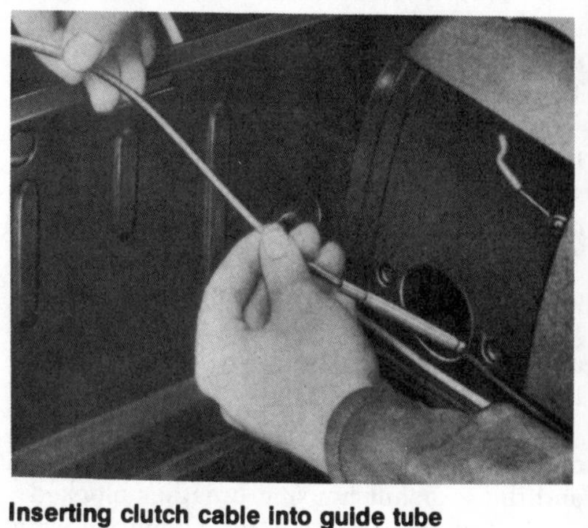

Inserting clutch cable into guide tube

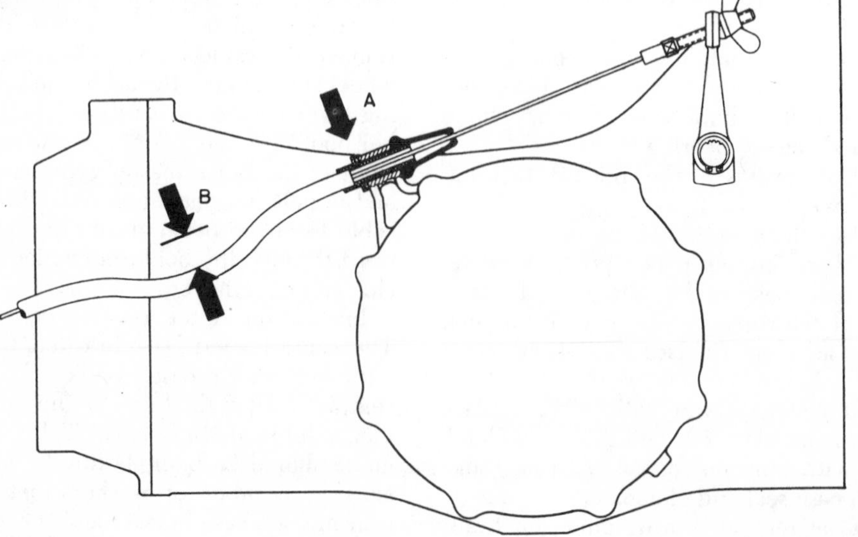

Smooth clutch action requires a slight sag in the cable. Dimension B should be between 1.0 and 1.7″. Adjustment is made via washers at point A

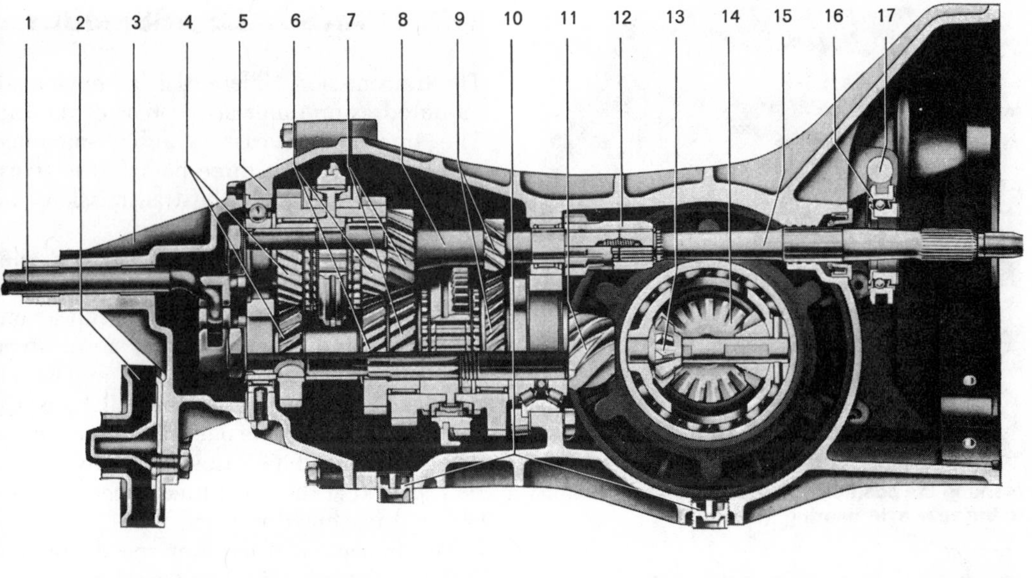

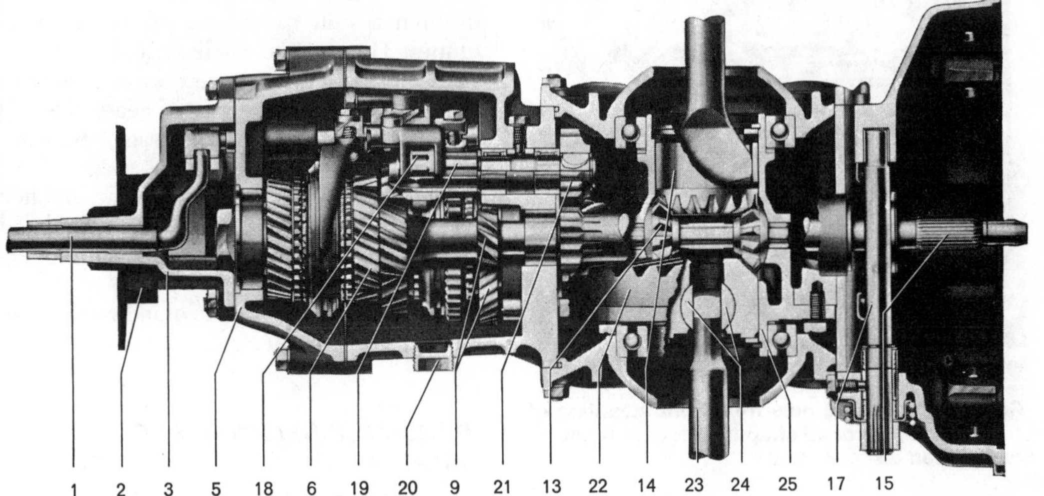

1. Transmission shift lever
2. Bonded rubber mounting
3. Gearshift housing
4. 4th speed
5. Gear carrier
6. 3rd speed
7. 2nd speed
8. Main drive shaft, front
9. 1st speed
10. Oil drain plugs
11. Drive pinion
12. Reverse gear
13. Differential pinion
14. Differential side gear
15. Main drive shaft, rear
16. Clutch release bearing
17. Clutch operating shaft
18. Reverse sliding gear
19. Reverse shaft
20. Oil filler plug
21. Reverse drive gear
22. Ring gear
23. Rear axle shaft
24. Fulcrum plate
25. Differential housing

Cross-sectional view, rear axle and standard transmission

Marking the position of the spring plate in relation to the rear axle bearing housing

Removing retaining nuts from front mounting of transmission. Ground strap (to left of nut) has already been disconnected

Loosening transmission carrier nuts with a 27 mm. wrench

THE TRANS-AXLE ASSEMBLY

The transmission, differential and engine are mounted as one unit at the rear of the car. The transmission case is rubber-mounted and is supported at three points. The transmission case contains the transmission, the differential and ring gear.

Recent transmission cases are of one-piece, die-cast construction. Transmissions of 1960 and earlier models (36 hp. with a non-synchromesh first gear) are of a split-type construction. With the 40 hp. engine introduced on the 1961 models, all transmissions have been of the one-piece type. In the case of the split-type cases, both halves must be replaced at the same time, since they are cast and machined in pairs.

The transmission has four speeds forward and one reverse, with various ratios.

Selection of gears in the Volkswagen transmission is by a floor-mounted lever working through a shift rod contained in the frame tunnel. The gears are helical, and are in constant mesh. In every speed, engine power is transmitted through a pair of gears. There is no direct drive in the Volkswagen transmission.

The drive pinion and ring gear are helically-cut. These gears must be perfectly adjusted in order that long life and silent operation will be ensured.

Transmission work of any kind requires removal of the engine.

TRANS-AXLE REMOVAL AND INSTALLATION

Standard Transmission with Swing Axles

1. With the engine removed from the car, remove the rear wheels and disconnect the brake lines at the rear wheels and plug the lines.

2. Disconnect the parking brake cables from the push bar at the frame and withdraw the cables from their conduit tubes.

3. Remove the bolts at the rear axle shaft bearing.

4. Disconnect the clutch release cable from the operating shaft lever and pull it from its guide plate.

5. From the access hole under the rear seat, disconnect the shift rod in back of the coupling.

6. Remove the nuts from the mounting studs at the front of the transmission.

Transmission Gear Ratios

Model	4th	3rd	2nd	1st	R	Final Drive	Reduction Gears or Torque Converter
1951-54 Type 1	.79	1.22	1.88	3.60	4.63	4.375 or 4.43	–
1954-60 Type 1	.82	1.23 ④	1.88 ③	3.60	4.63	4.375	–
1961-67 Type 1 and 3	.89	1.32	2.06	3.80	3.88	4.375 ①	–
1968-70 Type 1 and 3	.89	1.26	2.06	3.80	3.61	4.125	–
Automatic Stickshift	–	.89	1.26	2.06	3.07	4.375	2.1
Fully Automatic	–	1.00	1.59	2.65	1.80	3.670	2.5
Type 2 1,500 cc.	.82	1.22	2.06	3.80	3.88	4.375	1.26 ②

① Type 3, 4.125

② 1,200cc. Type 2, 1.4 or 1.39

③ 1.94 also used.

④ 1.22 also used.

Additional final drive ratios available for special purposes: 3.875 - type 181; 5.375 - type 2 (1 ton); 5.857 - type 2 (1 ton).

7. Remove the lower shock absorber mounting bolts and mark the position of the rear torsion bar radius arm in relation to the rear axle bearing housing by using a chisel.

8. Disconnect the wires from the starter motor.

9. Disconnect the ground strap from the frame and remove the nuts from the auxiliary spring rods (1966 Squareback and 1967–68 beetles).

10. Place a suitable jack under the unit, and remove with a 27 mm. wrench the two bolts at the transmission attachments.

11. Withdraw the trans-axle toward the rear of the car. Be sure that the main drive shaft is not damaged or bent when the unit is placed on the ground.

Installation of the trans-axle unit is accomplished by reversing the above procedure. The two bolts at the transmission carrier should be greased before being tightened. When a new rear axle is being installed, it is advisable that the retaining nuts of the transmission cradle be tightened fully only after the front mounting has been securely tightened. This tightening sequence is necessary to prevent distortion and premature wear of the rubber mountings.

When the shift rod coupling is reinstalled, the point of the coupling screw should be correctly engaged in the recess. The screw should be secured with a piece of wire. After replacing the ground strap, install the rear axle tubes in their correct positions. The mounting bolts on the spring plate should be tightened to a torque of about 80 ft.lbs. Tighten securely the lower mounting bolts of the shock absorbers. Install the engine and adjust the clutch pedal free play to .4–.8″ and tighten the rear axle shaft nuts to 217 ft. lbs. If the cotter pin cannot be lined up, turn further until it can be inserted. Bleed the brakes and adjust the hand brakes. Note: when a new axle, frame, spring plate or front transmission mounting is installed, the rear wheels must be re-aligned. A special optical alignment gauge is necessary for this purpose. An accurate setting is not otherwise possible.

Standard Transmission with Double Jointed Axles

This procedure is similar to that for vehicles with swing axles; however, the rear wheels and brakes need not be removed or disconnected. The driveshafts should be unbolted at both ends and removed. If the vehicle is

Removing lower mounting bolt of shock absorber

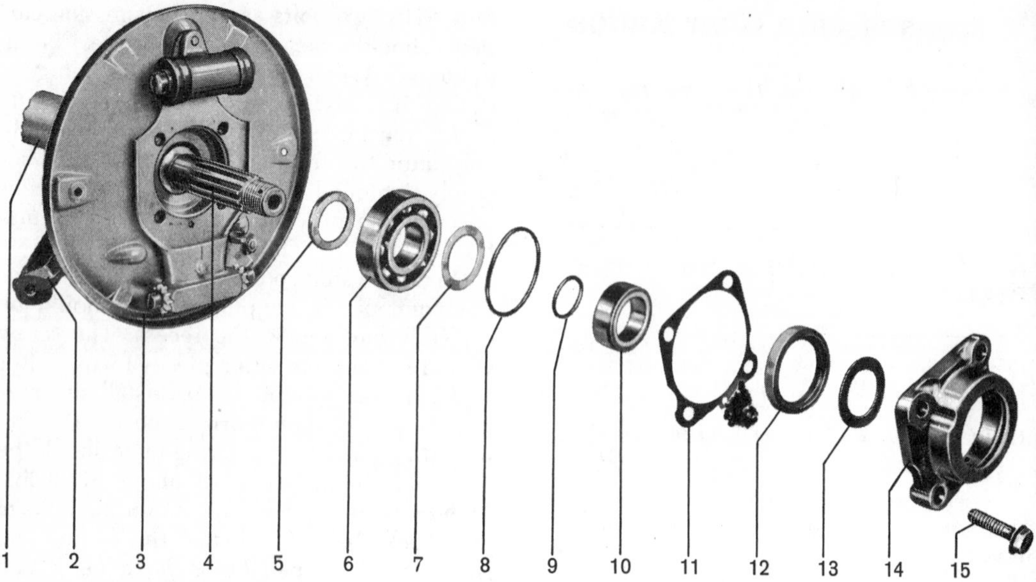

1. Rear axle tube
2. Shock absorber bracket
3. Brake back plate
4. Axle shaft
5. Inner spacer
6. Ball bearing
7. Washer
8. Sealing ring
9. Sealing ring
10. Outer spacer
11. Paper gasket
12. Oil seal
13. Oil deflector
14. Cover
15. Cover retaining screw

Exploded view, rear wheel bearing and rear axle assembly

not to be moved, the driveshafts may be unbolted at the inner ends only and wired up to the body. It is a good idea to cover the axle joints with plastic bags to keep out dirt.

Automatic Stickshift

All Automatic Stickshift models have double jointed axles. After removing the engine:

1. Detach gearshift rod coupling.
2. Remove or disconnect and support driveshafts.
3. Disconnect ATF hoses from transmission. Seal openings. Disconnect temperature switch, neutral safety switch, and backup light switch.
4. Pull off vacuum servo hose.
5. Disconnect starter cables. (Battery ground strap was disconnected during engine removal.)
6. Remove front trans-axle mounting nuts.
7. Loosen rear trans-axle mounting bolts. Support unit and remove bolts.
8. Remove trans-axle.

To replace the trans-axle:

9. Raise trans-axle into place. Tighten

Rear axle shaft nuts should be tightened with a torque wrench to 217 ft. lbs. If the holes do not line up for the cotter pin, turn on to next hole

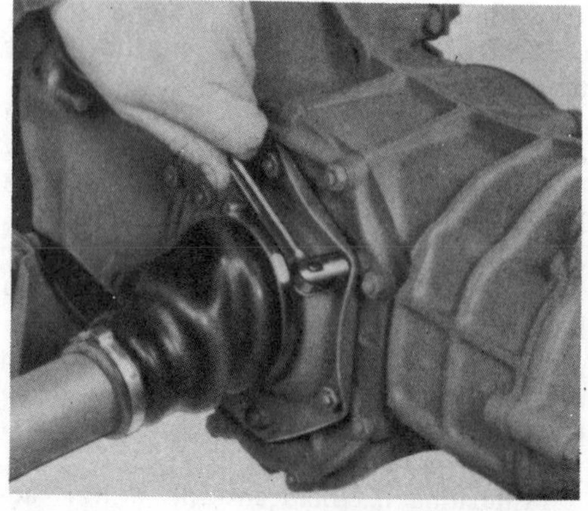

Removing nuts from rear swing axle tube retainer

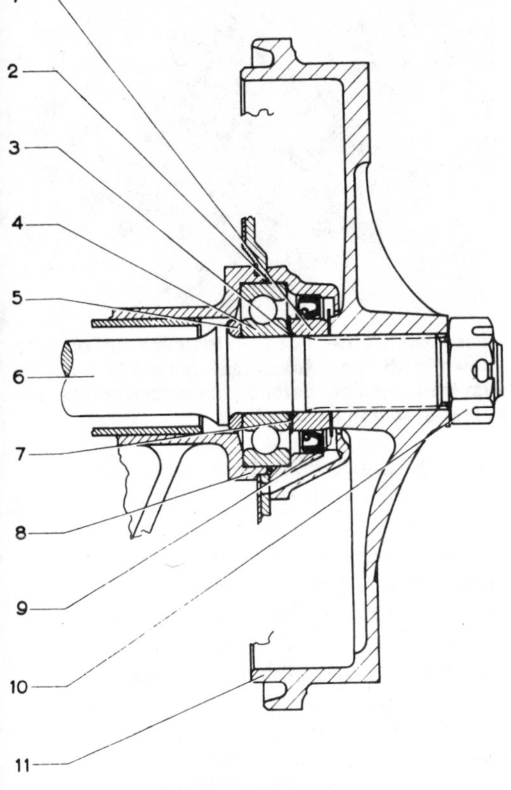

1. Outer spacer
2. Sealing ring
3. Sealing ring
4. Ball bearing
5. Inner spacer
6. Axle shaft
7. Washer
8. Bearing housing
9. Oil seal
10. Nut
11. Brake drum

Wheel bearing assembly, sectional view

nuts for front mounting. Insert rear mounting bolts loosely.

10. Replace vacuum servo hose.

11. Connect ATF hoses, using new washers.

12. Connect temperature switch and starter cables.

13. Install driveshafts, using new lockwashers. Turn the convex sides of the washers toward the screw heads.

14. Align trans-axle and tighten mounting bolts, being careful that the axle joints cannot rub on the frame fork.

15. Insert shift rod coupling, tighten screw and secure with wire.

16. After installing engine, bleed the ATF lines if return flow has not started after 2–3 minutes.

R & R, REAR WHEEL BEARING, OIL SEAL

Details of the rear wheel bearing and oil seal are shown in an exploded view. To remove the oil seal and bearing, remove the rear axle nut, raise the car and take off the brake drum. The hand brake should be disengaged to make this easy. Remove the retaining screws from the cover and take off the cover along with the oil seal. Remove brake line, and take off back plate, outer spacer, gasket between bearing and spacer, washer, and cover gasket. Remove the rear wheel bearing and inner spacer.

Installation is the reverse of the foregoing, but in addition, certain other steps should be taken. The condition of the bearing should be examined, and the bearing replaced if necessary. Replace the two sealing rings. If the oil seal is damaged or uneven, it should also be replaced. When installing a new oil sea, coat it with oil and press it into the bearing cover. The outer spacer should be examined for wear, replaced if scored or cracked, and lightly coated with oil when installed. Clean the oil hole in the cover and replace cover. The splines in the brake drum hub should be inspected and the brake drum replaced if the splines show signs of excessive wear. Tighten the rear axle shaft nut to a torque of 217 ft. lbs., using a new cotter pin and turning nut slightly tighter if necessary to line up holes for cotter pin.

Check the level of lubricant in the transmission and top up if necessary. The oil should be at a level even with the lower edge of the filler hole. Bleed and adjust the brakes.

R & R, REAR AXLE TUBE AND SHAFT—SWING AXLES

The rear axle tube and shaft can be removed while the transmission is still in the car.

1. Remove the brake drum, bearing cover, back plate and rear wheel bearing.
2. Remove the nuts of the axle tube retainer and remove the axle tube and retainer.
3. Take off the gasket and plastic packing.
4. Remove the differential side gear lock ring, the differential side gear thrust washer and the axle shaft.
5. After removing the differential side gear and fulcrum plates from the differential housing, knock the dowel pin from the bearing flange.
6. Remove the rear axle dust sleeve.

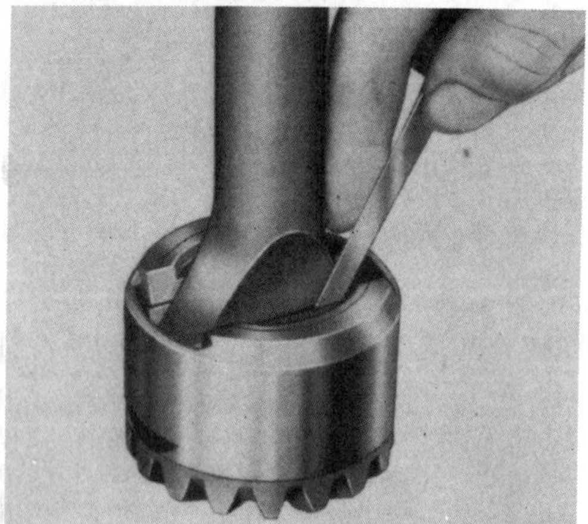

Checking clearance of rear axle shaft/ 2 fulcrum plates/differential side gear (4 parts).

7. Press the axle tube out of its bearing flange.

Installation is mainly the reverse of the preceding. The rear axle boot should be checked for wear and replaced if necessary. The tube retainer and its seat should be cleaned thoroughly. The clearance between the flat end of the rear axle shaft and the inner diameter of the side gear should be .03–.1 mm. (.0012–.004″). The axles and gears are coded according to color, and fall into four tolerance groups: yellow, blue, pink and green. Only parts in the same size group should be mated.

Paint Mark	*Inner Diameter Side Gear*	*Outer Diameter Axle Shaft*
Yellow	59.93–59.97 mm (2.3200–2.3610″)	59.87–59.90 mm (2.357–2.3582″)
Blue	59.98–60.00 mm (2.3610–2.3622″)	59.91–59.94 mm (2.3583–2.3598″)
Pink	60.01–60.04 mm (2.3626–2.3638″)	59.95–59.97 mm (2.3602–2.3610″)
Green	60.05–60.07 mm (2.3642–2.3650″)	59.98–60.00 mm (2.3614–2.3622″)

The maximum allowable run-out for the rear axle is .05 mm. (.002″). This measurement is taken at the seat of the ball bearing. Axles that are slightly bent can be straightened cold. A feeler gauge is used to measure the side clearance between the flat ends of the axle and the fulcrum plates. This clearance should be .035–.244 mm. (.0014–.0096″). Excessive clearance can be taken care of by installing oversize fulcrum plates, which have a groove on the face.

Install the differential side gear, axle and thrust washer in differential housing and in-

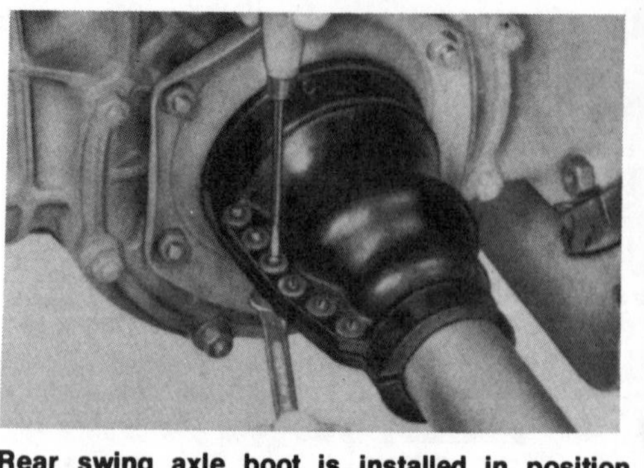

Rear swing axle boot is installed in position shown, with seam horizontal. If boot is replaced with transmission installed in vehicle, screws are easier to install from bottom

sert lock ring. Install the retainer gasket and the axle tube with retainer. There should be no end play between the axle tube and the axle tube retainer. This is accomplished by choosing a gasket of suitable thickness. The axle tube retainer nuts should be tightened to a torque of 14 ft. lbs. Over- or under-tightening should be avoided, for this will lead either to rapid wear or to leaks. Axle boots should not be tightened before the car is on the ground, axle intact. Otherwise, the boots may become twisted and damaged.

R & R, REAR AXLE BOOT SWING AXLES

The original rear axle boots (dust sleeves) are of a one-piece design and must be cut open in order to be removed for replacement. A split-type axle boot is available for replacement which can be installed and then tightened down. To remove the axle boot, take off the retaining clip at each end, and cut off the damaged boot. Clean thoroughly both the axle tube and the axle tube retainer so that the new boot will fit securely.

Upon installation, put a light coating of sealing compound on the joining faces of the boot and ensure that the smaller diameter of the boot is equal to 89 mm. When positioning the new boot, keep the joining faces in a horizontal plane and on the rear of the axle. Tighten the joining screws and the retaining clips (do not overtighten) only after the rear axle is in a loaded condition, and be sure that the boot is not twisted.

DISASSEMBLY AND ASSEMBLY OF TUNNEL-TYPE TRANS-AXLE

(The general repairman should not do extensive work on this unit unless he has special tools and experience.)

Disassembly

1. Remove the gear selector housing and pry off the lock plates that secure the drive pinion and drive shaft nuts.
2. Lock the transmission by engaging both reverse and high gears.
3. Remove the drive pinion and main drive shaft nuts, and remove and discard the lock plates.
4. Remove the gear carrier stud nuts, the ground strap, and the accelerator cable retainer.
5. Position the assembly so that the left-hand final drive cover faces up.
6. Remove the stud nuts from the left-hand final drive cover, then remove the cover.
7. Attach tool VW 297 to the right hand final drive cover studs, and press out the differential. Note the thicknesses and positioning of the differential shims to simplify reassembly.
8. Loosen the retaining ring that secures reverse gear on the main drive shaft.
9. Slide reverse gear toward the rear and screw apart the main drive shaft.
10. Remove the reverse gear and the retaining ring and withdraw the rear main shaft toward the rear, taking care not to damage the oil seal.
11. Remove tool VW 297 and right-hand final drive cover.
12. Release the lock tabs and remove attaching screws, then remove drive pinion ball bearing retainer.
13. Press the transmission out of case with tool VW 296. Note thickness of pinion shims to simplify reassembly.
14. Spread and remove snap ring, then pull off reverse drive gear.
15. Remove woodruff key and withdraw reverse gear shaft and thrust washer from the transmission case.
16. Remove the security screw of the needle bearing spacer sleeve from the reverse gear shaft.
17. With a suitable drift, drive out the reverse gear shaft needle bearings and spacer sleeve.
18. Remove security screw from the needle bearing of the main drive shaft.
19. With a suitable drift, drive out the main drive shaft needle bearing.
20. Press out the ball bearings from both final drive covers, and remove the clutch release bearing and operating shaft.

Assembly

Clean and inspect the case and all components for wear, damage or any indication of malfunction, and replace as necessary. The starting motor armature, brushes and bushings should be inspected and dealt with accordingly. The clutch operating shaft and bushings should be checked and, if necessary, replaced.

1. Press ball bearings into both final drive covers.
2. Insert needle bearings for reverse gear shaft and spacer sleeve, then secure.
3. Install main drive shaft needle bearing with a suitable drift, then secure.
4. Install reverse shaft, woodruff key thrust washer and gear, then secure with a snap ring.
5. Locate drive pinion shims over bearing, then turn two 4″ guide studs into bearing retainer to assure retainer and shim alignment during transmission-to-case assembly.
6. Push reverse selector and sliding gear onto reverse lever and engage reverse gear.
7. With a new carrier gasket in place, carefully insert the transmission into the case (the 4″ guide screws will help at this time).
8. Remove guide screws, then install transmission-to-case attaching screws and lock plates. Torque to 36 ft. lbs.
9. Lubricate lip of oil seal, and install rear half of main drive shaft.
10. Screw both halves of the drive shaft together.
11. Back them off until the splines of the reverse gear are in line, then install reverse gear snap ring.
12. With new gasket in place, install right-hand final drive cover and torque to 18 ft. lbs.
13. With shims properly inserted, install differential in case.
14. Install gear carrier nuts and torque to 14 ft. lbs.
15. Lock transmission by engaging both reverse and fourth gears at the same time.
16. Torque the main drive shaft nut to 87 ft. lbs.; then loosen the nut and retighten to a final 43 ft. lbs. Secure with lock plate.
17. Torque the drive pinion nut to 43 ft. lbs. and secure with lock plate.

CAUTION: *when installing gear shift housing, make sure that the three selector shafts are in neutral.*

Removing of nuts holding final drive cover

Main drive shaft and pinion nuts are tightened to 87 ft. lbs., backed off, and then tightened to 43 ft. lbs. before securing with locking plate

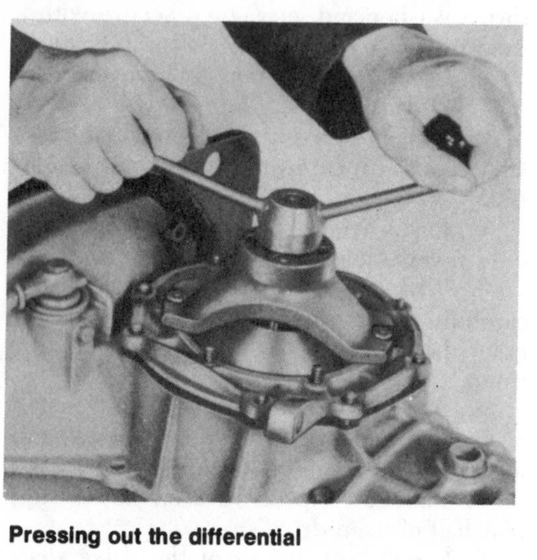

Pressing out the differential

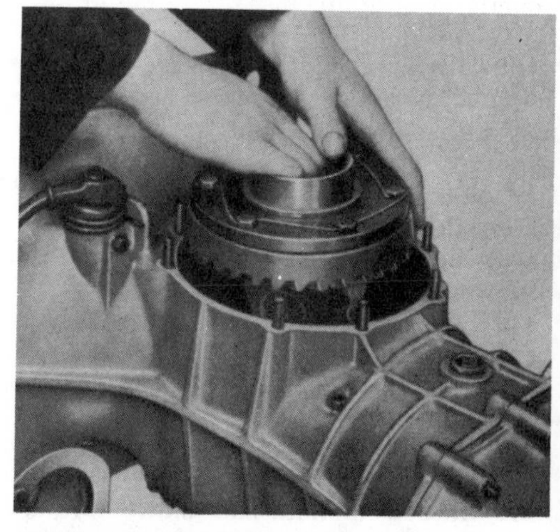

Inserting differential into transmission case

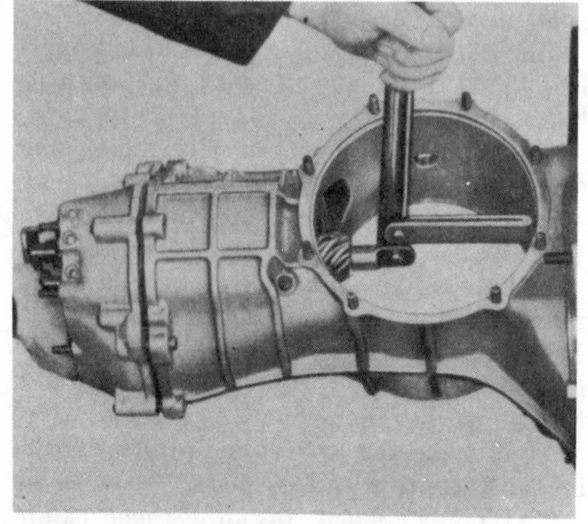

Using special tool to remove transmission from case

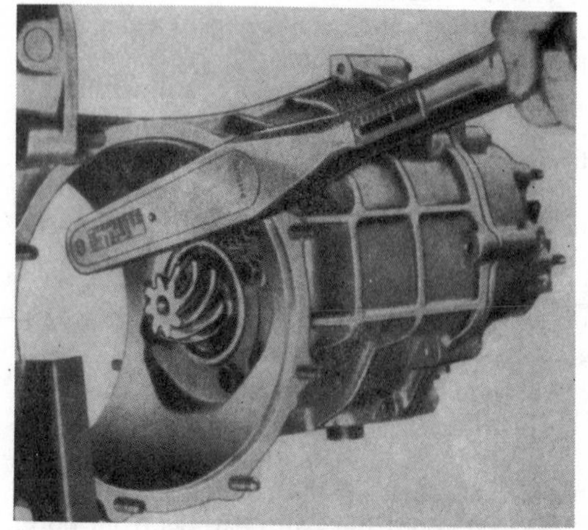

Use new lock plates after tightening ball bearing retaining bolts to 36 ft. lbs.

GEAR CARRIER, DISASSEMBLY AND ASSEMBLY

Disassembly

1. Remove the reverse selector fork including the reverse sliding gear from the reverse lever.
2. Remove and note the thickness of drive pinion ball bearing shims.
3. Clamp gear carrier in vise equipped with soft jaws.
4. Loosen and withdraw shifting fork lock screws, and remove first-second shifting fork.
5. Withdraw the shifting fork shaft from third-fourth shifting fork.
6. For security, place a strong rubber band around first-second operating sleeve and main shaft, mount the assembly in a press, case end up, and press on the main shaft to remove transmission from gear carrier.
7. Remove the screw that holds drive pinion needle bearing, and press out bearing.
8. Press out main drive shaft bearing.
9. Clamp gear carrier in vise with soft jaws, and remove reverse lever guide screws.
10. Withdraw reverse gear selector shaft and remove reverse lever guide.
11. Withdraw first-second selector shaft and remove reverse lever from support.
12. Withdraw third-fourth selector shaft.
13. Remove plungers and detent balls, and hook out detent springs with a small screwdriver.

When the transmission is being pressed into position, the drive pinion and main drive shaft are held together with a rubber band

The selector fork locking screws and the reverse lever guide screw are tightened to a torque of 18 and 14 ft. lbs., respectively

With gear carrier clamped in soft-jawed vise, locking screws of 1st–2nd and 3rd–4th selector forks are loosened prior to the removal of selector fork for 1st and 2nd gears

Assembly

All components should be checked for damage and wear, and replaced if necessary. Free length of detent springs should be 1.0″. The wear, or fatigue, limit is 0.9″. A force of 33–44 lbs. applied to the ends of the selector shafts should be required in order to unseat the detent balls when shifting.

1. Insert detent springs through the selector shaft holes.

   NOTE: *due to design, the springs for first-second and reverse gear detents can be more easily installed by inserting them into the top halves first.*
2. Install reverse selector shaft, including reverse lever and reverse lever guide.
3. Install selector shafts for first-second

and for third-fourth gears. Do not forget the two interlocking plungers. This is a safety assurance against shifting two gears at the same time.

4. Check drive needle bearing and main drive shaft ball bearing for wear and damage, and replace if necessary.

5. Secure drive pinion needle bearing in the gear carrier.

6. Position gear carrier on a suitable support and press main drive shaft ball bearing into position.

7. Check selector forks for wear. Fork-to-operating sleeve clearance should be 0.004"–0.012". Greater clearance warrants parts replacement.

8. Position the selector fork for third-fourth gears.

9. Press transmission into the gear carrier. While pressing, take care that the third-fourth selector fork does not become jammed. Also, with a heavy rubber band, secure first-second gears to the main drive shaft.

10. Install first-second selector fork.

11. Attach reverse gear fork with reverse sliding gear onto selector lever and adjust selector forks, as described in the following section.

SELECTOR FORK ADJUSTMENT

(In order to adjust the selector forks, special equipment is required.)

1. Place transmission, drive pinion shims and gasket for gear carrier on test tool VW 294 and secure gear carrier with four screws.

2. Tighten drive pinion bearing retainer with two screws located diagonally, to 36 ft. lbs. torque.

3. Push crank of the test tool onto splines of main drive shaft so that the main shaft is locked by the crank.

4. Engage first and second gears.

5. With a torque wrench, tighten the main drive shaft nut to 87 ft. lbs.; then loosen the nut and retighten to 43 ft. lbs. and lock it.

6. Attach gearshift housing and shifting handle. By attaching the gearshift housing, correct seating of the main drive shaft bearing in its recess in the gear carrier is guaranteed.

7. Position first-second and third-fourth selector forks so that they move freely in the operating sleeve while in neutral, and when various gears are engaged.

8. Position reverse gear selector fork so that reverse sliding gear is centered between the operating sleeve and second gear of the main drive shaft with second gear engaged. The fork must also engage properly in reverse gear of the drive pinion when reverse gear is engaged.

9. Using a T-handle torque wrench and socket, tighten the selector forks locking screws to 18 ft. lbs. Tighten the reverse lever guide screw to 14 ft. lbs.

10. Remove gearshift housing and transmission from tool VW 294.

MAIN DRIVE SHAFT OIL SEAL, REPLACEMENT

The main drive shaft oil seal can be replaced with the rear axle installed or removed. Remove the engine, clutch release bearing, and the seal from the transmission case.

Before installing the new seal, lightly coat the outer edge of the seal with stealing com-

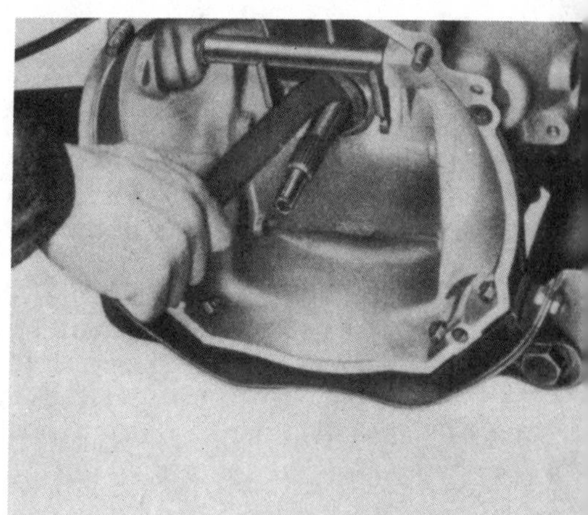

Removal of main drive shaft oil seal

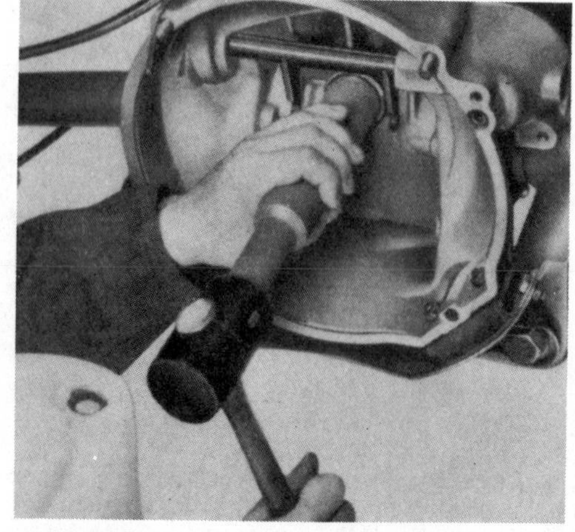

Installation of main drive shaft oil seal

ɔund, and lubricate the main drive shaft ɑnd the lip of the seal. Then, slide the oil seal onto the main drive shaft, and drive it into ɔosition with a suitable driving sleeve or ɔipe. The seal should be slid onto the shaft very carefully in order to avoid mis-positioning the spring around the lip.

DRIVE PINION, RECONDITIONING

Disassembly

1. Press out inner race of needle bearing and fourth gear, then remove woodruff key from the shaft.
2. Remove spacer sleeve, concave washer shims and the concave washer.
3. Remove second and third gears with needle cage and second gear synchronizer stop ring.
4. Remove clutch gear for first and second gears, including springs, shifting plates and operating sleeve.
5. Disassemble parts.
6. Inspect all components for wear and damage; replace as necessary.

If pinion and ring gear require replacement, a matched set is in order. (Note matching number on both gears.) If drive pinion or ball bearing are replaced, the drive pinion and ring gear must be adjusted. Whenever a damaged gear is replaced, the mating gear should also be replaced. Worn or otherwise damaged first and second speed gears require a replacement of the front main drive shaft.

Clean and check all synchronizer components for wear. Clearance between the synchronizer stop ring face and the clutch teeth of the corresponding gear should be about 043". If the wear limit of .024" has been reached, the stop ring should be replaced. If a gear will not engage, even though the clutch is fully released, the probable cause is wear in the slots of the stop ring. Worn parts should be replaced.

Assembly

In preparation, the inner races of the ball bearing and the needle bearing inner race for first gear should be heated in an oil bath to about 194°F.

1. Slide the ball bearing onto the drive pinion.
2. Slide the second inner race on so that the bearing parts numbers are exactly opposite each other.
3. Slide first gear thrust washer and needle bearing inner race onto the drive pinion.
4. With components mounted in a press, press all parts into correct position.
5. Tighten the round nut to 108–144 ft. lbs.
6. Install shims for first gear.
7. After the clutch gear for first and second gears has been installed, check for end

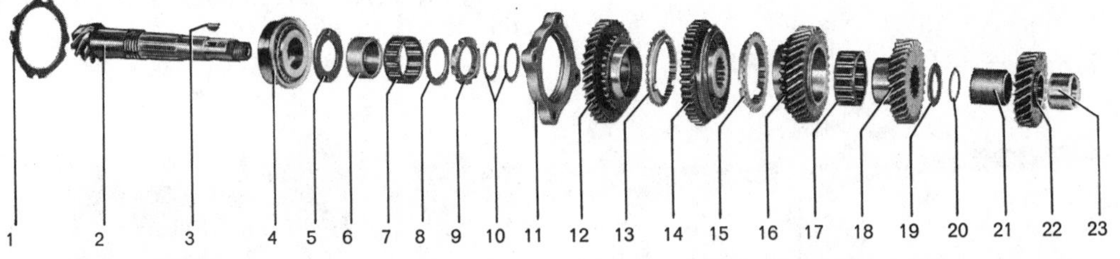

1. Shim
2. Drive pinion
3. Woodruff key for 4th gear
4. Roller bearing
5. Thrust washer for 1st gear
6. Needle bearing inner race (1st gear)
7. Needle cage (1st gear)
8. Thrust washer for needle bearing (1st gear)
9. Round nut
10. Shims, end play 1st gear
11. Roller bearing retainer
12. 1st gear
13. Synchronizer stop ring (1st gear)
14. Clutch gear 1st and 2nd gears, and reverse gear
15. Synchronizer stop ring (2nd gear)
16. 2nd gear
17. Needle cage (2nd gear)
18. 3rd gear
19. Concave washer
20. Shims for concave washer
21. Spacer sleeve
22. 4th gear
23. Inner race, needle bearing in gear carrier

Exploded view, drive pinion and components

play of .004″–.010″ between thrust washer and first gear. Correct if necessary; shims of various thicknesses are available for this purpose.

8. Position first speed stop ring on the cone surface of the gear. (First and second synchronizer stop rings are not interchangeable.)

9. Assemble the synchronizer unit for first and second gears.

10. Slide operating sleeve on the clutch gear so that its shifting plate slots are in line with the slots in the clutch gear.

11. With the shifting plates in position, install the two snap rings, offset to each other.

12. Slide the synchronizer assembly onto the drive pinion. The longer hub should be toward the face of the drive pinion splines.

13. Turn first speed stop ring until shifting plates engage with the slots.

14. Adjust the concave washer to produce the prescribed spring travel of .007″-plus or minus .0004″.

15. Heat the fourth speed gear and needle bearing inner race in an oil bath to 194°F. before pressing into position.

16. Insert woodruff key for fourth gear into drive pinion.

17. Slide fourth gear onto the drive pinion, wide shoulder facing the spacer sleeve.

18. Press fourth speed gear and needle bearing inner race fully into position.

MAIN DRIVE SHAFT, RECONDITIONING

Disassembly

1. Remove thrust washer, fourth gear, needle bearing cage and stop ring.

2. Remove fourth speed needle bearing inner race, clutch gear for third and fourth speed and third gear.

3. Remove needle bearing cage for third gear.

4. Strip down synchronizing unit for third and fourth gears.

5. Clean and inspect all parts for wear and damage.

6. Place front main drive shaft between two centers and, with a dial indicator, check for run-out at the contact surface of the third gear needle bearing. Run-out must not exceed .0006″. Note: if excessive run-out warrants replacement of the front main drive shaft, the gear wheels for first and second speeds on the drive pinion must also be replaced at the same time.

7. Check clearance between the stop ring face and the clutch teeth of the corresponding gear with a feeler gauge. Normal clearance is .043″. If a wear limit of .024″ has been reached, stop rings need replacement. If a gear resists engagement, even though the clutch is fully released, it may be due to misalignment of the teeth of the stop ring with the splines of the operating sleeve. This is caused by wear in the slots of the stop ring.

8. Check fourth gear thrust washer for wear, and replace if necessary.

Assembly

1. Assemble synchronizing unit for third and fourth gears. To hold lash between the clutch gear and operating sleeve to a minimum, the sleeve and clutch gear are matched and etched for identification.

2. Position the shifting plates and install

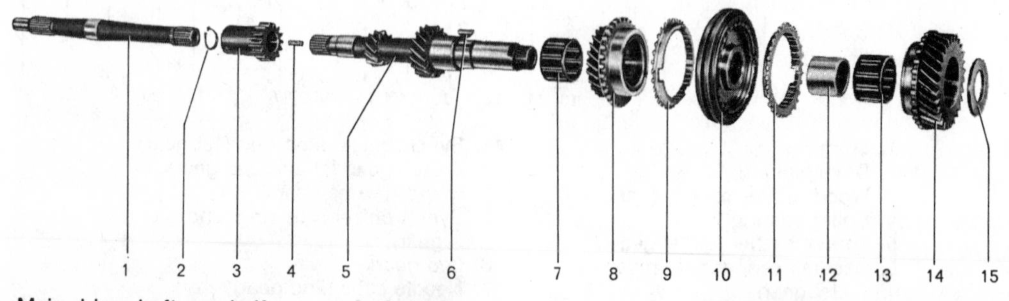

1. Main drive shaft rear half
2. Circlip for reverse gear
3. Reverse gear on drive shaft
4. Stud
5. Main drive shaft front half
6. Woodruff key for clutch gear
7. Needle cage (3rd gear)
8. 3rd gear
9. Synchronizer stop ring (3rd gear)
10. Clutch gear (3rd and 4th speeds)
11. Synchronizer stop ring (4th gear)
12. Needle bearing inner race (4th gear)
13. Needle cage (4th gear)
14. 4th gear
15. Thrust washer (4th gear)

Main drive shaft, exploded view

the two snap rings, offset to each other. Be sure that the ring ends engage behind the shifting plates.

3. Insert clutch gear woodruff key into the main drive shaft.

4. Place third gear synchronizer stop ring on the cone of the gear.

5. Press clutch gear for third and fourth gears into position. The identifying figure 4 on the clutch gear must be toward fourth gear. Third gear is lifted slightly and turned until the stop ring engages in the shifting plates.

6. Press fourth gear needle bearing inner race into position.

DIFFERENTIAL, RECONDITIONING

Disassembly

1. Put differential into holding fixture.
2. Cut and remove safety lock wire and ring gear attaching screws.
3. Lift off ring gear.
4. After driving out the lock pin, push out the differential pinion shaft, and remove differential pinions.

Assembly

1. Check the differential pinion concave thrust surfaces in the differential housing. If scored or worn, replace differential housing.
2. Install differential pinion gears and shaft, then install the pinion shaft lock pin and peen it into place.
3. Examine ring gear for wear or damage. If necessary, replace. Ring and drive pinion must be replaced only in pairs, which are matched. Note: replacement of drive pinion and ring gear or differential housing requires readjustment of the transmission.
4. Install and tighten ring gear attaching screws to a torque of 43 ft. lbs.
5. Insert ring gear attaching screws safety wire to effect a clockwise force on the attaching screws. Twist ends of safety wire and cut off.

PINION AND RING GEAR, ADJUSTMENT

Quiet operation with minimum wearing of the final drive is directly dependent upon pinion and ring gear relationship. For this reason, drive pinion and ring gears are produced in matched pairs and are so identified. Silent operation is obtained by adjusting the drive pinion endwise with the ring gear lifted enough out of the fully engaged position (without backlash) to ensure backlash being within the prescribed tolerance of .0067"–.0098". Any tolerance difference from standard is measured and marked on the pinion face.

Normally, it is necessary to readjust the ring gear and drive pinion only if parts have had to be replaced which directly affect the adjustment. It is satisfactory to readjust the ring gear if the differential housing, a final drive cover or a differential bearing have been replaced. The pinion and ring gear must be readjusted if the transmission case, the gear itself, or the drive pinion ball bearing have been replaced. To be sure of silent operation, the pinion must first be adjusted by installing shims between the ball bearing and the contact surface at the transmission case. This is to reestablish the factory setting

Removal of ring gear attaching bolts

Ring gear attaching bolts are tightened to a torque of 43 ft. lbs.

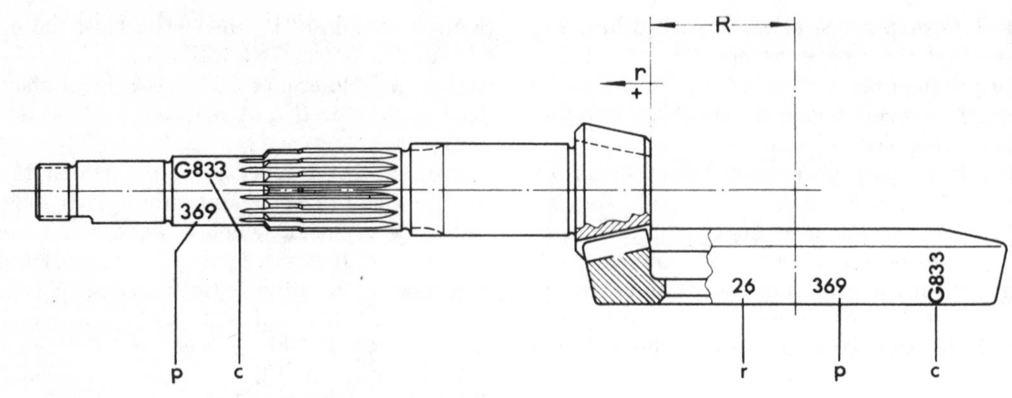

R. Standard fitting dimension/ring gear center line to drive pinion face:
r. Deviation from R (given in hundredths of a millimeter)
p. Matching number of gear set
c. Type of teeth (G = Gleason, K = Klingelnberg, and number of teeth (8:33)

Explanation of dimensions, pinion and ring gear

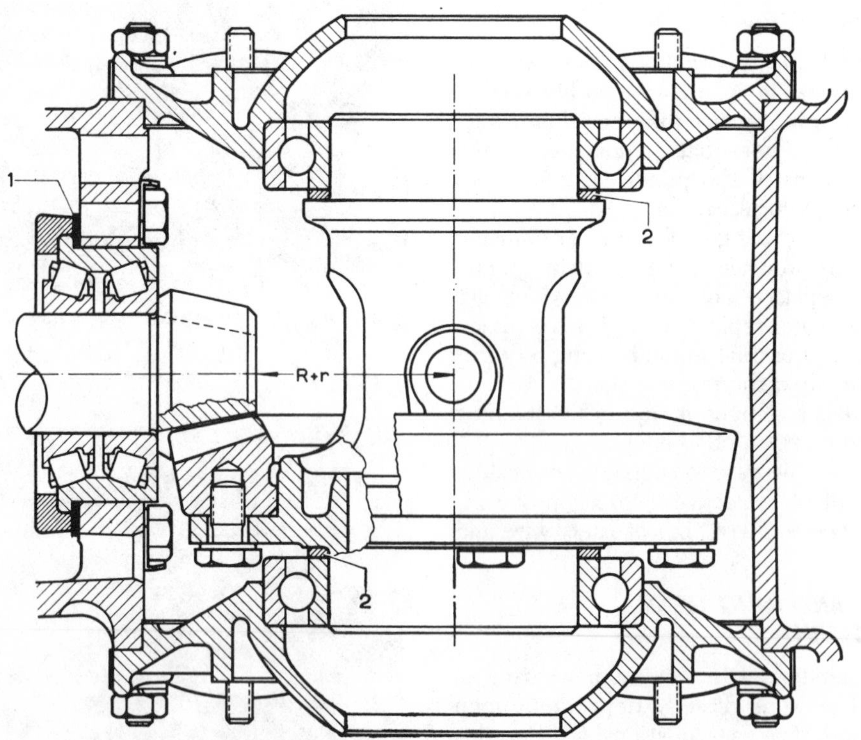

1. Pinion setting shims
2. Shims S1 (ring gear side) and S2 for the differential

Cross-section of pinion and ring gear

of distance from the center line of the ring gear to the drive pinion face.

Both final drive covers must be installed with a preload of .0055″. After determining the thickness of the shims, a preload of .0028″ must be considered on both sides.

Cross-section view, gearshift, lever assembly

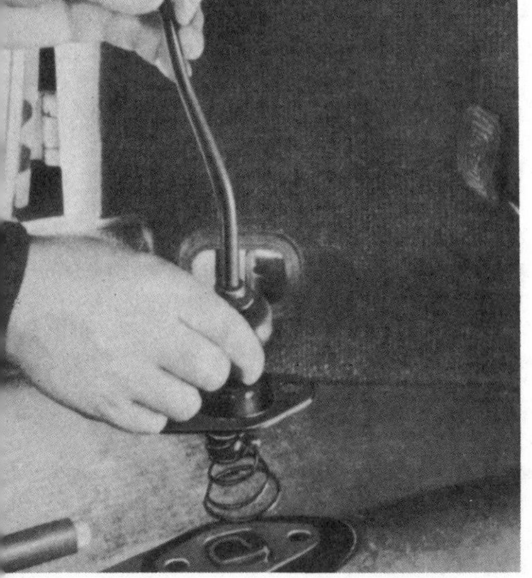

Removal of gearshift lever, housing, boot and spring as a unit

R & R, GEAR SHIFT LEVER—STANDARD TRANSMISSION

The gear shift lever can be removed after the front floor mat has been lifted and the screws removed that attach the gear shift lever ball housing to the central frame tunnel. After the two retaining screws have been removed, the gear shift lever, ball housing, rubber boot, and spring are removed as a unit. The spring will have to be turned in order to clear the pin. Remove the stop plate and clean all components and check them for wear.

Installation of the gear shift lever is the reverse of the preceding. Replace any worn parts. Be sure that the locating pin is a firm fit, but not overly tight. The spring in the steel ball should be checked for tension and replaced if necessary. When installing the stop plate, be sure that the turned-up ramp is on the right-hand side. Lubricate all parts generously with universal grease. After installation is completed, operate the various gears in order to check ease of movement.

SPLIT-TYPE TRANS-AXLE, RECONDITIONING

While the split-type trans-axle is no longer manufactured, there are a sufficient number of units in operation to warrant the following summary of the disassembly and assembly operations:

Disassembly

1. Remove the gear selector housing.
2. Remove clutch release bearing assembly.
3. Remove bolts holding the trans-axle halves together.
4. With a rubber hammer, carefully separate the case halves, then lift off the right half.
5. Remove the main drive shaft (the long, clutch-driven shaft).
6. With a rubber hammer, drive the axle and differential unit from the case.

   (NOTE: *many shims and special purpose washers are used in this unit. It is advisable to lay out, or otherwise identify these parts to help in assembly.*)
7. Remove lock pin at reverse sliding gear shaft and drive out the shaft.
8. Lift out the reverse gear.

TO DISASSEMBLE THE DRIVE PINION SHAFT

1. Straighten out the lockplate, and remove retaining nut.

Pin in gearshift lever pin should engage slot in ball socket. Assembly must be installed so that lower portion of lever is vertical when in neutral position

2. Remove the ball bearing, fourth gear, third-fourth synchronizer hub, and the roller bearing assembly.

TO DISASSEMBLE THE MAIN DRIVE SHAFT

1. Straighten out the lockplate, and remove retaining nut.
2. Remove the ball bearing and the high speed gear with a press.
3. Spread the spacer with a screwdriver, and press off third speed gear.
4. Remove woodruff keys, and remove the ball bearing at the first speed gear end of the shaft.

TO DISASSEMBLE THE DIFFERENTIAL

1. Cut lock wire and remove.
2. Remove ring gear retaining bolts.
3. Remove differential housing cover, axle shaft, differential side gears, fulcrum plates (trunnion blocks), and the ring gear.
4. Remove the lock pin, and pull out the differential shaft and the differential pinion gears.

When stop plate is installed, the turned-up edge should be at the right side, as shown

TO ASSEMBLE THE DRIVE PINION SHAFT

1. Install the roller bearing inner race by expanding it in an oil bath of 190°F., then sliding it over the shaft and into position.
2. Install the roller bearing.
3. Install the end play shim that was originally used. However, some modifications may be necessary, as will be described later.
4. Slide the second speed clutch gear over the splines.
5. Install synchronizer and second speed gear.
6. Slide bushing into second speed gear, then install third speed gear and synchronizer ring over the bushing.
7. Assemble synchronizer hub for third and fourth gears by sliding the operating sleeve onto the clutch gear, at the same time pulling the three plates into position and securing with the two snap rings. The ring ends must be located in one sector between two shifter plates.
8. Slide the synchronizer unit onto the drive pinion shaft and rotate the synchronizer ring until the shifting notches engage the slots. The top of the synchronizer hub should be even with the top end of the shaft splines by plus or minus .002″.
9. Place fourth speed synchronizer ring against the hub, then slide fourth speed gear bushing into position followed by fourth speed gear.
10. Install thrust washer, and measure end play of the gear train. End play should be from .004″-.010″. Shims are available in various sizes for this purpose.
11. Install the double row ball bearing.
12. Position and hold the drive pinion assembly so that the lock nut on the end of the shaft may be torqued to 80–87 ft. lbs. Do not lock the nut at this time.
13. Complete assembly of first gear by installing the three coil springs and shifter plates. Be sure the plates are positioned with their ends under the snap ring.
14. Press all shifter plates down and slide first gear over the hub.

TO ASSEMBLE THE MAIN DRIVESHAFT

1. Install the two woodruff keys and position third speed gear on the driveshaft.
2. Separate the spacer tube with a screwdriver and locate it over the woodruff keys.
3. Install fourth speed gear, then with an arbor press, push the gears into position until

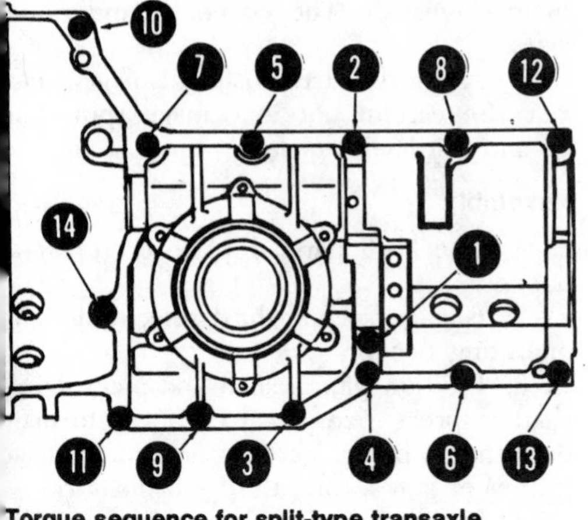

Torque sequence for split-type transaxle

third gear is tightly seated against second gear.

4. Install both bearings, the lock ring, lock plate, and the retaining nut.

5. Torque the lock nut to 30–35 ft. lbs., and bend the lock plate to secure the nut.

TO ASSEMBLE THE DIFFERENTIAL

1. Insert each axle shaft into its corresponding side gear and fulcrum plates. The play between axle and fulcrum plates should be from .002″–.009″. Oversize fulcrum plates are available.

2. Install axle shaft and side gear assembly, differential gears, shaft and lock pin. Stake the pin to secure it.

3. Install the other axle, side gear, and housing assembly. Torque bolts to 43–45 ft. lbs. Safety wire these bolts as a security measure.

At this point special equipment is required to relate the ring gear accurately with the pinion. According to design, the face of the drive pinion is positioned 59.22 mm. from the centerline of the ring gear. This measurement must be flexible to the extent of manufacturing tolerances, and the deviation from standard is stamped on the edge of the ring gear. The ring gear and pinion gear, as on the tunnel-type trans-axle, are matched in sets. Backlash value is also etched on the edge of the ring gear.

In the absence of special differential gauges and measuring equipment, the red lead tooth patterning method has been used, however, the practice is not advisable. The following is a brief description of the recommended procedure, using special Volkswagen tools.

To establish the location of the pinion in the case, install and hold the pinion into the case as far and firmly as possible. Install the mandrel of the gauging tool in one half of the case. Install the other case half and bolt them together.

Rotate the mandrel until the spring-loaded plunger of the mandrel is at right angles to the face of the pinion. Now, release the plunger to permit contact with the face of the pinion. Lock the plunger in this position, then rotate the mandrel so that the plunger is away from contact with the pinion. Separate the two case halves so that the mandrel may be removed for measurement.

Half the diameter of the mandrel, plus the length of the extended pin, should correspond with the value etched on the edge of the ring gear. If these values do not agree, the pinion-positioning shim installed in previous Step No. 10 under To Assemble Drive Pinion Shaft must be changed.

Carrier bearings must carry a preload sufficient to spring the case .005–.007″, while while maintaining a good tooth pattern and a backlash value corresponding to that etched on the ring gear. This is controlled by the selection of spacers used at the differential pedestal bearings. Proper thickness of spacer rings can be determined by using the special measurement tools supplied by VW.

After installing the differential assembly into its recess in the left-hand housing, install reverse sliding gear and the shaft. Insert the lock pin through the bearing recess. Bend the lock plate over the main drive pinion shaft retaining nut, then install the assembly in the case. Before the case halves are assembled, gears should be shifted to check for free and full tooth mesh. If full mesh is not made, loosen the positioning set screw and move the shifter fork enough to centralize the gear. Reverse shaft lock screw is accessible from inside the case, the other two being reached by removing threaded plugs from outside the case.

Coat the mating surfaces of the housing halves with sealer. Assemble the two halves and torque the retaining bolts to 15 ft. lbs. The double row rear pinion bearing must be preloaded by .001–.004″. This is done by inserting shims between the bearing and the gear shift housing at the rear of the transmission. To do this, take a depth gauge reading of the bearing recess in the gear shift housing, then measure the amount that the bearing race extends beyond the surface of the case. Paper shims are available to make up this specified preload.

Repeat the above measuring and shimming procedure at the mainshaft bearing and add enough shims to produce a .001–.004″ preload. Install the gearshift cover and test shift the unit.

Install the trans-axle by reversing the removal procedure.

THE TRANSPORTER, AN IMPORTANT DEVIATION

NOTE: *in the differential assembly of the VW Transporter, the ring gear is positioned on the opposite side of that in passenger cars, being on the right side of the unit instead of on the left. The reason for this difference is the presence of reduction gears on the rear of the transporter. These gears serve to make possible increased ground clearance in the Transporter and also to reduce the road speed at any given engine RPM to handle the loads allowed for in design. If the ring gear of the Transporter is accidentally installed on the wrong side of the differential unit, the result will be a Transporter with one speed forward and four in reverse.*

AUTOMATIC STICKSHIFT REPAIR

Disassembly

1. Remove gearshift housing with inner transmission shift lever.
2. Remove hex nuts holding gear carrier.
3. Remove transmission cover and gasket.
4. Take out locking clip and loosen roller bearing retaining ring at pinion gear until it just contacts the ring gear. Special wrench VW 183 is normally used.

NOTE: *the transmission can also be removed with the differential in place.*

5. Press out the transmission until the retaining ring touches the case. Alternately loosen retaining ring and press out transmission until ring has been completely screwed clear of the bearing. Hinged lever VW 281 is required to press out the transmission. Press out the bearing with the transmission. Note thickness and number of drive pinion adjusting shims
6. Support gear carrier in a vise. Remove selector fork clamping screws and remove first-reverse selector fork.
7. Remove second-third selector shaft from fork.
8. Remove circlip and dished washer from main driveshaft. The washer is under tension.
9. Press main driveshaft out of gear carrier. Be careful not to damage splines on second-third selector fork.

Assembly

1. Check all parts; replace or repair as needed.
2. Engage second-third selector fork in operating sleeve.
3. Position pinion shaft and main driveshaft in press. Press gear carrier onto main driveshaft, being careful not to damage splines or jam second-third selector fork.
4. Install dished washer and new circlip on main driveshaft. Press circlip down until it snaps into groove. Squeeze circlip all round with water pump pliers until it bottoms in the groove.

Install and adjust selector forks as follows:

5. Install the gear carrier and pinion shaft in setting appliance VW 294b. The pinion adjusting shims, but not the paper gear carrier gasket, must also be installed in the appliance.
6. Screw retaining ring on pinion roller bearing and hand tighten with C-wrench VW 183.
7. Push selector shaft into second third fork. Install clamp screw. Install first-reverse selector fork and clamp screw.
8. Move first-reverse lower selector shaft into first gear detent groove. Slide operating sleeve and fork over synchronizer teeth until it is against first gear. Centralize fork in operating sleeve groove and tighten clamp screw. The selector forks must not rub on the sides of the groove in the sleeve when in either neutral or a gear position.
9. Select first, neutral, and reverse several times while turning the transmission. Check for clearance between fork and sleeve groove in each position. In reverse, the sleeve contacts a stop pressed into the hub. If necessary, alter the selector fork setting until there is the same clearance between sleeve and gear sleeve and stop in both end positions. Tighten clamp screw.
10. Move upper selector shaft into detent groove for third. Adjust fork as for first-reverse. Tighten clamp screw.
11. Check interlock mechanism. It must not be possible to engage two gears at once.

Resume transmission assembly:

12. Insert transmission with pinion shims and gear carrier gasket into transmission

case. Drive pinion and mainshaft in with a rubber hammer. On transmission with locating screw for pinion shaft bearing, align bearing outer race hole with hole in housing.

13. If differential is still in place, the pinion bearing retaining ring must be inserted and screwed on while transmission is driven in.

14. Tighten retaining ring to 108 ft. lbs.

15. Tighten gear carrier nuts diagonally. Insert retaining ring locking clip and tighten screw. On transmission with pinion shaft bearing locating screw, insert and align locking clip so screw can be installed when cover is fitted.

16. Insert gearshift housing and transmission shift lever with new gasket. Tighten nuts.

17. Install transmission cover with gasket and tighten screws diagonally. Coat end of bearing locating screw with sealing compound and insert screw.

Gear Carrier Details

If difficult shifting was noted, check selector shaft detent springs. To remove the plugs holding in the springs, cut a 6 mm. thread in each. Spring free length should be 0.9–1.0″. The force required to overcome the grooves should be 33–44 lbs.

When using a replacement gear carrier from a four speed manual transmission, the holes for the reverse shift rod must be plugged. Only the old type of gear carrier with the long guide for the first-second shift rod is supplied as a replacement. When using this carrier for the Automatic Stick-shift, the hole for the first-second shift rod must be drilled about 16 mm. deep from inside with a 16 mm. dia. drill. If this is not done, the shift rod will probably jam.

Main Driveshaft Disassembly

1. Remove thrust washer, third gear, needle bearing, and synchronizer stopring.
2. Press off needle bearing inner race, clutch gear with operating sleeve, and second gear.
3. Take out shaft key.
4. Disassemble clutch gear.

Main Driveshaft Assembly

1. Check gears, synchronizer teeth, thrust washer, main driveshaft, and key for wear and damage.
2. Press synchronizer stop-rings onto gears and measure clearance between synchronizer ring and gear with a feeler gauge.

Gear	*Installation Clearance*	*Wear Limit*
First	.043–.070″	.023″
Second, Third	.040–.075″	.023″

3. Install second gear with needle bearing and synchronizer stop-ring.
4. Install key.
5. Fit operating sleeve and clutch gear for second and third gears together, aligning marks. Sleeve and clutch gear may be replaced in matched sets only. Install springs with ends overlapping 120°. The angled spring ends must fully engage over the shift plates.
6. Seat reassembled clutch gear. The 1 mm. deep groove on the operating sleeve must point toward third gear and the wide chamfer on one side of the clutch gear must be toward second gear.
7. Heat inner race of third gear needle bearing to about 212°F and press into position.
8. Install needle bearing, gear with synchronizer stop-ring, and thrust washer for third gear.

Drive Pinion Shaft Disassembly

1. Remove circlip, while holding third gear down with a press.
2. Press third gear and needle bearing inner race off together.
3. Take off spacer spring and remove second gear circlip. Take off second gear, first gear with synchronizer ring, first gear needle bearing, clutch gear with operating sleeve, and shim.
4. Unscrew round nut. Tool VW 293 may be used.
5. Press off bearing. Remove operating sleeve, shift plates, and spring from clutch gear.

Drive Pinion Shaft Assembly

1. Check all parts for wear and damage. Second and third gears may be replaced only in pairs. Press synchronizer ring over cone on gear and measure clearance. Clearances and wear limits are as given in Step 2 under Main Driveshaft Dissassembly.
2. Heat inner races of double taper roller bearing to about 212°F and install bearing on shaft. Cool to room temperature and press on with 3 tons pressure.

3. Screw on new round nut and tighten to 159 ft. lbs. Tool VW 293 should be used. Check bearing turning torque. On used bearings, there should be no end-play. To check turning torque, install pinion shaft in transmission housing without shim, fit retaining ring and tighten to 108 ft. lbs. (87 ft. lbs. when using VW 183). Turn pinion with a torque gauge, oiling bearings lightly with hypoid oil. Turn pinion rapidly in each direction about 15–20 turns, then take reading while turning. Turning torque should be .43–1.5 ft. lbs. (6–21 cmkg) for a new bearing or .21–.51 ft. lbs. (3–7 cmkg) for a used bearing. Peen locking shoulder of round nut into pinion splines at three places 120° apart, using a blunt chisel. Be careful not to crack or burr the shoulder.

4. Find thickness of shim for round nut as follows: Measure from end of pinion gear to base of bearing race. This is dimension a. Measure from end of pinion gear to top of bearing inner race. This is b. Measure from bearing contact shoulder on pinion to upper edge of shim. This is X. X should be 44.40–44.50 mm. Shim thickness $= X \times b - a$.

5. Assemble pinion shaft up to second gear. The clearance between second gear and its circlip should be .10–.25 mm. (.0039–.0098"). Circlips of various sizes are available.

6. Fit spacer spring and third gear.

7. Heat needle bearing inner race to about 212°F and press on with third gear.

8. Install circlip.

Differential Details

Before removing the differential, the transmission gears must be removed. Replacing and adjusting the differential requires numerous special tools and procedures. For this reason, these operations are best left to an authorized repair facility.

Differential specifications are as follow:

Backlash—.15–.25 mm (.0059–.0098")

Side bearing turning torque (preload)—New bearings, 18–22 cmkg (1.3–1.59 ft. lbs.); used bearings, 3–7 cmkg (.21–.51 ft. lbs.)

Torque Specifications—Transmission and Rear Axle

Fastener	Thread Size	Torque (ft.lbs.)
Transmission and Rear Axle (Standard and Partly-synchronized) Transmission) Type 1 and 2		
Drive pinion nut (Partly-synchronized transmission) up to Chassis No. 1 454 550/238 499	M 22 x 1.5	80-87 ①
Drive pinion nut (Partly-synchronized transmission /new lockwasher) from Chassis No. 1 454 551/238 500	M 22 x 1.5	58-65 ①
Slotted nut for pinion (Standard transmission)	M 18 x 1.5	36 ②
Main drive shaft nut	M 16 x 1.5	30-36
Reverse selector fork screw	M 7 x 12	14
Ring gear screws	M 10 x 1.5	43
Selector fork clamp screw	M 8 x 1.25	18
Transmission housing nuts and bolts ③	M 8 x 1.25	14
Oil drain plug	M 18 x 1.5	22-29
Oil filter plug	M 24 x 1.5	14
Axle shaft nut	M 24 x 1.5	217
Transmission carrier to frame	M 18 x 1.5	166
Spring plate nuts/bolts	M 12 x 1.5	72
Transmission and Rear Axle (fully synchronized) all Types		
Drive pinion round nut:		
1-for double ball bearing.	M 35 x 1.5	87
2-for double taper roller bearing	M 35 x 1.5	144
Pinion bearing retainer screws	M 10 x 1.5	36
Pinion nut	M 22 x 1.5	43 ④
Drive shaft nut	M 22 x 1.5	43 ④
Reverse lever guide screw	M 7 x 1	14
Selector fork screws	M 8 x 1.25	18
Nuts for gearshift housing	M 7 x 1	11
Ring gear screws	M 10 x 1.5	43
Final drive cover nuts	M 8 x 1.25	22
Axle tube retainer nuts	M 8 x 1.25	14
Rear wheel bearing retainer screws	M 10 x 1.5	43
Oil drain plug	M 24 x 1.5	14
Oil filter plug		
Rear axle shaft nut (Type 1 and 3)	M 24 x 1.5	217

Torque Specifications—Transmission and Rear Axle

Fastener	Thread Size	Torque (ft.lbs.)
Nut on driven shaft (Type 2 from August 1963)	M 30 x 1.5	108
Nut on rear axle driven shaft (Type 2) up to Chassis No. 1144302	M 24 x 1.5	217 ⑤
from Chassis No. 1144303	M 30 x 1.5	217 ⑤
Transmission carrier on frame	M 18 x 1.5	166
Spring plate/reduction gear housing screw (Type 2)	M 12 x 1.5	72-87
Additional torques for transmission and rear axle (Stickshift automatic)		
Temperature switch/Selector switch/Starter inhibitor switch	M 14 x 1.5	18
Converter to drive plate screws	M 8 x 1.25	18
Retaining nut for taper roller bearing	M 80 x 1	159
Nut for converter housing	M 8 x 1.25	14
Screw for one-way clutch support	M 6 x 1	11 ⑥
Screw for clutch	M 6 x 1	11
Lock screw	M 8 x 1.25	7
Clamp screw for clutch lever	M 8 x 1.25	18
Screw for transmission oil pan and lock plate	M 7 x 1.25	7
Union for oil pressure line	M 12 x 1.5	25
Union for oil return line	M 14 x 1.5	25
Screw for drive shaft	M 8 x 1.25	25
Fitted screw in diagonal arm	M 14 x 1.5	87
Additional torques for transmission and rear axle (Type 3 Automatic)		
Screw for oil pump on transmission case	M 6 x 1	3
Screw for valve body on transmission case	M 6 x 1	3
Screw for transfer plate on valve body	M 5 x 0.8	2
Screw for oil strainer on valve body	M 6 x 1	2
Screw for oil pan on transmission case	M 8 x 1.25	7
Pin for operating lever on transmission case	M 10 x 1.5	4
Plug for pressure connections/transmission case	M 10 x 1	7
Vacuum unit/transmission case	M 14 x 1.5	18
Screw for bearing cap/diff. carrier	M 10 x 1.5	40
Screw for ring gear/differential housing	M 9 x 1	32
Screw for converter on drive plate	M 8 x 1.25	14
Screw for drive shaft on flange	M 8 x 1.25	25
Screw for front band	M 12 x 1.75	3.5 ⑦
Screw for rear band	M 12 x 1.75	3.5 ⑧
Lock nut for band adjusting screw	M 10 x 1.75	14
Nut for differential carrier on rear axle housing	M 6 x 1	6
Nut for side cover on rear axle housing	M 6 x 1	6
Nut for transmission/final drive housing	M 8 x 1.25	14
Nut and screw for spring plate	M 12 x 1.75	80
Screw for bearing cover	M 10 x 1.5	43
Fitted bolt for diagonal arm	M 10 x 1.5	87
Transmission and Rear Axle (fully synchronized) Type 2-from Chassis No. 218 000-001		
Retaining ring for double taper roller bearing/transmission case	M 80 x 1	109
Round nut/pinion	M 35 x 1.5	144
Union nut/clamp sleeve	M 14 x 1.5	18-22
Bracket/reverse shifter shaft on gear carrier	M 8 x 1.5	18
Support/rocket lever on on gear carrier	M 8 x 1.5	18
Shift fork on shift rod	M 8 x 1.25	18
Locking screw with dog point	M 8 x 1.25	11
Clamp sleeve on gear carrier	M 14 x 1.5	32
Shift housing on gear carrier	M 7x 1	11
Nuts on gear carrier, transmission and clutch housing	M 8 x 1.25	68
Ring gear to differential housing	M 9 x 1	32
Double taper roller bearing retainer	M 9x 1.25	22 ⑨
Final drive side covers	M 8 x 1.25	14
Brake back plate to housing	M 8	18
Brake back plate to housing	M 10	25
Slotted nut on rear wheel shaft	M 30 x 1.5	230-253 ⑩
Joint to flange (socket head screw)	M 8	25
Control arm to frame	M 12 x 1.5	58
Cover/spring plate mounting	M 10	32

Torque Specifications— Transmission and Rear Axle

Fastener	*Thread Size*	*Torque (ft.lbs.)*
Control arm to bearing housing	M 14 x 1.5	94
Shock absorber to frame and bearing housing	M 12 x 1.5	43

① *The nut should be tightened and not backed off.*

② *First tighten to 108 ft. lbs., then back off and tighten to 36 ft. lbs.*

③ *Note tightening sequence, illustrated in Power Train Chapter.*

④ *Tighten first to 86 ft. lbs. then back off and finally tighten to 43 ft. lbs.*

⑤ *If cotter pin holes are not in line, tighten to a maximum of 250 ft. lbs. If hole is still not in line, fit a different nut.*

⑥ *Use new screws*

⑦ *Tighten to 7 ft. lbs. first, loosen and tighten again. Turn out 1 3/4 - 2 turns from this position.*

⑧ *Tighten to 7 ft. lbs. first, loosen and tighten again. Turn out 3 1/4 - 3 1/2 turns from this position.*

⑨ *Tighten to 32 ft.lbs. first, slacken off and tighten to 22 ft. lbs.*

⑩ *With reinforced spacer sleeve: at least 253 ft. lbs. then turn on to cotter pin hole.*

Suspension, Brakes and Steering

SUSPENSION

Trailing Arm Front Suspension

The trailing arm type front suspension of the Volkswagen has taken two basically different forms over the years. Models prior to 1966 used link (king) pins to connect the front wheel spindles to the suspension trailing arms. All Volkswagens since the 1966 model year employ ball joints in the front end along with the transverse torsion bars which had always been used. The principle of torsion bars is that of springing action taking place via twisting of the bars. When a front wheel goes up or down, the torsion bars are twisted, causing a downward or upward force in the opposite direction.

The supporting part of the Volkswagen front axle is the axle beam, which is two rigidly joined tubes attached to the frame with four screws. At each end of the tubes there is a side plate designed to provide additional strength and serve as the upper mounting point for the shock absorbers. Because the front axle is all-welded, it is replaced as a unit whenever damaged.

Strut Front Suspension

The type 4 and the type 1 Super Beetle use a strut front suspension. Each wheel is suspended independently on a shock absorber strut surrounded by a coil spring. The strut is located at the bottom by a track control arm and a ball joint, and at the top by a ball bearing which is rubber mounted to the body. The benefits of this type of suspension include a wider track, a very small amount of toe-in and camber change during suspension travel, and a reduced turning circle. The strut front suspension requires no lubrication. It is recommended, however, that the ball joint dust seals be checked every 6,000 miles and the ball joint play every 30,000 miles.

Swing Axle Rear Suspension

The rear wheels of the Volkswagen are independently sprung by means of torsion bars. The inside ends of the torsion bars are anchored to a body cross member via a splined tube which is welded to the frame. The torsion bar at each side of the rear suspension has a different number of splines at each end. This makes possible the adjustment of the rear suspension.

The torsion bars of different models may be slightly different in diameter, depending on the loads designed to be carried. For example, the torsion bars at the tear of the 1967 type 1 are 21 mm. in diameter compared to

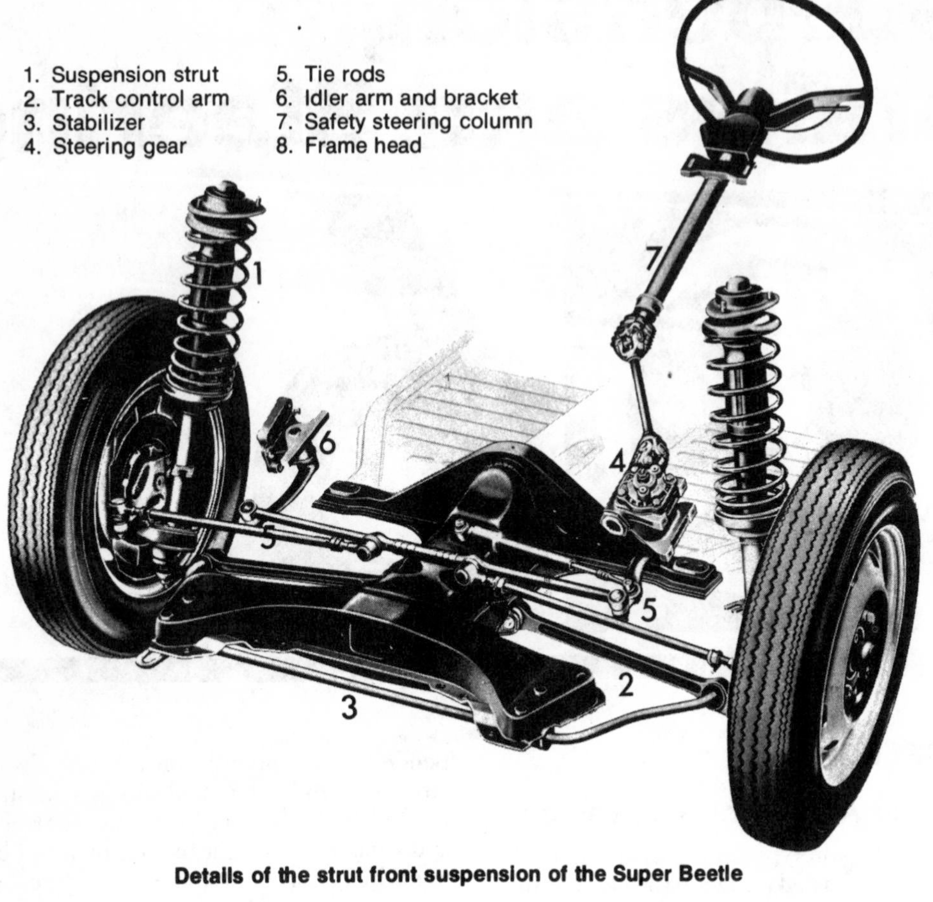

Details of the strut front suspension of the Super Beetle

23 mm. for the Squareback sedan. The length of the torsion bar also has an effect on its springing properties, and Volkswagens have, through the years and models, had torsion bars ranging in length from 21.7" (1967 type 1) to 24.7" (the first type 1 produced).

The suspension of the Squareback sedan is reinforced by a transverse torsion bar which is located above the rear axle. This bar acts progressively to soften the bumps in proportion to their size, and also to add to the handling qualities and lateral stability of the rear axle. This reinforcing spring is also present on all 1967 and 1968 models. For earlier models, there is available an accessory known as the "Camber Compensator."

This device is a transverse leaf spring which is installed below the rear axle. It reduces oversteer by resisting the tendency of the rear wheels to tuck under the body on hard cornering.

The rear shock absorbers of the Volkswagen are of the double-acting type which dampen the shocks of the road as well as prevent excessive rebound when the wheel(s) are in the unloaded position.

Double Jointed Axle Rear Suspension

This rear suspension system was first introduced on the 1968 type 2 and on the Automatic Stickshift type 1. It is currently used on all Volkswagen vehicles. The axle shafts each have two constant velocity joints. The rear wheels are located by trailing arms as on swing axle models, and by diagonal control arms from the rear crossmember. The axle shafts and final drive therefore do not absorb any thrust forces. In this design, there is only a very slight change in rear wheel track and camber during suspension travel. This results in more stable handling, since rear wheel traction remains constant regardless of the suspension position.

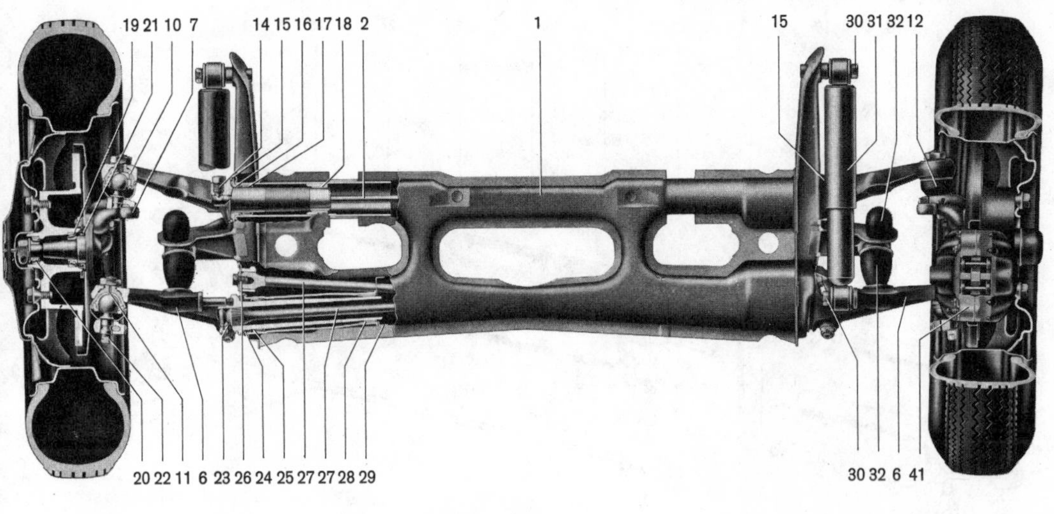

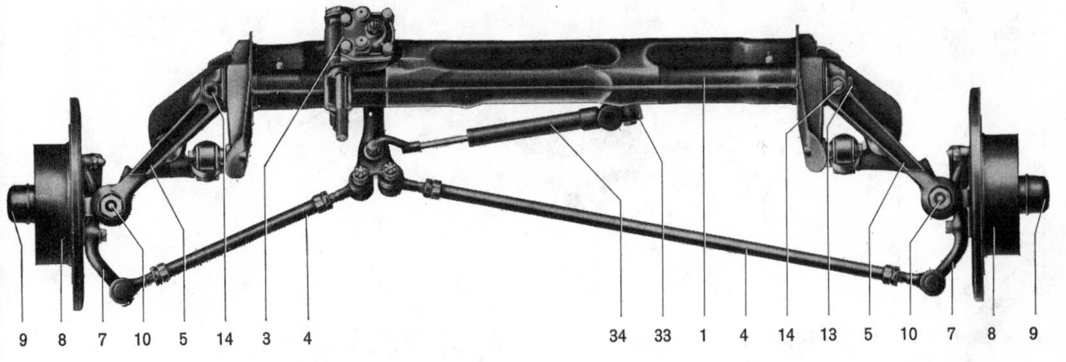

2 1 35 36 37 38 39 40 7

1. Front axle beam
2. Stabilizer
3. Steering gear
4. Tie rods
5. Torsion arm, upper
6. Torsion arm, lower
7. Steering arm
8. Brake disc
9. Grease cap
10. Upper ball joint
11. Lower ball joint
12. Dust seal
13. Adjust screw for upper torsion arm axial play
14. Grub screw
15. Seal, upper
16. Thrust ring
17. Needle bearing, upper
18. Plastic sleeve with metal bush
19. Front wheel bearing, inner
20. Front wheel bearing, outer
21. Seal
22. Eccentric for camber adjustment
23. Grub screw
24. Seal, lower
25. Needle bearing, lower
26. Retaining bolt
27. Torsion bars
28. Plastic sleeve with metal bush, lower
29. Reinforcement plate
30. Shock absorber mounting bolt
31. Shock absorber
32. Rubber stop
33. Steering damper mounting bolt
34. Steering damper
35. Steering gear mounting clamp
36. Steering drop arm
37. Clamping screw
38. Steering knuckle
39. Steering arm mounting bolt
40. Brake back plate
41. Caliper

Cross-sectional view, ball joint front suspension incorporated in current Volkswagen

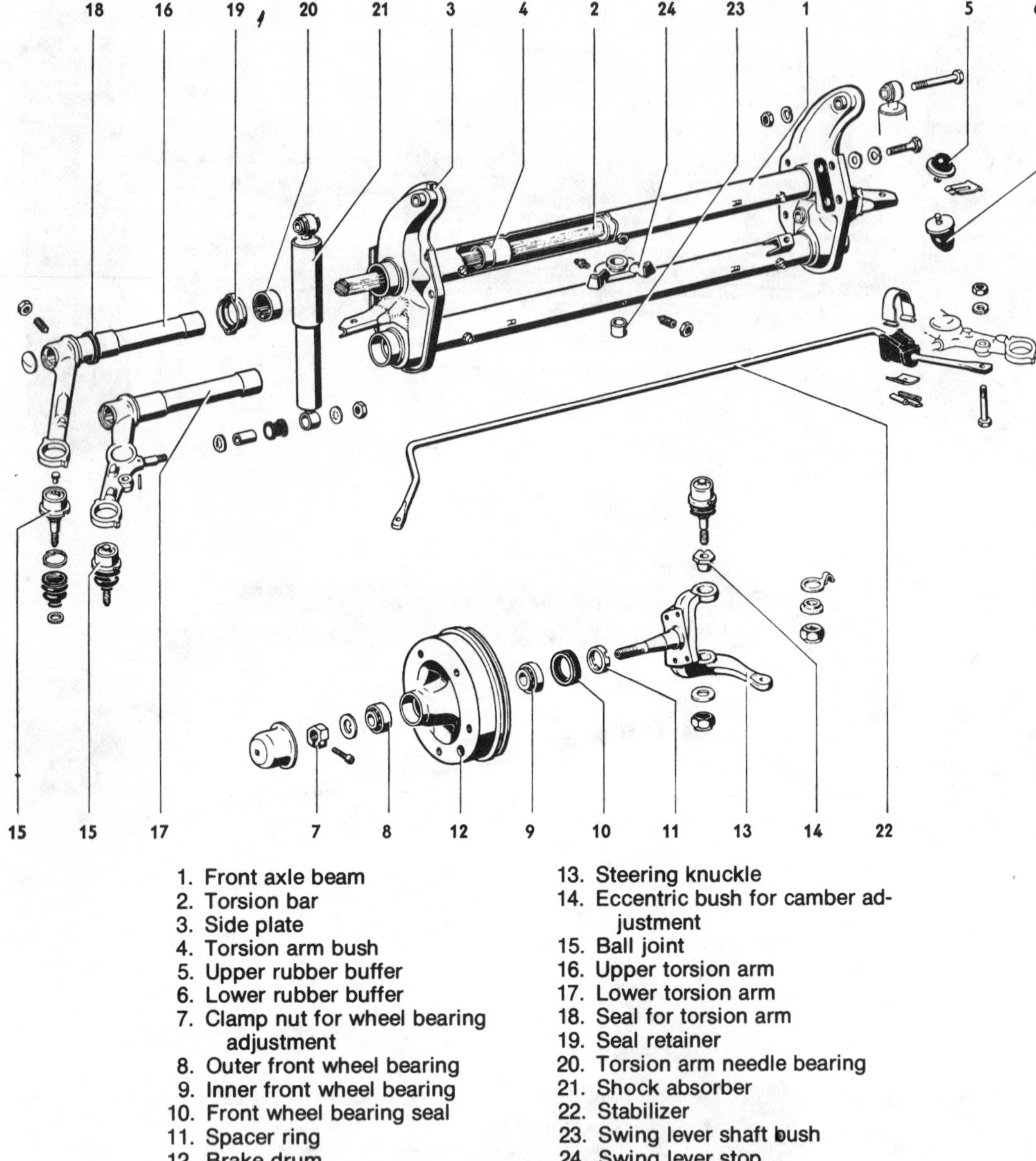

1. Front axle beam
2. Torsion bar
3. Side plate
4. Torsion arm bush
5. Upper rubber buffer
6. Lower rubber buffer
7. Clamp nut for wheel bearing adjustment
8. Outer front wheel bearing
9. Inner front wheel bearing
10. Front wheel bearing seal
11. Spacer ring
12. Brake drum
13. Steering knuckle
14. Eccentric bush for camber adjustment
15. Ball joint
16. Upper torsion arm
17. Lower torsion arm
18. Seal for torsion arm
19. Seal retainer
20. Torsion arm needle bearing
21. Shock absorber
22. Stabilizer
23. Swing lever shaft bush
24. Swing lever stop

Exploded view, front suspension of Transporter models. Note steering gear swing lever in middle of lower torsion arm housing

BRAKES

The Hydraulic Brake System

Since 1950, all Volkswagens imported to the U.S. have been equipped with hydraulic brakes. The brakes of the Squareback and Fastback sedans are of the disc/drum type, with discs on the front and conventional drums at the rear. The 1500 Karmann Ghia is also provided with discs at the front, while the beetle models are, at this writing, still equipped with drums front and rear. The type 2 models were equipped with front discs starting in 1971.

The hydraulic braking system functions as follows:

When the brake pedal is depressed, force is transmitted to the master cylinder via the push rod. The pressure generated at the master cylinder then travels through the system to the wheel cylinder or caliper, depending on the type of brake at the end of the line. With the drum brake arrangement, the

Rear suspension, Fastback Sedan with swing axles. Note the transverse auxiliary spring seen above flywheel housing

wheel cylinder expands and forces the brake shoes against the inside of the brake drum. In the disc brake, the caliper pinches the friction pads against the disc. Because the disc is out in the open, rather than enclosed like the drum, the heat is dissipated more rapidly, and brake fading is experienced only under the most unusual conditions. The rear brakes, which are generously proportioned relative to the work required of them, are also difficult to fade.

Because of the rearward weight distribution of the Volkswagen, braking is aided considerably. With the conventional car, braking transfers weight to the front, making the weight distribution grossly unequal between the front and the rear. As a result, the front brakes do more than their share of the work while the rear brakes, with little or no weight on their wheels, simply lock up and skid during panic stops. This is where the Volkswagen's rear weight bias really becomes an advantage. When a Volkswagen is stopped in a hurry, the transfer of weight to the front only serves to equalize the weight on all four wheels. Under severe braking conditions, the conventional 60/40 car may become a 70/30 car, with 70% of its weight on the front

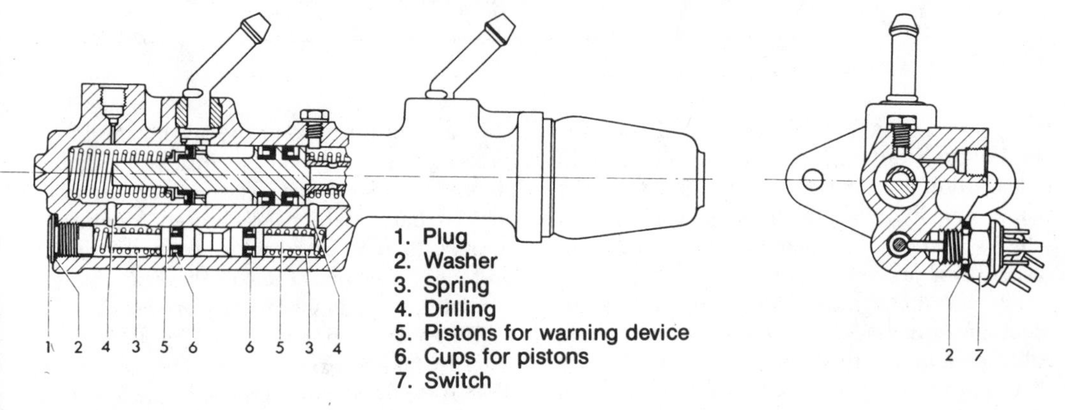

Cross-sectional view of dual circuit brake system—if one circuit fails, the other will stop the car. A warning light tells when either system is not operational

Brake Specifications

Vehicle	Model	Type		Brake Cylinder Bore (in.)			Brake Drum or Disc Diameter (in.)	
		Front	Rear	Master Cylinder	Wheel Cylinder Front	Wheel Cylinder Rear	Front	Rear
Type 1	25 hp., 36 hp. 1,200cc.	Drum ①	Drum	.750	.750	.690	9.05 ±.008	9.05 ±.008
	40hp. 1,200 and 1,300cc.	Drum	Drum	.687	.874	.750	9.059 ±.008	9.055 ±.008
	1,500 and 1,600cc. Single Master Cylinder	Drum	Drum	.687	.875	.687	9.059 ±.008	9.055 ±.008
	1,500 and 1,600cc.– Tandem Master Cylinder	Drum	Drum	.750	.875	.687	9.059 ±.008	9.055 ±.008
	1971 Models	Drum	Drum	.750	.94	.69	9.76	9.06
	Karmann Ghia	Disc	Drum	NA	1.574	.687	10.9	NA
	Karmann Ghia, 1971	Disc	Drum	NA	NA	NA	10.9	9.06
Type 2	Tandem Master Cylinder	Drum	Drum	.875	1.00	.875	9.843 +.008	9.843 +.008
	1971 Models	Disc	Drum	.813	.874	.875	10.9	9.92
Type 3	Tandem Master Cylinder	Disc	Drum	.750	1.653	.875	10.9	9.768 +.008
	1971 Models	Disc	Drum	.813	NA	.875	10.9	9.92

① *Some early models have mechanical brakes.*

wheels and only 30% on the rear. However, the Volkswagen, with its normal 40/60 weight distribution, approaches the 50/50 mark when heavily braked, thus giving all four wheels an equal chance to help in the slowing-down process.

The VW hand brake is mechanically actuated, and operates on the rear wheels via a cable running to the rear.

Disc Brakes

The principal components of the disc brakes are the disc, friction pad, caliper and splash shield. The purpose of the splash shield is to protect the inside of the disc from damage due to stones or dirt. The caliper housing is in two parts, which are bolted together by four bolts. The disc brakes are self-adjusting and need no maintenance except changing the friction pads when they are worn.

When friction pads need replacing, it is best to take it easy on the new ones for the first 100 miles or so. This is because the surfaces of the pads become very hard during this period of normal usage. If the brakes are used severely during the first 100 miles after installing new friction pads, the lives of the

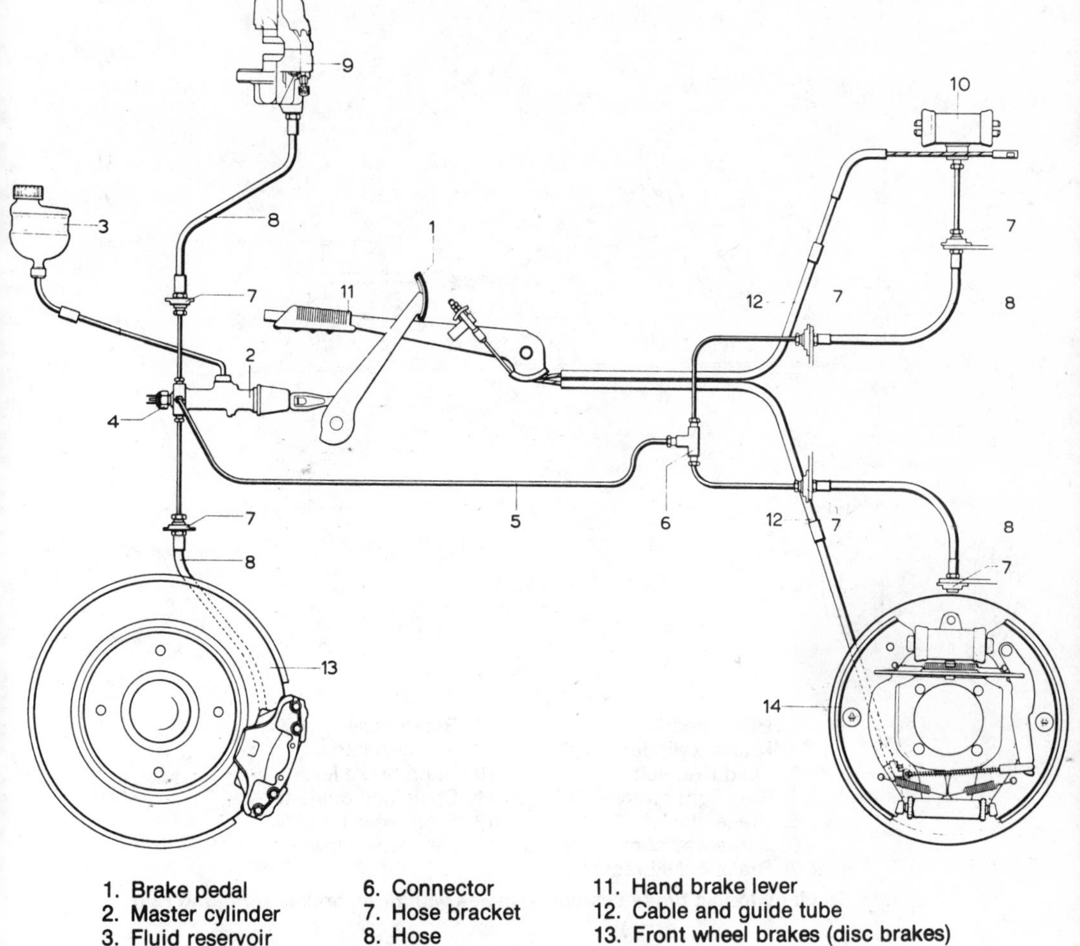

1. Brake pedal
2. Master cylinder
3. Fluid reservoir
4. Stop light switch
5. Brake line
6. Connector
7. Hose bracket
8. Hose
9. Brake caliper
10. Wheel cylinder
11. Hand brake lever
12. Cable and guide tube
13. Front wheel brakes (disc brakes)
14. Rear wheel brakes (drum brakes)

Single circuit hydraulic brake system, vehicles with the disc/drum brakes front/rear

pads will be significantly shortened. When friction pads are replaced, it is good practice to replace both pads on each of the front wheels. A special VW repair set is available for this purpose.

R & R FRICTION PADS

Replacement of the friction pads is easily done. After raising the front of the car, remove the wheel. Use a punch to drive out the upper retaining pin. Remove the friction pad expander spring, and drive out the lower retaining pin. The friction pads can now be removed via a special extractor tool.

On installation of friction pads, discard pads that are dirty or badly scored and put in four new ones. If the old pads are to be reused, they should be carefully cleaned.

Using a special tool, push the pistons away from the disc. Before carrying out this part of the operation, however, it is a good idea to remove some fluid from the brake fluid reservoir so that it does not overflow. Clean the calipers with alcohol. Sharp edged tools and mineral based solvents should not be used. The retaining plates are removed for the purpose of cleaning, and should be replaced if damaged or corroded. When replacing the retaining plate, be sure that it is installed so that the center part is firmly pressed into the center of the piston, and is below the piston cutaway. The piston should be at an angle of 20°.

The brake pads may now be inserted. Care should be taken to ensure that they move freely in the caliper housing. Insert the lower retaining pin, using a punch of a larger diameter than the pin itself. Install a new friction pad expanding spring. Insert the upper retaining pin while at the same time pressing

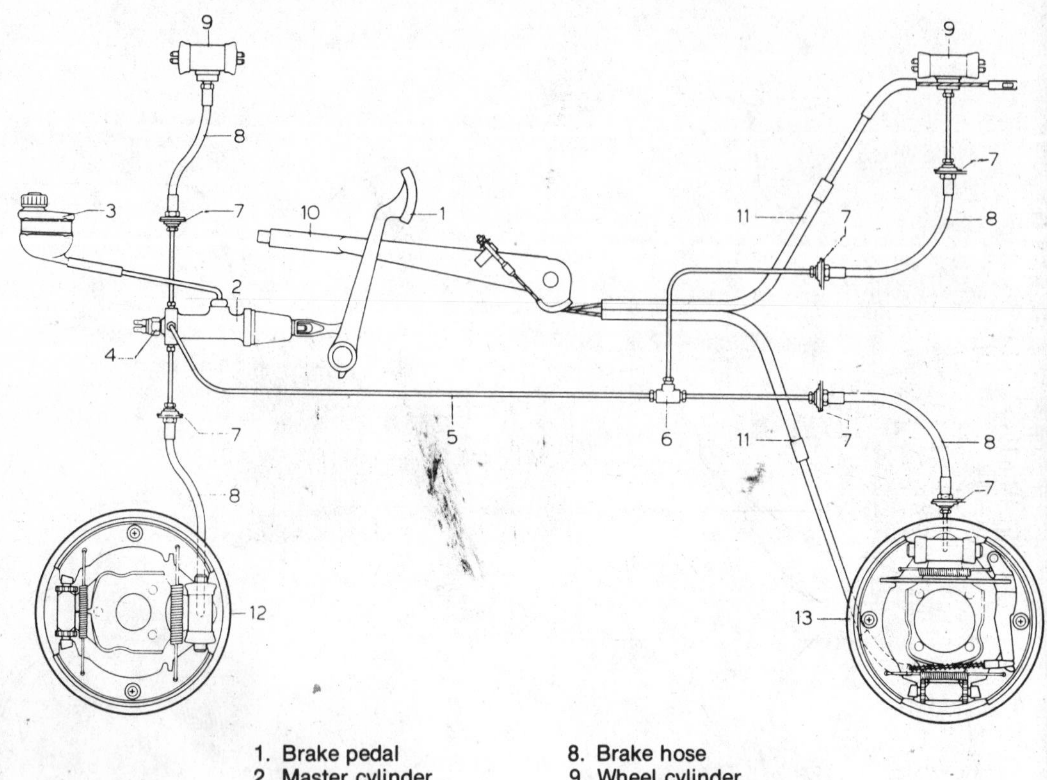

1. Brake pedal
2. Master cylinder
3. Fluid reservoir
4. Stop light switch
5. Brake line
6. Three-way connection
7. Brake hose bracket
8. Brake hose
9. Wheel cylinder
10. Hand brake lever
11. Cable and guide tube
12. Front wheel brake
13. Rear wheel brake

Single circuit hydraulic brake system, vehicles with drum brakes front and rear

down on the expander spring. While the vehicle is stationary, depress the brake pedal several times to enable the brake pads to settle into their correct positions. The level of brake fluid in the reservoir should be checked and the car taken on a test run.

Drum Brakes

The drum brakes of the type 1 Volkswagen are of the conventional type, with one leading and one trailing shoe per brake drum, and should present no unusual problem to anyone familiar with this type of system. The amount of brake lining remaining can be checked by looking through the holes provided in the drums.

SHOE REPLACEMENT—DRUM BRAKES (FRONT)

Remove the front wheel and grease cap. Remove the cotter pin from the speedometer drive cable (left wheel) before removing the grease cap. Remove the brake drum, the shoe retainer spring assemblies and the front shoe return springs. Take one brake shoe out of the slot of the adjuster, and remove both shoes from the back plate. When the brake drum has been removed and the brake shoes taken out, care should be taken to ensure that the brake pedal is not depressed through accident or carelessness. If this occurs, the result will be an unchecked expansion of the wheel cylinder and its parts, and a loss of brake fluid.

Before installing new brake shoes, be sure that both front wheels are using the same type of lining. Any difference in lining type, or the use of a lining of the wrong width, can lead only to uneven braking at best, and to a dangerous accident at worst. Care should also be taken to install the shoes correctly. The stronger return spring and the slots in the brake shoes should be at the wheel cylinder side of the assembly. The adjustor slots should be positioned as shown in the accompanying illustration. The brake shoe return springs should be positioned as shown in the

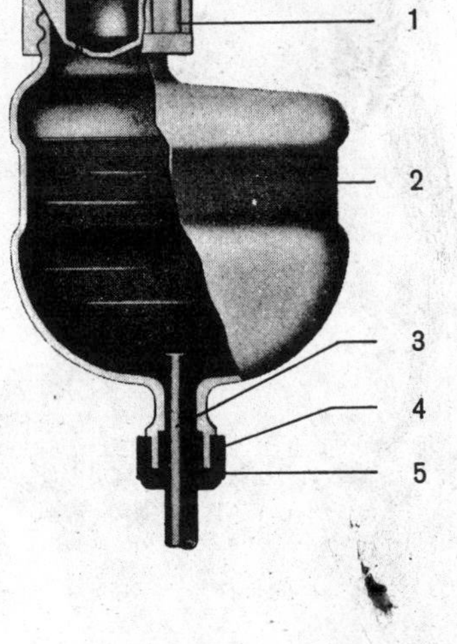

1. Screw cap
2. Fluid reservoir
3. Brake line
4. Line attaching nut
5. Seal for brake line
6. Stop light switch
7. Master cylinder body
8. Special check valve
9. Piston return spring
10. Main cup
11. By-pass port
12. Piston washer
13. Rubber plug
14. Washer for rubber plug
15. Intake port
16. Piston
17. Secondary cup
18. Piston stop plate
19. Lock ring
20. Piston push rod
21. Rubber boot

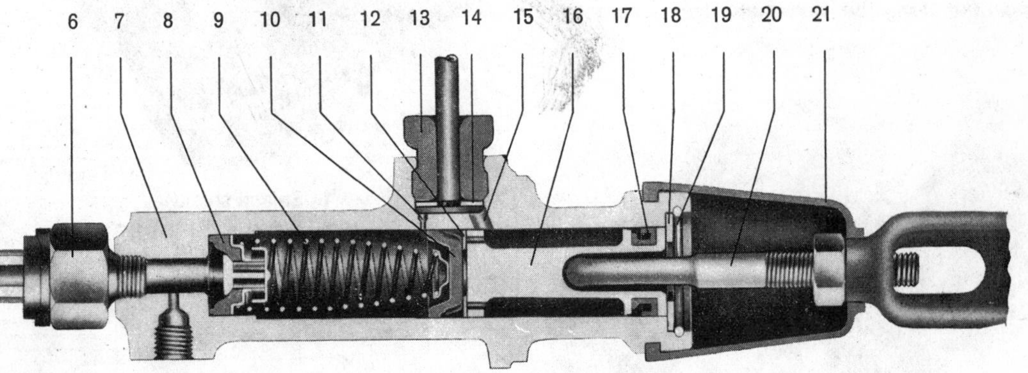

Cross-sectional view, single circuit master cylinder and reservoir

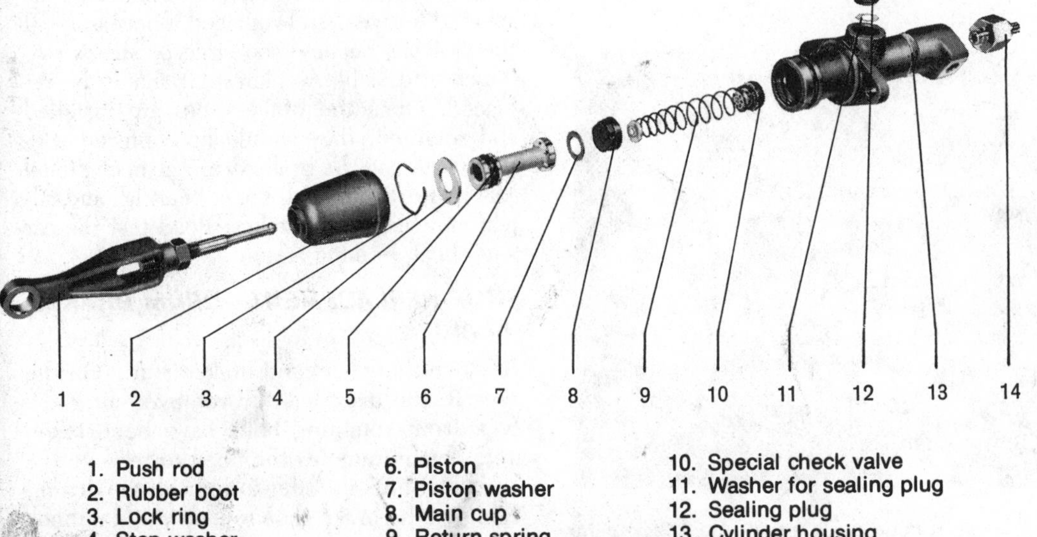

1. Push rod
2. Rubber boot
3. Lock ring
4. Stop washer
5. Secondary cup
6. Piston
7. Piston washer
8. Main cup
9. Return spring
10. Special check valve
11. Washer for sealing plug
12. Sealing plug
13. Cylinder housing
14. Stop light switch

Exploded view, single circuit master cylinder

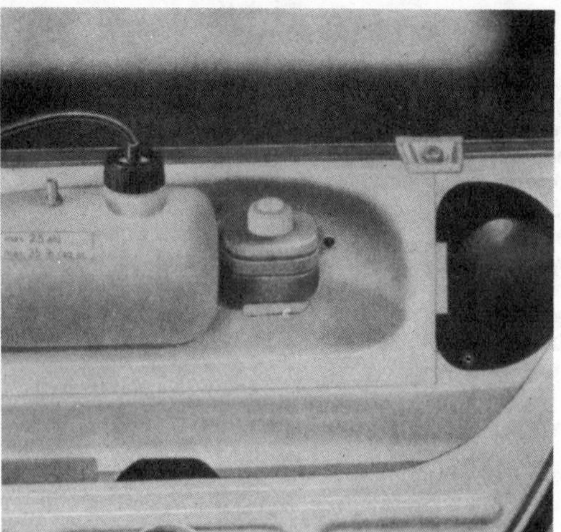

On pre-1968 type 1 models, brake fluid reservoir is mounted alongside windshield washer container

Friction pads, disc brakes. Each brake uses two friction pads

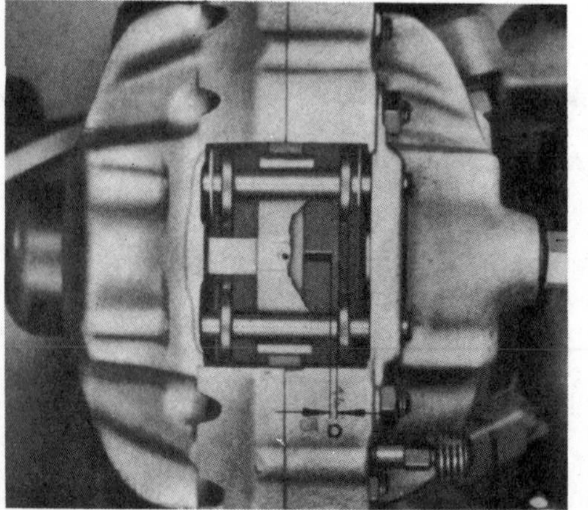

Disc brake friction pads should be checked for wear every 6,000 miles. Pads that have a thickness (dimension "a") of 2mm. or less should be replaced

1. Splash shield
2. Brake disc
3. Brake caliper

Disc brakes are standard equipment on all Type 3 Volkswagens

accompanying illustration. The brake shoe return springs should be hooked in from the front so that there is no chance of interference with shoe operation. The two brake shoe retainers should also be replaced at this time. The slotted retainer cup should be inspected for wear and replaced if necessary. If the slot has become too large or shows evidence of possible weakness, it should be replaced. Once the brake shoes are installed and retained, they should be centered. Before replacing the brake drum inspect the oil seal. Adjust the front wheel bearings and adjust and bleed the brakes. Road test the car and check braking action.

SHOE REPLACEMENT—DRUM BRAKES (REAR)

Remove the wheel and brake drum. (On the type 3, the drum can be removed after the two drum retaining bolts have been taken out. This eliminates the need to remove the axle shaft nuts in order to remove the drum.) Remove the brake shoe retainers and unhook the lower return spring. (There are two lower return springs on the rear brakes of the type 3.) Remove upper return spring, handbrake

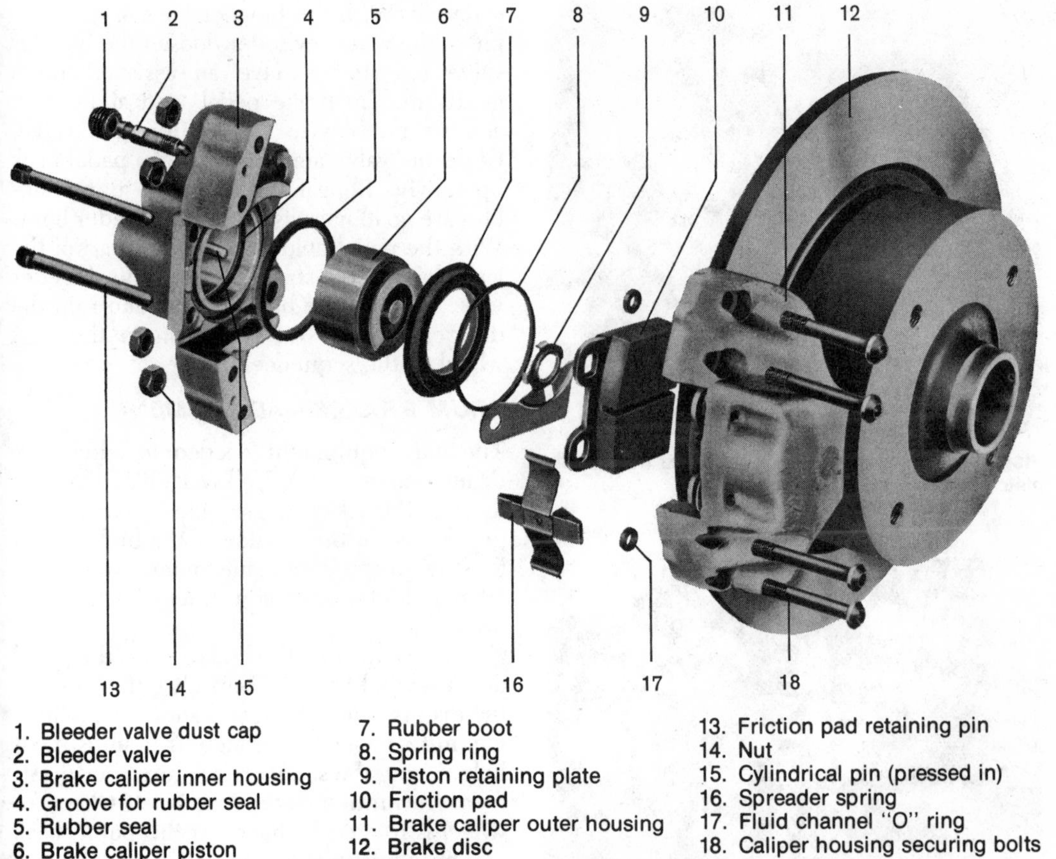

1. Bleeder valve dust cap
2. Bleeder valve
3. Brake caliper inner housing
4. Groove for rubber seal
5. Rubber seal
6. Brake caliper piston
7. Rubber boot
8. Spring ring
9. Piston retaining plate
10. Friction pad
11. Brake caliper outer housing
12. Brake disc
13. Friction pad retaining pin
14. Nut
15. Cylindrical pin (pressed in)
16. Spreader spring
17. Fluid channel "O" ring
18. Caliper housing securing bolts

Exploded view, disc brake as used on type 3

cable, and the brake shoe with lever. The lever is held onto the rear brake shoe by a circlip.

Installation of the rear brake shoes is in the opposite sequence. Be sure to install the proper linings on each of the rear wheels. Install the front brake shoe and attach its retaining assembly. The front brake shoe of the type 3 should be positioned as shown in the accompanying picture. Install the rear brake shoe with handbrake lever, connecting link, and upper return spring and clip. Fasten retainer assembly to the rear brake shoe, and attach the handbrake cable end to the lever on the rear shoe. Be sure to position the adjuster slots properly. Install lower return spring(s), adjust the brakes and bleed the brake system. If the axle nut was removed to allow removal of the brake drum, tighten it to a torque of 217 ft. lbs.

BRAKE SHOES—RELINING

A VW parts department is the most reliable place to obtain replacement linings or shoes.

When removing linings from shoes, take care not to damage or distort the shoes. Clean the shoes and remove any burrs from the rivet holes. The linings should fit squarely on the shoe and the rivets be pressed in vertically from the center outwards.

BLEEDING THE BRAKES

When a brake line is disconnected for any reason or the brake pedal action becomes spongy, the hydraulic brake system must be bled and the fluid reservoir topped up. The usual cause of a spongy brake is the presence of air somewhere in the system. Only Lockheed or Genuine VW brake fluid should be used.

An assistant will make the job easier when bleeding the brakes. Remove the dust caps from the bleeder valves at the wheel cylinders. As shown, place a container of brake fluid atop the fluid reservoir to keep it full during the bleeding operation. The cylinders may be bled satisfactorily in the sequence suggested by the diagram, beginning with the wheel cylinder farthest from the master

Piston retaining pliers are needed to push both pistons back

Insertion of friction pads into caliper

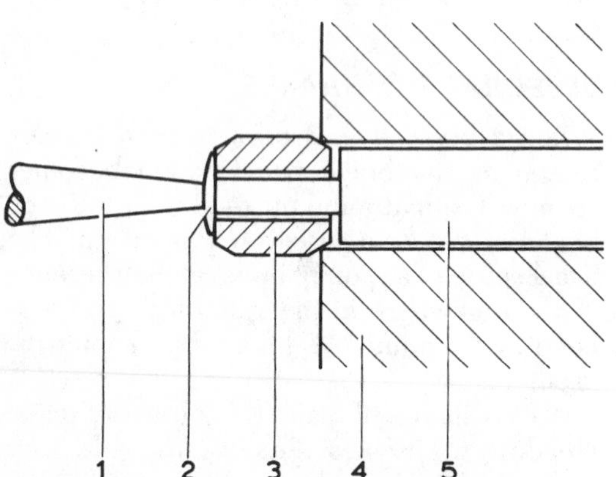

1. Punch (too small)
2. Endangered retaining pin shoulder
3. Split clamping bush
4. Housing
5. Retaining pin

Punch shown is too small to drive in friction pad retaining pin. The split clamping bush could shear off the shoulder of the pin.

cylinder. With the bleeder hose on the nipple of the wheel cylinder, loosen the bleeder valve one turn. Have an assistant press gently on the brake pedal, and allow fluid and air bubbles to escape from the valve. Close the valve and let the brake pedal back up slowly. Repeat the operation until bubbles are no longer visible in the bleeder hose. With the pedal held in the lowest part of the last downward stroke, close the bleeder valve, remove the bleeder hose and refit the dust cap to the valve. Go on to the next wheel in the sequence.

DRUM BRAKES—ADJUSTMENT

The only equipment needed to adjust the drum brakes of the Volkswagen is a screwdriver. Pre-1966 Volkswagens have an adjuster hole in the outside of the brake drum for the purpose of adjustment. Models of 1966 and later have adjustment holes in the back plate.

Before adjusting the brakes press the pedal down several times to centralize the shoes in the drums. Turn the wheel so that an adjusting nut is visible through the adjustment hole. Using the screwdriver, turn the adjustment nut until a slight drag is felt when the wheel is rotated by hand. At this point, back off the adjusting nut until the wheel turns freely (about 3 or 4 teeth of the adjusting nut will pass the adjustment hole). Move on to the other adjusting nut of the wheel. The adjustment nuts on each wheel turn in opposite directions, so whichever direction of rotation was needed to tighten one shoe will loosen the adjustment of the other shoe. The handbrake is adjusted by means of adjusting nuts at the rear of the control lever inside the car. However, when the rear brakes are adjusted, the handbrake is automatically adjusted also. If this is not enough to hold the rear wheels at 4 notches, the hand brake should be adjusted by means of the adjusting nuts. When the brake lever is applied by 2 notches, both rear wheels should resist turning by an equal amount of force. If for some reason, it were necessary to use the handbrake to stop in an emergency, it could be dangerous if both rear wheels did not tend to lock equally.

Wheels and Tires

Maximum tire life depends on proper care and on good driving habits.

Tire pressures should be checked often. The correct pressures are given in the

Front wheel brake

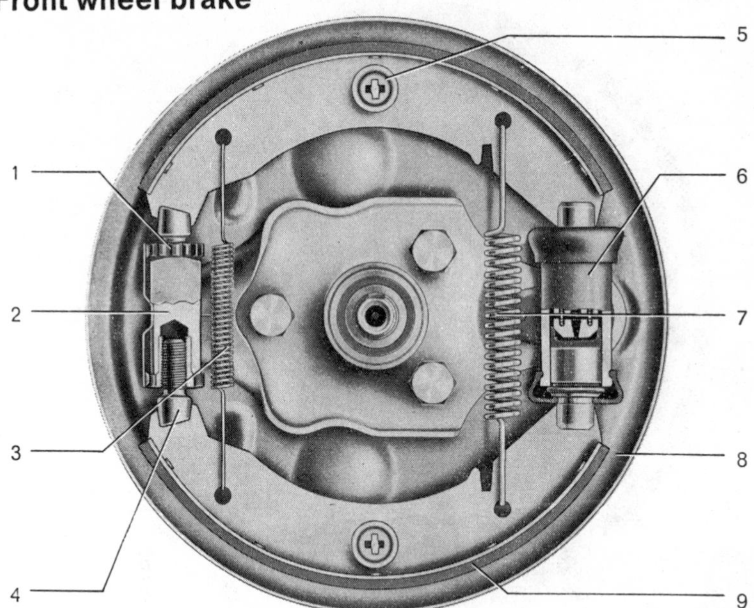

Rear wheel brake

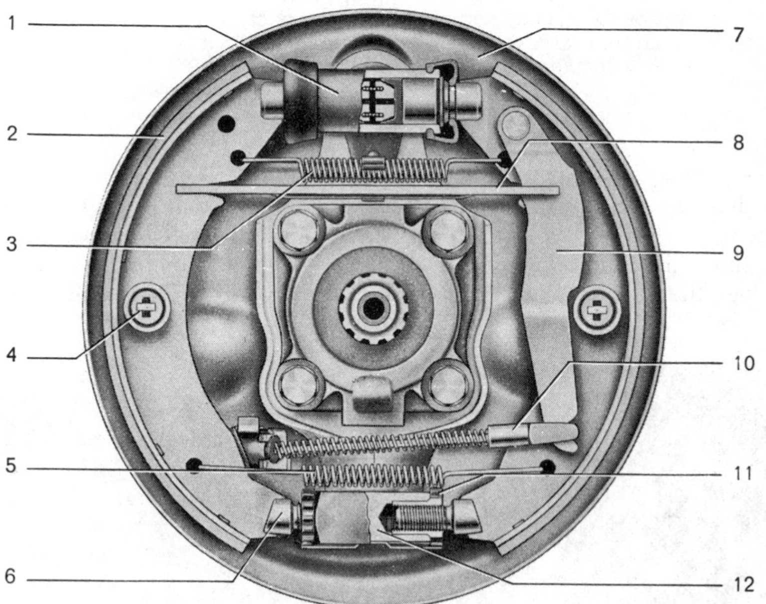

FRONT
1. Adjusting screw
2. Anchor block
3. Front return spring
4. Adjusting nut
5. Guide spring with cup and pin
6. Cylinder
7. Rear return spring
8. Back plate
9. Brake shoe with lining

REAR
1. Cylinder
2. Brake shoe with lining
3. Upper return spring
4. Spring with cup and pin
5. Lower return spring
6. Adjusting screw
7. Back plate
8. Connecting link
9. Lever
10. Brake cable
11. Adjusting nut
12. Anchor block

Cross-sectional view, front and rear drum brakes as used on Type 1 vehicles

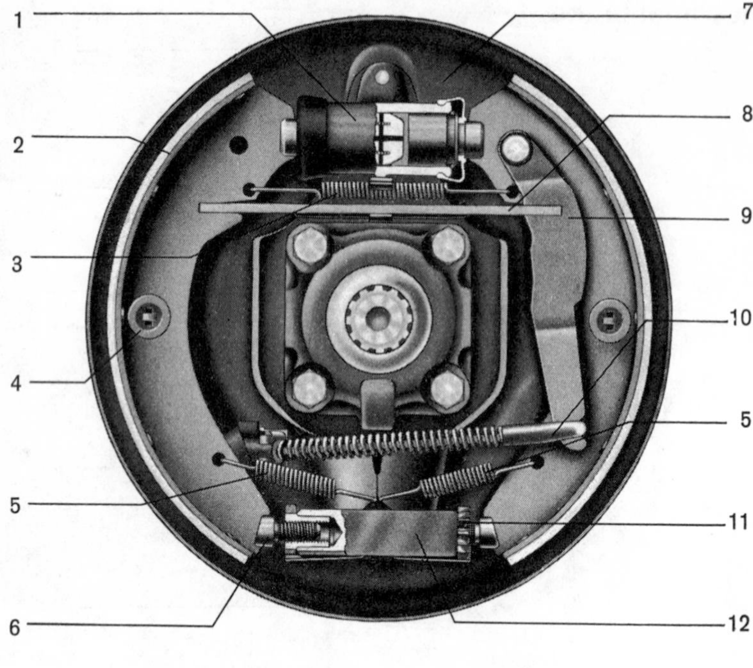

1. Cylinder
2. Brake shoe with lining
3. Upper return spring
4. Spring with cup and pin
5. Lower return spring
6. Adjusting screw
7. Back plate
8. Connecting link
9. Lever
10. Brake cable
11. Adjusting nut
12. Anchor block

Rear brake of Type 3 Volkswagen

owner's manual and on a sticker inside the glove compartment.

The pressures should be checked when the tires are cold. When the tires have been running, pressures will be higher. Air pressure should not be reduced in a warm tire in order to achieve the recommended cold pressure, because the tire will then be under-inflated

Rear brake cable (for handbrake) must be removed from operating lever before brake shoe can be removed. Brake shown is rear brake of Type 3 vehicle

Type 1 vehicle, disconnecting brake cable from operating lever

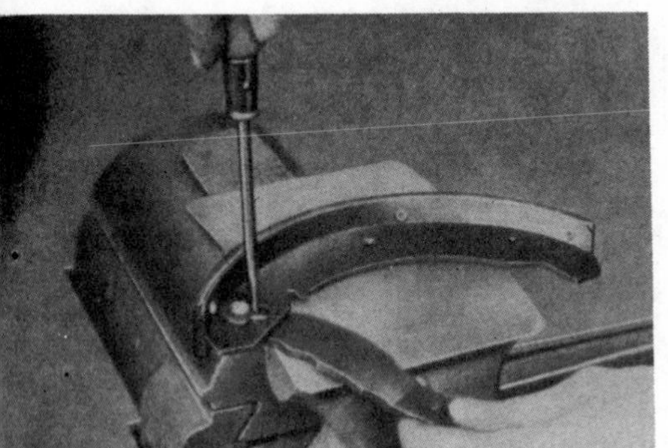

Lever can be removed from brake shoe after retaining clip is taken off

Rivets should be pressed in vertically to prevent tension in the linings

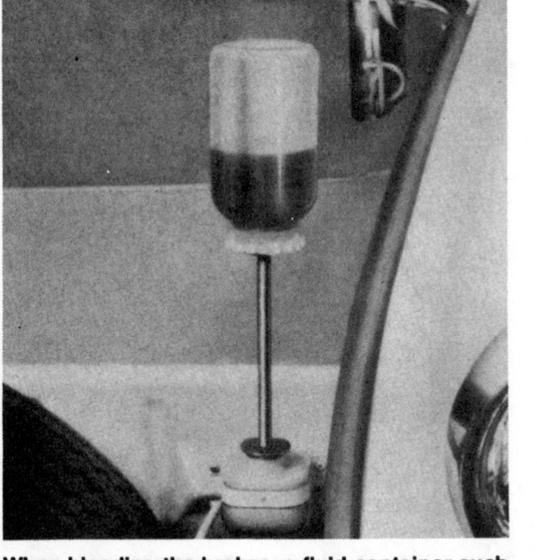

When bleeding the brakes, a fluid container such as this is used to keep the reservoir full of fluid

Brake bleeder hose and container

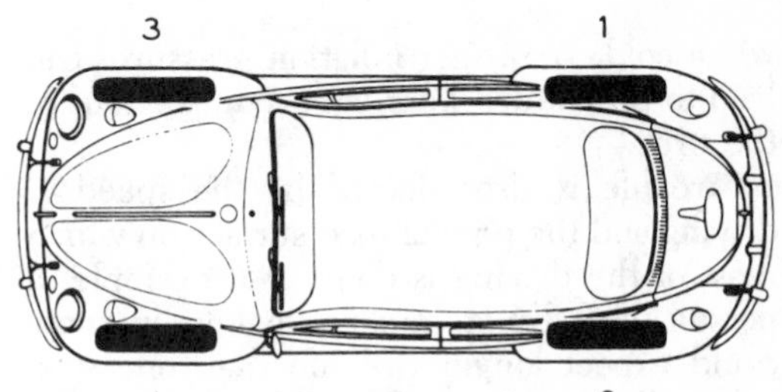

Suggested sequence of brake bleeding starts at the wheel cylinder farthest from the master cylinder

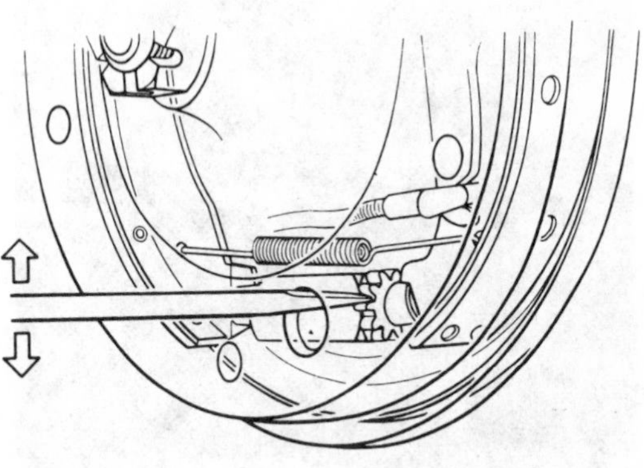

Brake adjustment nuts, drum brakes. When the wheel drags slightly, the adjusting nut should be backed off 3 or 4 notches until the wheel turns freely

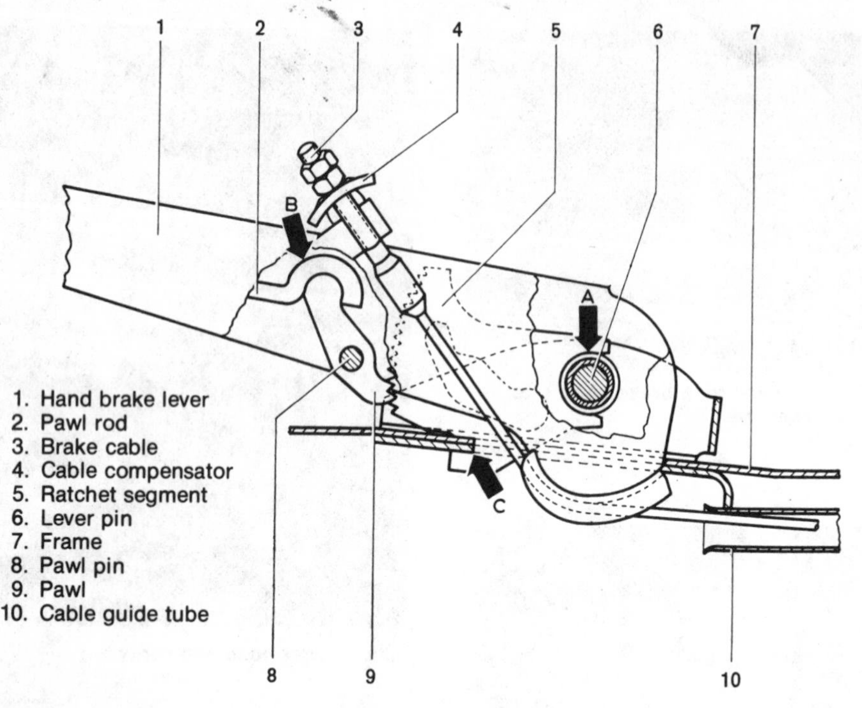

Cross-sectional view, hand brake

when cold. Improper inflation pressures can lead to premature wear in certain sections of the tires.

Tire life is also affected by the speed of driving and the type of road surface on which most of the driving is done. For example, a person who drives at slow speeds on snow could expect longer tire life than one who habitually drives at full speed across steaming Death Valley. The effects of speed and heat on tire life are expressed in the tables included in this section.

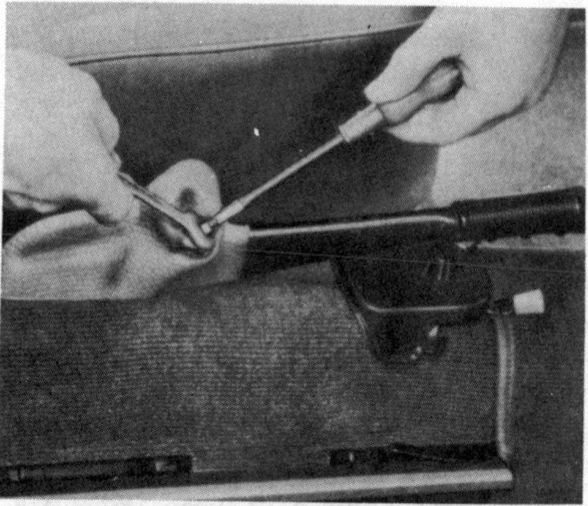

Adjusting the hand brake. When the brake is pulled up 4 notches, it should not be possible to turn the rear wheels by hand

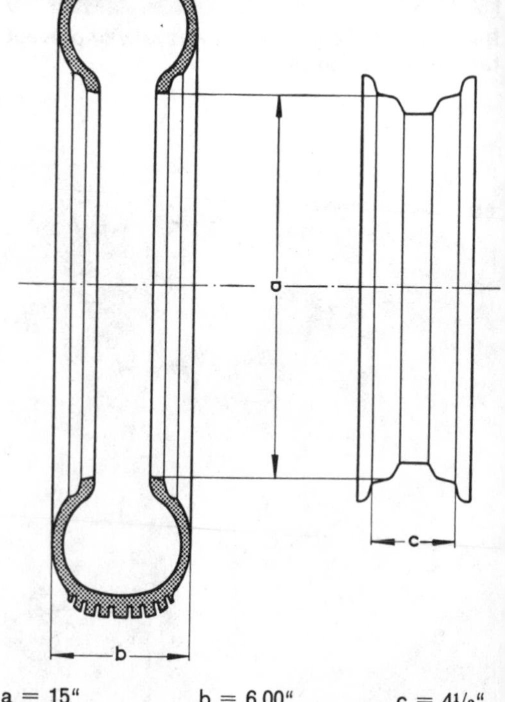

Cross-sectional view of 6.00 x 15 wheel and tire used on type 3

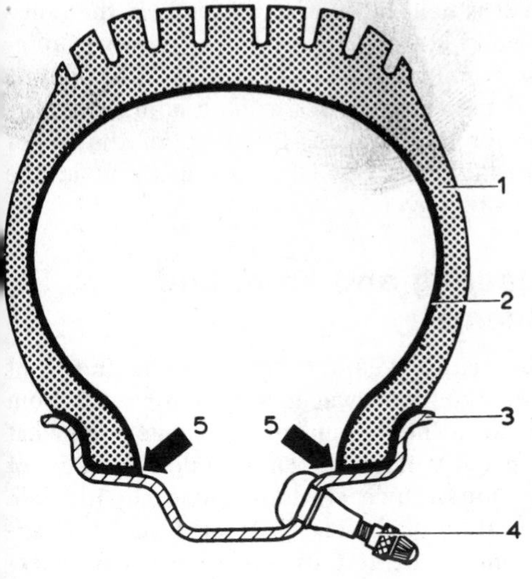

1. Tubeless tire
2. Air retaining lining
3. Rim flange
4. Valve
5. Rim sealing surface

Cross-section of tubeless tire as used on all Volkswagens

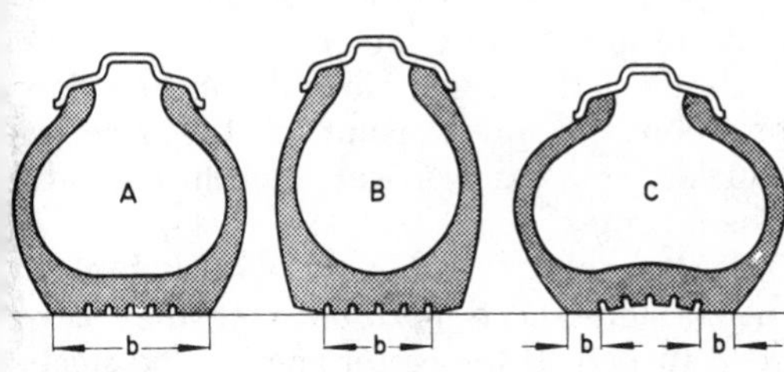

The effects of normal (A), too-high (B), and too-low (C) inflation. Dimension "b" is the contact with the road surface

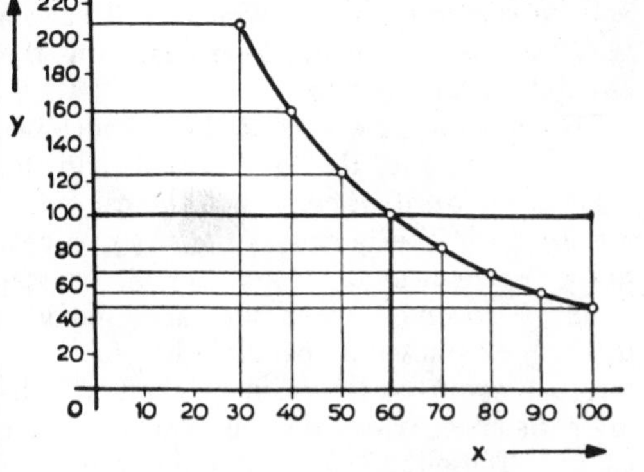

x = average speed (kph).
y = tire life as a % of normal value

The effect of speed on tire life. Normal tire life (100%) is based on average speed of 60 kph (37 mph)

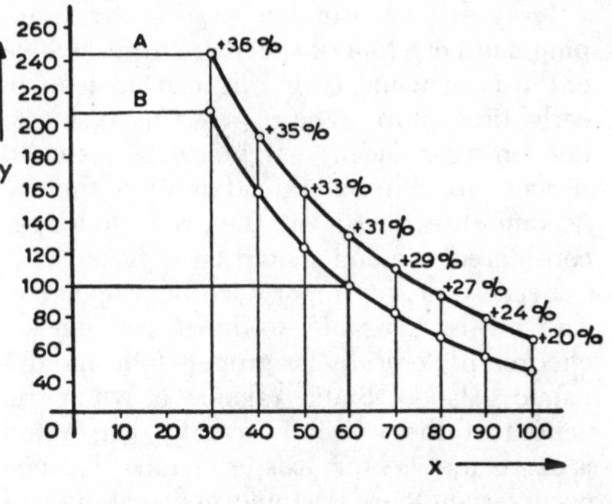

A = Winter B = Summer
x = average speed (kph).
y = Life of tire as a % of normal.

Effect of temperature on tire life. Note that tire wear is significantly greater during the summer months

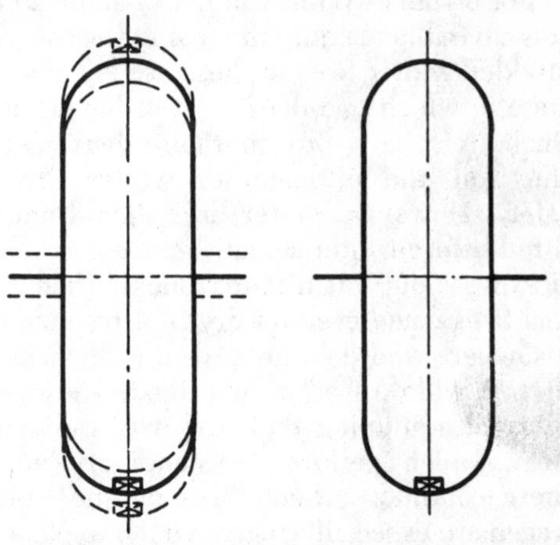

Wheel shown is out of balance statically; weight is not evenly distributed about the axis of the wheel

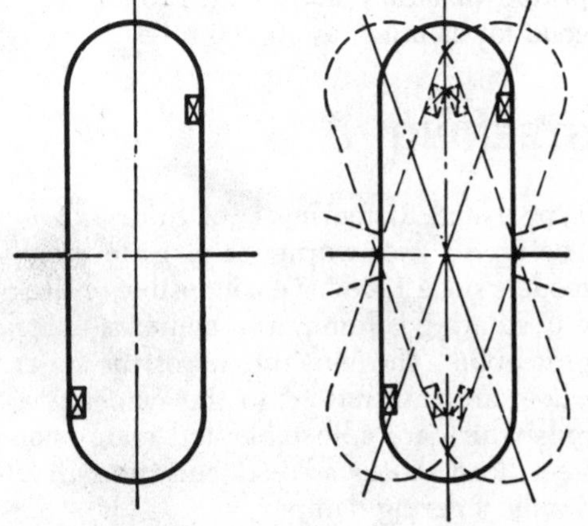

Wheel shown is not balanced dynamically; weight is not uniformly distributed in relation to the vertical centerline of the wheel

Jerky driving—sudden starting and stopping and changing of speeds—and excessive enthusiasm while cornering can all lead to early tire failure. These practices result in uneven wear and in a significantly lessened service life. When the tread depth of the tire becomes less than 1/16″, the tire is no longer considered safe and should be replaced.

Because of the importance of proper tire care, it is advisable to have the wheels checked periodically for proper static and dynamic balance. Static balance is when the weight of the wheel is evenly distributed around the center axis; dynamic balance occurs when there is a uniform distribution of weight relative to the vertical centerline running through the wheel and tire. The accompanying illustrations are examples of tires that are out of balance both statically and dynamically.

For owners who live in heavy-snow areas, it is advisable to equip the rear of the car with studded winter tires, if these are legal in the state in which one does most of his driving. Such tires have proven themselves to be, thus far, the ultimate for winter driving safety. However, winter tires should not be fitted before winter actually arrives, for snow tires wear out much more quickly than normal tires when used on dry, hot pavement.

Owners who do a great deal of highspeed driving will do well to investigate the possibility of equipping their car with radial-ply tires, which perform outstandingly under these conditions. Such tires on the Volkswagen are especially attractive if one plans to keep his car for a long period of time. Radial ply tires usually last much longer than normal tires, so on the Volkswagen, it can be expected that they may, with proper care, be good for as much as 80,000 miles.

STEERING

Type 1 and 3 steering is of the roller type. The type 2 uses worm and peg steering. All models since 1968 have collapsible or breakaway steering column arrangements for crash protection. The movements of the steering wheel are transmitted to the wheels via tie rods which are adjustable and maintenance-free. Road shocks are reduced through a hydraulic steering damper.

The worm in the steering case is adjustable, and is engaged by a roller shaft with a needle bearing mounted roller. The roller shaft is held by bronze bushings in the housing and housing cover, while the worm spindle is mounted in ball bearings. The spindle and the roller shaft are both adjustable, the former by a washer fitted under the upper bearing, and the latter by a screw in the housing cover.

Steering and Front-End Geometry

The critical geometrical angles in the front end of the Volkswagen vary significantly from model to model and even change somewhat from early models to later models. Because of the importance of these angles to the safe operation of the car, it is suggested that adjustments be left to one's local VW workshop. However, for the enlightenment of technical-minded readers, a description of the relevant angles follows:

Camber is the angle, viewed from the front of the car, that the wheel is inclined from the vertical.

King pin inclination is the angle between a line perpendicular to the road and the pivot point of the steering knuckle.

Caster is the angle, viewed from the side, between the pivot point of the steering knuckle and the vertical line through the wheel center.

Caster helps to bring the wheels back to the straight-ahead position after they have been turned. If the caster angle is too small, the result will be a tendency for the car to wander and be excessively influenced by cross winds and uneven road surfaces.

If the camber angle is too great, steering will be difficult, for the wheels will have a very strong tendency to remain in the straight-ahead position.

Toe-in is the difference in the distance between the rear of the front wheels and the front of the front wheels when the car is facing forward. Toe-in causes the front wheels to be "pigeon-toed" when the car is stationary. However, when the car is moving, the wheels move in parallel due to being forced outward at the front by camber, rolling resistance, wheel bearing play and other factors. Toe-out occurs naturally when the wheel is turned in cornering so that there is a common center point around which all four wheels will turn when a curve is negotiated. If the critical angles are not what they should be, the result will be excessive tire scuffing and wear.

Chassis and Wheel Alignment Specifications

Vehicle	Model	Chassis (in.) Wheel-base	Track Front	Track Rear	Wheel Alignment Caster (deg.) (or in.)	Camber (deg.)	Toe-in. (in.) (or deg.) ④	King-Pin Inclination (deg.)	Rear Wheel Camber (deg.)	Wheel Pivot Ratio (deg.) Inner Wheel	Outer Wheel
Type 1	25 hp. and 36 hp. 1,200cc.	94.5	51	49.2	2°30′ ±30′	0°40′ ±30′	.04-.12	4°20′	NA	NA	NA
	42 hp. 1,200cc.	94.5	51.4	50.7	2°±15′	0°40′ ±30′	.08-.16	4°20′	3°±30′	34	28
	42hp. 1,200 and 1,300 cc.-after August, 1965	94.5	51.4	51.2	2°±15′	0°30′ ±15′	.08-.18	4°20′	3°±30′ ①	34	28
	1,500 cc. -Swing Axles	94.5	51.4	53.5	2°±15′	0°30′ ±15′	.08 -.18	4°20′	① 1°±1°	34	28
	1,500cc. and 1,600cc - Double Jointed Rear Axles	94.5	51.57	NA	3°20′ ±1°	30′ ±20′	30′± 15	5°	-1°20′ ±40′	34±2	28-1
	1971 Super Beetle with suspension struts	95.3	54.3	53.2	.008 in.	1°20′ ±20′	20′ ±15	NA	-1°20′ ±40′	40	35
Type 2	Pre-1968 -Swing Axles	94.5	54.1	53.5	3°±40′	40 ±30′	±.04 (5′±10′)	NA	3°±30′ ②	NA	NA
	After 1968- Double Jointed Rear Axles	94.5	54.5	56.2	3°±40′	40′±15′	10′ ±10′	5°	-50′ ±30′	32	24
	1971 -Disc brakes	94.5	54.6	56.6	NA	NA	NA	NA	NA	NA	NA
Type 3	With Swing Axles	94.5	51.58	52.99	4°±40′	1°20′ ±20′	40′ ±5′	NA	2°30′ ±1° ③	NA	NA
	With Double Jointed Rear Axles	94.5	51.58	53.14	4°±40′	1°20′ ±20′	40′ ±15′	5°10′	-1°20′ ±40′	30	27-1

NA - Information not available

① 1967 sedan: 1°±1°
1967 Karmann Ghia and VW convertible: 15′±1°

② After chassis No. 117 901:
Van: 4°±30′
Kombi: 3°30′±30′
Bus: 3°±30′

③ 1967 and later Notchback and Type 3 Karmann Ghia: 1°45′±1°

④ Size Wheel	*10′ toe-in equals:*
14in.	*.043 in.*
15in.	*.047 in.*
16in.	*.051 in.*

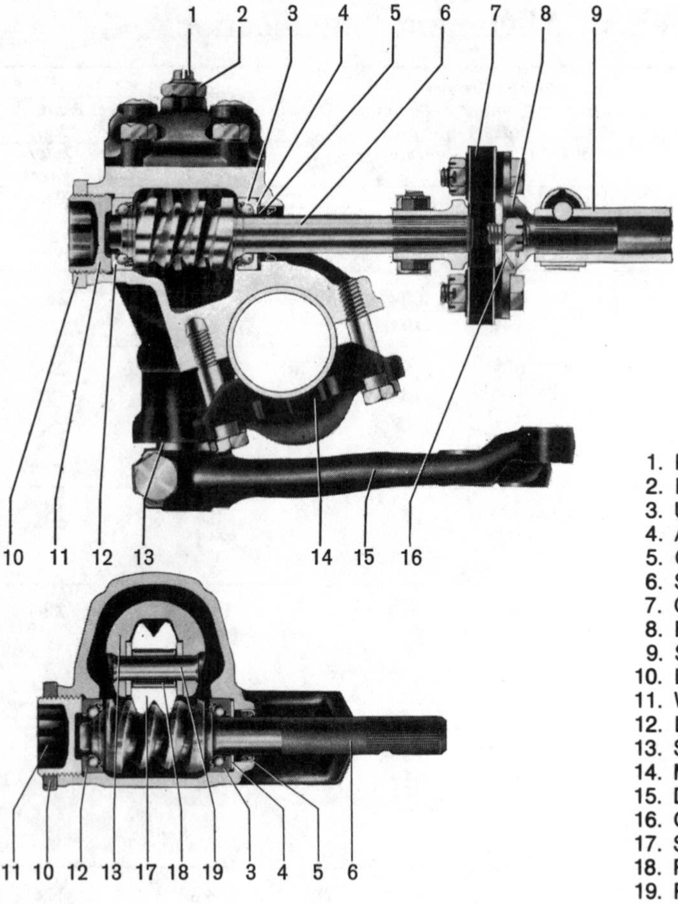

1. Roller shaft adjusting screw
2. Lock nut
3. Upper worm bearing
4. Adjusting shim for worm
5. Oil seal for worm
6. Steering worm
7. Coupling
8. Flange for coupling disc
9. Steering column
10. Lock nut
11. Worm adjusting screw
12. Lower worm bearing
13. Steering roller shaft
14. Mounting clamp
15. Drop arm
16. Ground connection terminal
17. Steering roller
18. Roller needle bearings
19. Roller support pin

Cross-sectional view, roller type steering gear

Steering Wheel—Correction of Angles

If the steering wheel spokes are not parallel to the floor of the car when the car is being driven in a straight line, it is necessary to reposition the wheel. This should never be carried out by simply altering the position of the wheel on the column. It requires that one tie rod be lengthened and the other shortened by the same amount. If the tie rod lengths are not changed by the same amount, the result will be a change in the toe-in of the car. The diagrams shown illustrate the direction in which to turn the two tie rods in case the steering wheel is slanted in either direction.

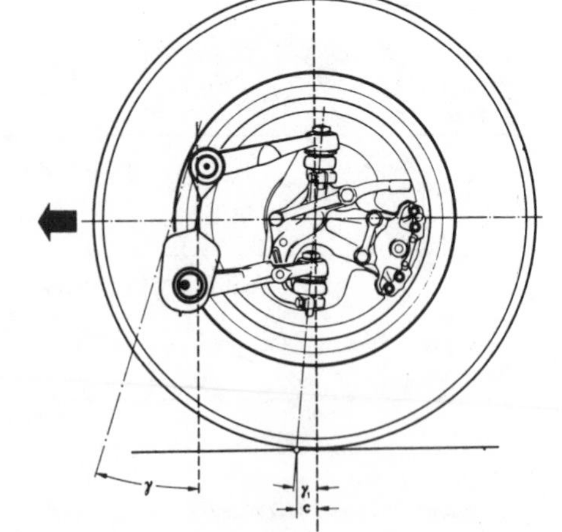

Angle γ = Axle beam angle
Angle γ_1 = Caster angle of steering knuckle (varies as suspension moves)

Caster and axle beam angles. Dotted lines are perpendicular to the road surface

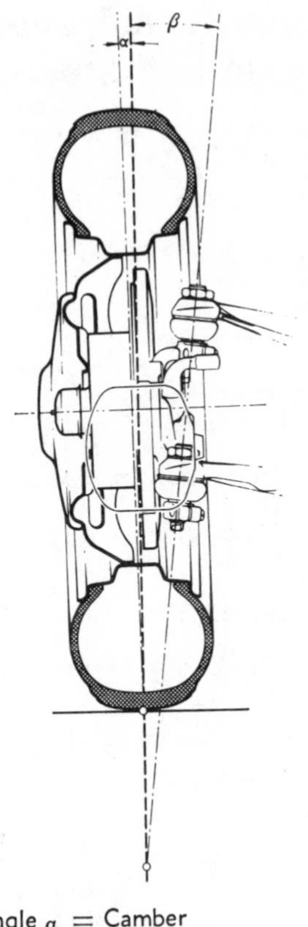

Angle α = Camber
Angle β = King pin inclination

Camber and king pin angles. Dotted line is perpendicular to the road surface

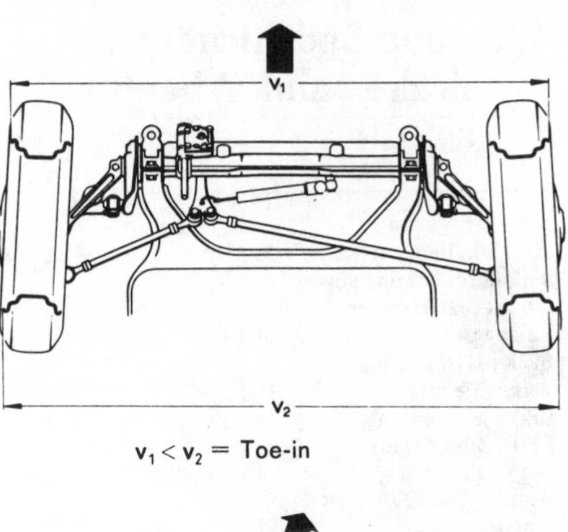

$v_1 < v_2$ = Toe-in

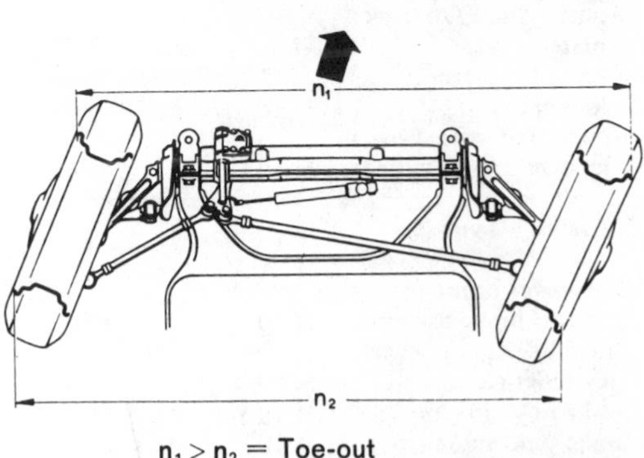

$n_1 > n_2$ = Toe-out

Toe-in and toe-out. Toe-out is designed into the steering system so that it occurs when the steering wheel is turned from the straight-ahead position

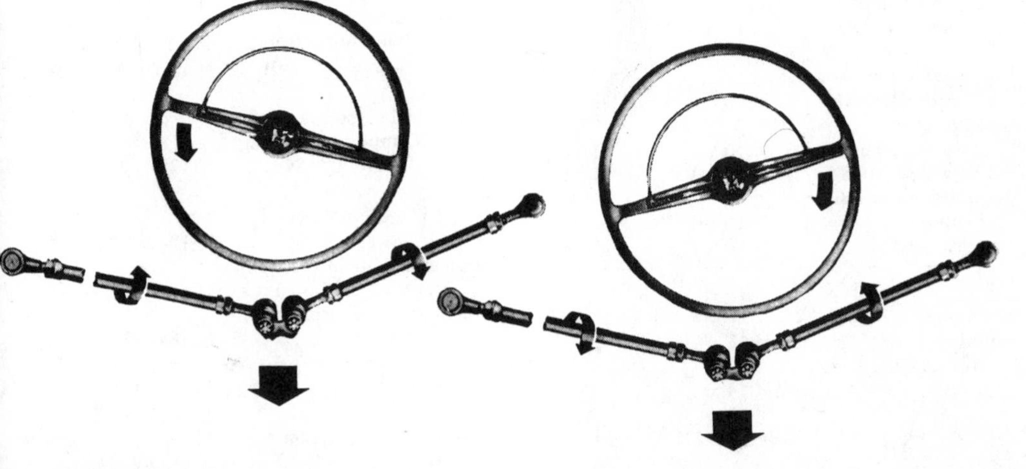

Steering wheel spokes should be in a horizontal position when the car is traveling in a straight line. If they are not, one tie rod must be shortened, and the other lengthened by the same amount so that toe-in is not affected

Torque Specifications— Brakes and Wheels

Fastener	Thread Size	Torque (ft.lbs.)
Brakes Type 1		
Master cylinder to frame	M 8	14-22
Screws for bearing cover/ back plate/bearing flange.	M 10	40-47
Back plate/steering knuckle screws	M 10	36
Brake hose unions	M 10 x 1	11-14
Brake pipe unions	M 10 x 1	11-14
Stop light switch	M 10 x 1	11-14
Wheel cylinder to back plate	M 8	14-22
Caliper to steering knuckle	M 10	36
Residual pressure valve in tandem master cylinder	M 12 x 1	14
Brakes Type 2		
Screws for bearing cover to rear brake back plate	M 10	40-43
Brake back plate/wheel cylinder front	M 10	40-43
Brake hose unions	M 10 x 1	11-14
Brake pipe unions	M 10 x 1	11-14
Stop light switch	M 10 x 1	11-14
Tandem master cylinder to brake servo	M 8	9
Brake servo to retaining retaining plate/front axle	M 8	9
Brakes Type 3		
Master cylinder to frame	M 8	14-22
Screws for bearing cover/ back plate rear	M 10 x 1.5	40-47
Wheel cylinders		
a - rear on back plate	M 8	18
b - front on back plate/steering knuckle	M 10 x 1	32
Disc brake caliper housing to steering knuckle	M 10	43
Brake hose at		
a - brake pipe	M 10 x 1	11-14
b - wheel cylinder	M 10 x 1	11-14
c- disc brake caliper housing	M 10 x 1	11
Stop light switch	M 10 x 1	11-14
Wheels		
Wheel bolts		
Type 1	M 12 x 1.5	72
from August 1965 (four hole wheel) ①	M 14 x 1.5	108
Type 2	M 14 x 1.5	94
Type 3	M 12 x 1.5	72
from August 1965 (four hole wheel)	M 14 x 1.5	108

① *Only on vehicle with disc brakes. For all from Chassis No. 118 000 001.*

Torque Specifications— Front Axle and Steering Gear

Fastener	Thread Size	Torque (ft.lbs.)
Type 1 Front Axle		
Front axle to frame	M 12 x 1.5	36
Shock absorber screw on side plate	M 12 x 1.5	22-25
Shock absorber nut on side plate	M 10	14
Shock absorber nut on lower tension arm	M 10	22-25
	M 12 x 1.5	36-50
Hexagon nuts for steering ball joints ⑤	or M 10 x 1	29-36
Inner wheel bearing nut	M 18 x 1.5	29 ①
Lock nut for wheel bearing	M 18 x 1.5	50 ①
Socket head screw in	M 7	
clamp nut	M 12 x 1.5	7-max. 9
Slotted nut on tie-rod	M 10 x 1	22 ③
Steering damper nut on tie-rod ⑤	M 10 x 1	18 ③
	M 10 x 1	18
Steering damper screw on axle tube	M 10	29-32
Setscrew for torsion bars	M 14 x 1.5	29-36
Locknut for setscrew	M 14 x 1.5	29-36
Caliper to steering knuckle	M 10	36
Clamping screw link pin to torsion arm	M 10	32
Screw for front axle support/front axle	M 12 x 1.5	40-43
Screw for front axle/ frame	M 10	40-43
Type 2 Front Axle		
Front axle/frame bolts (side member)	M 12 x 1.5	65-90
Shock absorber nut and bolt upper (from Chassis No. 971550)	M 12 x 1.5	36
	M 10	29-32
Shock absorber securing bolt, upper (up to Chassis No. 971549)	M 12 x 1.5	25-32
Shock absorber securing nut, lower	M 10	18-22
Steering knuckle/torsion arm (link pin bolts)	M 10	29-32
Ball joints to steering knuckle ⑤	M 18x 1.5	72
Inner wheel bearing nut	M 18 x 1 or M 22 x 1.5	25 ④
Wheel bearing locknut	M 18 x 1 or M22 x 1.5	50 ④
Tie-rod and draglink nuts	M 12 x 1.5	22 ③
	M 10 x 1	18 ③

Torque Specifications—Front Axle and Steering Gear

Fastener	Thread Size	Torque (ft.lbs.)
Type 1 and 3 Steering Gear		
Steering gear to axle-Type 1	M 10	18-22
Steering gear to axle-Type 3	M 10	18-22
Locknut for roller shaft adjusting screw	M 10 x 1	18
Steering gear cover screws	M 8 x 1.25	14-18
Screw securing drop arm to roller shaft	M 12 x 1.5	50
Steering wheel nut	M 18 x 1.5	36
Lock nut for steering worm adjustment screw	M 35 x 1.5	36-43
Hex. bolt for steering coupling to steering worm	M 8	14-18
Hex. nut. flange to coupling disc	M 8	11
Fillister head screw for self-cancelling ring on steering wheel	AM 3.5	3.6
Lock nut for tapered ring to tie rod	M 14 x 1.5	18
Clamping screw for tie rod retaining clip	M 8 x 1	11
Hex. bolt for steering column mounting plate to instrument panel	M 8	11
Screw for retainer eccentric bearing	M 8	11
Type 2 Steering gear		
Bracket to frame screws	M 10 x 22	29-32
Steering bos to bracket	M 10 x 40	25-36
Drop arm nut	M 20 x 1.5	58-80
Swing lever pinch bolt (from Chassis No. 20-117 901)	M 12 x 1.5	43
Upper and lower steering arm bolts (up to Chassis no.20-117 901)	M 12 x 1.5	47-54
Steering wheel nut	M 16 x 1.5	18-22
Hex. nut for flange to steering worm	M 8	14
Castellated nut for coupling disc to flange	M 8	11
Cheese head screw for steering column cap to floor plate	M 6	3.6
Steering gear case cover bolt	M 8	18
Steering gear and cover bolt	M 6	11

Fastener	Thread Size	Torque (ft.lbs.)
Steering damper/frame bolt and nut (up to Chassis No. 851 389)	M 10 x 45	32
Steering damper/axle tube screw (from Chassis No. 851 390)	M 10 x 40	29-32
Steering damper/ swing lever screw	M 10 x 72	29-32
Setscrew for torsion bars	M 14 x 1.5	29
Lock nut for setscrew	M 14 x 1.5	29
Stabilizer to torsion arm	M 10	25-36
	M 8	18
Screw for brake back plate to steering knuckle	M 10	36-43
Clamping screw for link pins to torsion bar	M 10	29-36
Type 3 Front axle		
Front axle securing bolts		
a - upper and lower	M 10	22
b - center	M 10	29
Grub screw securing torsion bars	M 14 x 1.5	22
Grub screw securing stabilizer	M 14 x 1.5	32-40
Lock nut for grub screw	M 14 x 1.5	29
Torsion bar to axle beam screws	M 10	29
Clamp screw stabilizer	M 10	29
Adjusting screw for stabilizer	M 8	7 ⑥
Shock absorber to axle beam screws	M 12 x 1.5	22-25
Shock absorber nut on torsion arm	M 10	22-25
Steering arm on steering knuckle	M 10 x 1	40
Nuts for upper and lower ball joints	M 20 x 1.5 or M 18 x 1.5	80
Clamp screws for upper and lower ball joints	M 10x 40	40
up to Chassis No. 0273513 (October 1963)	M 8 x 40	25
Socket head screw in split nut	M 7	7-max. 9
Inner wheel bearing nut up to Chassis No. 315 220 883	M 16 x 1.5	11 ②
Wheel bearing locknut	M 16 x 1.5	50 ②
Tie rod nuts	M 12 x 1.5	22 ④
	M 10 x 1	18 ④
Steering damper screw on axle	M 10	29-32
Steering damper nut on drop arm	M 10	18

Torque Specifications— Front Axle and Steering Gear

① *Tighten inner nut to 29 ft. lbs. first, fit new lock plate and slacken nut 72° (distance from one wheel bolt hole in drum to next). Then tighten outer nut to 50 ft. lbs.*

② *Tighten nut while turning wheel. Then slacken nut off until the specified axial play of. 03 - .12 mm (.001 - .005 in.) is obtained. If front axle tends to be noisy, keep play to lower limit (.03 - .06 mm.) When play is correct, tighten socket head screw to the correct torque.*

③ *Turn on to cotter pin hole.*

④ *Tighten inner nut to 25 ft. lbs. first while turning wheel. Then fit new lock plate and slacken nut off until specified axial play of .03 - .12 mm. (.001 - .005 in.) is obtained. If front axle tends to be noisy, keep play to lower limit (.03 - .06 mm.) When play is correct, tighten outer lock-nut to 50 ft. lbs.*

⑤ *Always use new self-locking nuts after removal.*

⑥ *Tighten clamp screw to 29 ft. lbs. first, then tighten adjusting screw to 7 ft. lbs. and lock it.*

Chassis Electrical

The six-volt electrical system was standard on all Volkswagens through the 1966 models. Beginning with the 1967 models—August 1966—the change was made to the 12-volt system.

DESCRIPTION

The Volkswagen electrical system is fairly conventional, consisting of generator, starter, battery, ignition and lighting systems and electrical accessories. Most of the electrical equipment is supplied by Bosch, although VW also produces some of its own components. The output of the generator is, as in most systems, controlled by a voltage regulator. In case of belt failure or other generator problems, a warning light in the speedometer dial lights.

The starting motor produces about ½ horsepower and is of the overrunning-clutch type. It is actuated by the ignition key and incorporates a solenoid which engages the pinion of the starter.

The electrical system of the Volkswagen is of the negative-ground type, the negative terminal of the battery being grounded. In most VW models, the battery is located under the right-hand side of the rear seat. In the Karmann Ghia and Transporter models it is in the engine compartment.

GENERATOR

Different types of generators have been used throughout the years and models. Refer to the Generator and Regulator Electrical Equipment Specifications Chart for details.

The generator warning light in the speedometer housing connects to the voltage regulator by means of terminals in the ignition switch. The warning lamp lights as soon as the ignition is turned on, and goes out when the voltage of the generator approaches that of the battery. The warning lamp simply gives a yes-no answer to the question of weather the generator is charging or not. As such, it is potentially useful in detecting broken fan belts, because when a fan belt is broken, the generator is no longer being turned and will not charge. In the type 1 or 2, a broken belt means that the entire car is out of commission, but with the type 3 the fan is mounted directly on the crankshaft and the car can be driven until the battery runs out of electricity.

The generator is equipped with ball bearings that are packed with special high melting point grease. Lubrication of the generator is not necessary under normal conditions. However, if the unit has been disassembled and/or overhauled, it is then necessary to provide new lubricant for the bearings.

Electrical Specifications—Generator and Regulator

Generator				Regulator		
Part Number	*Brush Spring Pressure (oz.)*	*Field Resistance (ohms.)*	*Max. Output*	*Part Number*	*Cut-in Voltage*	*Voltage Setting (No Load)*
25 hp.- Bosch RED 130/ 6-2600 AL 16	16-21	1.20-1.32	NA	Bosch RS/G130/ 6/11 (on generator)	NA	7.3-8.6
36 hp. 1,200 cc. Bosch LJ/ REF 160/ -2500 L4	16-21	1.20-1.32	NA	Bosch RS/TA 160/ 6/A1 (on generator)	5.5-6.3	7.3-8.6
36 hp. 1,200 cc. Bosch LJ/ REF 160/6/ 2500 L17	16-21	1.20-1.32	NA	Bosch RS/TAA 160/ 6/1 (on generator)	6.4-6.7	7.4-8.1
40 hp. 1,200 cc. Bosch 111 903 021 G	16-21	1.20-1.32	270 WATTS	Bosch RS/TAA 180 /6/A4	6.2-6.8	7.3-8.0
40 hp. 1,200 cc. -VW 113 903 021 C	16-21	1.20-1.32	270 WATTS	VW 113 903 801 C	6.4-6.7	7.4-8.1
Late 1,200 and 1,300 cc.- Bosch 113 903 021 H	16-21	1.20-1.32	NA	Bosch 113 903 801F	6.2-6.8	7.4-8.1
Late 1,200 and 1,300 cc.- VW 111 903 021 J	16-21	1.20-1.32	NA	VW 113 903 801G	6.4-6.7	7.4-8.1
Karmann Ghia 1,300 and Type 1 1,500- Bosch 131 903 021	16-21	NA	30 AMPS	Bosch 131 903 801	6.2-6.8	7.3-8.0
Bosch 450 M 12/ 3700-14 38A 32 (12 Volt)	16-21	NA	38 AMPS	Bosch UA 14 V 38A	12.5-13.2	13.5-14.5
Bosch E(L) 14V 38A 32, EG (R) 14V 38A 32 (12 Volt)	16-21	NA	38 AMPS	Bosch RS/VA 14V 38A	12.4-13.1	13.6-14.4
Bosch G(L) 14 V 30A 20	16-21	NA	30 AMPS	Bosch RS/VA 14V 30A	12.4-13.1	13.6-14.4

NA - Information not available.

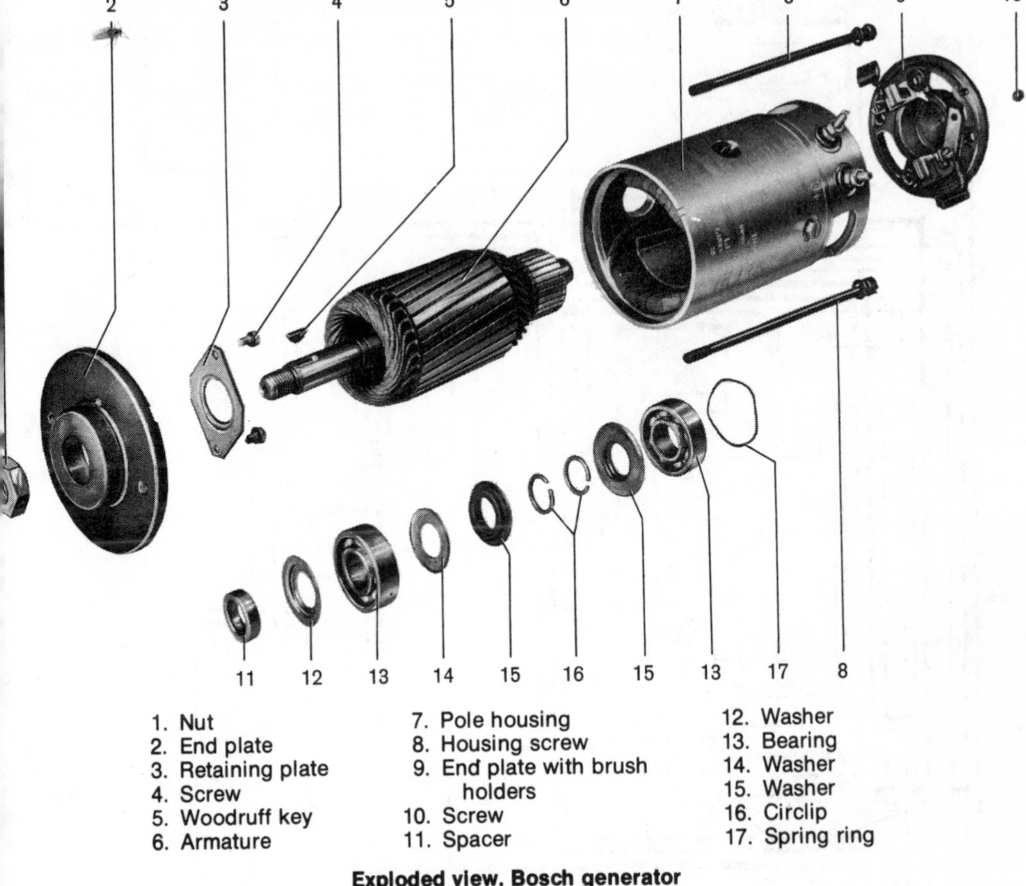

1. Nut
2. End plate
3. Retaining plate
4. Screw
5. Woodruff key
6. Armature
7. Pole housing
8. Housing screw
9. End plate with brush holders
10. Screw
11. Spacer
12. Washer
13. Bearing
14. Washer
15. Washer
16. Circlip
17. Spring ring

Exploded view, Bosch generator

Under no circumstances should ordinary grease be used, for it will not hold up under operating conditions.

GENERATOR—TESTING NO-LOAD VOLTAGE

In testing the no-load voltage of the generator, the cable from terminal B + (51) at the regulator must first be disconnected. The positive lead of the voltmeter to be used should be attached to terminal B + (51) of the regulator and the negative lead of the meter grounded. With the engine running, the speed should be increased gradually until the reading of the voltmeter peaks out. If the regulator is functioning properly, the peaking point of the no-load voltage should be approximately 7.4 to 8.1 volts for the 6-volt system and 13.6 to 14.4 for the 12-volt system. When the engine is turned off, the needle of the voltmeter should drop from 6 volts (12 volts) to zero just before the engine stops.

GENERATOR—TESTING WITHOUT REGULATOR

The generator can be given a very quick check without the regulator. It is most important that the duration of the test be very brief (only a few seconds) in order that the generator field windings will not be overloaded during the test.

Disconnect the two leads from the generator. Connect terminal DF of the generator to ground. Connect the positive terminal of the voltmeter to terminal D+ and the negative terminal to the generator ground. For 6 volt systems, approximately 6 volts should be generated at 1500 RPM and about 15 at 3000 RPM. A circuit diagram for this test is included in this section.

REGULATOR—R & R

On pre-1967 models, the regulator is located on top of the generator. Take off the connections from terminals B + (51) and 61 at the

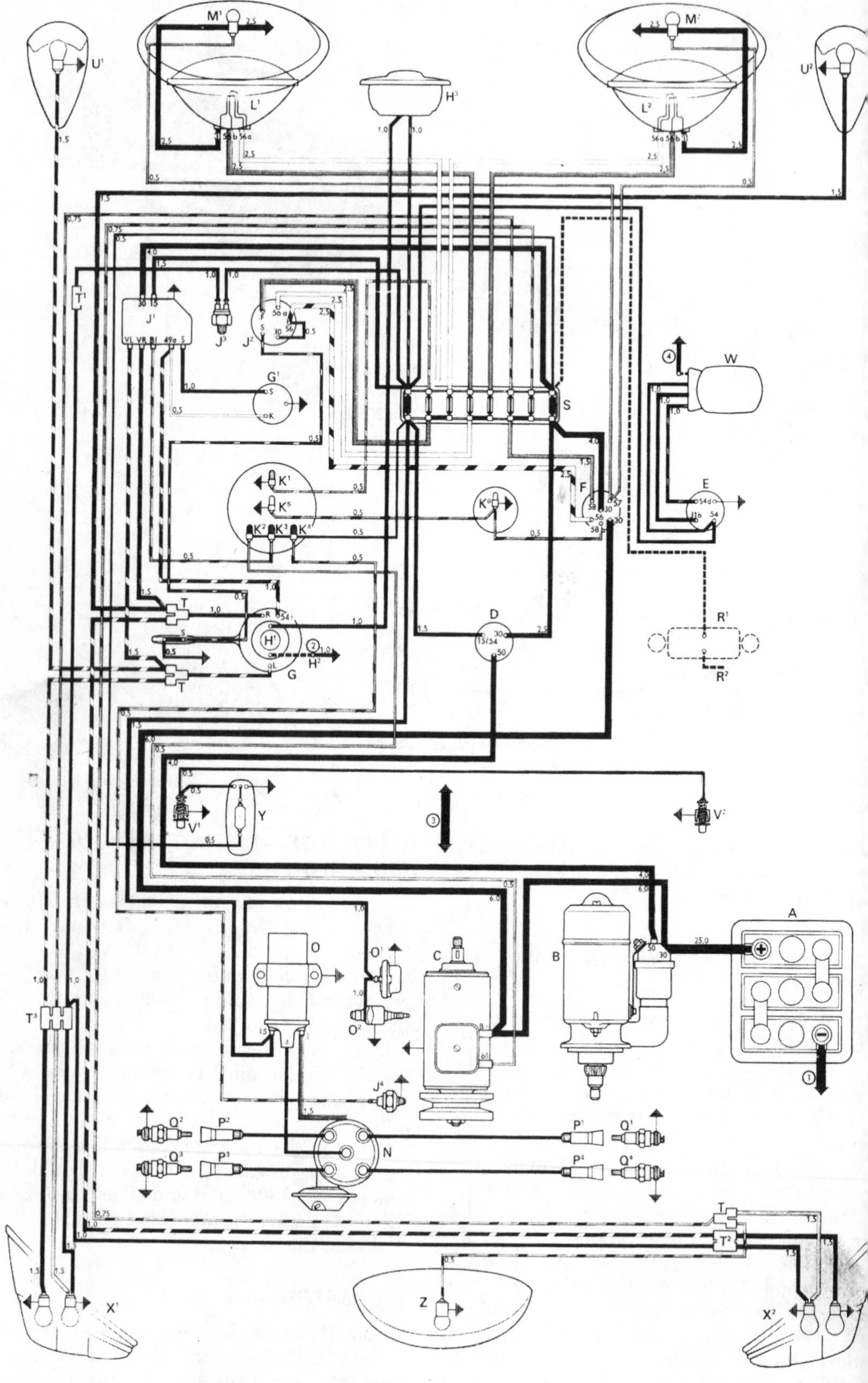

M¹
M²
U¹
U²
L¹
L²
H³
J¹
J²
J³
J⁴
G¹
S
W
E
F
K¹
K⁵
K²
K³
K⁴
K⁶
T
T¹
T²
T³
H¹
H²
G
D
R¹
R²
V¹
V²
Y
O
O¹
O²
C
B
A
N
P¹
P²
P³
P⁴
Q¹
Q²
Q³
Q⁴
X¹
X²
Z

A Battery
B Starter
C Generator
D Ignition/starter switch
E Windshield wiper switch
F Lighting switch
G Turn signal switch with dimmer switch
G^1 Emergency light switch
H^1 Horn half ring
H^2 Steering column connection
H^3 Horn
J^1 Flasher and emergency light relay
J^2 Dimming relay
J^3 Brake light switch
J^4 Oil pressure switch
K^1 High beam warning light
K^2 Generator warning light
K^3 Turn signal warning light
K^4 Oil pressure warning light
K^5 Speedometer light
K^6 Fuel gauge light
L^1 Sealed-beam unit, left
L^2 Sealed-beam unit, right
M^1 Parking light, left
M^2 Parking light, right
N Distributor
O Ignition coil
O^1 Automatic choke
O^2 Electro-magnetic pilot jet
P^1 Spark plug connector, No. 1 cylinder

Black dotted line = Service installation

P^2 Spark plug connector, No. 2 cylinder
P^3 Spark plug connector, No. 3 cylinder
P^4 Spark plug connector, No. 4 cylinder
Q^1 Spark plug for No. 1 cylinder
Q^2 Spark plug for No. 2 cylinder
Q^3 Spark plug for No. 3 cylinder
Q^4 Spark plug for No. 4 cylinder
R^1 Radio
R^2 Aerial connection
S Fuse box
white fuses: 8 Ampere
red fuses: 16 Ampere
T Cable adaptor
T^1 Cable connector, single
T^2 Cable connector, double
T^3 Cable connector, triple
U^1 Turn signal, left
U^2 Turn signal, right
V^1 Door switch, left
V^2 Door switch, right
W Windshield wiper motor
X^1 Brake, turn signal and tail lights, left
X^2 Brake, turn signal and tail lights, right
Y Interior light
Z License plate light
① Battery to frame ground strap
② Horn ring to steering coupling ground connection
③ Transmission to frame ground strap
④ Wiper motor to body ground strap

Wiring diagram, VW 1,300 type 1 (from August, 1965)

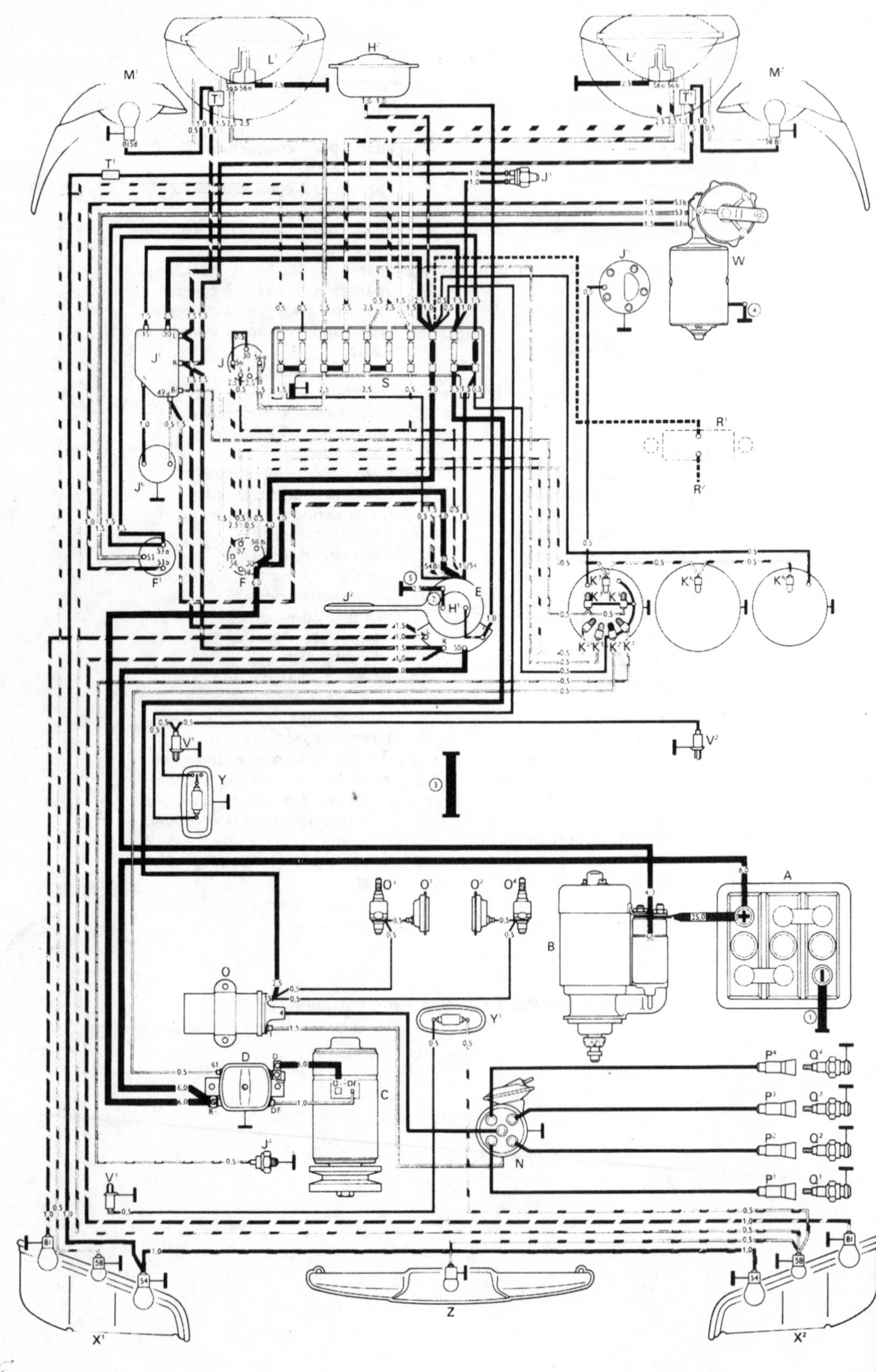

M¹
L¹
H²
L²
M²
T¹
J³
W
J⁵
J¹
J
S
R¹
R²
J⁶
F¹
F
E
J²
H¹
K²
K¹
K³
K⁴
K⁵
K⁶
V¹
V²
Y
A
B
O
O¹
O²
O⁴
Y¹
D
C
J²
N
P¹
P²
P³
P⁴
Q¹
Q²
Q³
Q⁴
X¹
X²
Z

A Battery
B Starter
C Generator
D Regulator
E Turn signal switch with ignition starter lock
F Lighting switch
F^1 Windshield wiper switch
H^1 Horn half ring
H^2 Horn
J Hand dimmer relay
J^1 Flasher and emergency light relay
J^2 Headlamp flasher button
J^3 Brake light switch
J^4 Oil pressure switch
J^5 Fuel gauge sender unit
J^6 Emergency light switch
K^1 High beam warning light
K^2 Generator warning light
K^3 Turn signal warning light
K^4 Oil pressure warning light
K^5 Parking light warning light
K^6 Speedometer light
K^7 Fuel gauge light
K^8 Clock light
L^1 Headlamp, left
L^2 Headlamp, right
M^1 Parking light and turn signal light, left
M^2 Parking light and turn signal light, right
N Distributor
O Ignition coil
O^1 Automatic choke, left
O^2 Automatic choke, right
O^3 Electro-magnetic pilot jet, left
O^4 Electro-magnetic pilot jet, right
P^1 Spark plug connector, No. 1 cylinder
P^2 Spark plug connector, No. 2 cylinder
P^3 Spark plug connector, No. 3 cylinder
P^4 Spark plug connector, No. 4 cylinder
Q^1 Spark plug for No. 1 cylinder
Q^2 Spark plug for No. 2 cylinder
Q^3 Spark plug for No. 3 cylinder
Q^4 Spark plug for No. 4 cylinder
R^1 Radio
R^2 Aerial connection
S Fuse box—10 fuses
T^1 Cable connector, single
T^2 Cable connector, double
V^1 Door switch, left
V^2 Door switch, right
V^3 Luggage compartment light switch
W Windshield wiper motor
X^1 Tail light, left
X^2 Tail light, right
Y Interior light
Y^1 Luggage compartment light
Z License plate light
① Battery to frame ground strap
② Horn half ring steering coupling ground connection
③ Transmission to frame ground connection
④ Windshield wiper motor to body ground strap
⑤ Front axle to frame ground strap

Black dotted lines = Service installation
1.5; 0.5 etc.: Cable cross section

Wiring diagram, VW type 3 (from August, 1965)

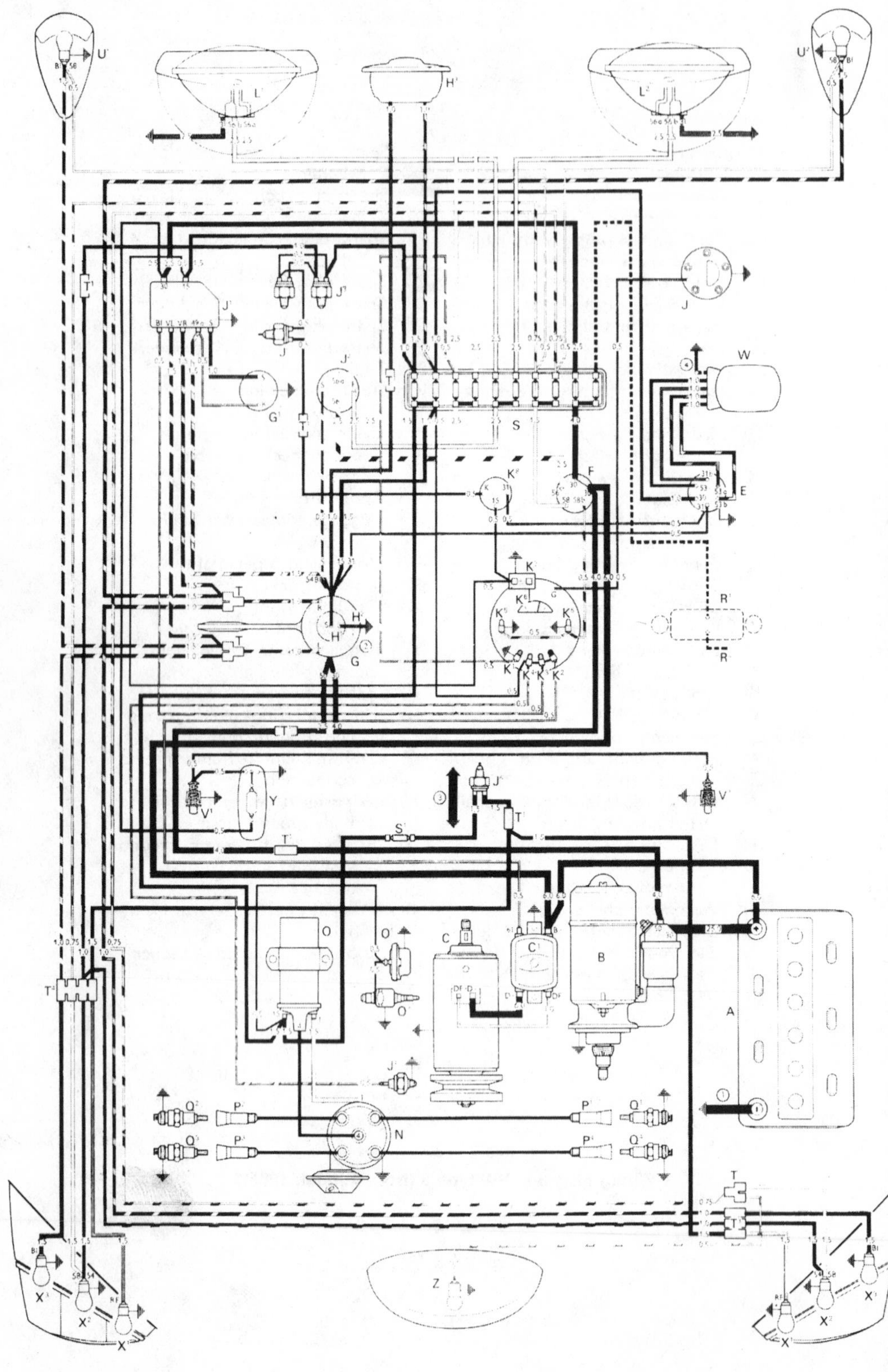

Wiring diagram, VW 1,500 type 1 sedan and convertible for 1968

- A Battery
- B Starter
- C Generator
- C^1 Regulator
- E Windshield wiper switch
- F Lighting switch
- G Turn signal switch with automatic canceling, hand dimmer button and ignition/starter switch
- G^1 Emergency light switch
- H^1 Horn half ring
- H^2 Steering column connection
- H^3 Horn
- J^1 Turn signal and emergency light relay
- J^2 Dimmer relay
- J^3 Brake light switch (2 X)
- J^4 Oil pressure switch
- J^5 Back-up light switch
- J^6 Warning switch for brake system
- J^7 Fuel gauge sender unit
- K^1 High beam warning light
- K^2 Generator warning light
- K^3 Turn signal warning light
- K^4 Oil pressure warning light
- K^5 Speedometer light
- K^6 Fuel gauge light
- K^7 Resistance for fuel gauge
- K^8 Brake warning lamp with test button
- L^1 Sealed-beam insert, left
- L^2 Sealed-beam insert, right
- N Distributor
- O Ignition coil
- O^1 Automatic choke
- O^2 Electro-magnetic pilot jet
- P^1 Spark plug connector, No. 1 cylinder
- P^2 Spark plug connector, No. 2 cylinder
- P^3 Spark plug connector, No. 4 cylinder
- P^4 Spark plug connector, No. 3 cylinder
- Q^1 Spark plug for No. 1 cylinder
- Q^2 Spark plug for No. 2 cylinder
- Q^3 Spark plug for No. 4 cylinder
- Q^4 Spark plug for No. 3 cylinder
- R^1 Radio
- R^2 Aerial connection
- S Fuse box
- T Cable adapter
- T^1 Cable connector, single
- T^2 Cable connector for horn under front luggage compartment lining
- T^3 Cable connector, triple
- U^1 Front turn signal and parking light, left
- U^2 Front turn signal and parking light, right
- V^1 Door contact switch, left
- V^2 Door contact switch, right
- W Windshield wiper motor
- X^1 Back-up lights
- X^2 Brake and tail lights
- X^3 Turn signal lights
- Y Interior light
- Z License plate light
- ① Battery to frame ground strap
- ② Horn ring to steering coupling ground connection
- ③ Transmission to frame ground strap
- ④ Wiper motor to body ground strap

Black dotted line = Optional extras or service installation

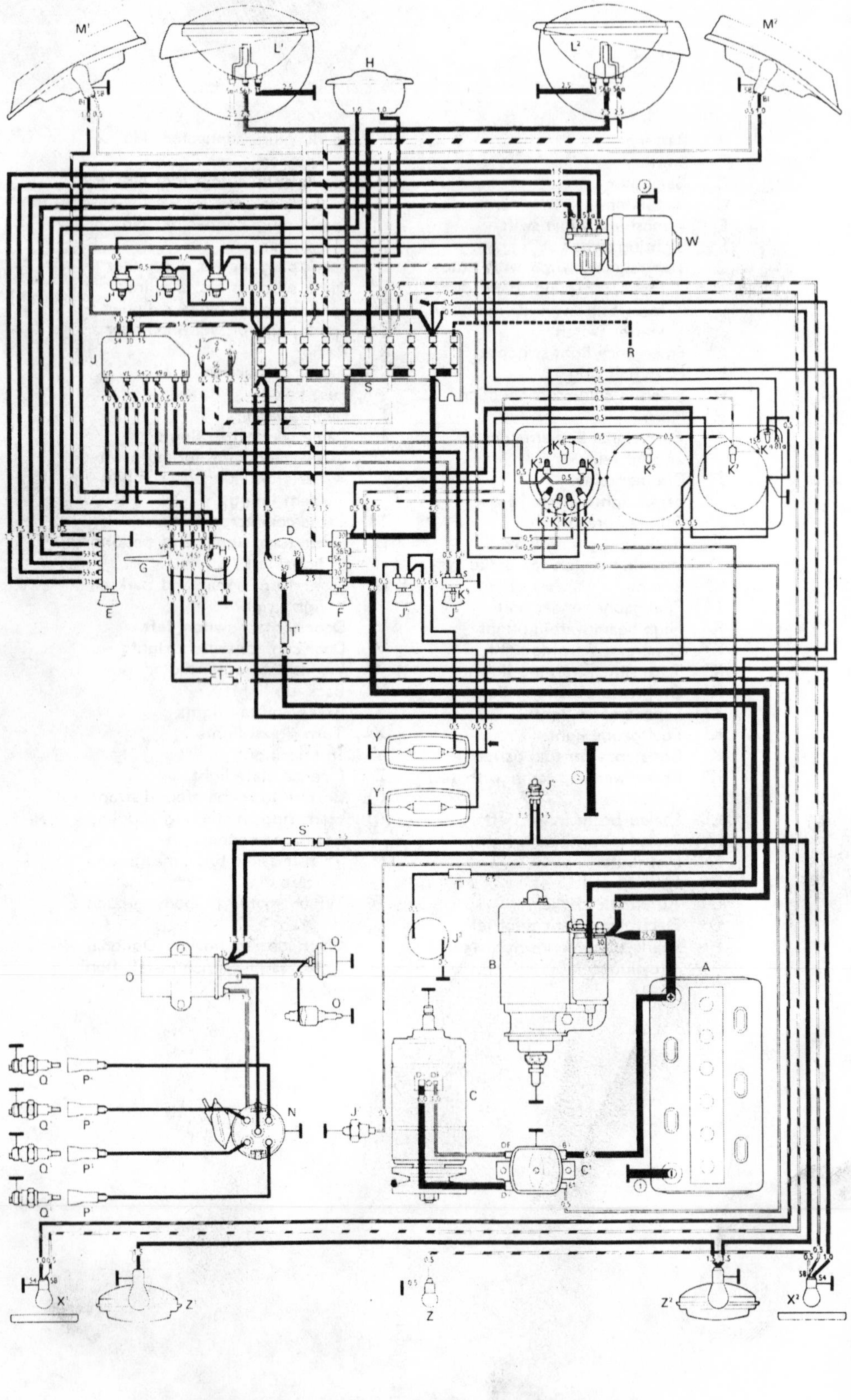

Wiring diagram, VW Transporter (from August, 1967)

A Battery
B Starter
C Generator
C^1 Regulator
D Ignition/starter switch
E Windshield wiper switch
F Lighting switch
G Turn signal switch and hand dimmer
H Horn
H^1 Horn button
J Emergency light relay
J^1 Brake light switch (2 X)
J^2 Oil pressure switch
J^3 Fuel gauge sender unit
J^4 Warning switch for brakes
J^5 Emergency light switch
J^6 Interior light switch
J^7 Dimmer relay
J_9 Back-up light switch
K^1 High beam warning lamp
K^2 Generator and fan warning lamp
K^3 Turn signal warning lamp
K^4 Oil pressure warning lamp
K^5 Speedometer light bulb
K^6 Fuel gauge light bulb
K^7 Clock light bulb
K^8 Emergency light warning lamp
K_9 Brake system warning lamp
L^1 Sealed beam unit, left
L^2 Sealed beam unit, right
M^1 Parking light, left
M^2 Parking light, right
N Distributor
O Ignition coil
O^1 Automatic choke
O^2 Electro-magnetic pilot jet
P^1 Spark plug connector, No. 1 cylinder
P^2 Spark plug connector, No. 2 cylinder
P^3 Spark plug connector, No. 3 cylinder
P^4 Spark plug connector, No. 4 cylinder
Q^1 Spark plug for No. 1 cylinder
Q^2 Spark plug for No. 2 cylinder
Q^3 Spark plug for No. 3 cylinder
Q^4 Spark plug for No. 4 cylinder
R Radio
R^1 Aerial connection
R^2 Rear loudspeaker connection
S Fuse box
S^1 Back-up light fuse
T^1 Cable connector, single
U^1 Turn signal, front left
U^2 Turn signal, front right
W Windshield wiper motor
X^1 Brake, turn signal and tail light, left
X^2 Brake, turn signal and tail light, right
Y Interior light, front
Y^1 Interior light, rear
Z License plate light
Z^1 Back-up light, left
Z^2 Back-up light, right
① Battery to body ground strap
② Transmission to body ground strap
③ Windshield wiper motor ground connection

Black dotted lines = Optional extras
All fuses: 8 amps

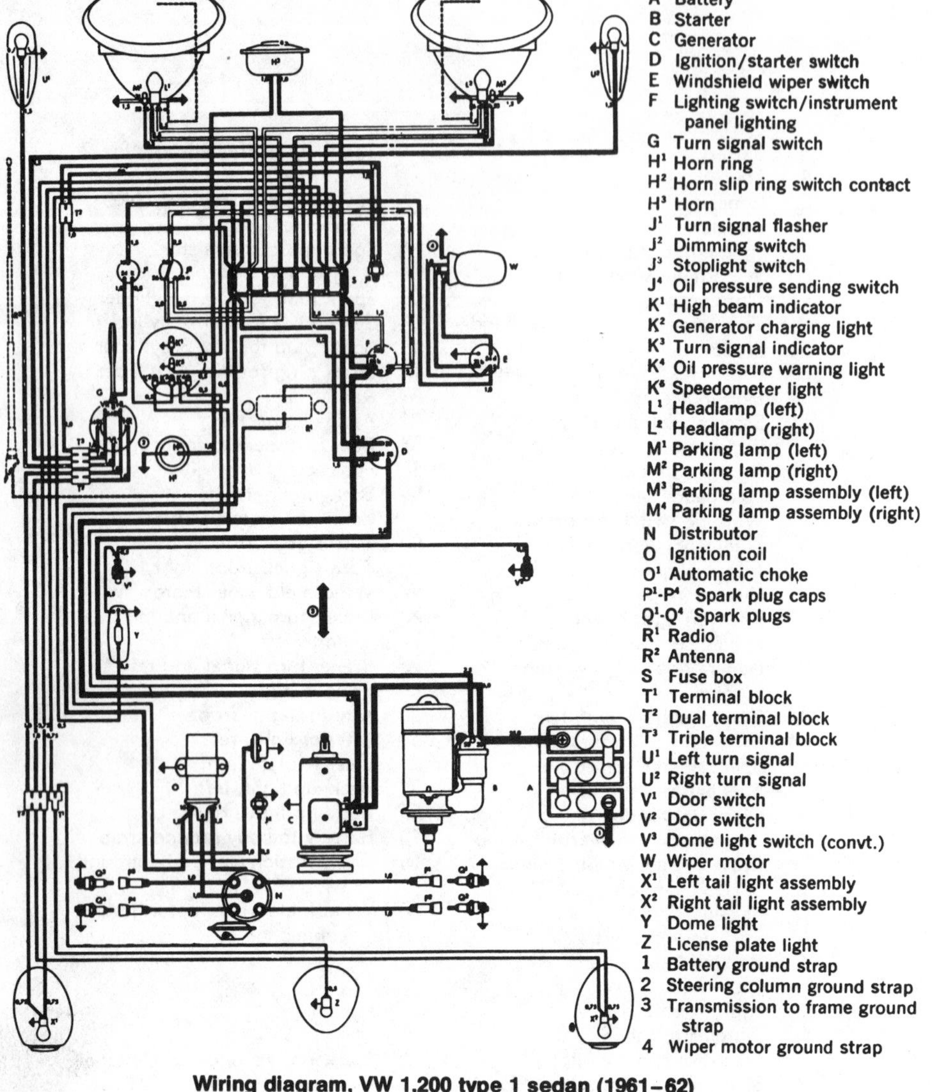

Wiring diagram, VW 1,200 type 1 sedan (1961–62)

regulator. Remove the screws that hold the regulator onto the generator and remove the regulator from its position on the generator. Disconnect the electrical cables from the bottom of the regulator. These are marked + (D+) and F(DF).

Installation of the regulator is the reverse of the preceding, but it should be noted that the thicker cable (coming from the positive brush of the generator) must be attached at the regulator bottom to terminal + (D+). The thin cable coming from the generator field windings should be attached to the F (DF) terminal at the bottom of the regulator. If the replacement of the regulator does not correct a deficiency in the charging system, chances are that the generator itself is defective.

GENERATOR—CHECKING BRUSHES

The generator brushes should be examined periodically for wear. If they are worn to the point where they no longer extend from their holders, they should be replaced.

GENERATOR—R & R

Disconnect the ground strap of the battery and disconnect the leads from the regulator. Remove the air cleaner and the carburetor and take off the fan belt. Remove the retaining strap from the generator. Remove the

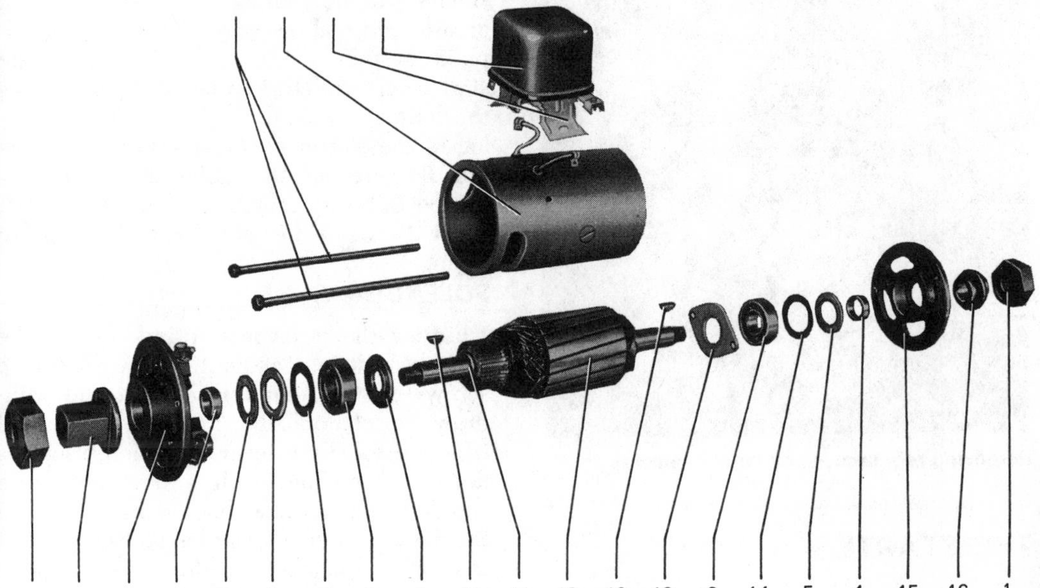

1. Nut
2. Pulley hub
3. Brush holder end plate
4. Spacer ring
5. Felt washer
6. Retainer
7. Thrust ring
8. Ball bearing
9. Washer
10. Key
11. Spacer
12. Armature
13. Bearing retainer
14. Thrust ring
15. End plate
16. Fan hub
17. Housing screws
18. Housing and field assembly
19. Slotted screw
20. Regulator

Exploded view, VW generator

cooling air thermostat. Remove hot air hoses from the fan housing, take out the fan housing screws and lift off the housing. After removing the fan housing screws, the generator can be lifted off along with the fan.

Installation is the reverse of the preceding.

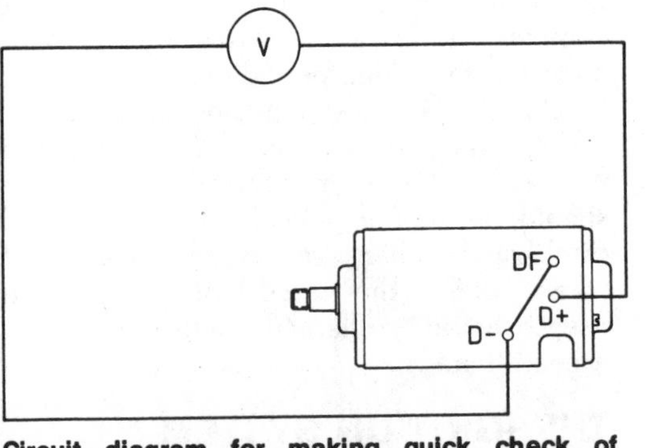

Circuit diagram for making quick check of generator without regulator. Test must not take longer than a few seconds, otherwise generator will be damaged

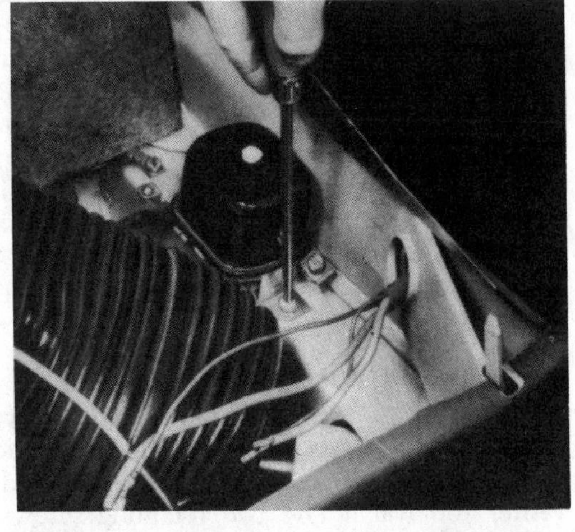
Removing regulator, Type 3 and post-1967 Type 1. Regulator is secured by two screws

Removing regulator, early type 1 vehicles

THE STARTER

The starter motor of the Volkswagen is of the sliding gear type and is rated at about ½ horsepower. The motor used in the starter is a series wound type and draws a heavy current in order to provide the high torque needed to crank the engine during starting. The starter cannot be switched on accidently while the engine is still running—the device responsible for this safeguard is a non-repeat switch in the ignition switch. If the engine should stall for any reason, the ignition key must be turned to the "off" position before it is possible to re-start the engine.

The starter is flange-mounted on the right-hand side of the transmission housing. Attached to the starter motor housing is a solenoid which engages the pinion and connects the starting motor to the battery when the ignition key is turned on. When the engine starts, and the key is released from the start position, the solenoid circuit is opened and the pinion is returned to its original position by the return spring. However, if for any reason the starter is not switched off immediately after the engine starts, a pinion free-wheeling device stops the armature from being driven so that the starter will not be damaged.

STARTER—R & R

Disconnect the ground strap of the battery and remove the cable from terminal 30 and the lead from terminal 50 of the solenoid. After removal of the two retaining screws, the starter can be taken out.

Prior to installation, the outboard bushing should be lubricated with special lithium grease, and sealing compound should be applied to the mating surfaces between the starter and the transmission. After putting the long screw into the hole in the flange, locate the starter on the transmission housing. Be sure that the cables are tightly connected to the terminals and that the contact points between the cables and terminals are clean.

SOLENOID—R & R

Unscrew the hexagon nut and remove the connector strip. Take out the two retaining screws on the mounting bracket and withdraw the solenoid after it has been unhooked from its actuating lever. When replacing a defective solenoid with a new one, care should be taken to see that the distance "a" in the accompanying diagram is 19+ or −.1 mm. when the magnet is drawn in. The actuating rod can be adjusted after loosening the lock nut.

Installation of the solenoid is the reverse of the preceding. Be certain that the rubber seal on the starter mounting bracket is properly seated. A small strip of VW Sealing Compound D 14 should be placed on the outside of the switch. In order to facilitate engagement of the actuating rod, the pinion should be pulled out as far as possible when the solenoid is inserted.

BATTERY STORAGE

If a battery is not used for a prolonged period of time, it tends to discharge itself at a slow rate. This rate varies according to the temperature—high temperatures cause stored batteries to discharge more quickly. At room temperature, the rate of battery discharge is about 1% per day. When a discharged battery is stored at room temperature, it also tends to "sulphate", or form layers of lead sulphate on the battery plates. When storing a battery for a long period of time, it should be charged before storage and the acid level and specific gravity checked and corrected if necessary. Once in storage the battery should be kept in a cool, dry location and discharged, then recharged, every 6–8 weeks. Before the stored battery is put into use, it should be charged at a low rate, not to exceed 3 amps.

THE IGNITION SYSTEM

The Volkswagen is equipped with a 6 or 12-volt battery-operated ignition system. The

Electrical Specifications—Battery and Starter

Model	Battery			Starter						
	Capacity (Amp Hours)	Volts	Grounded Terminal	Model	Lock Test			No Load Test		
					Amps	Volts	Torque (ft.lbs.)	Amps	Volts	RPM
Type 1 up to Chassis No. 929745	70	6	Neg.	25, 36 hp. Bosch EED 0.4/6L/4	500	3.5	NA	80	5.5	5,400
Type 1 from Chassis No. 929746	66	6	Neg.	40 hp. 1,200cc. Bosch EEF 0.5/ 6L/1	450-520	3.5	8	60-80	5.5	5,500-7,300
Type 1 from Chassis No. 118000001 ①	36	12	Neg.	40 hp. 1,200 and 1,300cc.- VW 113 911 021 A	450-520	3.5	8	60-80	5.5	5,500-7,300
Type 2 up to Chassis No. 117901	84	6	Neg.	40 hp. 1,200 and 1,300 cc. -Bosch 113 911 021 B	450-520	3.5	8	60-80	5.5	5,500-7,300
Type 2 from chassis No.117902	77	6	Neg.	Bosch AL/EEF 0.8/12L1 (12 Volt)	250-285	6.0	6.5 8.2	38-45	12	6,400-7,900
Type 2 from chassis No.217000001	45	12	Neg.	1,500cc.- 111 911 021 G (12 Volt) ②	250-285	NA	NA	38-45	12	7,150
Type 3 from chassis No.0000001	77	6	Neg.	–	–	–	–	–	–	–
Type 3 from chassis No. 317000001	36	12	Neg.	–	–	–	–	–	–	–

① *Excluding VW 1,200, Type 1.*

② *Test figures for 6 Volt units on 1,500 cc. engines should be the same as for previous 6 volt units.*

NA - Not Available

major parts of the system are the battery, coil, distributor, spark plugs and wiring. The job of the ignition system is to convert the 12 volts of the battery into voltage large enough to force a spark to jump across the .025–.028" gap of the spark plug.

The ignition coil has two circuits—a primary circuit and a secondary circuit. The primary circuit consists of heavy wire wrapped around the iron core of the coil, while the secondary circuit is made up of similar windings of fine wire. The separating of the contact points causes the current through the primary winding to cease, which in turn causes the magnetic field to collapse and induce a high-voltage surge to flow through the rotor to a spark plug. The condenser serves to help increase the surge in the circuit. Maintenance of the coil is limited to keeping the insulating cap clean and dry so that short circuits and "tracking" do not occur.

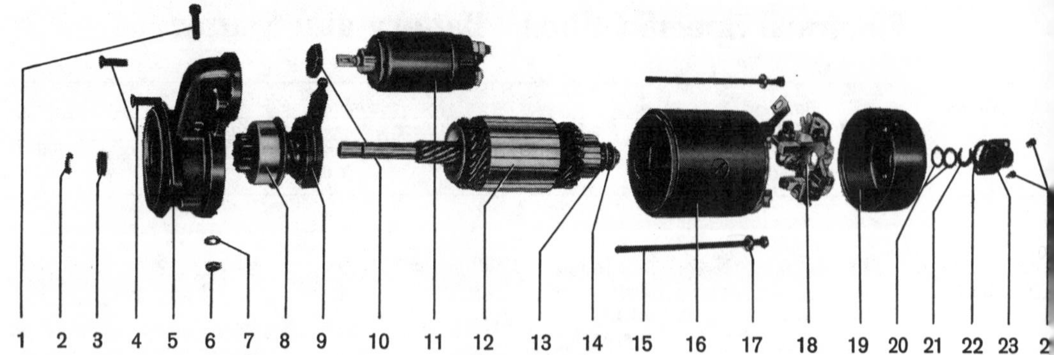

1. Lever bearing pin
2. Circlip
3. Stop ring
4. Securing screws
5. Mounting bracket
6. Nut
7. Spring washer
8. Pinion
9. Operating lever
10. Rubber seal
11. Solenoid
12. Armature
13. Steel washer
14. Synthetic washer
15. Housing screw
16. Pole housing
17. Washer
18. Brush holder
19. End plate
20. Shims
21. Lock washer
22. Sealing ring
23. End cap
24. Screws

Bosch starter, exploded view

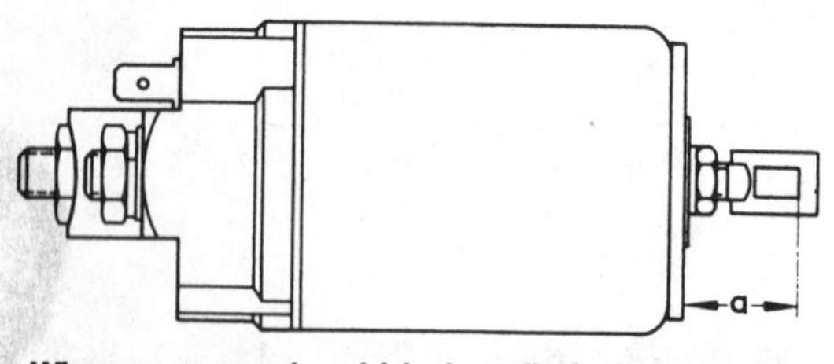

When a new solenoid is installed, distance "a" should be 19 + or − .1mm from the switch flange to the pull rod eye with the magnet drawn in

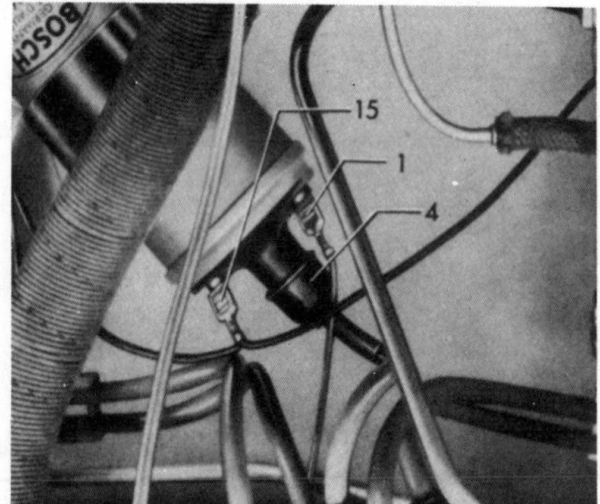

Connections at coil: (15) to ignition/starter switch, (1) to distributor contact breaker points, and (4) high tension lead to the distributor cap

DISTRIBUTOR

The distributor is of the four-cam type, with a single set of breaker points. The distributor

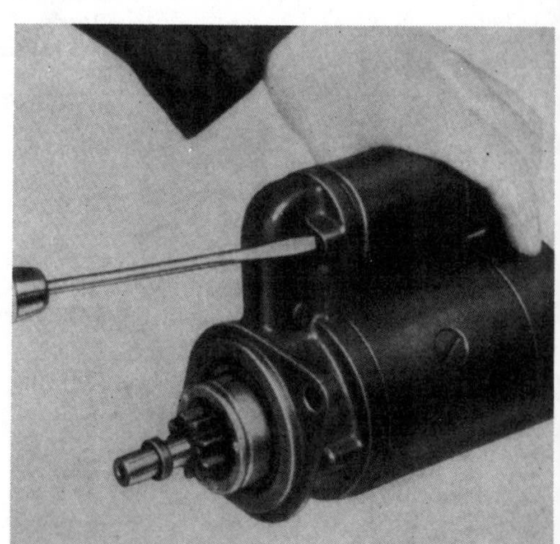

Solenoid may be withdrawn after removal of two screws that secure it to the intermediate bracket of the starter motor

cam shaft rotates at a speed of one-half that of the crankshaft. The fiber block of the movable breaker point should be lubricated periodically with lithium grease. In using the lubricant, care should be taken to ensure that no grease gets onto the contact points—only a small amount of grease should be used. The vacuum advance mechanism requires no maintenance, but should be checked periodically for leakage of the vacuum diaphragm. Sucking air from the vacuum tube should cause the interior of the distributor to rotate slightly. When air is sucked out and the tube

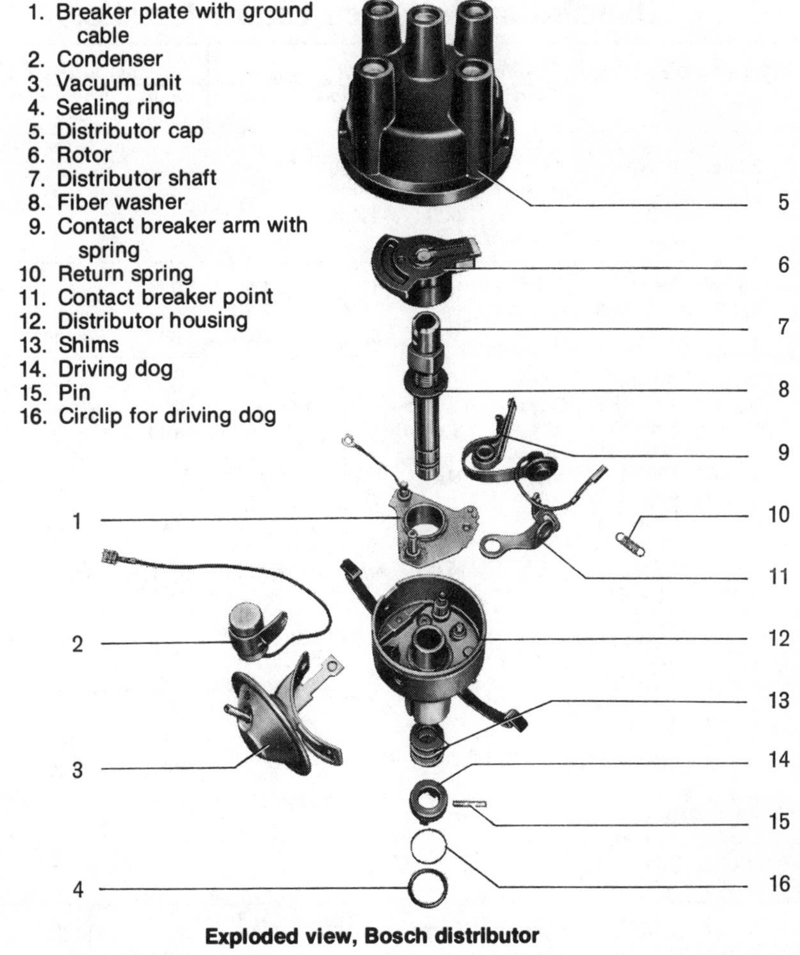

Exploded view, Bosch distributor

blocked off, the interior plate of the distributor should not move from its advanced position until the air passage is opened.

The contact breaker points are adjusted as described in the tune-up chapter, and should have a clearance of .016″.

DISTRIBUTOR—R & R

Take off the vacuum hose at the distributor. Disconnect cable 1 at the ignition coil and remove the distributor cap. Mark the relationship between the distributor body and the engine case. Unscrew the distributor retaining screw on the crankcase and lift out the distributor.

(NOTE: *before removing the distributor, it is best to turn the engine until the rotor points to number one cylinder lead; i.e., toward the notch in the distributor housing. In this way one can be sure of having the rotor pointing in the proper direction when the distributor is reinstalled.*)

Installation is in the reverse sequence. Align the marks made before removal. When the distributor is reinstalled in the engine, the timing must then be adjusted.

SPARK PLUGS

Plugs recommended for the Volkswagen are listed in the Tune-Up Specifications Chart. Spark plugs should be cleaned and their gaps checked at intervals of 6000 miles. Their appearance should also be checked, for the appearance of a spark plug tells a lot about what is going on inside the cylinder.

Spark plugs can experience—and tell about—many different conditions. Some of these are described:

• *Normal operating conditions* are apparent when the plug has no evidence of electrode burning and its body coloration is light tan or gray. Under normal conditions, the plug gap will not increase more than about .001″ every 1000 miles. When a plug is functioning normally, it can be taken out at 6000

Distributor Advance Characteristics

Vehicle	Engine	Distributor	Centrifugal Advance (deg. @ rpm.) Start	Intermed-iate	Intermed-iate	End	Vacuum Advance (deg. @ mm. hg.) Start	Intermed-iate	Intermed-iate	End
Type 1	25 hp.	Bosch VE 4 BRS 383	5@ O rpm	5-9 @ 600	15-20 @ 1,400	32-37 @ 2800	–	–	–	–
Type 1	36 hp. 1,200	Bosch VJU 4BR 3 mk	7.5@ O rpm	8-13 @ 1,200	13.5-16.5@ 2,000	31.5-34.5@ 3,300	0 @ 80	8.0-11.5 @200	17.5-19.5 @300	18-22 @ 370
Type 1	36 hp. 1,200	Bosch VJU 4BR 8 mk	7.5@ O rpm	10-14 @ 1,800	–	23-27 @ 3,400	0 @ 100	5-7.5 @200	11-14.5 @300	13-17 @ 350
Type 1	40 hp. 1,200	VW 113 905 205H	NA	NA	NA	NA	0 @ 140	7-13 @ 300	15-21 @ 400	19-25 @ 450
Type 1	50 hp. 1,300	Bosch 113 905 205K or VW113 905 2051	NA	NA	NA	NA	0 @ 40-110	5-11 @ 200	14-20 @ 400	23-28 @ 620-650
Type 1	53 hp. 1,500	Bosch 113905 205M	–	–	–	–	@ 40-80	17-19 @300	–	32-35 @ 800
Type 1	53 hp. 1,500, 57 hp. 1,600	Bosch 113 905 205T								
Type 1	53 hp. 1,500 Auto-matic	Bosch 113 905 205P	14-23 @ 1,500	19-23 @ 1,600	19-23 @ 2,100	30-33 @ 3,750	@ 50-100	14-20 @ 300	–	8-12 @ 230
Type 1	53 hp. 1,500 Auto-matic	Bosch 113 905 205AA	14-23 @ 1,500	19-23 @ 1,600	19-23 @ 2,100	30 -33@ 3,750	@ 50-100	3-7 @ 150	–	8-12 @ 230
Type 1	57 hp. 1,600 Auto-matic	Bosch 113 905 205AD	@ 1,050-1,200	13-15 @ 1,700	13-16 @ 2,200	25-28@ 3,900	@ 70-120	–	–	8-12@ 240
							@ 60-100	–		6-8(retar @170
Type 2	57 hp. 1,600	Bosch 113 905 205M	–	–	–	–	@ 40-80	17-19 @ 300	–	32-35 @ 800
Type 2	57 hp. 1,600	Bosch 113 905 205T	–	–	–	–	@ 40-80	17-19 @ 300	–	32-35@ 800
Type 3	65 hp. 1,600	Bosch 311 905 205F	–	–	–	–	@ 10-70	–	–	23-28 @ 310-340
Type 3	65 hp. 1,600	Bosch 311 905 205G	–	–	–	–	@ 10-70	17-19 @ 300	–	23-28 @ 310-340

Vehicle	Engine	Distributor	Centrifugal Advance (deg. @ rpm.) Start	Intermed-iate	Intermed-iate	End	Vacuum Advance (deg. @ mm. hg.) Start	Intermed-iate	Intermed-iate	End
Type 3	65 hp. 1,600	Bosch 311 905 205L	@ 900 1,100	6-12 @ 1,350	10-14 @ 1,500	26-30 @ 2,600	@ 50-100	10-16 @ 300	–	8-12 @ 200
Type 3	65 hp. 1,600	Bosch 311 905 205AB	@ 900-1,100	10-14 @ 1,500	20-23 @ 2,300	27-30 @ 2,800	@ 60-100	2-8 @ 150	–	8-12 @ 200
Type 3	65 hp. 1,600	Bosch 311 905 205M	@ 900 1,050	19-22 @ 1,600	19-22 @ 2,100	27-30 @ 2,700	@ 60-100	17-19 @ 300	–	8-12 @ 200

NOTE: Figures given are for crankshaft degrees and rpm. To obtain distributor degrees and rpm, divide crankshaft figures by two.

NA - Not available.

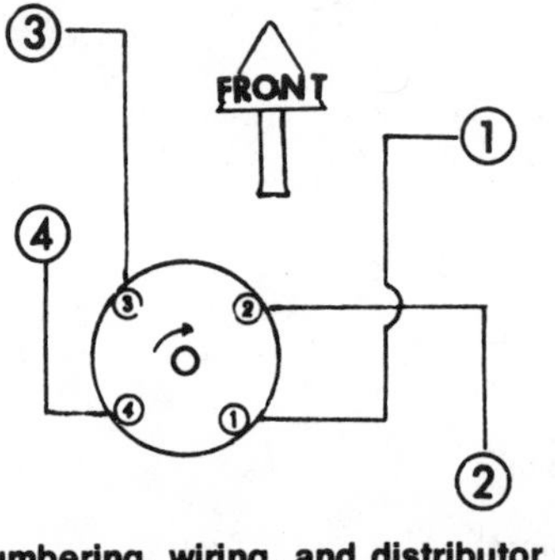

Cylinder numbering, wiring, and distributor rotation for all VW engines. The firing order is 1–4–3–2.

miles, cleaned, filed, regapped and put back into the engine with no ill effects.

• *Cold fouling* takes place when there is an extremely rich fuel-air mixture. It is characterized by a dry black appearance of the plug.

• *Wet fouling* gives much the same appearance as cold fouling, except that the plug shell and electrodes are covered with excess oil.

• *Splashed fouling* occurs when long-accumulating deposits in the combustion chamber are loosened and thrown onto the spark plug insulator surface.

• *Core Bridging* is a rare condition that occurs when a deposit is thrown against the plug and lodges between the center electrode and the shell of the plug. In effect, a bridge is formed between these parts and results in a shortening of the circuit.

• *Gap Bridging* is similar to core bridging except that the deposits bridge the gap between the center electrode and the side electrode, thus eliminating the air gap which is necessary for proper plug operation.

• *High speed glazing* occurs when plug temperature rises suddenly and normal deposits do not have their usual opportunity to "fluff" off the plug, but instead melt and form a conductive coating.

• *Scavenger deposits* are normal with some branded fuels, and may be white or yellow in color. Such deposits can be considered normal. And the plugs can be cleaned in the normal fashion.

• *Overheating* of the plug is indicated by a blistered condition of the insulator. In such cases the insulator will be found to be either white or very light gray in color. Spark plugs can be overheated by various engine malfunctions, such as over-advanced ignition, cooling system stoppages and other causes.

• *Chipped insulator* damage is usually the result of improperly adjusting the gap of a plug by bending the center electrode. A plug with a chipped insulator should be replaced.

• *Mechanical damage* occurs when a foreign object in the combustion chamber damages the spark plug.

• *Reversed coil polarity* is best detected by a tune-up oscilloscope, but can be identified by lack of wear of the center electrode and wear in a semi-circular pattern of the side electrode. When this condition exists, the primary coil leads are reversed from their proper positions and should be changed.

Fuses

Model	Circuit	Amps.
1,300 Type 1 (6 Volt)	Horn, flashers, stoplight, wipers	16
	High beam warning light, left high beam	8
	Right high beam	8
	Left low beam	8
	Right low beam	8
	Left parking light,left taillight	8
	Right parking light, right taillight license plate light	8
	Headlight dimmer, radio, interior light	16
1,500 Type 1 (12 Volt)	Turn signals, horn, Stoplights brake warning light, Automatic Stickshift and rear window defroster switch current	8
	Wipers	8
	High beam warning light, left high beam	8
	Right high beam	8
	Left low beam	8
	Right low beam	8
	Left parking light, left taillight	8
	License plate light, right parking light, right taillight	8
	Interior light, emergency blinkers	8
	Spare fuse	–
	Rear window defroster main current (under rear seat, left side)	8
	Backup lights (right side of engine fan housing)	8
	Automatic Stickshift control valve (left side of engine fan housing)	8
1,500 Type 2 (6 Volt)	Left low beam	8
	Right low beam	8
	Left high beam, high beam warning light	8
	Right high beam	8
	Left taillight	8
	Right taillight, license plate light, parking lights	8
	Stoplights, turn indicators	16
	Horn, interior lights, wipers, headlight dimmer	16
1,600 Type 3 (6 Volt)	Right parking light, left parking light left taillight, luggage compartment light	8
	Right taillight, license plate light	8
	Left low beam	8
	Right low beam	8
	Left high beam, high beam warning light	8
	Right high beam	8
	Spare fuse	–
	Emergency blinkers, interior light, horn, clock, radio	16
	Stoplights, turn signals	8
	Wipers, fuel gauge, warning lights	16

Light Bulbs

Model	Usage	U.S. Replacement Bulbs	VW Part No.	Wattage
36 hp.	Headlights	–	–	35/35
1,200	Parking lights	–	–	1.5
Type 1	Stoplights	–	–	15
(6 Volt)	Taillights	–	–	5
January,	License plate light	–	–	5
1954-August	Interior light	–	–	10
1955	All warning lights	–	–	1.2
	Instrument lighting	–	–	1.2
	Turn signals	–	–	3
36 hp.	Headlights	–	–	35/35
1,200 Type	Parking lights		–	2
1 (6 Volt)	Stoplights	–	–	20
from	Taillights	–	–	5
August, 1955	License plate light (tubular bulb)	–	–	5
	Interior light	–	–	10
	Semaphore-type	–	–	3
	Turn signals (tubular bulbs)	–	–	1.2
	All warning lights	–	–	1.2
	Instrument lighting	–	–	
36 hp.	Headlights	–	–	35/35
1,200 Type	Parking lights	–	–	3
1 (6 Volt)	Taillights	–	–	5
Karmann	Rear stop/turn signal	–	–	15
Ghia, from	License plate lights	–	–	5
August, 1955	Interior light	–	–	5
	Front turn signals	–	–	15
42 hp.	Headlights	–	N177051	45/40
1,200 and 1,300	Parking lights	–	N177171	4
Type 1	Stoplight/taillight	–	N177371	18/5
(6 Volt)	Turn signals	–	N177311	18
Sedan and	License plate light	–	N177191	10 ①
Convertible	Interior light	–	N177231	10
	Warning and instrument lights	–	N177221	1.2
42 hp.	Headlights	–	–	45/40
1,200 and 1,300	Parking lights	–	–	4
Type 1	Taillights	–	–	5
(6 Volt)	Stoplights	–	–	18
Karmann Ghia	Turn signals	–	–	18
	License plate lights	–	–	5
	Interior light	–	–	10
	Warning, instrument lights, clock	–		1.2
1,300 Type	Headlights	6012	11194126A	45/40
1 (12 Volt)	License plate light	–	–	10
	Interior light	–	–	10
	Instrument and warning lights	–	–	2
	Parking lights	–	–	4
	Turn signals	–	–	18
	Stoplight/taillight	–	–	18/5
1,500 and 1,600	Headlights	6012	111941261A	–
Type 1	Parking/turn signal, taillight/stoplight	1034	N177382	–
(12 Volt)	Rear turn signal	1073	N177322	–
Sedan and	License plate light	89	N177192	–
Convertible	Backup lights	1073	N177332	–
	Instrument and warning lights	–	N177222	–
	Sedan interior light	–	N177232	–
	Convertible interior light	–	N177252	–
	Warning lights for emergency flasher, brake, rear window defroster	–	N177512	–

Light Bulbs

Model	Usage	U.S. Replacement Bulbs	VW Part No.	Wattage
1,500 Type 2 (6 Volt)	Headlights	–	N177051	45/40
	Parking lights	–	N177171	4
	Turn signals	–	N177311	18
	Taillights/stoplights	–	N177371	5/18
	License plate light	–	N177191	10
	Warning lights, Instrument lights	–	N177221	1.2
	Dome light	–	N177251	5
	Clock	–	N177221	1.2
1,600 Type 3 (6 Volt)	Headlights	6006, Type 2	N177051	–
	Front parking/turn signal	1154	N177171	5/18
	Rear turn signal, stoplight	1129	N177311	18
	Taillight	81	N177181	5
	License plate light	81	N177191	10
	Warning, instrument lights	–	N177221	1.2
	Interior and luggage compartment lights	–	N177231	10

① *1,200 uses 5 watt bulb after August, 1965.*

Body 8

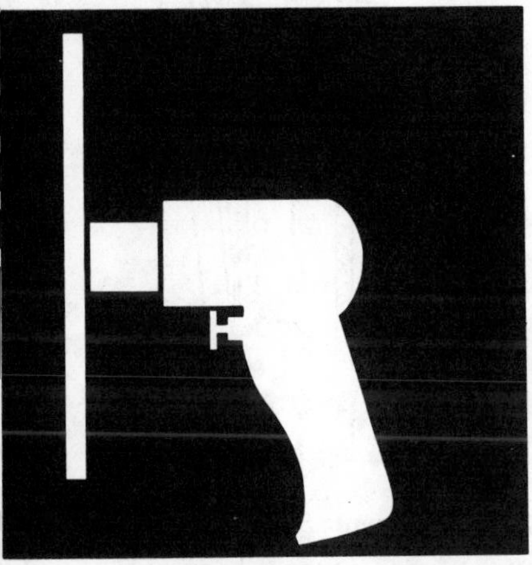

You can repair most minor auto body damage yourself. Minor damage usually falls into one of several categories: (1) small scratches and dings in the paint that can be repaired without the use of body filler, (2) deep scratches and dents that require body filler, but do not require pulling, or hammering metal back into shape and (3) rust-out repairs. The repair sequences illustrated in this chapter are typical of these types of repairs. If you want to get involved in more complicated repairs including pulling or hammering sheet metal back into shape, you will probably need more detailed instructions. Chilton's *Minor Auto Body Repair, 2nd Edition* is a comprehensive guide to repairing auto body damage yourself.

TOOLS AND SUPPLIES

The list of tools and equipment you may need to fix minor body damage ranges from very basic hand tools to a wide assortment of specialized body tools. Most minor scratches, dings and rust holes can be fixed using an electric drill, wire wheel or grinder attachment, half-round plastic file, sanding block, various grades of sandpaper (#36, which is coarse through #600, which is fine) in both wet and dry types, auto body plastic, primer, touch-up paint, spreaders, newspaper and masking tape.

Most manufacturers of auto body repair products began supplying materials to professionals. Their knowledge of the best, most-used products has been translated into body repair kits for the do-it-yourselfer. Kits are available from a number of manufacturers and contain the necessary materials in the required amounts for the repair identified on the package.

Kits are available for a wide variety of uses, including:

- Rusted out metal
- All purpose kit for dents and holes
- Dents and deep scratches
- Fiberglass repair kit
- Epoxy kit for restyling.

Kits offer the advantage of buying what you need for the job. There is little waste and little chance of materials going bad from not being used. The same manufacturers also merchandise all of the individual products used—spreaders, dent pullers, fiberglass cloth, polyester resin, cream hardener, body filler, body files, sandpaper, sanding discs and holders, primer, spray paint, etc.

CAUTION: ***Most of the products you will be using contain harmful chemicals, so be extremely careful. Always read the complete label before opening the containers. When***

you put them away for future use, be sure they are out of children's reach!

Most auto body repair kits contain all the materials you need to do the job right in the kit. So, if you have a small rust spot or dent you want to fix, check the contents of the kit before you run out and buy any additional tools.

ALIGNING BODY PANELS

Doors

There are several methods of adjusting doors. Your vehicle will probably use one of those illustrated.

Whenever a door is removed and is to be reinstalled, you should matchmark the position of the hinges on the door pillars. The holes of the hinges and/or the hinge attaching points are usually oversize to permit alignment of doors. The striker plate is also moveable, through oversize holes, permitting up-and-down, in-and-out and fore-and-aft movement. Fore-and-aft movement is made by adding or subtracting shims from behind the striker and pillar post. The striker should be adjusted so that the door closes fully and remains closed, yet enters the lock freely.

DOOR HINGES

Don't try to cover up poor door adjustment with a striker plate adjustment. The gap on each side of the door should be equal and uniform and there should be no metal-to-metal contact as the door is opened or closed.

1. Determine which hinge bolts must be loosened to move the door in the desired direction.
2. Loosen the hinge bolt(s) just enough to allow the door to be moved with a padded pry bar.
3. Move the door a small amount and check the fit, after tightening the bolts. Be sure that there is no bind or interference with adjacent panels.
4. Repeat this until the door is properly positioned, and tighten all the bolts securely.

Hood, Trunk or Tailgate

As with doors, the outline of hinges should be scribed before removal. The hood and trunk can be aligned by loosening the hinge bolts in their slotted mounting holes and moving the hood or trunk lid as necessary.

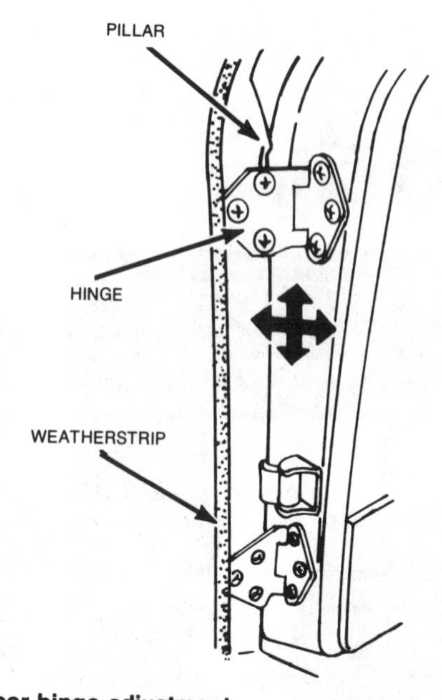

Door hinge adjustment

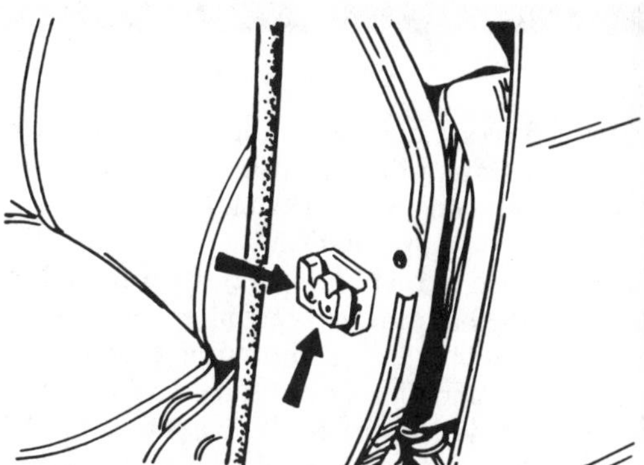
Move the door striker as indicated by arrows

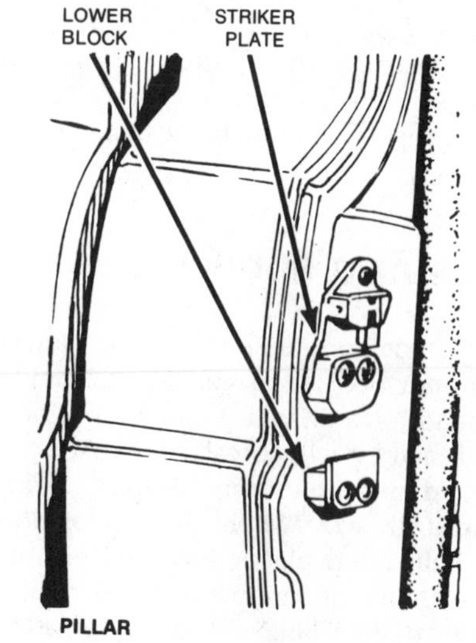

Striker plate and lower block

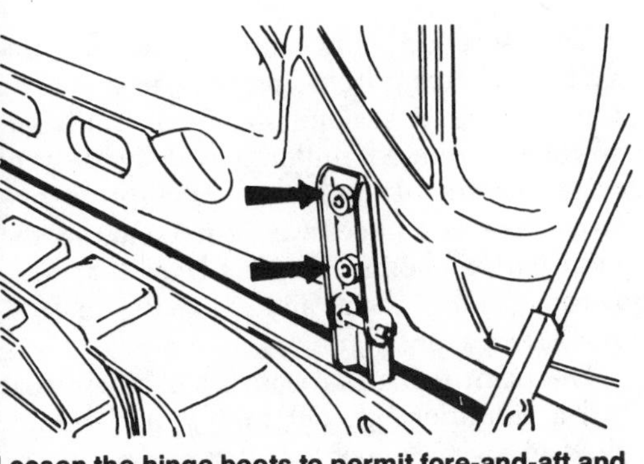

Loosen the hinge boots to permit fore-and-aft and horizontal adjustment

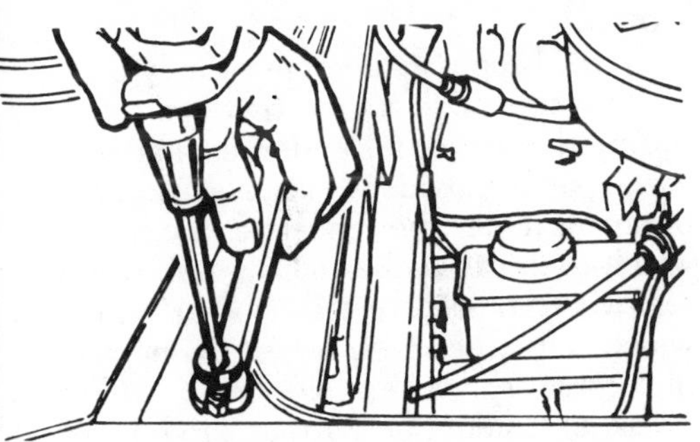

The hood is adjusted vertically by stop-screws at the front and/or rear

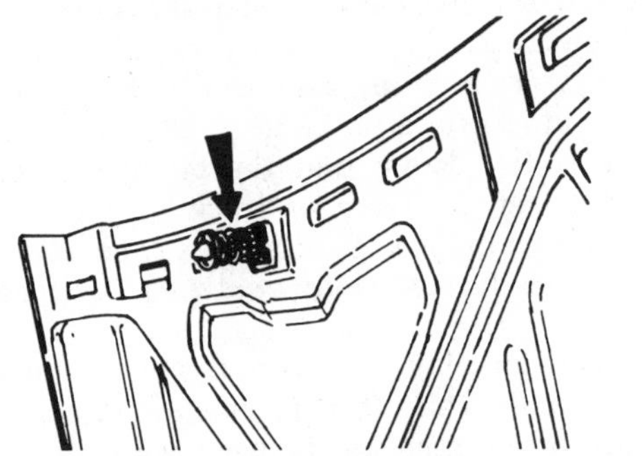

The hood pin can be adjusted for proper lock engagement

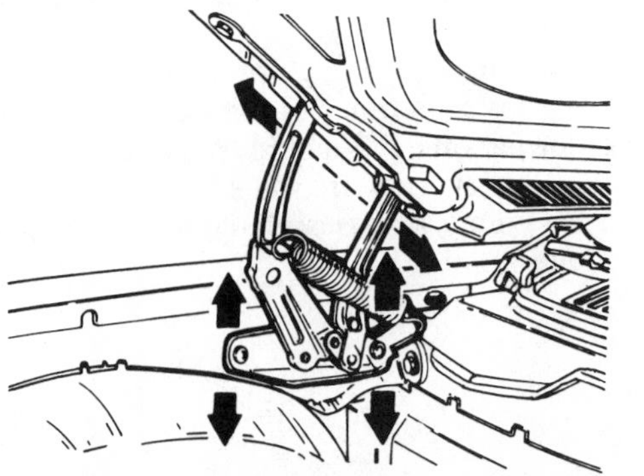

The height of the hood at the rear is adjusted by loosening the bolts that attach the hinge to the body and moving the hood up or down

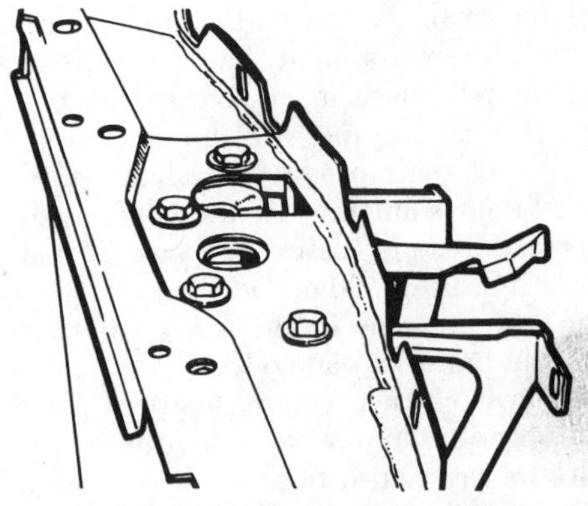

The base of the hood lock can also be repositioned slightly to give more positive lock engagement

The hood and trunk have adjustable catch locations to regulate lock engagement. Bumpers at the front and/or rear of the hood provide a vertical adjustment and the hood lockpin can be adjusted for proper engagement.

The tailgate on the station wagon can be adjusted by loosening the hinge bolts in their slotted mounting holes and moving the tailgate on its hinges. The latchplate and latch striker at the bottom of the tailgate opening can be adjusted to stop rattle. An adjustable bumper is located on each side.

RUST, UNDERCOATING, AND RUSTPROOFING

Rust

Rust is an electrochemical process. It works on ferrous metals (iron and steel) from the inside out due to exposure of unprotected surfaces to air and moisture. The possibility of rust exists practically nationwide—anywhere humidity, industrial pollution or chemical salts are present, rust can form. In coastal areas, the problem is high humidity and salt air; in snowy areas, the problem is chemical salt (de-icer) used to keep the roads clear, and in industrial areas, sulphur dioxide is present in the air from industrial pollution and is changed to sulphuric acid when it rains. The rusting process is accelerated by high temperatures, especially in snowy areas, when vehicles are driven over slushy roads and then left overnight in a heated garage.

Automotive styling also can be a contributor to rust formation. Spot welding of panels creates small pockets that trap moisture and form an environment for rust formation. Fortunately, auto manufacturers have been working hard to increase the corrosion protection of their products. Galvanized sheet metal enjoys much wider use, along with the increased use of plastic and various rust retardant coatings. Manufacturers are also designing out areas in the body where rust-forming moisture can collect.

To prevent rust, you must stop it before it gets started. On new vehicles, there are two ways to accomplish this.

First, the car or truck should be treated with a commercial rustproofing compound. There are many different brands of franchised rustproofers, but most processes involve spraying a waxy "self-healing" compound under the chassis, inside rocker panels, inside doors and fender liners and similar places where rust is likely to form. Prices for a quality rustproofing job range from $100–$250, depending on the area, the brand name and the size of the vehicle.

Ideally, the vehicle should be rustproofed as soon as possible following the purchase. The surfaces of the car or truck have begun to oxidize and deteriorate during shipping. In addition, the car may have sat on a dealer's lot or on a lot at the factory, and once the rust has progressed past the stage of light, powdery surface oxidation rustproofing is not likely to be worthwhile. Professional rustproofers feel that once rust has formed, rustproofing will simply seal in moisture already present. Most franchised rustproofing operations offer a 3–5 year warranty against rust-through, but will not support that warranty if the rustproofing is not applied within three months of the date of manufacture.

Undercoating should not be mistaken for rustproofing. Undercoating is a black, tar-like substance that is applied to the underside of a vehicle. Its basic function is to deaden noises that are transmitted from under the car. It simply cannot get into the crevices and seams where moisture tends to collect. In fact, it may clog up drainage holes and ventilation passages. Some undercoatings also tend to crack or peel with age and only create more moisture and corrosion attracting pockets.

The second thing you should do immediately after purchasing the car is apply a paint sealant. A sealant is a petroleum based product marketed under a wide variety of brand names. It has the same protective properties as a good wax, but bonds to the paint with a chemically inert layer that seals it from the air. If air can't get at the surface, oxidation cannot start.

The paint sealant kit consists of a base coat and a conditioning coat that should be applied every 6–8 months, depending on the manufacturer. The base coat must be applied before waxing, or the wax must first be removed.

Third, keep a garden hose handy for your car in winter. Use it a few times on nice days during the winter for underneath areas, and it will pay big dividends when spring arrives. Spraying under the fenders and other areas which even car washes don't reach will help remove road salt, dirt and other build-ups which help breed rust. Adjust the nozzle to a high-force spray. An old brush will help break up residue, permitting it to be washed away more easily.

It's a somewhat messy job, but worth it in the long run because rust often starts in those hidden areas.

At the same time, wash grime off the door sills and, more importantly, the under portions of the doors, plus the tailgate if you have a station wagon or truck. Applying a coat of wax to those areas at least once before and once during winter will help fend off rust.

When applying the wax to the under parts of the doors, you will note small drain holes. These holes often are plugged with undercoating or dirt. Make sure they are cleaned out to prevent water build-up inside the doors. A small punch or penknife will do the job.

Water from the high-pressure sprays in car washes sometimes can get into the housings for parking and taillights, so take a close look. If they contain water merely loosen the retaining screws and the water should run out.

Repairing Scratches and Small Dents

Step 1. This dent (arrow) is typical of a deep scratch or minor dent. If deep enough, the dent or scratch can be pulled out or hammered out from behind. In this case no straightening is necessary

Step 2. Using an 80-grit grinding disc on an electric drill grind the paint from the surrounding area down to bare metal. This will provide a rough surface for the body filler to grab

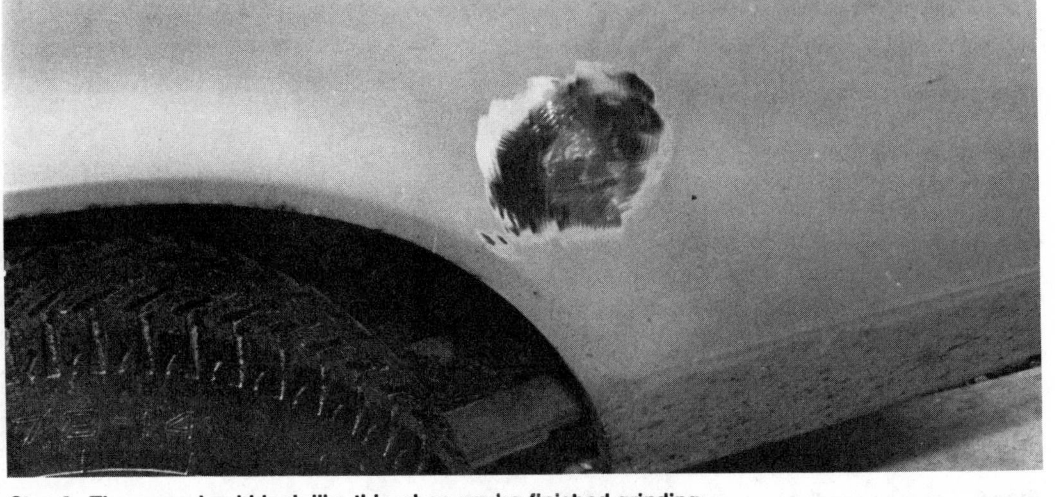

Step 3. The area should look like this when you're finished grinding

Step 4. Mix the body filler and cream hardener according to the directions

Step 5. Spread the body filler evenly over the entire area. Be sure to cover the area completely

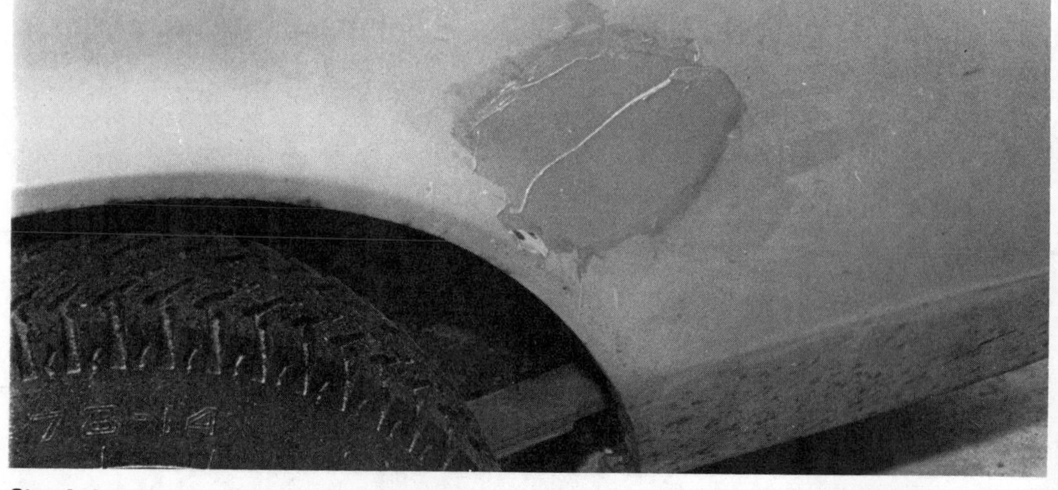

Step 6. Let the body filler dry until the surface can just be scratched with your fingernail

Step 7. Knock the high spots from the body filler with a body file

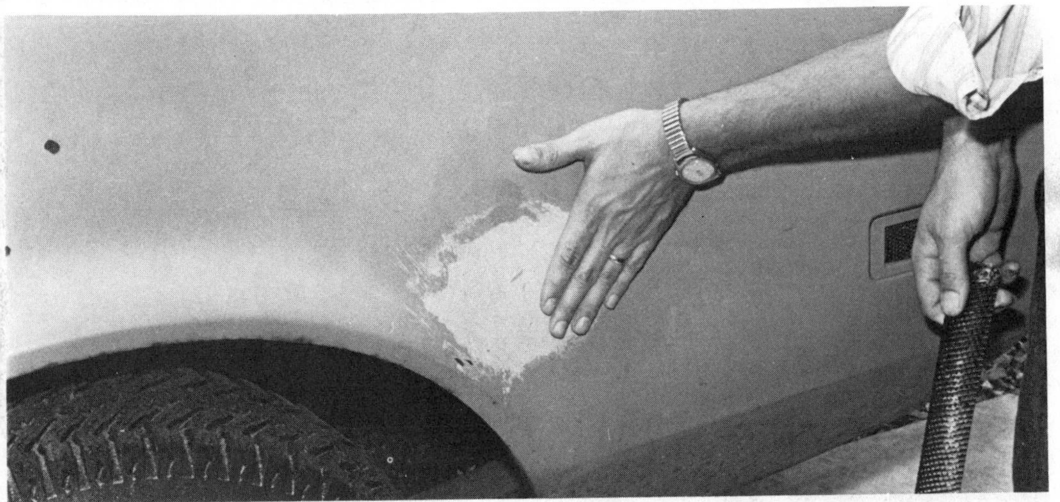

Step 8. Check frequently with the palm of your hand for high and low spots. If you wind up with low spots, you may have to apply another layer of filler

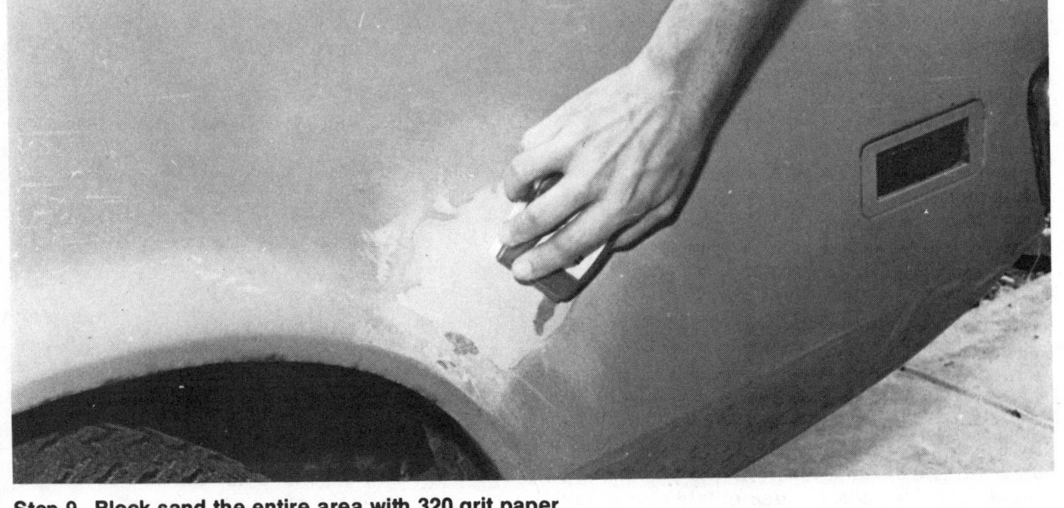

Step 9. Block sand the entire area with 320 grit paper

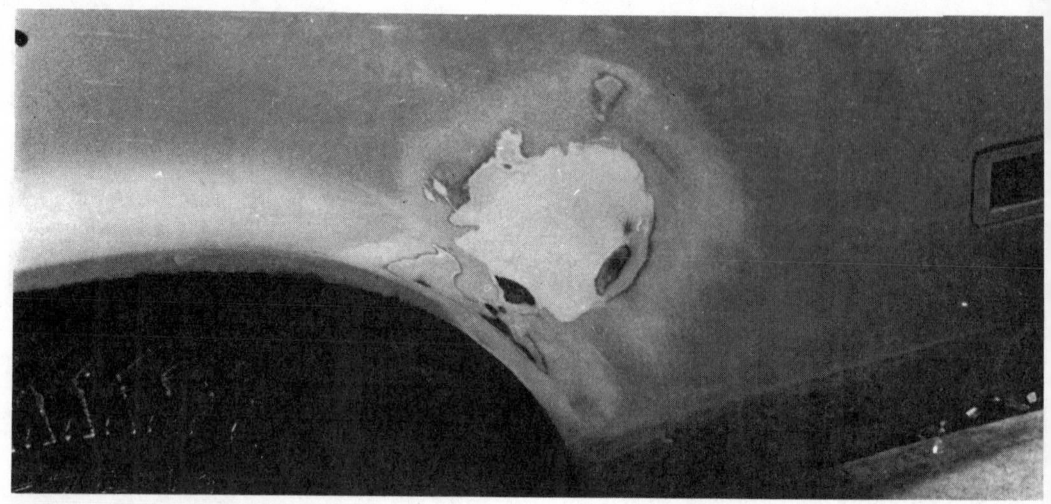

Step 10. When you're finished, the repair should look like this. Note the sand marks extending 2—3 inches out from the repaired area

Step 11. Prime the entire area with automotive primer

Step 12. The finished repair ready for the final paint coat. Note that the primer has covered the sanding marks (see Step 10). A repair of this size should be able to be spotpainted with good results

REPAIRING RUST HOLES

One thing you have to remember about rust: even if you grind away all the rusted metal in a panel, and repair the area with any of the kits available, *eventually* the rust will return. There are two reasons for this. One, rust is a chemical reaction that causes pressure under the repair from the inside out. That's how the blisters form. Two, the back side of the panel (and the repair) is wide open to moisture, and unpainted body filler acts like a sponge. That's why the best solution to rust problems is to remove the rusted panel and install a new one or have the rusted area cut out and a new piece of sheet metal welded in its place. The trouble with welding is the expense; sometimes it will cost more than the car or truck is worth.

One of the better solutions to do-it-yourself rust repair is the process using a fiberglass cloth repair kit (shown here). This will give a strong repair that resists cracking and moisture and is relatively easy to use. It can be used on large or small holes and also can be applied over contoured surfaces.

Step 1. Rust areas such as this are common and are easily fixed

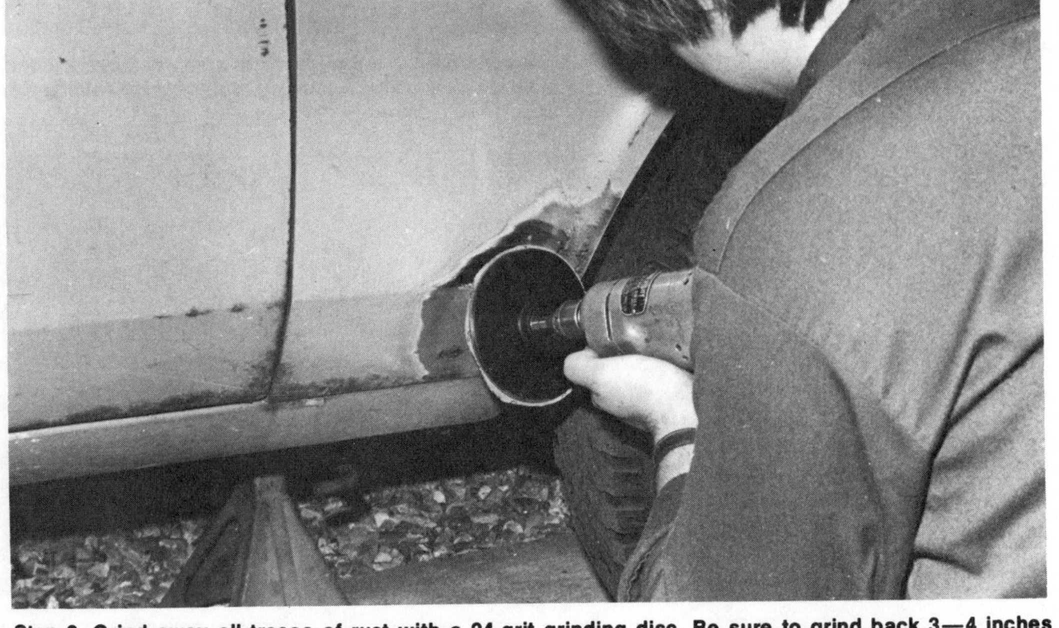

Step 2. Grind away all traces of rust with a 24-grit grinding disc. Be sure to grind back 3—4 inches from the edge of the hole down to bare metal and be sure all traces of rust are removed

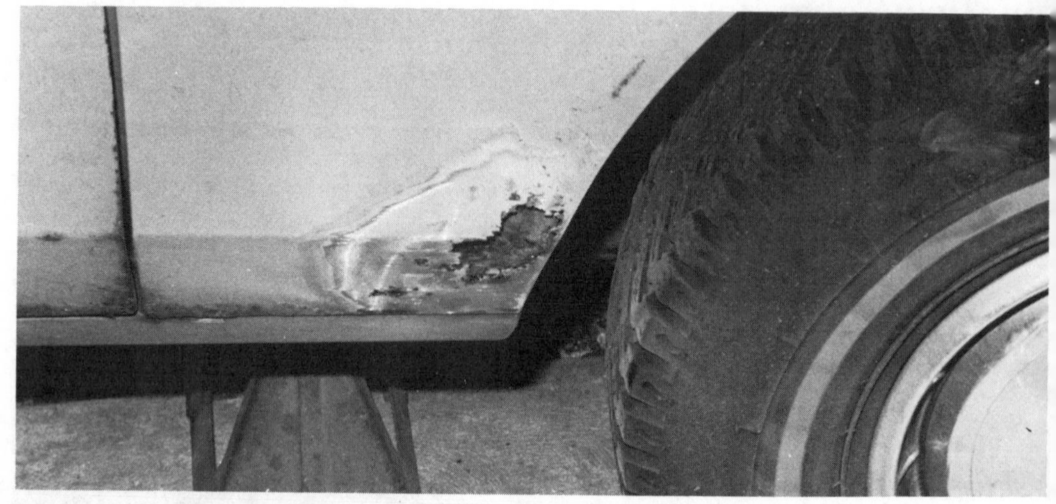

Step 3. Be sure all rust is removed from the edges of the metal. The edges must be ground back to un-rusted metal

Step 4. If you are going to use release film, cut a piece about 2″ larger than the area you have sanded. Place the film over the repair and mark the sanded area on the film. Avoid any unnecessary wrinkling of the film

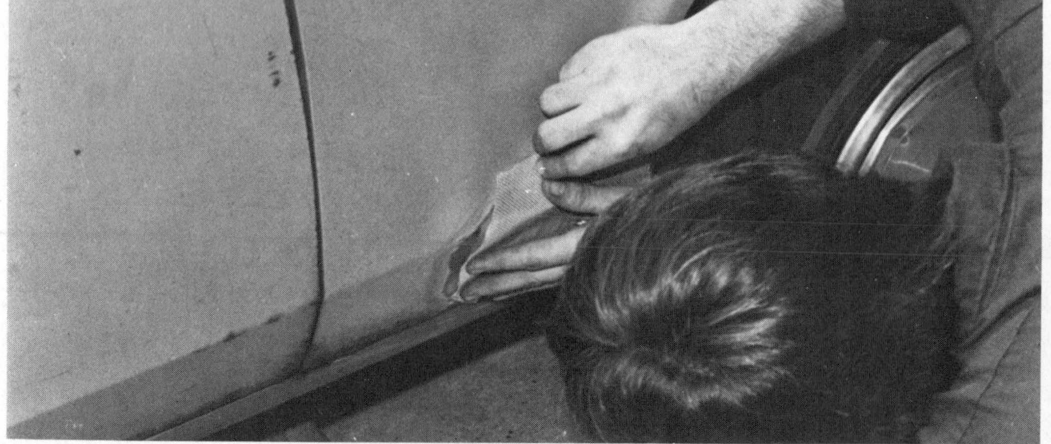

Step 5. Cut 2 pieces of fiberglass matte. One piece should be about 1″ smaller than the sanded area and the second piece should be 1″ smaller than the first. Use sharp scissors to avoid loose ends

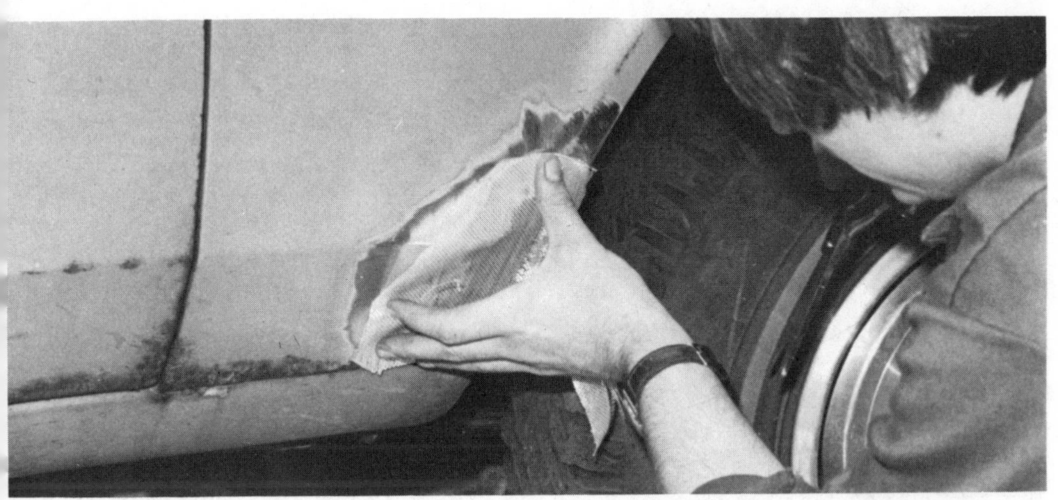

Step 6. Check the dimensions of the release film and cloth by holding them up to the repair area

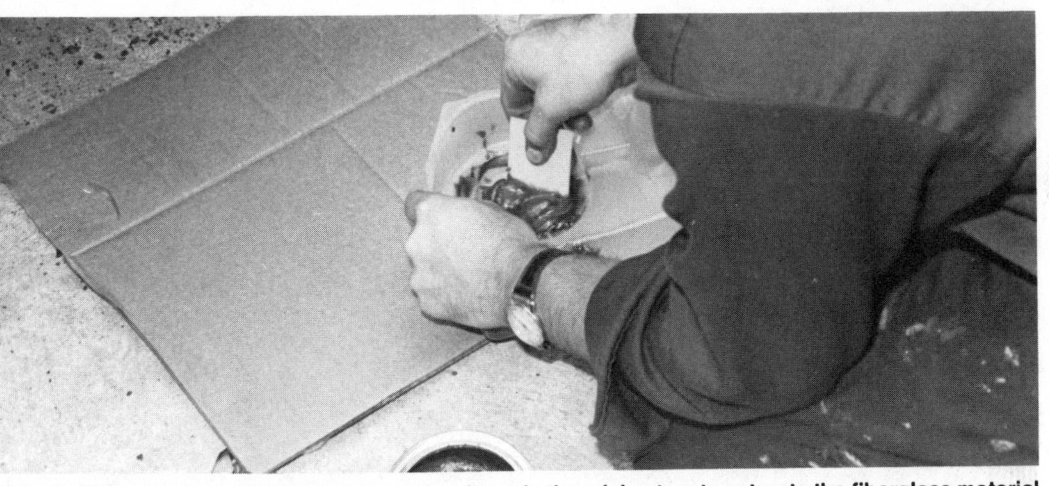

Step 7. Mix enough repair jelly and cream hardener in the mixing tray to saturate the fiberglass material or fill the repair area. Follow the directions on the container

Step 8. Lay the release sheet on a flat surface and spread an even layer of filler, large enough to cover the repair. Lay the smaller piece of fiberglass cloth in the center of the sheet and spread another layer of repair jelly over the fiberglass cloth. Repeat the operation for the larger piece of cloth. If the fiberglass cloth is not used, spread the repair jelly on the release film, concentrated in the middle of the repair

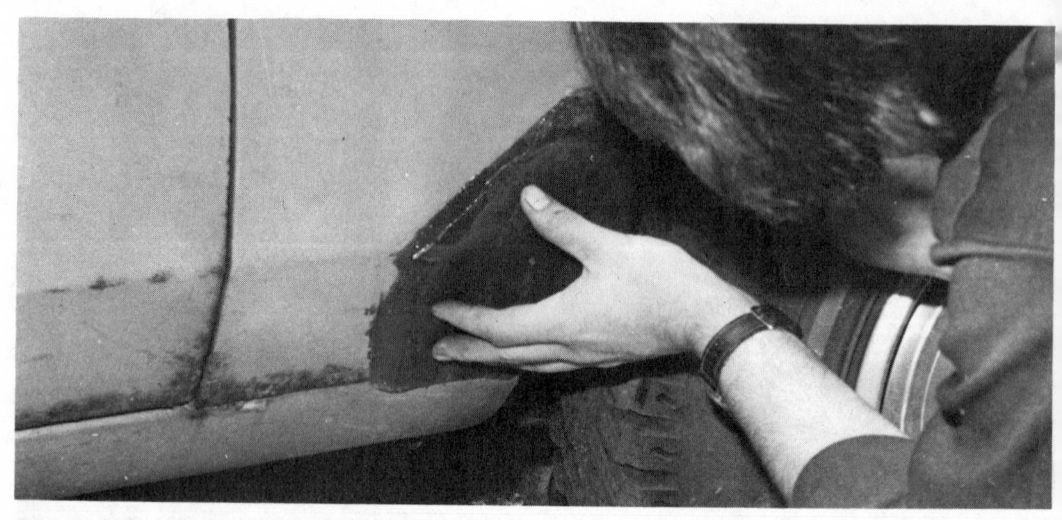

Step 9. Place the repair material over the repair area, with the release film facing outward

Step 10. Use a spreader and work from the center outward to smooth the material, following the body contours. Be sure to remove all air bubbles

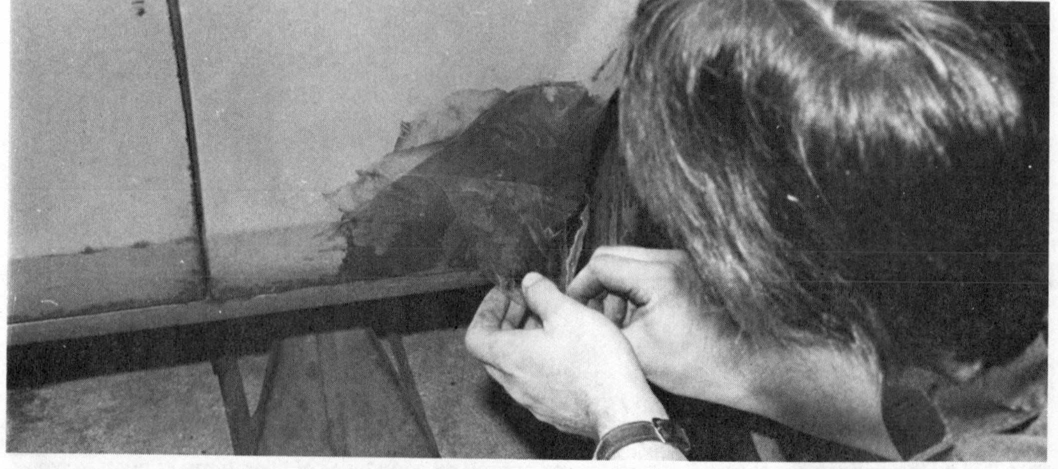

Step 11. Wait until the repair has dried tack-free and peel off the release sheet. The ideal working temperature is 65—90° F. Cooler or warmer temperatures or high humidity may require additional curing time

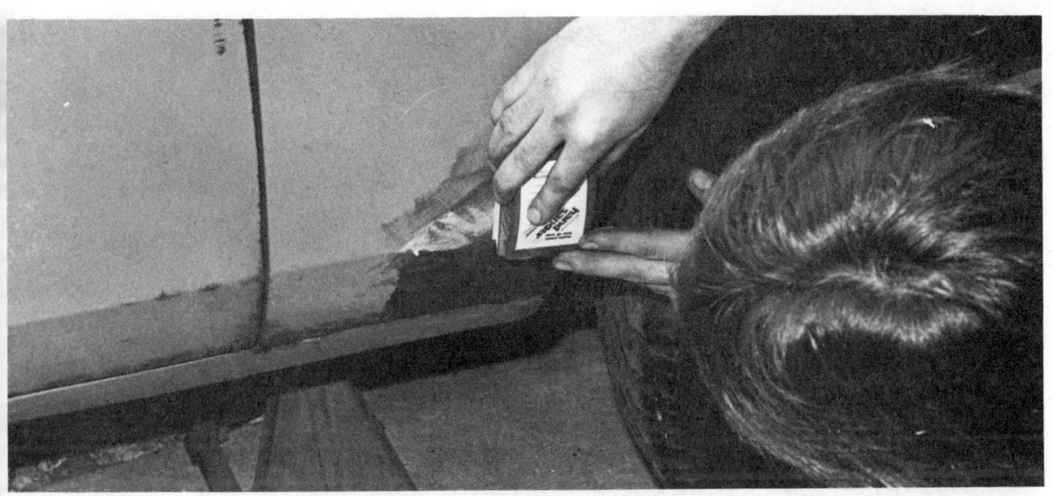

Step 12. Sand and feather-edge the entire area. The initial sanding can be done with a sanding disc on an electric drill if care is used. Finish the sanding with a block sander

Step 13. When the area is sanded smooth, mix some topcoat and hardener and apply it directly with a spreader. This will give a smooth finish and prevent the glass matte from showing through the paint

Step 14. Block sand the topcoat with finishing sandpaper

Step 15. To finish this repair, grind out the surface rust along the top edge of the rocker panel

Step 16. Mix some more repair jelly and cream hardener and apply it directly over the surface

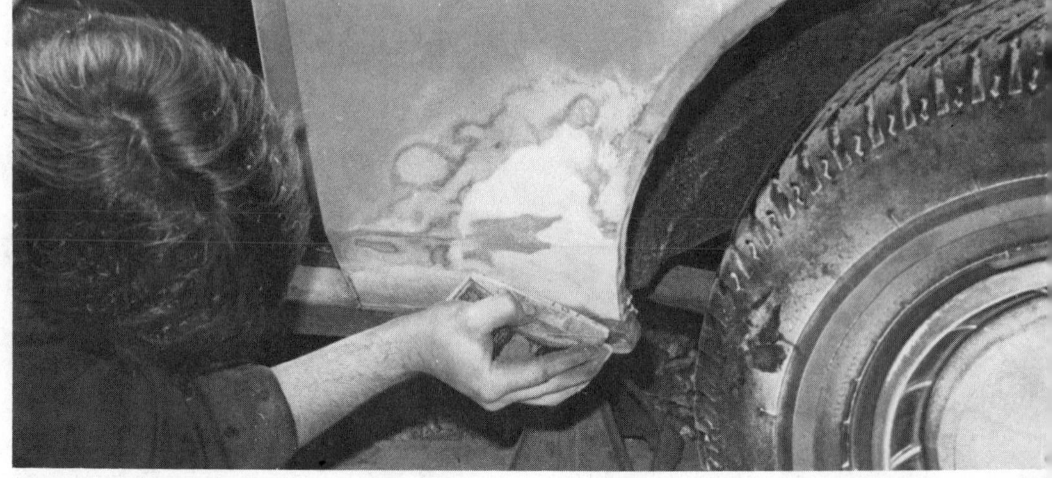

Step 17. When it dries tack-free, block sand the surface smooth

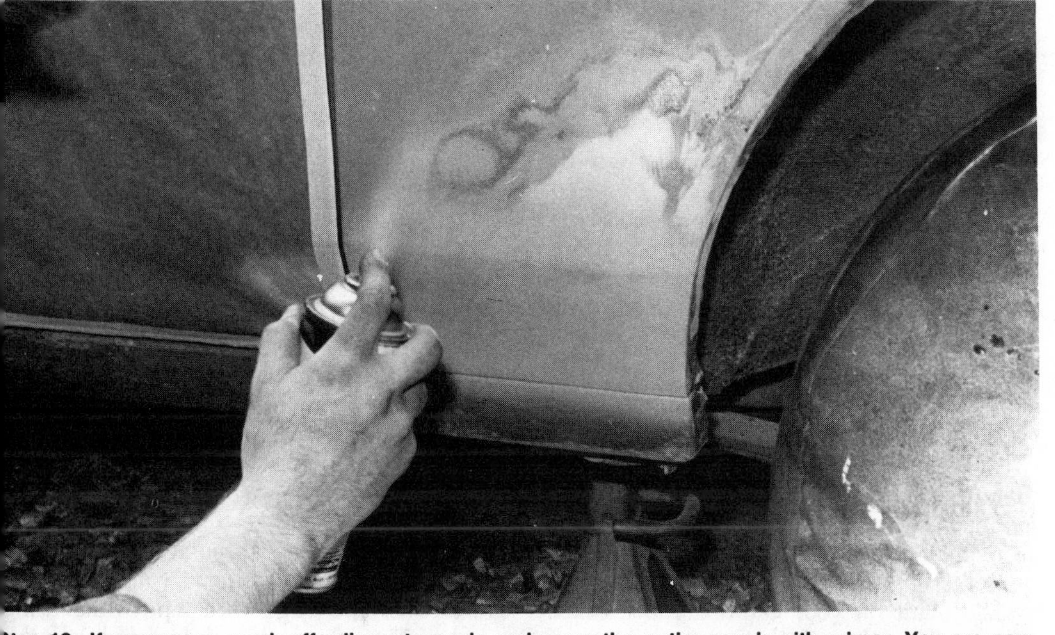

Step 18. If necessary, mask off adjacent panels and spray the entire repair with primer. You are now ready for a color coat

AUTO BODY CARE

There are hundreds—maybe thousands—of products on the market, all designed to protect or aid your car's finish in some manner. There are as many different products as there are ways to use them, but they all have one thing in common—the surface must be clean.

Washing

The primary ingredient for washing your car is water, preferably "soft" water. In many areas of the country, the local water supply is "hard" containing many minerals. The little rings or film that is left on your car's surface after it has dried is the result of "hard" water.

Since you usually can't change the local water supply, the next best thing is to dry the surface before it has a chance to dry itself.

Into the water you usually add soap. Don't use detergents or common, coarse soaps. Your car's paint never truly dries out, but is always evaporating residual oils into the air. Harsh detergents will remove these oils, causing the paint to dry faster than normal. Instead use warm water and a non-detergent soap made especially for waxed surfaces or a liquid soap made for waxed surfaces or a liquid soap made for washing dishes by hand. Other products that can be used on painted surfaces include baking soda or plain soda water for stubborn dirt.

Wash the car completely, starting at the top, and rinse it completely clean. Abrasive grit should be loaded off under water pressure; scrubbing grit off will scratch the finish. The best washing tool is a sponge, cleaning mitt or soft towel. Whichever you choose, replace it often as each tends to absorb grease and dirt.

Other ways to get a better wash include:

• Don't wash your car in the sun or when the finish is hot.

• Use water pressure to remove caked-on dirt.

• Remove tree-sap and bird effluence immediately. Such substances will eat through wax, polish and paint.

One of the best implements to dry your car is a turkish towel or an old, soft bath towel. Anything with a deep nap will hold any dirt in suspension and not grind it into the paint.

Harder cloths will only grind the grit into the paint making more scratches. Always start drying at the top, followed by the hood and trunk and sides. You'll find there's always more dirt near the rocker panels and wheelwells which will wind up on the rest of the car if you dry these areas first.

Cleaners, Waxes and Polishes

Before going any farther you should know the function of various products.

Cleaners—remove the top layer of dead pigment or paint.

Rubbing or polishing compounds—used to remove stubborn dirt, get rid of minor scratches, smooth away imperfections and partially restore badly weathered paint.

Polishes—contain no abrasives or waxes; they shine the paint by adding oils to the paint.

Waxes—are a protective coating for the polish.

CLEANERS AND COMPOUNDS

Before you apply any wax, you'll have to remove oxidation, road film and other types of pollutants that washing alone will not remove.

The paint on your car never dries completely. There are always residual oils evaporating from the paint into the air. When enough oils are present in the paint, it has a healthy shine (gloss). When too many oils evaporate the paint takes on a whitish cast known as oxidation. The idea of polishing and waxing is to keep enough oil present in the painted surface to prevent oxidation; but when it occurs, the only recourse is to remove the top layer of "dead" paint, exposing the healthy paint underneath.

Products to remove oxidation and road film are sold under a variety of generic names—polishes, cleaner, rubbing compound, cleaner/polish, polish/cleaner, self-polishing wax, pre-wax cleaner, finish restorer and many more. Regardless of name there are two types of cleaners—abrasive cleaners (sometimes called polishing or rubbing compounds) that remove oxidation by grinding away the top layer of "dead" paint, or chemical cleaners that dissolve the "dead" pigment, allowing it to be wiped away.

Abrasive cleaners, by their nature, leave thousands of minute scratches in the finish, which must be polished out later. These should only be used in extreme cases, but are usually the only thing to use on badly oxidized paint finishes. Chemical cleaners are much milder but are not strong enough for severe cases of oxidation or weathered paint.

The most popular cleaners are liquid or paste abrasive polishing and rubbing compounds. Polishing compounds have a finer abrasive grit for medium duty work. Rubbing compounds are a coarser abrasive and for heavy duty work. Unless you are familiar with how to use compounds, be very careful. Excessive rubbing with any type of compound or cleaner can grind right through the paint to primer or bare metal. Follow the directions on the container—depending on type, the cleaner may or may not be OK for your paint. For example, some cleaners are not formulated for acrylic lacquer finishes.

When a small area needs compounding or heavy polishing, it's best to do the job by hand. Some people prefer a powered buffer for large areas. Avoid cutting through the paint along styling edges on the body. Small, hand operations where the compound is applied and rubbed using cloth folded into a thick ball allow you to work in straight lines along such edges.

To avoid cutting through on the edges when using a power buffer, try masking tape. Just cover the edge with tape while using power. Then finish the job by hand with the tape removed. Even then work carefully. The paint tends to be a lot thinner along the sharp ridges stamped into the panels.

Whether compounding by machine or by hand, only work on a small area and apply the compound sparingly. If the materials are spread too thin, or allowed to sit too long, they dry out. Once dry they lose the ability to deliver a smooth, clean finish. Also, dried out polish tends to cause the buffer to stick in one spot. This in turn can burn or cut through the finish.

WAXES AND POLISHES

Your car's finish can be protected in a number of ways. A cleaner/wax or polish/cleaner followed by wax or variations of each all provide good results. The two-step approach (polish followed by wax) is probably slightly better but consumes more time and effort. Properly fed with oils, your paint should never need cleaning, but despite the best polishing job, it won't last unless it's protected with wax. Without wax, polish must be renewed at least once a month to prevent oxidation. Years ago (some still swear by it today), the best wax was made from the Brazilian palm, the Carnuba, favored for its vegetable base and high melting point. However, modern synthetic waxes are harder, which means they protect against moisture better, and chemically inert silicone is used for a long lasting protection. The only problem with silicone wax is that it penetrates all layers of paint. To repaint or touch up a panel or car protected by silicone wax, you have to completely strip the finish to avoid "fish-eyes."

Under normal conditions, silicone waxes will last 4–6 months, but you have to be careful of wax build-up from too much waxing. Too thick a coat of wax is just as bad as no wax at all; it stops the paint from breathing.

Combination cleaners/waxes have become popular lately because they remove the old layer of wax plus light oxidation, while putting on a fresh coat of wax at the same time. Some cleaners/waxes contain abrasive cleaners which require caution, although many cleaner/waxes use a chemical cleaner.

Applying Wax or Polish

You may view polishing and waxing your car as a pleasant way to spend an afternoon, or as a boring chore, but it has to be done to keep the paint on your car. Caring for the paint doesn't require special tools, but you should follow a few rules.

1. Use a good quality wax.
2. Before applying any wax or polish, be sure the surface is completely clean. Just because the car looks clean, doesn't mean it's ready for polish or wax.
3. If the finish on your car is weathered, dull, or oxidized, it will probably have to be compounded to remove the old or oxidized paint. If the paint is simply dulled from lack of care, one of the non-abrasive cleaners known as polishing compounds will do the trick. If the paint is severely scratched or really dull, you'll probably have to use a rubbing compound to prepare the finish for waxing. If you're not sure which one to use, use the polishing compound, since you can easily ruin the finish by using too strong a compound.
4. Don't apply wax, polish or compound in direct sunlight, even if the directions on the can say you can. Most waxes will not cure properly in bright sunlight and you'll probably end up with a blotchy looking finish.
5. Don't rub the wax off too soon. The result will be a wet, dull looking finish. Let the wax dry thoroughly before buffing it off.
6. A constant debate among car enthusiasts is how wax should be applied. Some maintain pastes or liquids should be applied in a circular motion, but body shop experts have long thought that this approach results in barely detectable circular abrasions, especially on cars that are waxed frequently. They advise rubbing in straight lines, especially if any kind of cleaner is involved.
7. If an applicator is not supplied with the wax, use a piece of soft cheesecloth or very soft lint-free material. The same applies to buffing the surface.

SPECIAL SURFACES

One-step combination cleaner and wax formulas shouldn't be used on many of the special surfaces which abound on cars. The one-step materials contain abrasives to achieve a clean surface under the wax top coat. The abrasives are so mild that you could clean a car every week for a couple of years without fear of rubbing through the paint. But this same level of abrasiveness might, through repeated use, damage decals used for special trim effects. This includes wide stripes, wood-grain trim and other appliques.

Painted plastics must be cleaned with care. If a cleaner is too aggressive it will cut through the paint and expose the primer. If bright trim such as polished aluminum or chrome is painted, cleaning must be performed with even greater care. If rubbing compound is being used, it will cut faster than polish.

Abrasive cleaners will dull an acrylic finish. The best way to clean these newer finishes is with a non-abrasive liquid polish. Only dirt and oxidation, not paint, will be removed.

Taking a few minutes to read the instructions on the can of polish or wax will help prevent making serious mistakes. Not all preparations will work on all surfaces. And some are intended for power application while others will only work when applied by hand.

Don't get the idea that just pouring on some polish and then hitting it with a buffer will suffice. Power equipment speeds the operation. But it also adds a measure of risk. It's very easy to damage the finish if you use the wrong methods or materials.

Caring for Chrome

Read the label on the container. Many products are formulated specifically for chrome, but others contain abrasives that will scratch the chrome finish. If it isn't recommended for chrome, don't use it.

Never use steel wool or kitchen soap pads to clean chrome. Be careful not to get chrome cleaner on paint or interior vinyl surfaces. If you do, get it off immediately.

Troubleshooting

TROUBLESHOOTING THE ENGINE

Troubleshooting is an orderly procedure in which possible causes of trouble are eliminated one by one until the fault is found.

Troubleshooting of the engine entails investigation of parts of four different subsystems: fuel, air, spark, and compression. Troubleshooting other parts of the car also includes basic mechanical logic applied to known symptoms, and if done methodically, should prove successful for the troubleshooter.

The accompanying chart, "Engine Diagnosis", is a flow diagram presentation of the logic involved in tracking down problems within the engine and narrowing down the field of possible engine ailments. The following engine conditions and possible causes should also prove helpful to the troubleshooter:

ENGINE WILL NOT START

Battery is weak.
Coil or condenser is faulty.
Cracked or shorted ignition cables.
Defective starter motor.
Starter solenoid defective.
Moisture contained in distributor cap.
Battery connections loose or corroded.
Blockage of fuel line.
Carburetor float setting incorrect.
Fuel pump inoperative.
Dirt in carburetor, blocking needle valve or jet.
Carburetor flooded due to extended starting attempts.
Distributor contact points dirty.
Ignition timing incorrect.
Spark plugs improperly gapped.

ENGINE MISSING—ACCELERATION

Ignition timing incorrect.
Spark plugs dirty or improperly gapped.
Faulty carburetor accelerator pump.
Distributor contact points dirty or burned.
Engine valves burned or warped.
Carburetor improperly adjusted.
Ignition coil or condenser faulty.
Distributor advance mechanism inoperative.

ENGINE MISSING—HIGH SPEED

Dirt in fuel line or carburetor.
Ignition timing incorrect.
Excessive play in distributor shaft.
Distributor cam or rotor burned or worn.
Ignition points incorrectly gapped.
Inoperative ignition coil or condenser.

ENGINE—POOR PERFORMANCE AT ALL SPEEDS

Ignition timing incorrect.
Ignition coil or condenser faulty.
Excessive play in distributor shaft.
Distributor shaft cam worn.
Malfunctioning of distributor advance mechanism.
Spark plugs dirty or incorrectly gapped.
Compression low or unbalanced in different cylinders.
Ignition cables cracked and shorting out.
Engine valves burned, warped, or pitted.
Carburetor float setting incorrect.
Fuel line or carburetor blocked by dirt.
Excessive back pressure in exhaust system due to clogged muffler or tail pipe.
Valve timing incorrect.
Leaky intake manifold or carburetor gasket.
Carburetor out of adjustment or broken.

STALLING OF ENGINE

Incorrect idle speed setting.
Choke adjustment incorrect.
Improper slow-speed mixture setting in carburetor.
Coil or condenser faulty.
Distributor points dirty or incorrectly gapped.
Carburetor float setting incorrect.
Leaky intake manifold or carburetor gasket.
Ignition wiring faulty.

LOW OIL PRESSURE

Oil thin or diluted.
Oil level too low.
Oil pump worn or not operating properly.
Bearing clearances excessive.
Oil pressure sending unit inoperative.
Oil pressure relief valve sticking.
Obstruction in oil pump suction tube.

ENGINE NOISES—VALVES

Sticky valves.
Bent valve stem.
Warped or burned valve head.
Valve spring broken.
Valve tappets out of adjustment.
Loose rocker arms.
Bent or worn push rod.
Worn or loose rocker arm shaft.
Worn valve or tappet guides.
Tappets dirty.
Valve springs of wrong specifications.

ENGINE NOISES—PISTON

Piston collapsed or broken.
Piston pin too tight.
Excessive clearance between piston and cylinder.
Piston or cylinder wall scored.
Broken piston rings.
Loose or broken piston pin.
Misalignment of piston and cylinder bore.

ENGINE NOISES—CRANKSHAFT BEARING

Loose connecting rod bearing.
Main bearing loose.
Connecting rod bent.
Flywheel loose.
Excessive crankshaft end play (noticeable when engaging clutch).
Loose crankshaft pulley. (Sounds like bearing.)
Crankshaft misalignment.

ENGINE NOISES—DETONATION

Denonation is a spontaneous combustion within the cylinder. It is caused by an imbalance of compression ratio, heat, fuel value, and timing. Detonation can be annoying, wasteful and also most destructive to engine parts.

Excessively high engine temperature.
Spark plugs that are too hot for their intended use.
Improper ignition timing.
Use of a fuel of a too low octane rating.
Carburetor mixture excessively lean.
Incandescence within the combustion area caused by carbon particles, sharp edges, burnt spark plugs, etc.

Troubleshooting Instruments

HYDROMETER

A specific gravity test is a practical indicator of the state of charge of the battery. As a battery is discharged, a chemical change takes place within each cell. The sulphate of the electrolyte combines chemically with the battery plates, thus reducing the weight of the electrolyte. For this reason the specific gravity of the acid, or electrolyte, of a partially charged battery will be less than that of one that is fully charged. The electrolyte in a fully charged battery is usually about 1.285 times as heavy as pure water at the same temperature. The following chart gives an in-

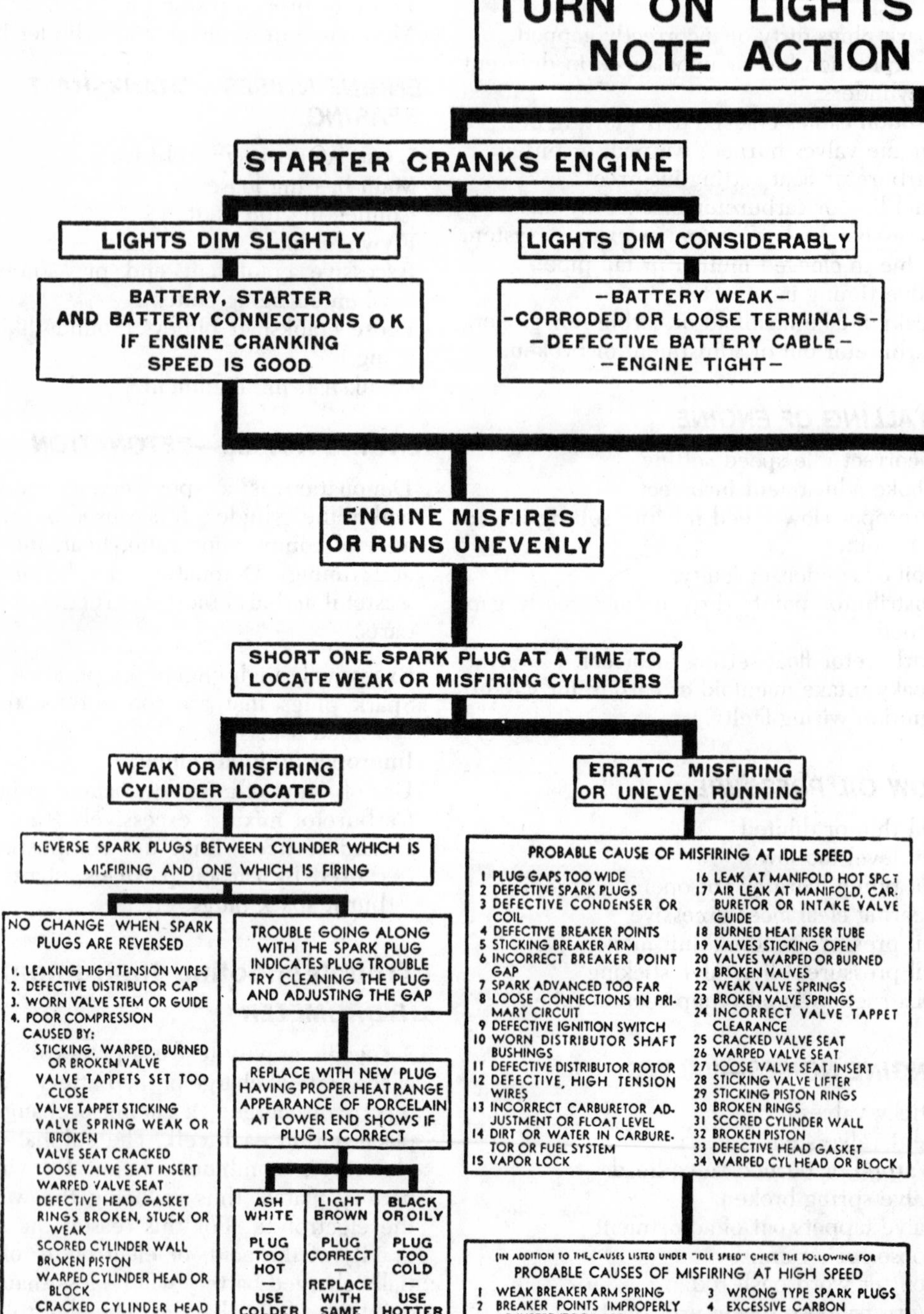
TROUBLE
ENGINE MISFIRING
TURN ON LIGHTS NOTE ACTION
STARTER CRANKS ENGINE
LIGHTS DIM SLIGHTLY
BATTERY, STARTER AND BATTERY CONNECTIONS O K IF ENGINE CRANKING SPEED IS GOOD
LIGHTS DIM CONSIDERABLY
-BATTERY WEAK- -CORRODED OR LOOSE TERMINALS- -DEFECTIVE BATTERY CABLE- -ENGINE TIGHT-
ENGINE MISFIRES OR RUNS UNEVENLY
SHORT ONE SPARK PLUG AT A TIME TO LOCATE WEAK OR MISFIRING CYLINDERS
WEAK OR MISFIRING CYLINDER LOCATED
REVERSE SPARK PLUGS BETWEEN CYLINDER WHICH IS MISFIRING AND ONE WHICH IS FIRING
NO CHANGE WHEN SPARK PLUGS ARE REVERSED
1. LEAKING HIGH TENSION WIRES
2. DEFECTIVE DISTRIBUTOR CAP
3. WORN VALVE STEM OR GUIDE
4. POOR COMPRESSION CAUSED BY:
STICKING, WARPED, BURNED OR BROKEN VALVE
VALVE TAPPETS SET TOO CLOSE
VALVE TAPPET STICKING
VALVE SPRING WEAK OR BROKEN
VALVE SEAT CRACKED
LOOSE VALVE SEAT INSERT
WARPED VALVE SEAT
DEFECTIVE HEAD GASKET
RINGS BROKEN, STUCK OR WEAK
SCORED CYLINDER WALL
BROKEN PISTON
WARPED CYLINDER HEAD OR BLOCK
CRACKED CYLINDER HEAD OR BLOCK
TROUBLE GOING ALONG WITH THE SPARK PLUG INDICATES PLUG TROUBLE TRY CLEANING THE PLUG AND ADJUSTING THE GAP
REPLACE WITH NEW PLUG HAVING PROPER HEAT RANGE APPEARANCE OF PORCELAIN AT LOWER END SHOWS IF PLUG IS CORRECT
ASH WHITE — PLUG TOO HOT — USE COLDER PLUG
LIGHT BROWN — PLUG CORRECT — REPLACE WITH SAME TYPE
BLACK OR OILY — PLUG TOO COLD — USE HOTTER PLUG
ERRATIC MISFIRING OR UNEVEN RUNNING
PROBABLE CAUSE OF MISFIRING AT IDLE SPEED
1 PLUG GAPS TOO WIDE
2 DEFECTIVE SPARK PLUGS
3 DEFECTIVE CONDENSER OR COIL
4 DEFECTIVE BREAKER POINTS
5 STICKING BREAKER ARM
6 INCORRECT BREAKER POINT GAP
7 SPARK ADVANCED TOO FAR
8 LOOSE CONNECTIONS IN PRIMARY CIRCUIT
9 DEFECTIVE IGNITION SWITCH
10 WORN DISTRIBUTOR SHAFT BUSHINGS
11 DEFECTIVE DISTRIBUTOR ROTOR
12 DEFECTIVE, HIGH TENSION WIRES
13 INCORRECT CARBURETOR ADJUSTMENT OR FLOAT LEVEL
14 DIRT OR WATER IN CARBURETOR OR FUEL SYSTEM
15 VAPOR LOCK
16 LEAK AT MANIFOLD HOT SPOT
17 AIR LEAK AT MANIFOLD, CARBURETOR OR INTAKE VALVE GUIDE
18 BURNED HEAT RISER TUBE
19 VALVES STICKING OPEN
20 VALVES WARPED OR BURNED
21 BROKEN VALVES
22 WEAK VALVE SPRINGS
23 BROKEN VALVE SPRINGS
24 INCORRECT VALVE TAPPET CLEARANCE
25 CRACKED VALVE SEAT
26 WARPED VALVE SEAT
27 LOOSE VALVE SEAT INSERT
28 STICKING VALVE LIFTER
29 STICKING PISTON RINGS
30 BROKEN RINGS
31 SCORED CYLINDER WALL
32 BROKEN PISTON
33 DEFECTIVE HEAD GASKET
34 WARPED CYL HEAD OR BLOCK
(IN ADDITION TO THE CAUSES LISTED UNDER "IDLE SPEED" CHECK THE FOLLOWING FOR
PROBABLE CAUSES OF MISFIRING AT HIGH SPEED
1 WEAK BREAKER ARM SPRING
2 BREAKER POINTS IMPROPERLY ADJUSTED (TOO WIDE)
3 WRONG TYPE SPARK PLUGS
4 EXCESSIVE CARBON
5 WEAK VALVE SPRINGS

SHOOTING
LACK OF POWER

—TRY STARTER OF LIGHTS

STARTER DOES NOT CRANK ENGINE

LIGHTS STAY BRIGHT
OPEN CIRCUIT AT STARTER SWITCH OR STARTING MOTOR BRUSHES MAY NOT MAKE CONTACT WITH ARMATURE

DIM VERY SLIGHTLY
STARTER MAY NOT ENGAGE WITH ENGINE
RESISTANCE AT STARTER OR STARTER SWITCH

VERY DIM OR GO OUT
—BATTERY DISCHARGED—
—POOR BATTERY CONNECTIONS—
—STARTER BINDS OR SHORTED—
—ENGINE TIGHT—

ENGINE LACKS POWER

1 POOR COMPRESSION (SEE CAUSES LISTED UNDER ITEM 4, FIRST COL.)
2 IGNITION IMPROPERLY TIMED
3 IGNITION POINTS NOT PROPERLY SYNCHRONIZED
4 AUTOMATIC ADVANCE NOT OPERATING PROPERLY
5 VACUUM SPARK CONTROL NOT OPERATING PROPERLY
6 INCORRECT CARBURETOR ADJUSTMENT
7 INCORRECT VALVE TIMING
8 VAPOR LOCK
9 CLOGGED MUFFLER
10 DENTED EXHAUST OR TAIL PIPE
11 CLOGGED AIR CLEANER
12 ENGINE OVERHEATING
13 EXCESSIVE INTERNAL ENGINE FRICTION
14 SLIPPING CLUTCH
15 DRAG IN CHASSIS WHICH RETARDS FREE RUNNING OF CAR

ENGINE WILL NOT RUN

REMOVE SPARK PLUG WIRE AND HOLD NEAR ENGINE WHILE CRANKING

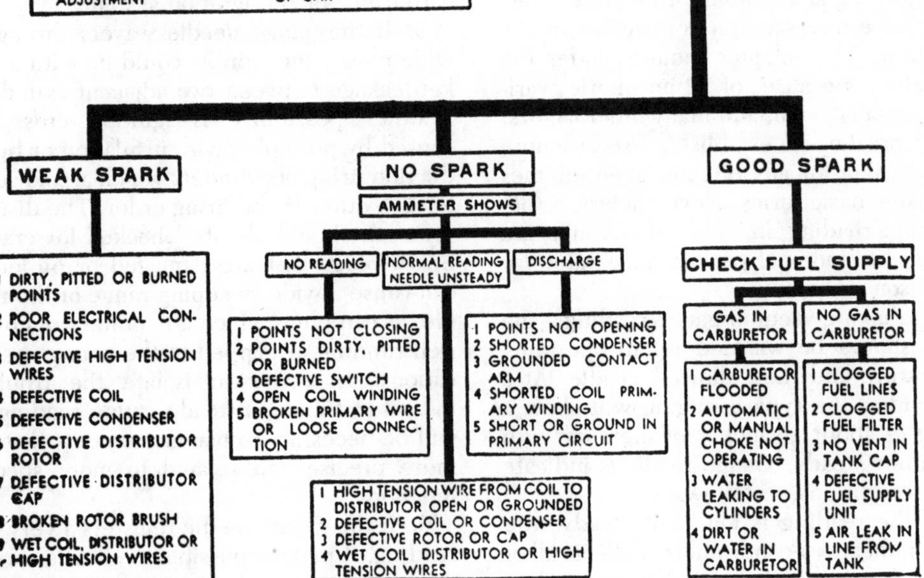

dication of specific gravity value and how it relates to battery charge condition:

Specific Gravity Reading	*Charge Condtion*
1.260–1.280	Fully charged
1.230–1.250	¾ charged
1.200–1.220	½ charged
1.170–1.190	¼ charged
1.140–1.160	Almost flat
1.110–1.130	Nil

The battery hydrometer consists simply of a glass cylinder, a moving float, and a calibrated scale. When acid is drawn into the glass cylinder, the calibrated float displaces its weight in acid, and thereby reveals the specific gravity of the battery acid and the condition of the battery. Hydrometers are available at auto supply houses at a fairly low price. It is always possible to have the specific gravity checked at a service station.

THE VACUUM GAUGE

Another useful instrument in troubleshooting and tuning the Volkswagen is the vacuum gauge which can be applied with the use of a T-connection to the vacuum take-off from the carburetor to the distributor advance mechanism. On engines with a throttle regulator, the vacuum gauge should be T-connected to the regulator hose which comes from the intake manifold. An adapter for a vacuum fitting is available for engines which do not have any vacuum connection to the distributor. This adapter mounts under the carburetor. Because of atmospheric variables, engine design, and many other factors, it is not practical to establish a fixed vacuum gauge reading for any engine, even engines of the same basic series. Nevertheless, a vacuum gauge reading, in inches of mercury, is a very reliable index of performance value for comparison purposes.

Before taking vacuum gauge readings, the engine should be warmed up to operating temperature and then allowed in idle. At a normal idle, the typical engine will show a reading of about 18 inches of mercury with the pointer steady. Gauge readings indicate various conditions, as follows:

1. If the reading is low, but steady, the trouble indicates a condition that affects all of the cylinders, such as, late valve timing, late ignition timing, or an intake manifold leak. Any of the above conditions can result in a reduction of up to 2 inches in vacuum gauge reading. A more severe condition (cracked intake manifold, warped intake manifold, or very bad carburetor to manifold gasket, depending upon cases) can result in an intake manifold vacuum reading drop of up to 15 inches.

2. If the reading fluctuates, with rhythm (needle continues to waver in a regular pattern) it indicates trouble in one area. This may be a fouled spark plug, a burned valve seat, a cracked distributor cap, or any number of things that would upset normal combustion in only one cylinder.

3. A wavering and *irregular* gauge reading may be caused by the conditions listed in (2.) but with the conditions existing in more than one cylinder. Possible causes here are a poorly adjusted carburetor, a high float level, excess wear in the distributor shaft or bushing, poorly adjusted ignition timing, too-wide spark plug gaps or poorly seating intake valves.

4. If the pointer wavers, with irregularity, as in (3.) and the range of the needle becomes greater with an increase in speed, weak or broken valve springs are a strong possibility. However, if the range of fluctuation of the needle decreases but the needle wavers more rapidly with increased engine speed, the trouble more than likely lies in an intake manifold leak. If the pointer tends to become more stable as the engine speed is increased, the indication would be toward trouble in the carburetor or the ignition system.

5. If the gauge needle wavers through a wide range, the trouble could lie with a gasket leakage between two adjacent cylinders. Another possibility is ignition cross-fire, caused by poor plug wire insulation or by induction firing of cylinders which are adjacent to each other in the firing order. The distributor cap should also be checked for cracks. Spark plugs that are damaged or oil-fouled can cause a wide sweeping range of the needle, as can plugs which are fouled from over-rich running or gapped to the wrong specifications. In order to isolate the troubles indicated by an unsteady gauge reading, it will be necessary to use instruments that are more precise and related to more specific functions.

6. If the gauge needle registers a very low reading, it may be possible to effect a correction by changing the ignition timing to the proper specification. If this does not correct the situation, the possibilities of a leak in the

intake system should be explored by the following procedure: (1.) Remove the carburetor air cleaner. (2.) Crank the engine for about 10 revolutions while holding a hand tightly over the air horn of the carburetor. A vacuum gauge reading during this cranking period should be roughly $^2/_3$ of the reading obtained at a normal engine idle. If the reading is low, it will be necessary to proceed further in order to narrow down the source of the leak. (3.) Remove the carburetor and seal off the carburetor opening to the intake manifold very tightly. Repeat the cranking test and watch the gauge reading. If the reading is higher than in the previous test, the leak is in the carburetor, or at the carburetor to manifold mounting flange. Carburetor vacuum leaks could be in the distributor vacuum control line, the throttle shaft, or the result of a cracked or broken carburetor body. A method of locating leaks is to squirt oil at a suspected point and watch the vacuum gauge needle at the same time. When oil is applied to the trouble spot, the vacuum gauge needle should rise significantly.

It is possible that exhaust restrictions can cause a low vacuum reading. Restrictions anywhere in the exhaust system (tail pipe, muffler, resonator, exhaust pipe, exhaust manifold or exhaust valve ports) can cause back pressure, especially at higher engine speeds. Such restrictions will cause the vacuum gauge reading at approximately 2,000 RPM to be only slightly, if any, higher than the reading at idle. Also, the needle may tend to hesitate in returning to the idle reading when the throttle is returned to the idle position.

Electrical Test Instruments

VOLTMETER

A voltmeter is an instrument used to measure the voltage (electrical pressure) which tends to push electrical current through a unit or circuit. The voltmeter is connected across the terminals of the unit or circuit being tested, and the meter reading is the difference in pressure (voltage drop) between the two sides of the unit.

AMMETER

An ammeter is an instrument used to measure the amount of electrical current flowing through a circuit or a unit. Ammeters are always connected in series with the unit or circuit being tested.

OHMMETER

The ohmmeter is used to measure the amount of electrical resistance in a unit or circuit. The ohmmeter has a self-contained power supply and is always connected across (in parallel with) the terminals of the unit being tested.

THE COMPRESSION GAUGE

The compression gauge is an instrument used to measure pressure in a cylinder or cylinders. With experience and skill, it is possible to combine the compression gauge with other tests in order to narrow down the source of trouble to specific problems such as poor valve seating, worn piston rings, broken pistons, or blown cylinder head gaskets. In addition, when used and the readings recorded on a periodic basis, it is possible for the compression gauge to tell a mechanical history of the comparative wear on individual cylinders.

THE OSCILLOSCOPE

Because it is time consuming to check individually all the possible sources of engine trouble, it may be advisable to have a troublesome engine put under the watchful screen of an oscilloscope. These instruments are widely used in engine diagnosis, and are even available in kits or fully built for the home mechanic or do-it-yourselfer. However, the cost places them out of the reach of the average home mechanic. With the oscilloscope, it is possible to test engine components while they are actually in operation. The oscilloscope, when connected to the proper wires of the engine, presents a television screen-type picture of the situation within the running engine.

By looking at this picture, a competent mechanic can translate the lines into engine functions which, though critical, mean little to the average driver. In addition, when an oscilloscope is used in conjunction with other pieces of test equipment, most engine problems can be brought to light and subsequently corrected quickly. A good oscilloscope in the hands of an average mechanic can determine conditions such as the following:

Compression balance.
Condition of spark plugs.
Condition of distributor points.
Ignition coil or condenser problems.
Bad ignition wiring.

Distributor point dwell measurement.
Cracked distributor cap.
Worn or broken rotor.
Worn distributor points.
Bad secondary wires and terminals.
Reversed coil polarity.
Distributor shaft "wobble".
Many other items, depending on the scope of the instrument and the experience of the mechanic.

THE ELECTRICAL SYSTEM

The major electrical components of the Volkswagen are the generator, the starting motor, the battery, the ignition system, the lighting system, and the electrical accessories. The electrical system is of the negative-ground type and is controlled by a voltage regulator which prevents the battery from discharging through the generator when the engine is not running and also controls the voltage produced by the generator. The regulator contains no replaceable wearing parts, and for this reason cannot be repaired in a normal workshop.

TROUBLESHOOTING THE STARTER

1. If starter does not operate when the ignition key is turned (switch on lights when testing):
   a. If lights do not burn, battery is run down or cables are loose or poorly grounded.
   b. If lights go out when key is turned to starting position, terminals are corroded or connections are loose.
   c. If lights go dim, battery is run down.
   d. If lights stay bright when key is turned, make a jumper contact between terminals 30 and 50 at the starter motor. If the starter operates, there is an open circuit.
   e. If lights stay bright and the solenoid switch operates, disconnect the battery cable from terminal 30 at the starter motor and connect to the connector strip terminal. If the starter motor operates, the solenoid is defective and should be replaced.
2. If starter does not operate when battery cable is connected directly to connector strip terminal:
   a. Sticking brushes.
   b. Worn brushes.
   c. Brushes not making contact, weak spring tension.
   d. Commutator dirty.
   e. Commutator grooved or burned.
   f. Defective armature or field coils.
   g. Jammed armature end bearings.
   h. Bent shaft.
   i. Broken starter housing.
3. If starter turns engine slowly or not at all:
   a. Run down battery.
   b. Loose connections.
   c. Sticking or worn starter motor brushes.
   d. Commutator dirty, grooved, or burned.
   e. Defective armature or field coils.
   f. Broken or seized engine parts, such as crankshaft seized in bearings, bent or broken connecting rod, or seized connecting rod bearing.
4. If starter engages, but cranks engine erratically:
   a. Defective drive pinion.
   b. Defective flywheel gear ring.
5. If starter drive pinion does not disengage:
   a. Dirty or damaged drive pinion or armature shaft.
   b. Defective solenoid switch.

TROUBLESHOOTING THE GENERATOR

1. Generator light does not light up when ignition switch is turned on with engine not running:
   a. Bulb burned out.
   b. Ignition switch defective.
   c. Battery terminals loose or corroded.
   d. Battery discharged or defective.
   e. Defective voltage regulator.
   f. Generator brushes not making contact with commutator.
2. Generator charging lamp remains on or comes on occasionally when engine is accelerated:
   a. Generator belt slipping.
   b. Defective voltage regulator.
   c. Commutator dirty.
3. Generator lamp goes out only at high speed:
   a. Defective generator or voltage regulator.

4. Generator lamp remains on when ignition switch is turned off:
   a. Voltage regulator contact points sticking.

TROUBLESHOOTING THE IGNITION SYSTEM

The ignition system is divided into two circuits: a low voltage or PRIMARY circuit, and a high voltage or SECONDARY circuit. The purpose of the primary circuit is to carry current at battery voltage. It includes the battery, ignition-starter switch, starter solenoid, primary winding of the coil, condenser, contact points, and ground. The secondary circuit begins with the ignition coil. The secondary voltage is a product of the coil and emerges from the secondary terminal of the coil and flows through a cable to the distributor cap. From the distributor cap, it flows through the rotor, through the distributor cables, to the spark plugs, and ultimately to the ground. The secondary circuit must be handled with a great deal of caution, as the electrical pressure (voltage) in this circuit can reach as high as 30,000 volts.

1. Burned or pitted distributor contact points:
   a. Dirt or oil on contact point surfaces.
   b. Voltage regulator setting too high.
   c. Contact points misaligned, or point gap too small.
   d. Defective coil.
   e. Defective condenser or condenser of wrong capacity.
   f. "Wobble" in distributor cam shaft.
2. Failure of ignition coil:
   a. Carbon tracking in coil tower.
   b. Voltage regulator setting too high.
3. Failure of condenser:
   a. Normal fatigue or damage due to heat or moisture.

TESTING COIL POLARITY

The polarity of the coil is predetermined, and designed to suit the rest of the ignition circuit. Electron flow through the spark plug is generally better from the hotter center plug electrode-to-ground than by the opposite route, i.e. from ground-to-center electrode. It is for this reason that negative to ground polarity is the most popular set-up. There is said to be about a 14% difference in required voltage of the two polarity systems at idle speed, with the differential increasing with increasing engine speed.

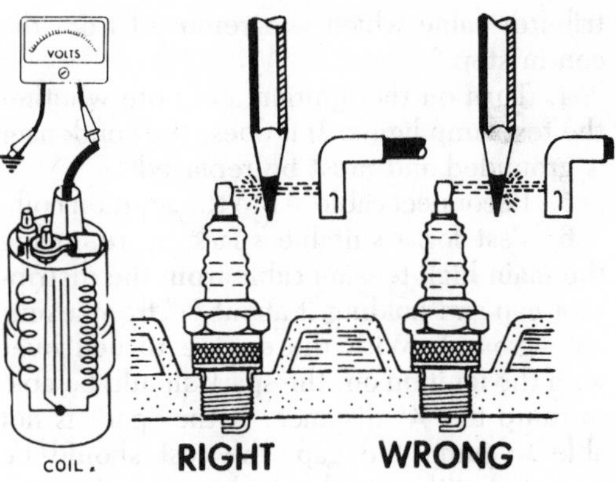

A tentative test of coil polarity

Correct coil polarity can be checked by the use of a voltmeter, in which case the voltmeter negative lead is connected to the secondary wire of the coil, and the positive voltmeter lead to the engine ground. If the voltmeter reading is up-scale, polarity is correct; if, however, the voltmeter reading is down-scale, the coil polarity is reversed. Another method of checking for correct coil polarity is to hold a regular carbon pencil in the gap between a disconnected spark plug wire and ground (or the plug). It is possible to observe the direction of spark flow from wire-to-pencil-to-ground when polarity is correct (see accompanying diagram). Although terminal sizes and cable lengths discourage improper battery installation, improper attachment of the battery and distributor terminals of the coil can still result in reversed polarity.

TESTING CONDENSER

The condenser helps the ignition system attain the high voltage necessary for plug sparking, and also serves to prevent the points from burning prematurely by reducing spark formation when the points are breaking. It is rare that a condenser will give trouble, but if one is suspected to be defective, and no condenser tester is available, the following procedure should be followed:

1. Remove the distributor cap and turn the engine until the contact points are fully open.
2. Disconnect cable #1 at the ignition coil.
3. Using a six or 12-volt test lamp, connect one lead of the lamp to terminal #15 of the ignition coil as shown in the wiring diagram, and connect the other lamp lead to the dis-

tributor cable which was removed from the coil in step 2.

4. Turn on the ignition and note whether the test lamp lights. If it does, the condenser is grounded and must be replaced.

5. Reconnect cable #1 to the ignition coil.

6. Test for a suitable spark by removing the main high tension cable from the distributor cap and holding it about ¼″ from a suitable ground. With the engine turned over with the ignition on, the spark should be able to jump the ¼″ distance. If the spark is not able to jump the gap, the test should be repeated with a condenser known to be non-defective.

TROUBLESHOOTING THE CLUTCH

While nothing can substitute perfectly for a careful examination and experience, it is nevertheless helpful to be aware of the symptoms which may accompany clutch problems so that they may be attacked in an orderly fashion. Some of these symptoms are:

Excessive noise.
Clutch chatter or grab.
Clutch slipping.
Clutch drag or failure to release.
Pulsation of the clutch pedal.
Low life of clutch facing.
Gear lockup or hard shifting.
Hard pedal.

For each of the above symptoms, there is a logical sequence of possible causes and remedies. Once the causes are known, the remedies should be relatively obvious. It is for this reason that in the troubleshooting portion of this book only the causes are discussed in any detail.

CAUSES OF EXCESSIVE CLUTCH NOISE

Release bearing When the engine is idling and the foot is resting on the clutch pedal, there will be a high-pitched rubbing noise. Usual causes of release bearing failure are age of bearing, riding the clutch, insufficient pedal free play, lack of lubricant in the bearing, and worn or out-of-true clutch release fingers.

Pilot bearing Clutch shaft pilot bearing noises are heard only when the bearing is in operation; in other words, when the crankshaft speed is different from the speed of the clutch shaft—when the clutch is disengaged and the transmission is in gear. The noise made by the pilot bearing is a high-pitched squeal and the bearing, which is probably dry, should be replaced.

Transmission pinion shaft bearing A rough or damaged input shaft bearing noise will be heard only when the clutch is engaged and the transmission is in any position. The noise is generally most noticeable when the transmission is in neutral. The noise should diminish and completely disappear when the clutch is disengaged and the pinion gear of the transmission slows down and stops.

Transmitted engine noises When the correct amount of free play is present in the clutch pedal, there should not be an unreasonable amount of noise transmitted to the passenger area via the clutch. Such noises, if they exist, are generally modified through a manipulation of the clutch pedal. Such problems rarely exist in the Volkswagen because of the relatively great distance between the clutch pedal and the engine compartments.

Clutch linkage noise Noise in the clutch linkage is generally a clicking or snapping sound heard or felt in the pedal itself when the pedal is moved completely up or down. If the noise is heard to occur within the center tunnel of the passenger compartment, there is a strong possibility that lubrication is needed at the pivot point just inside the tunnel. In this case, the pedal cluster (throttle, brake and clutch) must be removed by means of the two holding bolts, and the pivot point lubricated with a high quality grease such as the lithium-base type. If such grease is not used to lubricate this point, it will be a matter of only a few weeks before lubrication is again required.

CAUSES OF CLUTCH CHATTER OR GRAB

The cause of clutch chatter or grab is generally located within the clutch assembly and can be corrected only by removal of the engine and the clutch from the vehicle. To diagnose, follow procedure below:

1. Check to ensure that the clutch linkage is in adjustment and not ginding. If necessary, the linkage should be adjusted, aligned and lubricated.

2. Check for defective, worn, or loose engine and/or transmission mounts. If necessary, such mounts must be tightened or replaced.

3. Check the attaching bolts on the clutch

pressure plate for looseness. Also tighten or replace loose bolts on the transmission and clutch housings.

4. Check freedom of movement of clutch release bearing. Free up or replace as necessary.

5. Check the clutch and flywheel for oil or grease. The trouble may also be caused by oil or grease on the friction disc or pressure plate.

6. Check the friction disc for trueness, and ensure that the disc hub is not binding on the splines of the transmission input shaft.

7. Check the disc and pressure plate for breakage.

8. Examine the pressure plate and cover plate assembly for cracks or heat discoloration.

CAUSES OF CLUTCH SLIPPAGE

This condition is generally most noticeable when the car is started from a standing stop or when the gears are shifted quickly and the clutch "popped" for fast acceleration. This treatment of the clutch may well be the cause of clutch slippage sooner or later, for no clutch is designed to withstand such mistreatment for long. One way of testing for clutch slippage is to apply the parking brake with the car on a level surface, start the engine and put the transmission into second gear. With the foot brake also applied, accelerate the engine slightly and release the clutch pedal. If the clutch is in good condition, it will grip and the engine will be made to stall. If, however, the clutch is heard to slip, the cause may be one or more of the following:

Insufficient free play at the clutch pedal.
Broken or disconnected parts in the clutch.
Clutch linkage binding and not allowing full-pressure application of the clutch.
Oil or grease on the friction disc. Also a worn friction disc.
Worn pressure plate or weak springs from temper loss or failure. Such damaging heat as results in temper loss will usually cause the afflicted parts to appear blue.

In applying the clutch slippage test, it should be remembered that this test is most severe. In other words, one should not apply this test every other day in order to determine whether his clutch is slipping. After not too many of these tests, it is practically guaranteed that the clutch will slip if it wasn't slipping before.

CAUSES OF CLUTCH DRAG OR FAILURE TO RELEASE

Clutch drag is the condition that takes place when the clutch pedal is fully depressed and the clutch disc is not completely released. The clutch disc does not come fully to rest, but continues to be rotated due to the rotation of the engine. Dragging of the clutch generally causes difficult shifting and clashing of the gears, especially when shifting in the lower gears. Possible causes of clutch drag:

Insufficient pedal free play.
Clutch plate binding on the transmission input shaft.
Pressure plate or friction disc warped or bent.
Misalignment, engine to transmission.
Transmission lubricant too thick.

CAUSES OF CLUTCH PEDAL PULSATION

This condition is evident when, with a slight pressure applied to the pedal, and the engine running, the pedal is felt to vibrate or pulsate with every revolution of the engine. When the pedal is pushed down further, the pulsation is no longer evident. Clutch pedal pulsation may be caused by any of the following:

Clutch release fingers bent or uneven.
Flywheel runout excessive due to bent flywheel or crankshaft flange.
Release bearing cocked on transmission bearing retainer.
Poor alignment of engine and transmission.

CAUSES OF LOW CLUTCH-FACING LIFE

When low clutch-facing life is experienced, the first thing to look for is the presence of improper driving habits on the part of the operator(s) of the vehicle. These are the most likely reasons why the lining is not lasting as long as it should. The possible causes of low clutch facing life are:

Riding the clutch, i.e. driving with the left foot constantly on the clutch pedal, or slipping the clutch instead of shifting to a lower gear.
Jack-rabbit type starts from stop lights, etc.
Continuous overloading of the car, or the excessive hauling of heavy trailers or other equipment.
Using the clutch to keep from drifting backward while stopped on a grade. When

stopped on a grade, the handbrake should be applied rather than holding position by slipping the clutch.

Improper amount of clutch pedal free play.

The presence of a rough surface on the flywheel or the pressure plate.

The presence of oil or water on the clutch facing material.

Clutch creep or slip caused by weak pressure plate springs.

CAUSES OF GEAR LOCK UP OR HARD SHIFTING

The causes of this condition are similar to those that cause the "Clutch Drag or Failure to Release" condition, and should be diagnosed in the same manner. If, however, the elimination of all possible causes as listed in this section does not serve to locate the cause of the problem, it is most likely that the problem lies in the shifting assembly, the transmission cover, or in the transmission itself. In the latter case, it will be necessary to dismantle the transmission and correct the cause of the trouble.

CAUSES OF A HARD CLUTCH PEDAL

The presence of this condition is evidenced by a clutch pedal that requires an abnormal amount of pedal pressure in order to disengage the clutch. Possible causes are:

Dry or binding linkage.

Clutch linkage out of alignment.

Release bearing sleeve dry or binding.

Use of the wrong type of clutch assembly, especially one of the heavier duty than is required.

TRANSMISSION TROUBLESHOOTING

It is generally acknowledged that the Volkswagen transmission is one of the most durable parts of the automobile. Any well-treated VW transmission is capable of well over 100,000 trouble-free miles. In the event, however, that an owner should have transmission problems, here are some problems along with their possible causes:

CAR IS NOISY WHILE MOVING IN ANY GEAR

Insufficient lubrication.

One or more worn bearings in the transmission.

Mainshaft end play excessive.

Sliding gears worn or broken.

Misalignment of transmission case or clutch housing.

TRANSMISSION SLIPS OUT OF GEAR

Improper shifting procedure.

Worn shift detent parts.

Shift linkage improperly adjusted.

Misalignment between the transmission and the engine.

TRANSMISSION NOISY IN NEUTRAL

Insufficient lubrication.

One or more worn gears or bearings.

TRANSMISSION DIFFICULT TO SHIFT

Shift linkage improperly adjusted.

Clutch not releasing properly.

Improper lubricant in transmission.

Binding of shift linkage due to worn or damaged parts.

TRANSMISSION LEAKS LUBRICANT

Axle boot not sealing properly due to looseness, crack, or other damage.

Oil seals damaged.

Transmission axle retainer nuts loose. (Do not overtighten because the retainer will then be slightly distorted and may leak more than before.)

Transmission housing nuts loose.

Transmission filler and/or drain plugs loose or stripped of thread.

Use of a lubricant that tends to foam excessively.

Excessively high transmission oil level.

TROUBLESHOOTING REAR AXLE

The Volkswagen rear axle and transmission are combined in a single unit. Therefore, some of the possible problems may be hard to attribute to one assembly or the other, especially in the event of lubricant leakage. When lubricant leaks from one part of the unit, it may be blown onto another section or carried there by gravity while the car is in motion. However, like the transmission, the Volkswagen rear axle is a very sturdy piece of equipment, and not likely to give any trouble for a very, very long time. In the event of trouble, here are possible problems and causes:

REAR AXLE LEAKS LUBRICANT

Excess level of lubricant in unit.
Leakage at rear axle boots, caused by improper sealing or damaged boots.
Oil is too light or of poor quality.
Axle retainer not tightened down properly.
Improper sealing of seals or gaskets.

REAR AXLE NOISES

Because of the close proximity of the rear axle to the transmission and the engine, it should be ascertained that the rear axle is in fact making whatever noise is being heard. The following are possible causes of noise in the vicinity of the rear axle:

Tire noise—driving the car over various types of road surfaces will reveal the extent of tire noise. If tire noise is to be minimized for noise detection purposes, it is advisable to drive on a smooth asphalt or black top road while trying to pinpoint noise causes.
Rear wheel bearing noise can be checked by jacking up the car and rotating the rear wheels, by coasting at a low speed, or by driving at low speed and applying the brakes after disengaging the clutch. If, in the latter test, the noise diminishes, defective wheel bearings are a definite possibility.
Noise when accelerating in a straight line is generally caused by heavy heel contact on the gear teeth. It is necessary to move the ring gear nearer to the drive pinion.
If noise is most evident when coasting with the car in gear and the throttle closed, it is most likely that there is heavy toe contact on the gear teeth, in which case the ring gear must be moved away from the drive pinion. (NOTE: *the toe end of the gear tooth is the smaller of the two circles formed by the ends of the gear teeth, while the heel is the larger circle.*)
If the noise is present only when the car is driven around a curve, the cause of the noise is probably excessive backlash between gears, damaged gears or thrust washers, differential side gears that are tight in the case, or differential-pinion gears that are tight on the pinion shaft.
The cause of a knocking noise in the rear axle may be bearings or gears that are either damaged or badly worn.
The presence of a constant humming noise may indicate that the drive pinion or ring gear is out of adjustment. Such a condition should be remedied before gear-tooth wear becomes significant and the noise changes from a hum to a growl.
Excessive end play in the shafts of the rear axles will result in a thumping sound being heard when the car is driven around a corner on a rough road.

TROUBLESHOOTING THE FUEL SYSTEM

Problems in the fuel system are generally of two different types: fuel pump troubles and carburetor troubles.

FUEL PUMP TROUBLESHOOTING

Following are some of the problems and possible causes within the mechanically operated diaphragm fuel pump:

Pump leaking at joining faces and losing fuel.
  a. Screws insufficiently tightened.
  b. Torn fuel pump diaphragm.
Diaphragm leaking at rivets and losing fuel.
  a. Diaphragm is damaged and must be replaced.
Diaphragm material leaky.
  a. Diaphragm material is damaged by solvent substance in fuel, and must be replaced.
Excessive pump stroke overstraining diaphragm.
  a. Pump not installed correctly; gasket too thin.
Pump pressure low
  a. Pump incorrectly installed; gasket too thick.
  b. Spring pressure low.
Pump pressure excessive; float needle valve forced down.
  a. Pump installed incorrectly; gasket too thin.
  b. Spring pressure excessive.
Fuel pump inoperative or insufficient fuel delivery.
  a. Valves leaky or sticking; top half of pump must be renewed.

TROUBLESHOOTING THE CARBURETOR

Engine will not start (ignition in order and fuel in tank.)
  a. Automatic choke not working properly.

b. Choke valve sticking.
c. Bi-metallic spring broken or unhooked.
d. Ceramic plate broken.
e. Float needle valve sticking, causing flooding of carburetor.

Engine runs at a fast idle.
a. Automatic choke not switching off.
b. Defective heater element.
c. Throttle positioner incorrectly adjusted.

Engine runs unevenly, with tendency to stall.
a. Incorrect idle speed adjustment.
b. Carburetor pilot jet blocked.
c. Incorrect idle mixture adjustment.
d. Throttle positioner incorrectly adjusted.

Engine "runs on" after ignition is turned off.
a. Idling mixture too lean.
b. Idle speed too fast.
c. Electro-magnetic cut-off jet inoperative.

Banging in the exhaust when car is overrunning the engine.
a. Idle mixture too weak.
b. Throttle positioner incorrectly adjusted.

Poor transfer from idle speed to normal running.
a. Defective accelerator pump system; sticking ball or blocked passages.
b. Accelerator pump diaphragm torn.
c. Incorrect idle adjustment.
d. Accelerator pump system injecting too much or too little fuel.

Engine stalls when accelerator is suddenly released.
a. Idle mixture too rich.

Engine runs unevenly at low idle speed; exhaust soots excessively at high idle speed; spark plugs tend to soot up. (i.e. the mixture is too rich.)
a. Excessive fuel pump pressure causing needle valve to remain open.
b. Float leaking.
c. Float needle valve defective, not closing.

Engine runs unevenly, misfires at high speeds.
a. Fuel starvation, due to dirty main jet, needle valve, fuel tank, or insufficient fuel pump pressure.

Excessive fuel consumption.
a. Incorrect jet sizes.
b. Excessive fuel pump pressure causing float level to be too high.
c. Float leaking, causing high float level.
d. Float needle valve does not close.
e. Improper operation of automatic choke.

(NOTE: *in checking and adjusting the carburetors one should keep in mind that the engine will respond to fine carburetor adjustments only after the electrical and mechanical parts of the engine are set to the proper specifications. If such things as the ignition timing, valve clearance, compression balance, and point gap are not in order, fine carburetor tuning will be of little or no avail.*)

TROUBLESHOOTING THE BRAKE SYSTEM

Pedal goes to floorboard.
a. Normal lining wear. Adjust or renew shoes.

Spongy response at brake pedal.
a. Air present in the hydraulic system.
b. Lack of fluid in the master cylinder reservoir. Top up.

Without braking action, pedal goes to floorboard although system has been bled and adjusted.
a. Defective valve in master cylinder.
b. Dirty valve seat. Clean or renew.

Braking action is obtained only after pumping pedal several times.
a. Air is present in the system.
b. Piston return-spring weak.

Although brakes have been adjusted, brake action decreases and pedal goes to floorboard.
a. Fluid leak in the braking system.
b. Damaged or unserviceable cups in master or wheel cylinder.

Brakes drag and overheat.
a. Clogging of by-pass port in master cylinder.
b. Insufficient clearance between piston push rod and master cylinder piston.
c. Shoe return-springs broken or weak.
d. Rubber parts swollen because of improper brake fluid being used.

Poor stopping accompanied by excessive pressure required on pedal.
a. Oil on brake shoe lining.
b. Improper brake shoe lining.

Brakes bind while driving.
a. By-pass port in master cylinder not

free, possibly as the result of a swollen or deformed cup.

b. Improper brake fluid in use.

c. Incorrect position of brake pedal stop plate.

Brakes uneven in operation (car tends to pull to left or right when brakes are applied.)

a. Oil or grease on brake shoe linings.

b. Brake drums out of round or scored.

c. Different types of linings on opposite sides of car.

d. Incorrect and/or uneven tire pressures.

e. Brake drums distorted due to uneven tightening of wheel bolts.

f. Dirt in brake lines or hoses.

g. Different types of tires (especially new versus badly worn) on opposite sides of vehicle.

h. Natural causes, such as when the right track is through snow, while the left side is on dry road. Such conditions occur often during winter on narrow snow-covered roads.

Brakes chatter.

a. Brake shoe lining not chamfered at ends.

b. Brake shoe lining worn; rivets making contact with drum.

c. Brake drum eccentric (out of round).

Brakes noisy.

a. Improper brake shoe lining.

b. Lining not chamfered at ends.

c. Brake lining loose on shoe.

d. Brakes dirty.

(NOTE: *often brakes will squeak after the car has been in a damp atmosphere for some time. Such squeaking will occur only during the first few brake applications, and will then disappear. Sometimes brake squeaking can be stopped by inserting a high pressure air hose through the brake adjusting or inspection hole and blowing out the accumulation of dirt and brake dust. However, if such squeaking continues, other possible causes should be investigated.*)

TROUBLESHOOTING DISC BRAKES

Beginning in 1967, the Karmann Ghia models were equipped with front disc brakes, which had been standard on type 3 models since the 1966 model year. Type 2 models were equipped with front discs, starting in 1971. The following symptoms and possible causes relate to problems that sometimes develop in disc braking systems.

EXCESSIVE PEDAL TRAVEL

Excessive disc runout.
Air leak or insufficient fluid in system or in caliper.
Improper fluid (boils).
Damaged caliper piston seal.
Piston and/or lining not properly seated.

BRAKE ROUGHNESS OR CHATTER

Excessive disc runout.
Excessive thickness variation of disc.
Excessive thickness variation of lining.

EXCESSIVE PEDAL EFFORT

Brake fluid, oil or grease on lining.
Incorrect lining.
Seized or frozen piston.
Excessively worn lining.

BRAKES PULL TO ONE SIDE

Brake fluid, grease or oil on lining.
Caliper out of proper alignment to disc.
Pistons frozen or seized.
Improper tire pressures.
Restricted hose or line.

NOISES

Groaning noises: too slow brake release.
Rattles: excessive clearance between disc and caliper.
Scraping noises: mounting bolts too long, loose wheel bearings, or brake disc rubbing housing.

BRAKES HEAT UP AND FAIL TO RELEASE

Piston seized or frozen.
Residual pressure in master cylinder.

LEAKY WHEEL CYLINDER

Caliper seals damaged or worn.
Cylinder bore coroded or scored.
Scored or corroded piston surface.

NO BRAKING ACTION WHEN PEDAL IS DEPRESSED

Leak in system or caliper.
Leaks at rear brake system.
Improper rear brake adjustment.
Air in hydraulic system.

(NOTE: *on Volkswagens, adjusting the rear brakes automatically compensates for excessive movement of the handbrake lever. However, in the event that the handbrake operating cable has stretched, an adjustment is possible at the lever itself.)*

TROUBLESHOOTING STEERING AND SUSPENSION

Steering is stiff from lock to lock and front wheels do not automatically return to the straight-ahead position after a turn.
a. Inadequate lubrication of front axle.
b. Seizing or stiffening of king pins or ball joints.
c. Tight adjustment of steering gear.
d. Low level of lubricant in steering gear box.
e. Wheels out of alignment.
f. Tire pressure too low.

Hard steering accompanied by squeaking noise.
a. Steering wheel binding in steering column.
b. Steering column is not correctly centered in the steering column tube.

Although there is no binding in system, front wheels do not automatically seek the straight-ahead position after a turn.
a. Improper front alignment: caster, camber, or toe-in.
b. Steering arms of stub axles bent or twisted.

Excessive play in steering system.
a. Improper adjustment of steering gear.
b. Looseness in steering gear mounting.
c. Steering linkage worn excessively.

Car steers to one side at all times.
a. Incorrect alignment: caster, camber or king pin angle.
b. Unequal air pressure in tires or unequal tread on tires.
c. Unequal shock absorber control.
d. Bent or damaged steering components.

Excessive play in front suspension.
a. Worn bearing points: torsion arm link pins, front wheel bearings, stub axle.

Car wanders—steers erratically.
a. Front wheel bearings loose.
b. Improper tire pressure.
c. Incorrect caster.
d. Steering linkage loose.
e. Excessive wear or damaged suspension components.

Steering wheel spoke is at an angle when driving straight ahead.
a. Depending on which way the spoke is off the horizontal, one tie rod must be lengthened and the other shortened by the same amount in order that the toe-in is not changed. The steering wheel should not be removed, nor its position changed on the column.

TROUBLESHOOTING ABNORMAL TIRE WEAR

Tires wear at both sides of tread.
a. Underinflation for loads carried.

Tires wear at center of tread.
a. Overinflation.

Spotty or irregular wear at one side of the tread (gouges and/or waves).
a. Wheel assembly out of balance statically and dynamically.
b. Excessive lateral wheel runout.
c. Excessive play in wheel bearings or at king pins.

Lightly worn spots at the center of the tread.
a. Static unbalance of wheel and tire.
b. Excessive radial run-out.

Isolated flat spots at center of tread.
a. Brakes binding in panic application, or brake drums out of round. Check brakes.

Stepped tread wear. (One end of each tread block worn more than the other.)
a. Overloading. Inside of casing should be checked for cracks.

Side wear.
a. Incorrect camber.
b. Continual driving on steeply cambered roads.
c. Fast cornering.

NOTE: *for best total tire life, it is advisable to rotate all five tires, including the spare, at periodic intervals, say 5,000 miles.*

Appendix

Major Specifications—VW 1200, Type 1 (to July, 1965)

Engine

Design: 4 cylinder, 4 cycle, flat, horizontally opposed engine.
Bore: 77 mm. (3.03 in.)
Stroke: 64 mm. (2.52 in.)
Displacement: 1192 cc. (72.74 cu. in.)
Compression ratio: 7.0 : 1
Performance:
34 bhp at 3600 RPM (DIN)
41.5 bhp at 3900 RPM (SAE)
61 ft. lbs. at 2000 RPM (DIN)
65 ft. lbs. at 2400 RPM (SAE)
Engine weight, dry: 238 lbs.
Crankcase: magnesium alloy, two-piece.
Cylinders: individually cast; of special gray iron, finned.
Cylinder heads: one for each pair of cylinders, sintered steel valve seat inserts shrunk in; 14 mm. spark plug thread cut into cylinder head.
Crankshaft: steel forging, hardened journals. Four main bearings, aluminum-alloy bearing shells. Main bearings 1, 2 and 3 are sleeve-type. Numbers 1, 2 and 3 are 55 mm. diameter. Number 4 (at rear of engine) is 40 mm. diameter.
Flywheel: steel forging, integral starter ring.
Connecting rods: H-section, steel forgings. Connecting rod bearing 3-layer steel-backed. Pressed-in wrist pin bushing of bronze.
Pistons: aluminum alloy with steel inserts, 2 compression rings, 1 oil control ring. Fully floating wrist pin.
Camshaft: situated below crankshaft; gray cast-iron, running in three bearings. Gear driven.
Valves: one intake and one exhaust per cylinder. Exhaust valve has special heat-resistant seating surface.
Valve clearances: .004″. Cold when indicated by sticker. Older engines: .008″ intake and .012″ exhaust. (Engines without sticker on fan housing.)
Valve springs: one per valve.
Valve timing: with clearance for checking, .040″.
Intake opens: 6 degrees before TDC
Intake closes: 35° 30′ after BDC
Exhaust opens: 42° 30′ before BDC
Exhaust closes: 3° after TDC
Cooling: by forced air. Belt-driven fan on generator shaft. Drive ratio approximately 1 : 1.8, crankshaft/generator. Thermostatically controlled cooling. Capacity approximately 500 liters (19 cubic feet) per second at 3600 RPM.
Lubrication: wet sump, full pressure type with gear pump. Oil cooler in path of cooling air.
Ignition system: battery ignition with conventional distributor and coil.
Spark timing: 10° before top dead center.
Firing order: 1-4-3-2
Spark advance: under full vacuum control
Breaker point gap: .016″
Spark plugs: Bosch W 175 T 1 and other good quality plugs of same heat range.

Fuel System

Carburetor: Solex, single throat down-draft type. 28 PICT-1 with accelerator and automatic choke.

Venturi:	22.5 mm. diameter
Main jet:	122.5
Air correction jet:	130 y with emulsion tube 145 y Karmann Ghia (sedan and convertible)
Pilot jet:	g 55
Pilot jet air bleed:	2.0 mm. diameter
Pump jet:	0.5
Power fuel jet:	1.0 mm. diameter
Float needle valve:	1.5 mm. diameter
Float weight:	5.7 gram, plastic material

Pump feed: approx. 1.1-1.4 cc/stroke
Air cleaner: oil bath type with air preheater.
Fuel pump: diaphragm type, mechanical.
Fuel filter: filter in fuel pump.
Fuel gauge: float type, mechanical sender.

Clutch

Design: single dry plate.
Lining area: 41.6 square inches.
Free play: .4 to .8 in. at pedal

Transmission and Final Drive

Design: transmission and final drive integral with four speeds forward, all fully synchronized.
Gear ratios: 1st: 3.80:1 2nd: 2.06:1 3rd: 1.32:1 4th: .89:1 reverse 3.88:1 final drive: 4.375:1

Chassis

Frame design: flat platform with tubular backbone. Forked at rear to accommodate engine and trans-axle unit.

Front suspension: two trailing links at each wheel. Two torsion bar springs consisting of 8 leaves each. Anti-sway bar.

Rear suspension: trailing links, swing axles independently suspended.

Shock absorbers: front and rear are hydraulic, telescopic, double-acting.

Steering: worm and roller with divided tie rods and steering damper.

Steering ratio: 14.3:1 2.6 turns lock to lock.

Wheel angle at full lock: inside wheel: 34° + or – 2°. Outside wheel 28° – 1°.

Camber: 0° 40′ + or – 30′ with wheels straight ahead.

Toe-in: 2 to 4.5 mm.

Axle beam angle: 2° + or – 15′

King pin inclination: 4° 20′ at maximum permissible weight.

Rear wheel camber: 3° + or – 30′

Wheels: 4J x 15 steel discs.

Tires: tubeless, 5.60 x 15 inch.

Rolling radius: 309 mm. + or – 3 mm.

Brakes

Foot brake: hydraulic, acting on all four wheels.

Hand brake: cable operating, rear wheels.

Brake lining area: 96 square inches.

Specifications—1300 Model (differences from VW 1200 to Aug., 1965)

Engine

Stroke: 69 mm. (2.72 in.)

Displacement: 1285 cc. (78.3 cu. in.)

Performance:
40 bhp at 4000 RPM (DIN)
50 bhp at 4600 RPM (SAE)
63 ft. lbs. at 2000 RPM (DIN)
69 ft. lbs. at 2600 RPM (SAE)

Engine weight, dry: 244 lbs.

Camshaft bearings: replaceable steel-backed lead-coated shells.

Valve timing: with checking clearance of .040 in.

Intake opens: 7° 30′ before TDC

Intake closes: 37° after BDC

Exhaust opens: 44° 30′ before BDC

Exhaust closes: 4° after TDC

Cooling air delivery: approximately 556 liters per second (20 cubic feet per second) at 4000 RPM.

Ignition timing: basic ignition timing of 7.5° before TDC.

Fuel System

Carburetor: Solex 30 PICT-1

Venturi: 24 mm. in diameter

Main jet: 125

Air correction jet:
125 z for sedans and convertibles
170 z for Karmann Ghia

Pilot jet: g 55 (with electromagnetic shut-off valve).

Pilot jet air bleed: 150

Pump jet: 50

Power fuel jet: 75 mm. diameter, for Karmann Ghia models only.

Float needle valve: 1.5 mm. diameter

Float weight: 5.7 grams (plastic material)

Pump delivery: 1.3 – 1.6 cc/stroke

Fuel pump: diaphragm, mechanical, with cut-off valve in upper part.

Chassis

Steering ratio: 15:1

Wheels: perforated steel disc, 4J x 15.

Specifications—1500 Models (differences from 1300 models) from August, 1966

Engine

Bore: 83 mm. (3.27 in.)

Stroke: 69 mm. (2.72 in.)

Displacement: 1493 cc. (91.1 cu. in.)

Compression ratio: 7.5:1

Performance:
44 bhp at 4000 RPM (DIN)
53 bhp at 4200 RPM (SAE)
10.2 mkg at 2000 RPM (DIN)
78.1 ft. lbs. at 2600 RPM (SAE)

Engine weight, dry: 250 lbs.

Cooling fan drive ratio: 1.9:1 approximately

Air cleaner: oil bath with two intakes

Transmission and final drive:
3rd gear ratio 1.26:1 final drive ratio 4.125:1

Chassis

Rear suspension: equipped with overload compensator spring.

Rear radius arm setting: 20° + 50′.

Rear track: 1358 mm. (53.4″)

General Data—Type 1 Vehicles

Top speed:
78 mph (53 bhp engine) (3950 RPM)
75 mph (50 bhp engine) (4010 RPM)
72 mph (41.5 bhp engine) (3870 RPM
68 mph (36 bhp engine) (3400 RPM)

Hill climbing ability, with two occupants:

	53 bhp engine	*36 bhp engine*
1st gear	46%	40.0%
2nd gear	24%	20.5%
3rd gear	13%	12.0%
4th gear	7.5%	6.5%

Acceleration:
from 0 to 100 kph (0 to 62 mph):
53 bhp 23 sec.
50 bhp 26 sec.
41.5 bhp 37 sec.
36 bhp 50 sec.
from 80 to 100 kph (50 to 62 mph):
53 bhp 10 sec.
50 bhp 12 sec.
41.5 bhp 19 sec.
36 bhp 29 sec.

Fuel consumption:
53 bhp 26.7 mpg.
50 bhp 27.7 mpg.
41.5 bhp 30.4 mpg.
36 bhp 32.2 mpg.

Capacities

Fuel tank: 10.5 U.S. gallons
Crankcase: 5.3 U.S. pints
Transmission and final drive: 6.3 pints
Reduction gears (Transporter models) ½ pint each.
Steering: sector type .26 pint
roller type .4 pint
ross type .5 pint (transporters)
Brake fluid: .5 pint
Oil bath air cleaner: .5 pint

Dimensions, VW Sedan

Wheelbase: 94.5 in.
Track: front 51.4 in.
rear 53.4 in.
Length: 160.6 in.
Width: 60.6 in.
Height: unladen 59.1 in.
Ground clearance: 6.0 in.

1968 Models, Type 1

Length: 158.6 in.
Width: 61.0 in.
Height: 59.1 in.
Ground clearance: 5.9 in.
Unladen weight: 1807 lbs.
Permissible total weight: 2645 lbs.

Specifications—Type 3; major deviations from Type 1

Engine

Design: cooling fan is mounted directly on end of crankshaft.
Bore: 85.5 mm. (3.37 in.)
Stroke: 69 mm. (2.72 in.)
Displacement: 1584 cc. (96.7 cu. in.)
Compression ratio: 7.7:1
Performance:
54 bhp at 4000 RPM (DIN)
65 bhp at 4600 RPM (SAE)
81 ft. lbs. at 2200 RPM (DIN)
87 ft. lbs. at 2800 RPM (DIN)
Engine weight, dry: 276 lbs.
Cooling air delivery: 565 liters/second (20 cubic feet/second) at 4000 RPM.

Clutch

Lining area: 52 square inches.

Fuel System

Carburetion: Two Solex 32 PDSIT-2/3 carburetors with accelerator pumps and automatic chokes. Carburetor specifications, 1600 models to August 1967, when electronic fuel injection was introduced

Venturi: dia. (mm.)		24
Main jet:	X 132.5 (l. carb.)	X 130 (r. carb.)
Air correction jet:	150 (l. carb.)	120 (r. carb.)
Pilot jet:		50
Float needle valve: dia.		1.2
Float weight:		7.3 gr.
Pump capacity:		.35–.55 cc/stroke
Power fuel system:		none

Chassis

Front torsion bar setting: 39° 10′ + 50′
Rear torsion bar setting, unloaded:
Fastback Sedan: 20° 30′ + 50′
Squareback Sedan: 21° 30′ + 50′
Front wheel toe-in: 3.6 to 6 mm. toe-in- wheels not pressed together.
Front wheel camber: wheels straight ahead:
1° 20′ + or − 10′
Axle beam angle: 11° 50′
King pin inclination: 5° 15′
Rear wheel track: 0° + or − 5′
Rear wheel camber: 3° + or − 30′
Wheels: Perforated steel disc, 4½ J x 15
Tires: tubeless, 600 x 15, with dynamic rolling radius of 12.2 in.
Tire pressures:
Fastback Sedan with:

1 or 2 occupants 16 front/ 24 rear (psi)
3 to 5 occupants 18 front/ 27 rear (psi)
Squareback Sedan with:
half payload 17 front/26 rear (psi)
full payload 18 front/37 rear (psi)

Steering: overall ratio 14.8:1 with 2.8 turns lock to lock.

Brakes: disc front, drum rear. Lining area of discs: 12.5 square inches; lining area of drum brakes: 70 square inches.

General Data—Type 3 Vehicles

Top speed: 84 mph (4250 RPM)

Hill climbing ability:

	*Squareback**	*Fastback*
1st gear	39.5%	46.0%
2nd gear	20.5%	24.0%
3rd gear	12.0%	14.0%
4th gear	7.0%	8.0%

* with half payload

Acceleration:
from 0 to 100 kph (0 to 62 mph):
20.0 sec.
from 80 to 100 kph (50 to 62 mph):
7.5 sec.

Fuel consumption:
28.6 miles per gallon

Capacities:
Fuel tank: 10.5 U.S. gallons
Crankcase: 5.3 U.S. pints
Transmission and differential: 6.3 U.S. pints
Brake fluid: .53 pint
Oil bath air cleaner: .84 pint

Dimensions and weights:

	Fastback	*Squareback*
Length, in.	166.3	166.3
Width	63.2	63.2
Height	57.9	57.9
Ground clearance	5.9	5.9
Unladen weight	2116 lbs.	2116 lbs.
Permissible total weight	2998 lbs.	3108 lbs.

Specifications—1968 Commercial Vehicles (Type 2)

Engine

Bore: 3.36 in.
Stroke: 2.72 in.
Displacement: 96.6 cubic inches.
Compression ratio: 7.7:1
Output: 57 bhp at 4400 RPM (SAE)
Torque: 81.7 ft. lbs. at 3000 RPM (SAE)
Weight, with oil: 253 lbs.
Ignition timing: 0° (TDC)

Fuel System

Carburetor: downdraft Solex 30 PICT–2
Venturi: 24 mm.
Main jet: x 116
Air correction jet: 125 z with emulsion tube
Pilot jet: 55 with electromagnetic cut-off valve
Pilot air jet: 130
Pump jet: 50
Power fuel jet: 60
Float needle valve: 1.5 mm. dia.
Float weight: 8.5 grams

Rear Axle and Transmission

Hypoid gear differential with bevel gearing; ratio, 5.375:1.

Front End

Wheel alignment: (vehicle unladen) track – 5′ to + 10′ with wheels not pressed together.
Camber: + 40′ + or – 15′
Axle beam angle: 3°. Caster: 3° + or – 40′

Steering

Ratio: 14.7:1, 2.8 turns lock to lock. Angles at maximum wheel lock, inner wheel, 32°; outer wheel, 24°.

Wheels and Tires

Steel disc wheels, 5 JK x 14. 7.00 x 14 6 PR tires on Station Wagon, 7.00 x 14 8 PR on all other models.

Tire Pressures

Front: 28 psi. **Rear:** 36 psi up to ¾ load, 41 psi with full load. **Spare wheel:** 44 psi.

Weights and Dimensions

Wheelbase: 94.5 in.
Track: front 54.5 in.
rear 56.1 in.
Overhang: front 42.3 in.
rear 37.2 in.
Overhang angle: front 19°
rear 21°
Turning circle: between walls 40.4 feet
between curbs 37.1 feet
Length: 174 in.
Width: 69.5 in.
Height: 77.0 in. (unladen)

Load compartment volume:

Van, Kombi	177 cubic feet
Pick-up	166 cubic feet
Double Cab Pick-up	113 cubic feet

Load compartment length: Van, Kombi, 110.2 in. Pick-up 106.3 in., Double-Cab Pick-up 73.0 in.

Weights, Lbs

	Unladen Weight	Payload	Gross Weight
Station Wagon	2723	1962	4685
Kombi	2624	2171	4795
Van	2425	2370	4795
Pick-up (with tarp.)	2503	2292	4795
Double Cab (with tarp.)	2591	2204	4795

Capacities

Fuel: 15.8 U.S. gallons
Crankcase: 5.3 U.S. pints
Transmission and final drive: 7.4 pints
Steering gear: 160 cc
Brake fluid reservoir: .63 pint
Air cleaner: .95 pint
Windshield washer: 1.45 quarts, approx.

Performance

Maximum speed: 65 mph at 3900 RPM
Average piston speed at maximum speed: 1764 ft./min.

Road Speeds at 4000 RPM and Hill Climbing Ability

14.5 mph	1st gear	27%
27	2nd gear	14%
43.5	3rd gear	7%
65.5	4th gear	4%

Fuel Consumption

Approx. 22.6 miles per gallon (DIN 70 030)
Octane requirement: 91 octane (regular)

Conversion Factors

Conversion factors between British Gravitational ystem (foot-pound-second system) and metric ilogram-meter-second) system:

ength

Inches	x	25.40 = millimeters
Millimeters	x	.0394 = inches
Feet	x	.3048 = meters
Meters	x	3.281 = feet
Miles	x	1.609 = kilometers
Kilometers	x	.6214 = miles

rea

Sq. inches	x	6.452 = sq. centimeters
Sq. centimeters	x	.1550 = sq. inches

olume

Cubic inches	x	16.39 = cubic centimeters
Cubic centimeters	x	.0610 = cubic inches
Fluid ounces	x	29.57 = cubic centimeters
Cubic centimeters	x	.03381 = fluid ounces
Liquid pints	x	.4732 = liters
Liters	x	2.113 = liquid pints
Gallons	x	3.785 = liters
Liters	x	.2642 = gallons

Mass

Ounces	x	28.35 = grams
Grams	x	.0353 = ounces
Pounds	x	.4536 = kilograms
Kilograms	x	2.205 = pounds

Velocity

Miles per hour	x	1.609 = kilometers/hour
Kilometers/hr.	x	.6214 = miles per hour

Pressure

Pounds/sq. in.	x	.0703 = kilograms/sq. cm.
Kilograms/sq. cm.	x	14.22 = pounds/sq. in.
Atmospheres	x	14.70 = pounds/sq. in.
Pounds/sq. in.	x	.0680 = atmospheres

Power

Horsepower	x	.7457 = kilowatts
Kilowatts	x	1.341 = horsepower

WHEN IN DOUBT

If the reader is uncertain of the exact meaning of certain terms used in this book, he is urged to consult a competent VW mechanic in order to clear up any misunderstanding. It is important also to remember that he should never attempt a service operation if he has the slightest doubt of his ability or his supply of tools. Within the limited size of this book, it is of course impossible to teach the average owner to become an expert mechanic.

PARTS AND SERVICE

When replacing parts, it is always wise to get them from a VW dealer. Every VW parts department has detailed information about every part of every Volkswagen ever made. No other source is as good and as complete.

Because the intervals between service, and the type of service itself, has not remained unchanged over the years, it is always wise to consult the owner's manual of a new Volkswagen. If you own a used Volkswagen and do not have an owner's manual, your local VW dealer can inform you of the service required for your model.

When contemplating a major overhaul of a Volkswagen engine, transmission, or other principal component, it is smart to consider the excellent possibilities offered by the VW *Exchange Parts Service*. In light of today's labor costs, a factory rebuilt exchange could be a most favorable alternative to paying for heavy repairs. Factory exchange parts are every bit as good as brand new parts. A wornout engine can be replaced by a rebuilt one in less than two hours, whereas the old engine could take many hours to repair. Rebuilt parts available include engine, rear axle and transmission assembly, generator, starter, carburetor, fuel pump, clutch cover assembly, clutch disc, steering gear assembly, brake shoes, windshield wiper motor, and speedometer. These factory-rebuilt parts are available for all VW models and are covered by a full 6-month/6,000-mile warranty honored by any authorized Volkswagen dealership in the U.S.A.

General Conversion Table

Multiply by	*To convert*	*To*	
2.54	Inches	Centimeters	.3937
30.48	Feet	Centimeters	.0328
.914	Yards	Meters	1.094
1.609	Miles	Kilometers	.621
6.45	Square inches	Square cm.	.155
.836	Square yards	Square meters	1.196
16.39	Cubic inches	Cubic cm.	.061
28.3	Cubic feet	Liters	.0353
.4536	Pounds	Kilograms	2.2045
3.785	Gallons	Liters	.264
.068	Lbs./sq. in. (psi)	Atmospheres	14.7
.138	Foot pounds	Kg. m.	7.23
1.014	H.P. (DIN)	H.P. (SAE)	.9861
—	To obtain	From	Multiply by

Note: 1 cm. equals 10 mm.; 1 mm. equals .0394".

Conversion—Common Fractions to Decimals and Millimeters

Common Fractions	*Decimal Fractions*	*Millimeters (approx.)*	*Common Fractions*	*Decimal Fractions*	*Millimeters (approx.)*	*Common Fractions*	*Decimal Fractions*	*Millimeters (approx.)*
1/128	.008	0.20	11/32	.344	8.73	43/64	.672	17.07
1/64	.016	0.40	23/64	.359	9.13	11/16	.688	17.46
1/32	.031	0.79	3/8	.375	9.53	45/64	.703	17.86
3/64	.047	1.19	25/64	.391	9.92	23/32	.719	18.26
1/16	.063	1.59	13/32	.406	10.32	47/64	.734	18.65
5/64	.078	1.98	27/64	.422	10.72	3/4	.750	19.05
3/32	.094	2.38	7/16	.438	11.11	49/64	.766	19.45
7/64	.109	2.78	29/64	.453	11.51	25/32	.781	19.84
1/8	.125	3.18	15/32	.469	11.91	51/64	.797	20.24
9/64	.141	3.57	31/64	.484	12.30	13/16	.813	20.64
5/32	.156	3.97	1/2	.500	12.70	53/64	.828	21.03
11/64	.172	4.37	33/64	.516	13.10	27/32	.844	21.43
3/16	.188	4.76	17/32	.531	13.49	55/64	.859	21.83
13/64	.203	5.16	35/64	.547	13.89	7/8	.875	22.23
7/32	.219	5.56	9/16	.563	14.29	57/64	.891	22.62
15/64	.234	5.95	37/64	.578	14.68	29/32	.906	23.02
1/4	.250	6.35	19/32	.594	15.08	59/64	.922	23.42
17/64	.266	6.75	39/64	.609	15.48	15/16	.938	23.81
9/32	.281	7.14	5/8	.625	15.88	61/64	.953	24.21
19/64	.297	7.54	41/64	.641	16.27	31/32	.969	24.61
5/16	.313	7.94	21/32	.656	16.67	63/64	.984	25.00
21/64	.328	8.33						

Conversion—Millimeters to Decimal Inches

mm	inches	mm	inches	mm	inches	mm	inches	mm	inches
1	.039 370	31	1.220 470	61	2.401 570	91	3.582 670	210	8.267 700
2	.078 740	32	1.259 840	62	2.440 940	92	3.622 040	220	8.661 400
3	.118 110	33	1.299 210	63	2.480 310	93	3.661 410	230	9.055 100
4	.157 480	34	1.338 580	64	2.519 680	94	3.700 780	240	9.448 800
5	.196 850	35	1.377 949	65	2.559 050	95	3.740 150	250	9.842 500
6	.236 220	36	1.417 319	66	2.598 420	96	3.779 520	260	10.236 200
7	.275 590	37	1.456 689	67	2.637 790	97	3.818 890	270	10.629 900
8	.314 960	38	1.496 050	68	2.677 160	98	3.858 260	280	11.032 600
9	.354 330	39	1.535 430	69	2.716 530	99	3.897 630	290	11.417 300
10	.393 700	40	1.574 800	70	2.755 900	100	3.937 000	300	11.811 000
11	.433 070	41	1.614 170	71	2.795 270	105	4.133 848	310	12.204 700
12	.472 440	42	1.653 540	72	2.834 640	110	4.330 700	320	12.598 400
13	.511 810	43	1.692 910	73	2.874 010	115	4.527 550	330	12.992 100
14	.551 180	44	1.732 280	74	2.913 380	120	4.724 400	340	13.385 800
15	.590 550	45	1.771 650	75	2.952 750	125	4.921 250	350	13.779 500
16	.629 920	46	1.811 020	76	2.992 120	130	5.118 100	360	14.173 200
17	.669 290	47	1.850 390	77	3.031 490	135	5.314 950	370	14.566 900
18	.708 660	48	1.889 760	78	3.070 860	140	5.511 800	380	14.960 600
19	.748 030	49	1.929 130	79	3.110 230	145	5.708 650	390	15.354 300
20	.787 400	50	1.968 500	80	3.149 600	150	5.905 500	400	15.748 000
21	.826 770	51	2.007 870	81	3.188 970	155	6.102 350	500	19.685 000
22	.866 140	52	2.047 240	82	3.228 340	160	6.299 200	600	23.622 000
23	.905 510	53	2.086 610	83	3.267 710	165	6.496 050	700	27.559 000
24	.944 880	54	2.125 980	84	3.307 080	170	6.692 900	800	31.496 000
25	.984 250	55	2.165 350	85	3.346 450	175	6.889 750	900	35.433 000
26	1.023 620	56	2.204 720	86	3.385 820	180	7.086 600	1000	39.370 000
27	1.062 990	57	2.244 090	87	3.425 190	185	7.283 450	2000	78.740 000
28	1.102 360	58	2.283 460	88	3.464 560	190	7.480 300	3000	118.110 000
29	1.141 730	59	2.322 830	89	3.503 903	195	7.677 150	4000	157.480 000
30	1.181 100	60	2.362 200	90	3.543 300	200	7.874 000	5000	196.850 000

To change decimal millimeters to decimal inches, position the decimal point where desired on either side of the millimeter measurement shown and reset the inches decimal by the same number of digits in the same direction. For example, to convert 0.001 mm to decimal inches, reset the decimal behind the 1 mm (shown on the chart) to 0.001; change the decimal inch equivalent (0.039″ shown) to 0.000039″.

Tap Drill Sizes

National Fine or S.A.E.

Screw & Tap Size	Threads Per Inch	Use Drill Number
No. 5	44	37
No. 6	40	33
No. 8	36	29
No. 10	32	21
No. 12	28	15
1/4	28	3
5/16	24	1
3/8	24	Q
7/16	20	W
1/2	20	29/64
9/16	18	33/64
5/8	18	37/64
3/4	16	11/16
7/8	14	13/16
1 1/8	12	1 3/64
1 1/4	12	1 11/64
1 1/2	12	1 27/64

Tap Drill Sizes

National Coarse or U.S.S.

Screw & Tap Size	Threads Per Inch	Use Drill Number
No. 5	40	39
No. 6	32	36
No. 8	32	29
No. 10	24	25
No. 12	24	17
1/4	20	8
5/16	18	F
3/8	16	5/16
7/16	14	U
1/2	13	27/64
9/16	12	31/64
5/8	11	17/32
3/4	10	21/32
7/8	9	49/64
1	8	7/8
1 1/8	7	63/64
1 1/4	7	1 7/64
1 1/2	6	1 11/32

Decimal Equivalent Size of the Number Drills

Drill No.	Decimal Equivalent	Drill No.	Decimal Equivalent	Drill No.	Decimal Equivalent
80	.0135	53	.0595	26	.1470
79	.0145	52	.0635	25	.1495
78	.0160	51	.0670	24	.1520
77	.0180	50	.0700	23	.1540
76	.0200	49	.0730	22	.1570
75	.0210	48	.0760	21	.1590
74	.0225	47	.0785	20	.1610
73	.0240	46	.0810	19	.1660
72	.0250	45	.0820	18	.1695
71	.0260	44	.0860	17	.1730
70	.0280	43	.0890	16	.1770
69	.0292	42	.0935	15	.1800
68	.0310	41	.0960	14	.1820
67	.0320	40	.0980	13	.1850
66	.0330	39	.0995	12	.1890
65	.0350	38	.1015	11	.1910
64	.0360	37	.1040	10	.1935
63	.0370	36	.1065	9	.1960
62	.0380	35	.1100	8	.1990
61	.0390	34	.1110	7	.2010
60	.0400	33	.1130	6	.2040
59	.0410	32	.1160	5	.2055
58	.0420	31	.1200	4	.2090
57	.0430	30	.1285	3	.2130
56	.0465	29	.1360	2	.2210
55	.0520	28	.1405	1	.2280
54	.0550	27	.1440		

Decimal Equivalent Size of the Letter Drills

Letter Drill	Decimal Equivalent	Letter Drill	Decimal Equivalent	Letter Drill	Decimal Equivalent
A	.234	J	.277	S	.348
B	.238	K	.281	T	.358
C	.242	L	.290	U	.368
D	.246	M	.295	V	.377
E	.250	N	.302	W	.386
F	.257	O	.316	X	.397
G	.261	P	.323	Y	.404
H	.266	Q	.332	Z	.413
I	.272	R	.339		

Anti-Freeze Chart

emperatures Shown in Degrees Fahrenheit +32 is Freezing

Cooling System Capacity Quarts	Quarts of ETHYLENE GLYCOL Needed for Protection to Temperatures Shown Below													
	1	2	3	4	5	6	7	8	9	10	11	12	13	14
10	+24°	+16°	+ 4°	−12°	−34°	−62°								
11	+25	+18	+ 8	− 6	−23	−47								
12	+26	+19	+10	0	−15	−34	−57°							
13	+27	+21	+13	+ 3	− 9	−25	−45							
14			+15	+ 6	− 5	−18	−34							
15			+16	+ 8	0	−12	−26							
16			+17	+10	+ 2	− 8	−19	−34	−52°					
17			+18	+12	+ 5	− 4	−14	−27	−42					
18			+19	+14	+ 7	0	−10	−21	−34	−50°				
19			+20	+15	+ 9	+ 2	− 7	−16	−28	−42				
20				+16	+10	+ 4	− 3	−12	−22	−34	−48°			
21				+17	+12	+ 6	0	− 9	−17	−28	−41			
22				+18	+13	+ 8	+ 2	− 6	−14	−23	−34	−47°		
23				+19	+14	+ 9	+ 4	− 3	−10	−19	−29	−40		
24				+19	+15	+10	+ 5	0	− 8	−15	−23	−34	−46°	
25				+20	+16	+12	+ 7	+ 1	− 5	−12	−20	−29	−40	−50°
26					+17	+13	+ 8	+ 3	− 3	− 9	−16	−25	−34	−44
27					+18	+14	+ 9	+ 5	− 1	− 7	−13	−21	−29	−39
28					+18	+15	+10	+ 6	+ 1	− 5	−11	−18	−25	−34
29					+19	+16	+12	+ 7	+ 2	− 3	− 8	−15	−22	−29
30					+20	+17	+13	+ 8	+ 4	− 1	− 6	−12	−18	−25

For capacities over 30 quarts divide true capacity by 3. Find quarts Anti-Freeze for the ⅓ and multiply by 3 for quarts to add.

For capacities under 10 quarts multiply true capacity by 3. Find quarts Anti-Freeze for the tripled volume and divide by 3 for quarts to add.

To Increase the Freezing Protection of Anti-Freeze Solutions Already Installed

Cooling System Capacity Quarts	Number of Quarts of ETHYLENE GLYCOL Anti-Freeze Required to Increase Protection													
	From +20° F. to					From +10° F. to					From 0° F. to			
	0°	−10°	−20°	−30°	−40°	0°	−10°	−20°	−30°	−40°	−10°	−20°	−30°	−40°
10	1¾	2¼	3	3½	3¾	¾	1½	2¼	2¾	3¼	¾	1½	2	2½
12	2	2¾	3½	4	4½	1	1¾	2½	3¼	3¾	1	1¾	2½	3¼
14	2¼	3¼	4	4¾	5½	1¼	2	3	3¾	4½	1	2	3	3½
16	2½	3½	4½	5¼	6	1¼	2½	3½	4¼	5¼	1¼	2¼	3¼	4
18	3	4	5	6	7	1½	2¾	4	5	5¾	1½	2½	3¾	4¾
20	3¼	4½	5¾	6¾	7½	1¾	3	4¼	5½	6½	1½	2¾	4¼	5¼
22	3½	5	6¼	7¼	8¼	1¾	3¼	4¾	6	7¼	1¾	3¼	4½	5½
24	4	5½	7	8	9	2	3½	5	6½	7½	1¾	3½	5	6
26	4¼	6	7½	8¾	10	2	4	5½	7	8¼	2	3¾	5½	6¾
28	4½	6¼	8	9½	10½	2¼	4¼	6	7½	9	2	4	5¾	7¼
30	5	6¾	8½	10	11½	2½	4½	6½	8	9½	2¼	4¼	6¼	7¾

Test radiator solution with proper hydrometer. Determine from the table the number of quarts of solution to be drawn off from a full cooling system and replace with undiluted anti-freeze, to give the desired increased protection. For example, to increase protection of a 22-quart cooling system containing Ethylene Glycol (permanent type) anti-freeze, from +20° F. to −20° F. will require the replacement of 6¼ quarts of solution with undiluted anti-freeze.

Index

O

P

R

S

T

V

W

Chilton's Repair & Tune-Up Guides

The complete line covers domestic cars, imports, trucks, vans, RV's and 4-wheel drive vehicles.

CODE	TITLE
#7199	AMC 75–82; all models
#7165	Alliance 1983
#7323	Aries 81–82
#7344	Arrow 78–83
#7193	Aspen/Volaré 76–80
#5902	Audi 70–73
#7028	Audi 4000/5000 77–81
#6337	Audi Fox 73–75
#5807	Barracuda 65–72
#7203	Blazer 69–82
#5576	BMW 59–70
#7315	BMW 70–82
#7308	Buick 75–83 all full sized models
#7307	Buick Century/Regal 75–83
#7045	Camaro 67–81
#7317	Camaro 82–83
#6695	Capri 70–77
#7195	Capri 79–82
#7059	Cavalier 1982
#7309	Celebrity 82–83
#7309	Century 82–83
#5807	Challenger 65–72
#7343	Challenger (Import) 71–83
#7344	Champ 78–83
#6316	Charger/Coronet 71–75
#7162	Chevette 76–82 inc. diesel
#7313	Chevrolet 68–83 all full sized models
#7167	Chevrolet/GMC Pick-Ups 70–82
#7169	Chevrolet/GMC Vans 67–82
#7310	Chevrolet S-10/GMC S-15 Pick-Ups 82–83
#7051	Chevy Luv 72–81 inc. 4wd
#7056	Chevy Mid-Size 64–82 inc. El Camino, Chevelle, Laguna, Malibu & Monte Carlo
#6841	Chevy II 62–79
#7309	Ciera 82–83
#7059	Cimarron 1982
#7335	Citation 80–83
#7343	Colt 71–83
#7194	Continental 1982
#6691	Corvair 60–69 inc. Turbo
#6576	Corvette 53–62
#7192	Corvette 63–82
#7405	Cougar 65–73
#7190	Cutlass 70–82
#6324	Dart/Demon 68–76
#5790	Datsun 61–72
#7196	Datsun F10, 310, Nissan Stanza 77–82
#7170	Datsun 200SX, 510, 610, 710, 810 73–82
#7197	Datsun 1200, 210/Nissan Sentra 73–82
#7172	Datsun Z & ZX 70–82
#7050	Datsun Pick-Ups 70–81 inc. 4wd
#6554	Dodge 68–77 all full sized models
#7323	Dodge 400 1982
#6486	Dodge Charger 67–70
#7168	Dodge Vans 67–82
#7032	Dodge D-50/Plymouth Arrow Pick-Ups 77–81
#7055	Escort 81–82 inc. EXP & LN-7
#6320	Fairlane/Torino 62–75
#7312	Fairmont 78–83
#7042	Fiat 69–81
#6846	Fiesta 78–80
#7046	Firebird 67–81
#7345	Firebird 82–83
#7059	Firenza 1982
#7318	Ford 68–83 all full sized models
#7140	Ford Bronco 66–81
#7341	Ford Courier 72–82
#7194	Ford Mid-Size 71–82 inc. Torino, Gran Torino, Ranchero, Elite, LTD II & Thunderbird
#7166	Ford Pick-Ups 65–82 inc. 4wd

CODE	TITLE
#7171	Ford Vans 61–82
#7165	Fuego 82–83
#6935	GM Sub-compact 71–81 inc. Vega, Monza, Astre, Sunbird, Starfire & Skyhawk
#7311	Granada 78–83
#7204	Honda 73–82
#5912	International Scout 67–73
#7136	Jeep CJ 1945–81
#6739	Jeep Wagoneer, Commando, Cherokee 66–79
#7203	Jimmy 69–82
#7059	J-2000 1982
#7165	Le Car 76–83
#7323	Le Baron 1982
#7055	Lynx 81–82 inc. EXP & LN-7
#6634	Maverick/Comet 70–77
#7198	Mazda 71–82
#7031	Mazda RX-7 79–81
#6065	Mercedes-Benz 59–70
#5907	Mercedes-Benz 68–73
#6809	Mercedes-Benz 74–79
#7318	Mercury 68–83 all full sized models
#7194	Mercury Mid-Size 71–82 inc. Continental, Cougar, XR-7 & Montego
#7173	MG 61–80
#7311	Monarch 75–80
#7405	Mustang 65–73
#6812	Mustang II 74–78
#7195	Mustang 79–82
#6841	Nova 69–79
#7308	Oldsmobile 75–83 all full sized models
#7335	Omega 80–83
#7191	Omni/Horizon 78–82
#6575	Opel 71–75
#5982	Peugeot 70–74
#7335	Phoenix 80–83
#7027	Pinto/Bobcat 71–80
#8552	Plymouth 68–76 full sized models
#7168	Plymouth Vans 67–82
#7308	Pontiac 75–83 all full sized models
#7309	Pontiac 6000 82–83
#5822	Porsche 69–73
#7048	Porsche 924 & 928 77–81 inc. Turbo
#7323	Reliant 81–82
#7165	Renault 75–83
#7383	S-10 Blazer 82–83
#7383	S-15 Jimmy 82–83
#5988	Saab 69–75
#7344	Sapporo 78–83
#5821	Satellite/Roadrunner, Belvedere, GTX 68–73
#7059	Skyhawk 1982
#7335	Skylark 80–83
#7208	Subaru 70–82
#5905	Tempest/GTO/LeMans 68–73
#5795	Toyota 66–70
#7314	Toyota Celica & Supra 71–83
#7316	Toyota Corolla, Carina, Tercel, Starlet 70–83
#7044	Toyota Corona, Cressida, Crown, Mark II 70–81
#7035	Toyota Pick-Ups 70–81
#5910	Triumph 69–73
#7162	T-1000 1982
#6326	Valiant/Duster 68–76
#5796	Volkswagen 49–71
#6837	Volkswagen 70–81
#7339	Volkswagen Front Wheel Drive 74–83 inc. Dasher, GTI, Jetta, Quantum, Pick-Up, Rabbit, Scirocco
#6529	Volvo 56–69
#7040	Volvo 70–80
#7312	Zephyr 78–83

Chilton's Repair & Tune-Up Guides are available at your local retailer or by mailing a check or money order for **$10.95** plus **$1.00** to cover postage and handling to:

Chilton Book Company
Dept. DM
Radnor, PA 19089

NOTE: When ordering be sure to include your name & address, book code & title.